LIFE AND TRADITION IN WEST YORKSHIRE

LIFE AND TRADITION
IN
WEST YORKSHIRE

Marie Hartley and Joan Ingilby

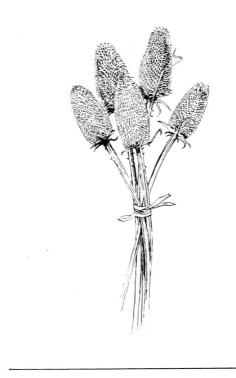

Smith Settle

First published in 1976 by
J M Dent & Sons Ltd

This new edition published in 1990 by
Smith Settle Ltd
Ilkley Road
Otley
West Yorkshire
LS21 3JP

ISBN Paper 1 870071 52 2
Cloth 1 870071 53 0

British Library Cataloguing in Publication Data
Hartley, Marie
Life & tradition in West Yorkshire – New ed.
1. (Metropolitan County) West Yorkshire. Social life
1901–1936
I. Title   II. Ingilby, Joan
942.810823
ISBN 1–870071–53–0
ISBN 1–870071–52–2 pbk

Printed and bound by
SMITH SETTLE
Ilkley Road, Otley, West Yorkshire LS21 3JP

Contents

Photographs

Drawings

Introduction

IN the eleven years from 1965 to 1976 we devoted the whole of our working lives to researching and writing a series of three books, *Life and Tradition in the Yorkshire Dales, Life and Tradition in the Moorlands of North-East Yorkshire,* and *Life and Tradition in West Yorkshire*. This book was the last of the three and in contrast to the first two was totally concerned with cities, towns and industrial life. It was not unknown territory to us, for we were both born in West Yorkshire (or rather in the old West Riding) and Marie Hartley came of a family of mill owners, so that there were many relations and friends to give us invaluable contacts.

The book followed the plan of the other two in that it was based on field-work, this time on tape-recorded interviews with many people of divers walks of life, and on personal visits to factories of all kinds. Information from printed sources was only used to back up our research. Although the textile industry dominates, the book is not, except where necessary for clarification, a history of that trade. It is rather concerned with people and their recollections. As some were born in the 1890s and others in the first decade of this century, a picture of life emerges which is vastly different from that of the present day and could no longer be recorded in such detail.

As we pursued our work in the 1970s the great textile industry was diminishing, and in 1986 only employed 40,000; and the great mills – Manningham at Bradford, Salt's at Saltaire and Dean Clough at Halifax – have closed and are being or about to be used as workshops, or art galleries or museums. Black Dyke Mills remains because of its specialised products.

We were fortunate in having introductions to several colliery officials and coal miners, also to many owners and managers of varied works, some of which have now gone. We look back on their co-operation with gratitude. In other spheres the huge chapels have for long been redundant and historic graveyards need preservation. Partially as a result of changes the once industrial valleys such as Calderdale – which includes Hebden Bridge – are now being promoted as tourist resorts, as is Bradford. We are pleased that this book is to be reprinted by Smith Settle as it serves to remind us in Yorkshire of a life in the not too distant past now gone.

M.H. and J.I. 1990

Foreword and Acknowledgments

THE territory under consideration, now called West Yorkshire, may briefly be described as the wool textile area of the old West Riding, for although many other industries exist in it, textiles dominate by importance and tradition. Geographically it is a complicated region, roughly encircled by the cities and towns of Leeds, Bradford, Halifax, Huddersfield and Wakefield, an area which may be divided into the lowlands to the east and the hill country of the Pennines to the west. In the past the latter shared a culture with the rural Yorkshire dales. Similarities once abounded: insularity, the farming, the love of homeland, the sporting character of pursuits, the use of by-names, the food—oatcake—and the real beauty in spite of industry still glimpsed in some valleys and on the extensive moors. One further geographical feature elucidates the pattern of settlement, the towns and hamlets clustered in five main valleys: the Colne and the Holme valleys to the south, Calderdale to the west, the Spen valley in the centre and Airedale skirting the northern boundary.

To describe in detail such a region with its many industries, thousands of firms and tens of thousands of inhabitants would result in a kind of gazetteer. Also many subjects, for example transport, cricket, trade unionism, vernacular architecture, have received full treatment elsewhere, and a wealth of information has been published by local historians, museums and the several distinguished antiquarian societies. We have endeavoured to take a cross-section of activities illustrated by individual personal experiences. It is as Defoe said 'a noble scene of industry and application', the kind of region manufacturing goods, many for export, on which the nation including those engaged in non-productive work have for long depended and still depend for their well-being, a fact too often disregarded.

We are concerned mainly here with the West Riding around the last decade of the nineteenth century and the first quarter of this. It was a time when the capitalist system prevailed, and private enterprise flourished but experienced more difficulties than heretofore, when wages were small but food and goods cheap, when hours of work were less than formerly, when measures of social security had been introduced but not enough, when the fearful slump of the 1920s is remembered rather than wars or the General Strike, and when the British Empire, whether we approve or not today, was a stabilizing factor.

We have used a tape recorder so that much is related in the speakers' own words. What has emerged is the resilience, the stamina, the sterling qualities, the wry humour, and by and large the happiness of men and women working hard, living in poor conditions, and with only the simplest pleasures attainable. Cynics say that people were only happy because they knew nothing better, but happiness is happiness in whatever circumstances or walk of life it is experienced. We have set down our findings without bias, and make no comment except to say that the sense of belonging to home, street, mill, chapel or church was all important and that material prosperity alone, however desirable, is not enough.

We are indebted to a great many people of whom most mentioned in the text are omitted here on account of space. Without the constant care and helpfulness of Mrs M. R. Hartley whose home in Leeds became ours for many weeks over a period of two years this book would not have been possible. In the Huddersfield district we received generous hospitality and introductions from Mrs P. D. Crowther of Lindley and Mr and Mrs J. D. Hartley of Fixby.

We also wish to thank the following for information and for introducing us to their staff: Mr A. G. Crowther of W. & E. Crowther Ltd, Crimble Mill, Slaithwaite and Mrs Crowther who encouraged us from first to last, Mr W. Asquith, Mr R. A. Hornshaw and Miss D. Blewitt of Lister and Co. Ltd, Manningham Mills, Bradford and Low Mills, Addingham, Mr T. P. Lambert and Mr W. Gallimore of John Foster and Son Ltd, Black Dyke Mills, Queensbury, Mr M. W. Shelton of Thomas Burnley and Sons Ltd, Gomersal Mills, Mr A. E. Pease of Lock Hill Mills, Sowerby Bridge and Mrs Pease and Mrs G. R. Stansfeld, Mr S. J. E. Huxley of Joshua Ellis and Co. Ltd, Batley Carr Mills, Mr M. Pearson of John Crossley and Sons Ltd, Dean Clough Mills, Halifax, Mr A. G. Wilson of Salts (Saltaire) Ltd.

Many have kindly shown us round their works, lent us unpublished material and in some cases read the MS: Mr J. F. Alcock of the Hunslet Engine Company Ltd, Mr J. G. Walker of James Walker and Sons Ltd, Mirfield, Mr M. D. Aykroyd of Firth Carpets Ltd, Heckmondwike, Mr W. Wormald of Wormalds and Walker Ltd, Dewsbury, Mr S. J. S. Walker of Joseph Sykes Bros (English Card Clothing Ltd), Lindley, the staff of James Holdsworth Bros Ltd, Mirfield, Mr R. L. Smith of George Hattersley and Sons Ltd, Keighley, Mr L. Barker of the C.W.S. Ltd, Hebden Bridge, Mr H. G. Marshall of Marshalls (Halifax) Ltd, Mr P. K. Stead and Mr E. H. Crack of Charles F. Stead and Co. Ltd, Leeds, Mr P. Schofield of

Schofields (Leeds) Ltd, Mr J. A. Horrox of Brown, Muff Ltd, Bradford, Colonel
A. Monteith, Ingleby Arncliffe, Mr W. Cook, formerly of Whitehead-Miller G-J
(Printers) Ltd, Leeds, Mr T. M. Little of David Little and Co. Ltd, Leeds, Mr A.
Summers of Cullingworth Summers, Batley, Mr D. Asquith of Emu Wools Ltd,
Keighley, Mr P. B. Haigh of John Haigh and Sons Ltd, Huddersfield, Mr P. Kirk
of Kirk and Steel Ltd, Morley, Mr G. Dracup of Samuel Dracup and Sons Ltd,
Bradford, Mr G. E. Phelon of David Crabtree and Son Ltd, Bradford, Mr H. S.
Sykes of Harding (Leeds) Ltd, Mr P. W. Sutcliffe and Mr Aquilla Morris of the
British Picker Company Ltd, Todmorden, Mr M. Popplewell of the BBA Group
Ltd, Cleckheaton, Mr T. Day of Henry Day and Sons Ltd, Dewsbury, Mr R.
Addis of John Fowler and Co (Leeds) Ltd, Mr C. T. Green of Thomas Green
(Silsden) Ltd, Mr W. A. Winter, Bingley, Mr W. Walton and Mr J. I. Hartley of
Walton Bros (Halifax) Ltd, Mr J. A. R. Maude of Boldron, Mr and Mrs F. Walkley
and Mr J. Uttley of Huddersfield and Hebden Bridge, Mr F. N. Drury of Joshua
Tetley and Son Ltd, Leeds.

We should like to thank in particular Mr G. W. Atkinson, Morley, Mr T. B.
Fletcher and Mr J. R. Hepper, Leeds, Mr and Mrs J. C. Atack, Hebden Bridge,
Mr and Mrs E. Walker, Batley, Mr and Mrs G. E. Buckley, Delph, Mr and Mrs
K. F. B. Roberts and Mr F. Burley, Holmbridge, Miss C. F. Wright, formerly of
Gomersal, Mrs O. M. Bedford and Miss M. G. Phillips, Gildersome, Mr B.
Barnes, Saddleworth, Mr J. Ogden, Mr I. Dewhirst and Mr E. D. Dewhirst,
Keighley, Mrs G. C. Roper, Pannal, Miss V. Watson, Scarcroft, Mr W. H. Murga-
troyd, Bramley, Mr H. N. Sykes, Almondbury, Sir Harry Hardy, Morley, Mr
S. Lee Vincent, formerly of Leeds, Mr J. Mitchell, Bradford, Mr R. Lingard,
East Bergholt, Mr G. E. Bowman, Bovingdon, Mr J. Bradley, Shelf, Mrs A.
Newell, Queensbury, Mr R. L. Sunderland, Halifax, Mr J. Mortimer, Mytholm,
Mrs A. O. Pullan and Mrs M. I. Rigg, Rawdon, Mr F. Else and Mr F. Horsfall,
Heptonstall, Mr and Mrs J. Mitchell, Pudsey, Mr H. Sykes, Slaithwaite.

We are indebted to Mr Stewart Sanderson for access to the records at the
Institute of Dialect and Folk Studies at the University of Leeds. Mr C. S. Fowler
of the *Halifax Courier* Ltd has shown us files in their library and Mrs Shirley Kaye
persuaded readers to send in life stories, many of which we have used. Several
directors, curators and keepers of museums have helped with information,
suggestions for research and old photographs: Mr C. M. Mitchell of Leeds City
Museums, Mr R.-A. Innes and Miss P. F. Millward of the Calderdale Museums,
Miss Anne Ward of Cliffe Castle Museum, Keighley, Mr E. W. Aubrook and
Mr R. A. McMillan of the Tolson Memorial Museum, Huddersfield, Mr S. W.
Feather and Mr G. Hollingshead of the Bradford Industrial Museum, Mr P. C. D.

Brears, then of Clarke Hall, Wakefield, Miss A. V. Diver of Bolling Hall Museum, Mr J. Goodchild then of Cusworth Hall Museum, Doncaster, Mr P. Kelley of the Museum of Industry and Science, Armley Mills, Leeds, Mr J. Stafford of Oldham Museum. We also thank and acknowledge information from the chief and reference librarians at the Central and Public libraries at Leeds, Bradford, Halifax, Huddersfield, Batley, Keighley, Oldham, Saddleworth at Uppermill, the County Library at Taunton, the archives department of Leeds Central Library, and the Yorkshire Archaeological Society.

M. H. and J. I.

Photographic Acknowledgments

Of the 147 photographs the fifty undated ones are the authors'. We acknowledge the loan of the remainder with the numbers of the plates as follows: Mr J. C. Atack, 6; Mrs G. E. Buckley, 7; Tolson Memorial Museum, Huddersfield, 10, 38; Bagshaw Museum, Batley, 11; Miss P. Smith, 12; Mr J. G. Walker, 15; Mr A. G. Crowther, 16; Mr M. Pearson, 17; Mr S. J. S. Walker, 18, 60; Miss H. Holmes, 19; Mr R. A. Hornshaw, 20, 21, 36, 67; Mr L. Barker, 24–8; Harding (Leeds) Ltd, 29; C. H. Wood, 30, 48; T. Burnley and Sons Ltd, 32; Bradford Industrial Museum, 33, 46; Mrs E. Taylor, 34; Mr R. L. Smith, 58, 66; Mr J. Jessop, 37; Mr M. D. Aykroyd, 59. Mr G. H. Gledhill, 39, 68; Mr J. Goodchild, 40, Bath and West and Southern Counties Society, 43; Mr B. Burrows, 49; Mr A. Summers, 50; Mr T. Day, 51; Mrs A. Marlow, 52; Mr G. W. Atkinson, 53, 136; Mr C. Westerby, 54, 133; Mr P. B. Haigh, 55, 56; Mr S. J. E. Huxley, 57; Mr P. W. Sutcliffe, 63; Mr M. Popplewell, 65; Mr H. Morton, 76, 121; Shibden Hall Museum, 77, 140; Mr W. A. N. Brooke, 74, 81; Mr P. V. Charlesworth, 73; National Coal Board, 72; Mr R. Addis, 78; Mr J. F. Alcock, 79; Kirkstall Forge Engineering Ltd, 75; Central Library, Bradford, 80, 82, 112; Mrs A. Tupman, 83, 90; Central Library, Leeds, 84; Mr W. Pickles, 85; Mr C. B. Pratt, 86, 138; Miss A. K. Sutton, 87, 139; Mr J. N. Charlesworth, 91; Public Library, Heckmondwike, 92, 132; Mr Ian Dewhirst, 93; Mr W. H. Murgatroyd, 94; Mrs F. Tomasso, 95; Mr T. Farmer, 96; Mrs M. H. Gartside, 97; Mr Peter Schofield, 111; Mr T. Beaumont, 113;

Mr W. A. Potts, 114; Mr W. Cook, 115; Mrs B. Smith, 118; Mr E. and Mr S. Coates, 120; Mr M. Anderson, 122, 123; Mr C. M. Mitchell, 124–7; *The Halifax Courier* Ltd, 128, Mr J. Uttley, 129; Mr C. T. Green, 130; *The Yorkshire Post*, 131; *Bradford Telegraph and Argus*, 135; Mr G. E. Crowther, 145; Mr R. Hall, 135; Miss E. Hinchliffe, 137; Mrs A. Longstaff, 141; Science Museum, London, drawing of the Crank Mill, Morley.

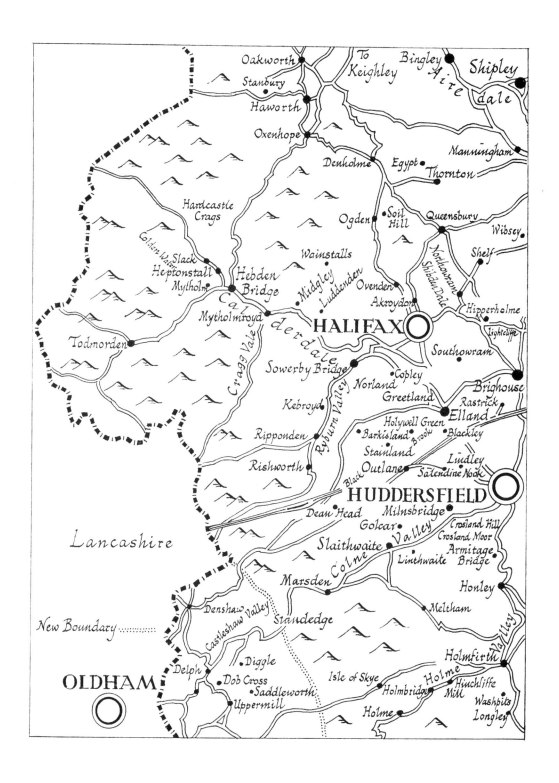

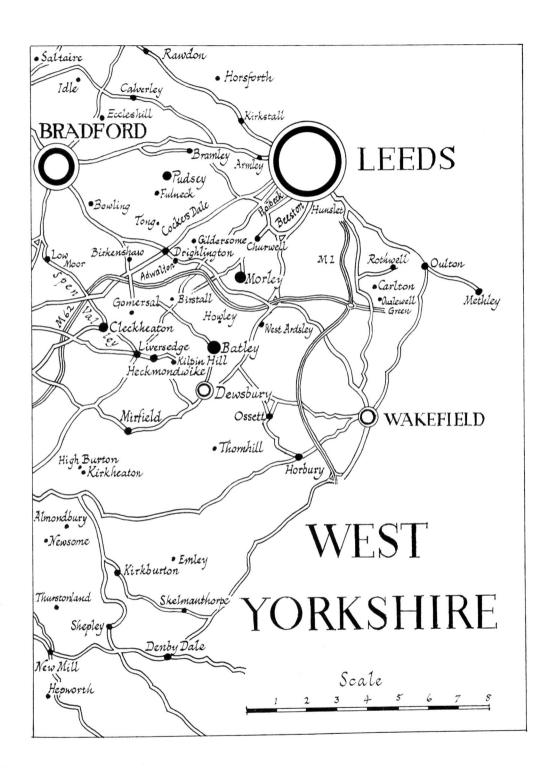

A noble scene of industry and application is spread before you here . . .

Defoe

1 Recollections of the Domestic System

THE antiquity and continuity of the wool textile industry is cause for marvel. Dating back as an industry in Yorkshire and widespread in the country in the Middle Ages, it was drawn in the eighteenth century to the West Riding where, formed by zealous merchants and a multitude of clothiers based on home-work-shops, a unique structure had developed.[1] This fragmentation, this mass of small units, by and large squeezed out in the last century and up to the 1920s, but still discernible, offered opportunity and encouraged enterprise, that allied with ample natural resources, carried people and industry triumphantly through the building of mills, the installation of machinery, the reorganization of the work force, immense if fluctuating trade, in short the travail of the Industrial Revolution and beyond.

In the last decades of the eighteenth century following on inventions, the many processes of cloth manufacture—spinning, carding, weaving, finishing—were being mechanized. At the same time the clothiers then enjoying rapidly expanding trade built three-storied houses with their full-width windows lighting workrooms for weaving broadcloth. These, to be seen in the Colne valley and the Saddleworth district, are still striking relics of the domestic system in transition (*see plates 1 and 3*). In the same period old corn and fulling mills were adapted for scribbling (carding), and new purpose-built water-driven mills, known as country mills, for one or more of the processes of scribbling, dyeing, fulling (milling), and spinning began to be erected on the rivers and tributary streams (*see plates 6–7*). As machinery was introduced it is well known that it was attended by strikes and by the Luddite, Chartist and Plug Riots.

A reminder of these disturbed times was the widespread practice of watchmen firing flintlocks or blunderbusses at nine o'clock at night as for example at Lee

---

[1] William White, *History, Gazetteer, and Directory of the West Riding of Yorkshire*, 1837, vol. I, p. 512, states that about 1800 there were from Leeds to the Lancashire border nearly 6,000 master clothiers who employed besides their wives and children 30,000 to 40,000 people.

Bridge Mills, Halifax, and Acre Mills, Lindley, near Huddersfield. When a watch-man was set on at Gillroyd Mills, Morley, in 1843, after the Plug Riots, he had 'to go on duty and Fire his Gun at nine o'clock at night from 1st October to 1st April and at ten o'clock for the rest of the year'.[1] At Black Dyke Mills, Queensbury, the custom only ceased in the 1930s and at Dewsbury Mills in the 1960s.

In this turmoil 'of all the operatives connected with the trade', wrote James in 1857, 'he [the piece-maker or weaver] was on the whole the most uncomplaining and praiseworthy'.[2] Weaving was the last major process to leave the home-work-shop. The clothier's house and the weaver's cottage, the pivot on which the domestic system had revolved, for long remained the places to which the warp and weft were brought, the places from which the woven cloth was taken to the mill to be scoured and fulled, and brought back to be stretched on tenters and then taken to be sold. (These processes undertaken in the home varied according to the period, the machinery introduced and the proximity of a mill.)[3] Some clothier's houses had dye houses near by, as at High Kinders, Saddleworth, and every village too had several small workshops for cloth dressing (finishing). 'The Clothiers,' wrote Baines, in 1858, 'by their industry and frugality, find themselves able to compete with the factory owners whose great works and complicated machinery incur heavy expenses.'[4]

None the less the adjustment from hand to power looms (like that from the employment of children in the home to the factory) was temporarily painful. It was only at first, following on the invention of the flying shuttle and when machinery was small, that the piece-makers benefited.[5] In 1795 because of the French war they could earn 39s. 6d. a week, a sum which dropped to 15s. in 1810 and to 5s. in 1830, both decades of national crises. They became known as poverty-knockers (a term derived from the sound of the loom), and lived on porridge, oatcake, barley bread, milk, potatoes and some bacon. Marauding parties in the Colne valley raided warehouses; others went in singing companies to the Sheffield district to earn money; children turned to begging.

A halfway stage was the erection of loom-shops to accommodate hand-loom

[1] MS. Committee Book, 1835–61, Gill Royds Company Mill, Archives Department, Leeds City Libraries.

[2] John James, *History of the Worsted Manufacture in England*, 1857, p. 479.

[3] See W. B. Crump and G. Ghorbal, *History of the Huddersfield Woollen Industry*, 1935; A. Easther, *A Glossary of the Dialect of Almondbury and Huddersfield*, 1883; B. Barnes, *Saddleworth Heritage*, 1975.

[4] E. Baines, *Yorkshire Past and Present*, 1858, vol. IV, p. 629.

[5] See P. E. Razzell and R. W. Wainwright, *The Victorian Working Class. Selections from the Morning Chronicle, 1849*, 1973.

HOUSES AND INDUSTRY

1. Golcar in the Colne valley showing some of the many late eighteenth-century clothiers' houses. In 1753 of the 166 clothiers in the valley, 111 lived in and around here. An example of an early trading estate, it is now a conservation area. The house in the centre, one of the many home-workshops, contains the Colne Valley Museum.

2. Hebden Bridge, upper Calderdale, showing the nineteenth-century development. Most of the terraces of houses were built in the 1890s. Many of them are in tiers with one house entered from the front and another above it entered from the back. On the hilltops are seen some of the old original settlements.

EARLY INDUSTRY

3. High Kinders, Greenfield, Saddleworth, dated 1642, a fine example of a clothier's house. It takes its name from the family who built it, and it has been extended several times. Hand-loom weaving continued here until the 1880s. Note the two 'takin' in' doors at the top of the flight of steps, one blocked up.

4. Wuzzing holes at Manor Farm, Thurstonland, near Huddersfield. A stick was put in the hole, and wet wool in a skep (basket) or a metal container was hung on the stick, which was swirled round and round, thus shaking out the water.

5. Tenter posts erected about 1840, a very late date, for Wall Clough Mill on Wall Hill, Saddleworth. They would have wooden bars with hooks on to which the cloth was fastened and stretched along the top and bottom.

6. Low Lumb Mill, built in 1805, and High Lumb Mill, built in 1815, on Colden Water, upper Calderdale. The latter had a little gasometer. Paved paths led through the woods to them from Heptonstall (date unknown).

EARLY MILLS

7. High and Low Broadhead, water-powered fulling mills in the Castleshaw valley, near Delph, built in the late eighteenth century. From here the Buckley family exported superfine broadcloth and fine shawls (c. 1875).

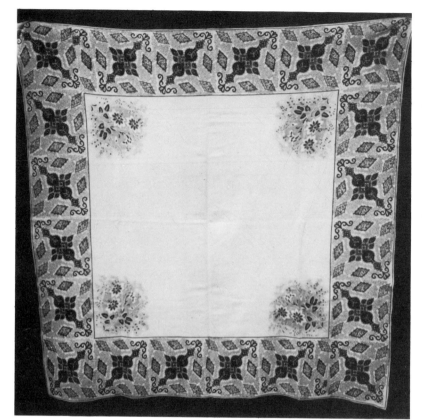

8 & 9. Two of a group of fine mostly woollen shawls, still preserved, made at Broadhead. They date from 1820 to 1850. The one with no fringe is white printed with a border of grey scrolling motifs and green, blue and red lozenges. The second with a long twisted fringe is elaborately printed in red, blue, orange, green, rose pink, dark and light browns and yellow.

weavers for convenience under one roof (*see plate* 19). In some cases a row of single-storied cottages was built with a chamber for looms across the whole of a floor above them.[1] Sir Harry Hardy of Morley recollects that in the last quarter of the nineteenth century his grandfather had a shed for sixty journeymen weavers at Skelmanthorpe, near Huddersfield.

Very many mills for long simultaneously employed both hand- and power-loom weavers. The former were now called in-weavers if employed in the mill and out-weavers if still working at home. In the 1840s a shed for hand looms was incorporated in a new mill built by the Akroyds at Copley. In 1858 Wormalds and Walker had 161 hand looms of which twenty-six were worked by in-weavers and the rest by out.[2] At Armley Mills, Leeds, the looms were never connected to a power supply, and were rented by the weavers. At Gillroyd Mills when new power looms were installed in 1860 they were let for 3*s*. 3*d*. a week, with all the parts found and a tuner engaged who earned 32*s*. a week. At Butt End Mills, Cleckheaton, Mrs D. White (b. 1883) remembers that her father, B. H. Goldthorp, employed six old hand-loom weavers working out their days. They used to give her Pomfret cakes covered with fluff out of their pockets.

In the worsted industry power looms could be used at faster speeds than hand looms and therefore replaced them in the first half of the century. But in the woollen trade hand looms were no less slow than power. 'Until well after 1866 the thud of the treadle and the clack of the picker against the shuttle was work-music in Batley homes.'[3] In 1860 there were in Batley 1,260 hand-loom weavers earning 9*s*. to 10*s*. a week.[4] But during the Franco-Prussian War power looms were rapidly installed, and hand looms continued only here and there (*see plates* 12–14). By this time women as spinners, weavers and menders had become essential to the running of a mill.

Certain districts by tradition made certain materials. In 1841 Thomas Cook, the main founder of Wormalds and Walker, blanket-makers of Dewsbury Mills, observed: 'This neighbourhood is studded with multitudes of small makers whose property may not, nor does, average £100.'[5] An enclave of the blanket-makers lived at Kilpin Hill, near Heckmondwike (which from 1811 for a few years had a

[1] H. A. Bodey, *Industrial History in Huddersfield*, 1972, for the beginning of the firm of George Mallinson & Sons, Linthwaite in the Colne valley.

[2] F. J. Glover, 'Dewsbury Mills, a History of Wormalds and Walker Ltd', University of Leeds, Ph.D. thesis, 1959.

[3] T. C. Taylor, *One Hundred Years*, 1946.

[4] S. Jubb, *History of the Shoddy Trade*, 1860.

[5] F. J. Glover, ibid.

blanket hall). Here the eighteenth- and early nineteenth-century cottages are remembered as home-workshops with loom chambers, scouring places and tenter fields 'once dressed out in snow-white drapery' of blankets. In 1850 the blanket weavers of Kilpin Hill and neighbourhood banded together to fix piecework rates (*see plate* 11).[1]

Only ten years later the movement down into the valley to the banks of the Calder began. In 1866 John Walker of Kilpin Hill was invited to become a partner of Hague Cook & Wormald, eventually to become Wormalds and Walker. Here, too, in 1750 another Walker, James, living on a small farm at Capas Heights and starting with one loom, began to employ weavers in cottages near by. He bought and scoured wool, wove blankets, milled, tentered and raised the pieces, which each gave some twenty blankets, and took them for sale to the piece hall at Halifax. When in 1868–72 his grandsons built Holme Bank Mills on the Calder at Mirfield, other people from Kilpin Hill moved down to work for them. In 1932 the firm built a mill at Witney. Similarly the Bruce family business was moved from Heckmondwike to Clive Mills on the Calder, and four daughters getting up at 5 a.m. are remembered going there to whip blankets.[2]

Clothiers and often weavers living on a farm or a smallholding kept a horse or a donkey, a cow or cows, and a pig, clothed themselves in their own stuffs, and in the Pennine hills dug peat for fuel. Living expenses were small, reckoned in the 1830s at 5s. 2d. a week a head to clothe and feed a family out of a combination of farming and cloth manufacture.[3] Donkeys for transporting pieces, coal and any other goods were part of the system. There were said to be as many of them as people in Thurstonland near Huddersfield.[4]

The upper floors of houses, often stone-flagged, held the loom or looms and a bobbin wheel, and where houses were built into the hillside access to loom chambers was gained directly at the back, or on flat ground by a flight of outside stone steps to the 'takin-in' door (*see plate* 3). Rockfold, a three-storied building at Golcar, now pulled down, was known as ''t sheet o' pins' because the long rows of windows resembled pins as they used to be sold on sheets of paper. In such a house processes such as beaming (preparing the warp for the loom), sometimes *lecking* (scouring the cloth with urine and pig's dung to cleanse it of grease), or spinning (by this time on a hand-spinning jenny) took place in the middle chamber.

[1] Leaflet at the Bagshaw Museum, Batley.
[2] Information from Mr Harold Walker, Mr J. G. Walker, and Mr and Mrs E. Walker.
[3] Beardsell, 'An historical account of our trade from the time of becoming a Partner in 1828'. Transcript of MS. lent by Mr S. Beardsell.
[4] Mary A. Jagger, *The History of Honley*, 1914.

10. *Mr Ishmael Whittell, hand-loom plush weaver, at Messrs Sykes and Tunnicliffe, Northfields Mill, Almondbury (1919).*

11. *Mr Joseph Pinder (d. 1910), the last of the Kilpin Hill blanket weavers (date unknown).*

12. Timothy Feather (1825–1910), of Buckley Green, Stanbury, near Keighley, seen sitting in his 'house'. He was the last hand-loom weaver in that neighbourhood. Note the bobbin winder, and oatcake hung on a flake.

HAND-LOOM WEAVING

Often smells and when raw wool was prepared fleas were endemic. A common piece of furniture in the downstairs living quarters was a put-up bed, even two, sometimes of solid mahogany. Children often slept in the loom chamber, and in one house in the Colne valley in a hammock, reached with difficulty, slung above the loom.

The loom itself was the property of the weaver, and in 1830 costing £2 11s., it strained a man's means.[1] They were made by local joiners such as the Stansfields of Almondbury, near Huddersfield, who generally had one on the bench for winter work. Latterly they were sold to technical colleges, foreign countries, and the last, made there in 1947 by Mr W. S. Schofield, who had worked for and followed the Stansfields, cost £120. The frame, 9 feet high, was of deal and the going part (*sley* board) beech, and they were finished with a high polish like the best furniture (*see diagram on page* 23).

In 1832 James Beardsell wrote from London to ask his wife to send him some papers 'in the Money drawer in our loom'. Women, when weaving, rocked their babies by fastening the cradle band to the sley board, and they washed and baked at night while the men wove by the light of 'a farding cannel at each end of the loom'.[2] When shuttles had to be thrown, all wore hooves on their hands, and children had to wind so many bobbins before going to school.

At Halifax the piece hall, opened on 1 January 1779, the only one left intact in Yorkshire, is undoubtedly the finest monument to the wool textile industry in the eighteenth century to be seen in England, and recollections of people carrying their pieces to it are numerous. Crowds of clothiers, who having paid £28 4s. owned one of the 315 rooms, and weavers, charged 1d. for each piece brought in, converged on it on market days. Nancy Ickeringill, 'a big powerful woman, six feet tall, and with a Roman nose', who lived on a farm at Haworth, carried her pieces to Halifax, and Grace Southwell of Denholme hired herself to transport pieces across the moors and was in consequence known as 'the packhorse'.

On the other side of Halifax at Longley near Norland Moor lived William Whitaker, a hand-loom weaver, who following a packhorse track down and up steep hillsides transported his pieces to Halifax. 'One shoulder was always lower than the other', says Mrs S. E. Grayshan, his granddaughter. 'They all were. One old man was quite down on one side.' The trough to which all neighbours brought urine is still there in front of the houses where William lived. Eventually he started work at Rawson's Mill in the Ryburn valley. During the Luddite Riots truncheons

[1] E. Sigsworth, *Black Dyke Mills*, 1958, p. 147.
[2] Mrs A. Tupman (b. 1882), Heptonstall.

had been issued to the work force, and one passed on to William has been handed down in the family.

In the Holme valley Mrs A. Howard remembers her grandmother, Mary Haigh (1826–1920) known as Mary a' t' Mount', who was born at Holme Woods, one of the high little moorland farms then usually occupied by hand-loom weavers. Down in the valley were the small mills for spinning, scouring and fulling, and Mary herself took the cloth there on horseback. Working when it suited, often until midnight, the family hung up a curtain so that people should not see in. But in some households here two buckets of peat were brought in every night, and when 'those were done it were bedtime'.

Many hand-loom weavers eventually found employment in quarries, in the building of reservoirs, and in such jobs as delivering goods for shops with a horse and cart. A few, earning mere pittances, wove to the end of their days supported by younger members of the family, or they took up secondary occupations such as baking oatcake or mangling clothes. The last in a district acquired fame (*see plates* 11–12).

Mr Joe France, the retired manager of Cellars Clough Mill, Marsden (b. 1882), recollects the Colne valley in his boyhood. 'Times were hard and it bred a hard people. But in those weaving hamlets on the hillsides they never thought of locking their doors, and if anyone fell on evil days the others always helped out.' His grandfather, Joseph Sykes, known as Knuckle, built Shaw Field, never so called but always referred to as New 'Oile (Hole), still to be seen tucked into the hillside between Slaithwaite and Marsden. He was a man of some means and education who pursued work and hunting in about equal parts. His house was furnished with the solid carved oak pieces of former days, and hounds generally basked on the hearthrug in front of the fire. 'When the weavers heard the bay of the hounds it was more than they could stand. They dropped their work and set off hunting. Later as candle lights glimmered from windows people said: "So-and-so's *inning* up [catching up]."'

Besides making cloth, Joseph set up hand looms whenever they were required and kept a stock of parts—sleys, beams, shuttles. He used to go a *a-bunting*, that is he fetched warp and weft from Longroyd Bridge, five miles away, on donkeys and delivered it round to the cottages. The general trade of the valley was then linsey, a cheap cloth with a cotton warp and a woollen weft, mostly a faded blue or natural brown in colour, sold in Lancashire and to miners. (Cotton warps were introduced in 1834.) Joseph Sykes had one special sixteen-treadle loom, on which an old man who was an expert designer, and who always wore a top hat when working, wove fancy waistcoating. Pieces were sent to Manchester, usually by train, although many people walked there across the moorlands. After a successful deal Knuckle declared a free house for the day at the Dartmouth Arms, Slaithwaite; but on Sundays he wore his best broadcloth and conducted Bible readings at teatime.

When he was very small Mr France helped his grandfather in various ways. If the yarns were snarling and difficult to handle, he *bruzzed* bobbins put in a frame. 'You filled your mouth with water and made a mist by blowing air and water out at the same time.' (Another method was to dip a basket of weft in water and *wuzz* it on a stick (*see plate* 4).) 'And when they were beaming another warp for the loom in the middle chamber they used to put me underneath on a little buffet. They were going through their *raddles* that is separating and opening out the warp into so many threads to go on the beam. [The raddle, of which the top bar was detach-able, was a long wooden framework with thick vertical wires through which the yarn was threaded.] The men put a *stang* [pole] through a hole in the centre of the beam, and turned it over, and at the other end the threads were running through these raddles. If a thread broke I had to shout and they stopped winding. They'd take their pieces to be scoured at Shaw Carr, an old mill no longer there. Tenter-gates were all over; sometimes stone, sometimes wooden posts carried them. A piece was between sixty and seventy yards long, and it was hooked on and held tight. They had to watch the weather.' Similarly the weaver looked for a fine day on which to size his warp, hanging it to dry between gate-posts or on pegs driven into walls.

Life at the end of the last century on the bleak Pennine plateau of green pastures, stone walls, and isolated weavers' houses between the Colne and Deanhead valleys is remembered by Mr J. T. Gee of Outlane. His parents, Tom and Alice Gee, and their five children lived in a cottage at Prospect Place on condition that Alice wove for the owner, George Brook, a clothier of Jacob's Well, Round Ings, less than a mile away.

Both parents could weave, but Tom was employed as a horseman for Edward Sykes, the owner of Gosport Mills at Outlane, built about 1860. Before then the Sykeses had put out their scribbling and spinning to the country mills and had taken in the pieces from the weavers all round. 'It was a busy spot.' Once Gosport Mills were built the workers left the country mills and went there. 'My grandad', says Mr Gee, 'was in at the building of it. Living in the Deanhead valley, he walked over, and became manager and designer. His children, ten of them, all worked at Gosport. He'd a big mending table, and they all took their own food and sat round having breakfast together.'

Alice wove the same cotton-warp cloth that was made in the Colne valley just over the hill. 'I went to bed many a time with the loom going and mother singing. Oh aye!' For Christmas they used to buy half a pig, curing it in the cellar. Alice had to have a 'double draw' to pay for it, that is to weave two pieces in a week and earn double the usual money which was 8*s*. 6*d*. a piece. When the shuttle had not run off clean, the bits were put in a little basket and one of Jack's jobs was to wind them steadily out on *coppins* (cops) to be used again. Three of the family beamed the warp (wound it on a beam). Usually a six-cut warp, this made six pieces, 'a fair length' which had to be *cuttled* up (folded backwards and forwards) and tentered on some light railings with nails on them. Those who had a donkey transported the piece tied on with a girth called a *wantey*. But young Gee took his in a wheelbarrow, held on tightly with a canvas belt, to Round Ings where it was taken in at the landing. George Brook weighed out the weft, that is the coppins, and wrapped them up in canvas to fit the shape of the barrow.

One of their friends used his donkey for cuttling pieces. Two people standing at each side drew the cloth across the animal's back, folding it on to a table. Then the donkey died. When the next piece was delivered, the clothier complained that it had not enough pile on it. The wooden stand substituted had failed to brush it up. 'My father said, "You'll have to buy another donkey."'

As in all these districts farming was linked with daily life. Milk was 2½*d*. a quart, 1*d*. for old milk for baking with. One of their neighbours, Sam Morton, a cattle dealer, journeyed regularly to Ireland, and Tom Gee helped out with the milking. 'It was surprising how the whole of the time was filled with doing something.' His wife, Polly Morton, was a big strong woman. They used to meet the cows which had arrived by train at Slaithwaite and had galloped off up Crimble Clough. 'Don't worry,' Polly used to say, 'they'll slow down before you get to the top of Crimble.'

'My mother worked all the year round. They were workers in those days. They were grand days though. We were happy. I can remember my first suit. It was blue. My father used to buy odd lengths at the mill [pattern lengths made for showing to customers] and mother made them up. When a lad was going to get married they used to say, "Can she bake and wesh?"'

At the age of thirteen Jack Gee started to work for his uncle at Parkwood Mill, Longwood, for 5*s*. a week, out of which his mother gave him 1*s*. for pocket money. The wage rose by 1*s*. a week until he was earning 12*s*.; 18*s*. to £1 was then a good wage. 'I was a big lad, and I'd always to work over [overtime]. I got all this and put half of it in the bank.' Mr and Mrs Gee were mayor and mayoress of Huddersfield in 1955–6, and Mrs Gee was mayor in her own right in 1964–5.

When William Cudworth wrote *Round About Bradford* in 1876 he had seen many disused hand looms 'awaiting their doom as firewood'. A hundred years later we

13. Mr G. H. Johnstone demonstrates weft winding from the hank to the bobbin at a small factory making heald rugs up to about 1953 in Pudsey.

14. The looms were arranged round the walls near the windows, and the weavers sat propped against the walls on two-legged buffets. Two beams were used—a pile beam seen at the top of the loom and a warp beam at the bottom.

found machinery and a hand loom, formerly one of six, in a small factory for making heald rugs at Pudsey, run for the first fifty years of this century by the Johnstone family. (Another of the looms is to be seen at the Moravian Museum, Fulneck.) Heald rugs have a long pile of twisted worsted dyed red, green, rust and black, and used in kitchens and farmhouses were valued for their hard-wearing qualities.

The three-storied house, probably originally occupied by a clothier, dates back at least to 1833, and is a reminder of the once populous clothing villages round about.[1] The top floor, 35 feet square, extending over the whole building, holds the machinery and the remaining looms (*see plates* 13–14). The Johnstones bought in yarn and processed it ready for weaving with the machines—a doubler, cheese winder and a hank winder—driven by a gas turbine and later by electricity, and they employed half-timers who learnt to weave in a fortnight by throwing the empty shuttle from side to side and treadling rhythmically with their feet. Older women working full time could each make three rugs, one yard by two, in a day.

[1] *Commercial Directory* 1816–17 gives '164 manufacturers who attended the Mixed and Coloured Cloth Halls at Leeds from Armley, Rawdon, Calverley, Churwell, Gildersome, Farsley, Bramley, Horsforth, Stanningley, Low Wortley, Pudsey'.

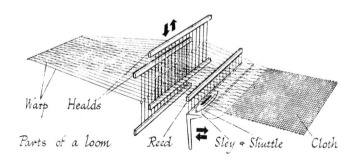

Warp   Healds

Parts of a loom   Reed   Sley & Shuttle   Cloth

2 Mills and Manufacturers

FROM the 1770s onwards mills to contain the new machinery began to be built. Opportunity to make a start was there for anyone who was capable, hard working, shrewd, far-sighted and as was said of Robert Moore, the mill-owner in *Shirley*, 'keen o' making brass and getting forrards'. Briefly mills were initially built by three means: by private individuals, by landlords who let 'room and power', and most often by groups of men who on the lines of friendly societies subscribed small sums of money to build and run company mills. Thus many gained a foothold.

Most were drawn from the ranks of the clothiers, some from landowning families, and a few from outside the county. Many borrowed from banks, which in the early nineteenth century were sometimes run by the large textile firms. Hague and Cook of Dewsbury Mills printed their own bank-notes. It was not until the 1850s to the 1870s, the climactic period of the industry, that large mills, of which foremost examples are Saltaire Mills (1853) and Manningham Mills (1873), were erected all at one time (*see plate* 21).

Nor was opportunity for the many confined to the early days. Mills constantly changed hands as the clothiers, now manufacturers, rose and fell. One man's disaster was another man's chance. An abandoned mill could be bought cheaply. Clogs to clogs in three generations (and sometime less) echoes down the years. Most eventually became family concerns with almost always a dominant member of one generation laying foundations for those who followed. Sometimes sons lost all that their fathers had built up. Manufacturers had constantly to install new machinery, change to new raw materials and new cloths, overcome the dire effects of tariffs imposed by foreign governments especially American, and the cycles of trade peculiar to the industry. 'Trade comes in the night' expresses their unpredictable nature. The awesome slumps of the early 1920s and 1930s put many out of business altogether. Wars from the eighteenth century onwards, bringing in their train army contracts for uniform cloths and blankets benefited trade, saved firms from disaster, and earned capital to surmount later recessions.

MILL-OWNERS
15. John Eli Walker (1848–1943) of Holme Bank Mills, Mirfield (c. 1925).

16. John Crowther (1817–1865), son of John Crowther (b. 1783) clothier and of Lees Mill, Golcar, Colne Valley, the founder of the Crowther dynasty.

18. Charlotte Sykes (1790–1852) who built Acre Mills, Lindley, near Huddersfield.

17. Martha Crossley (1775–1854), wife of and driving force behind John Crossley, founder in 1802 of Crossleys Carpets at Dean Clough Mills, Halifax. Rising daily at 4 a.m., she controlled 160 hand-loom weavers, was responsible for selling

the products of four looms making brace webs and body belts, and with assistance, made and stitched every carpet they sold retail.

EVOLUTION OF A FIRM

19. Loomshop for sixty hand looms in Chapel Lane, Addingham, built by John Cockshott in about 1780 for weaving calico. There were five Cockshotts, calico manufacturers, in Addingham in 1822. The building was later used for the making of clog irons.

20. Low Mills, Addingham, built in 1787 by John Cockshott and John Cunliffe, the second worsted mill to be built in England. The water-wheel was at the side of the building next to the river Wharfe, and two rows of cottages, in one of which a school was held, are seen behind. The projections on the front of the two main buildings contained closets (c. 1921).

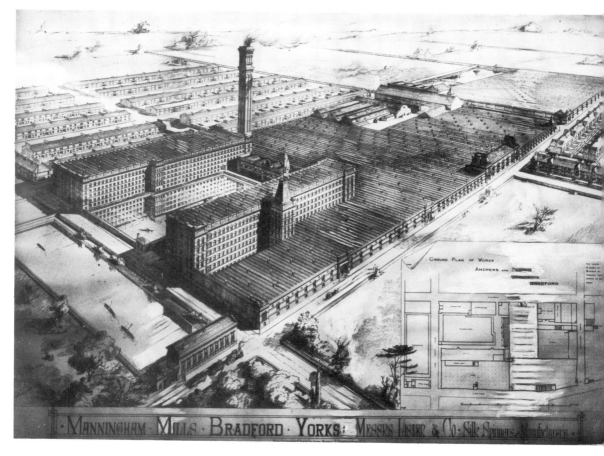

21. *Ground plan of Manningham Mills, Bradford, built by Samuel Cunliffe Lister, grandson of John Cunliffe, in 1873. The architects were Andrews and Pepper of Bradford and the works then covered eleven acres of flooring and required about 3,000 h.p. to drive the machinery. The lodges spaced at intervals along the frontage gave access to the various departments. Note the rows of back-to-back houses.*

MILL YARD AND DAM
22. *The mill yard at John Foster and Son, Black Dyke Mills, Queensbury. The office block is glimpsed on the left and the semi-round projection contains Shed Mill staircase and a lift. The chimney was built prior to 1868.*

Throughout the nineteenth century mills were added to, pulled down, burnt down, rebuilt and extended. Almost without exception they were destroyed by fire at least once. In cotton mills the spinners worked in bare feet, incurring the hazard of *spells* (splinters) from wooden floors as at Spring Mill in the Ryburn Valley, so that their clogs did not strike sparks. These disasters resembled a *blitzkrieg* from whose ashes new and better mills arose. Mill fires, an unforgettable sight of crashing beams and leaping flames, had dire effects on both owners and workers, and encouraged the provision of private fire-engines and brigades, and also fireproof building techniques for which cast-iron columns and girders were advocated as early as 1801 by James Watt. In this century water sprinkling systems were introduced.

Low Mills, Addingham, the second worsted spinning mill in the country, was built on the river Wharfe in 1790 by John Lister and John Cockshott (*see plate* 20). The first of the great steam-driven mills, Park Mills at Bean Ing, Leeds, built in 1792, was the vision of the first of the great entrepreneurs, Benjamin Gott. 'It sprang from nothing, an ideal, a dream of a new age of industrialization material-ized in brick and iron, in steam and machinery.'[1] Two years later John Marshall, also in Leeds, started the first of his flax-spinning mills that culminated in the Egyptian-style Temple Mill in 1840. Bradford's first worsted mill with a 15 h.p. engine was built in 1798[2] (and only fifty years later a writer in the *Morning Chron-icle* commented that 'fortunes have been made in Bradford with a rapidity almost unequalled even in the manufacturing districts'). In the 1830s the building of woollen mills in the Dewsbury area was 'immense, enough to astonish anybody'. At Batley, short of water power, the era of mill building dated from the late 1840s to 1860.

As we have noted many little mills, each with dams, goits and water-wheels, were built in the smaller Pennine valleys: twenty-four on the river Holme and its tributaries down to Holmfirth, now only three mills left;[3] eight cotton and two silk built between the 1780s and the 1840s on Colden Water in upper Calderdale, now none; eight cotton, one corn, and one woollen in Cragg Vale, now none; ten in the Blackburn valley on the Black Brook, south of Halifax, for corn, fulling, cotton, paper, wire, woollen, and worsted,[4] now six, three woollen, one waste, one paper and one carpet; and over 100 on the waters of the Tame and its tributaries in

[1] W. B. Crump, 'The Leeds Woollen Industry 1780–1820', *Thoresby Society* vol. XXXII, 1929.
[2] J. James, *History of Bradford*, 1866.
[3] J. M. Hinchliffe, 'A Dissertation on the Mills of the Upper Holme Valley', Huddersfield Poly-technic School of Architecture, unpublished thesis.
[4] See Augustus Muir, *The History of Bowers Mills*, 1969.

Saddleworth. In these areas bordering on Lancashire the manufacturers who built the cotton mills had changed from the woollen to the cotton trade, and many were to revert later to wool. In 1838 there were 140 cotton mills employing 10,000 persons in the West Riding.

Many of these mills were demolished when reservoirs were made. But also for several reasons—accessibility, the more efficient steam power needing coal, and transport provided by canals and railways—industry moved into the main valleys. The complex of huge mills in the Colne valley was developed from 1860 to 1890 and the last, called Titanic, was built as its name implies in 1912. By 1884 the total number of mill-owners had risen to 1,108.

Built from stone quarried near at hand and evolving in design from the corn mills, the clothiers' homes and the loomshops, mills were first small and square and developed into the familiar long, many-storied, many-windowed edifices. Like castles and abbeys they roughly conform to a basic design. Entering through a sometimes handsome gateway, the mill yard paved with setts allowed for the arrival and despatch of goods and was so large at Bean Ing that it held tenters. At the entrance was the time office or 'penny 'oile' (*see Chapter* 4), and on one side of the yard either adjoining the warehouse or a separate building stood the owner's house which in time was vacated for a new house built at a discreet distance. Because weaving came late into the mills, one-storied weaving sheds usually with saw-tooth roofs fill in available ground.

Interior stone spiral staircases in the corners to save space as at St Peg Mill, Cleckheaton, Clough House Mills, Slaithwaite, or Washpits Mill, Holmfirth, were common. Machinery was in fact too closely packed together. At Spring Mill in the Ryburn valley Mr Irvin Berry remembers that when the little piecer wanted to put bobbins in at the back of the spinning frames, he lay on the floor to let the mules run over him and lay down again to get out. In weaving sheds when a new warp was required, the beam had to be lifted shoulder high into position on the loom by several overlookers.

Shallow projecting gables as at Low Mills, Addingham, and Dean Clough Mills, Halifax, accommodated privies on each floor, with a cast-iron pipe down the full height. Towers, with later water tanks for the sprinklers put on top, contained hoists, and the engine house is distinguished by tall narrow windows. Those symbols of the power house and the Industrial Revolution, chimneys, rose higher and higher, and some of their owners, Samuel Cunliffe Lister of Manningham Mills, Bradford, Thomas Taylor of Blakeridge Mills, Batley, John Edward Crowther of Bank Bottom Mills, Marsden, and Armitage Haigh of Priestroyd Ironworks, Huddersfield, on their completion or when they were being repaired, climbed to the top. Dams once needed for water for the water-wheels (and remembered as paradise for skaters in frosty winters), were still essential to provide water for the various processes. Single-storied buildings are now regarded as more functional; yet, there the mills stand in the industrial landscape, grand and huge, monuments to human endeavour and endurance, symbols of an industry 'epic in its destiny and traditions'.

Innumerable examples might be given of the humble beginnings of large important firms. Jeremiah Ambler began in 1789 as a rope-maker and founded what was to become a large important mohair and worsted spinning firm at Bradford, and C. & J. Hirst began in a cottage at Longwood in the Colne valley, and eventually had five mills and 1,400 employees. In Batley J. T. and T. Taylor, who eventually were to employ 1,600 people, become famous for their profit-sharing scheme and for Theodore Taylor, who lived to be 102, started with £300 and an eight-day clock.

A diary describes how the Beardsell family business at Holme House in the Holme valley was built up. In 1828 James Beardsell, a small clothier, took his four sons into partnership, and one of them, Isaac, the hard-working member, increased the trade in three years from the making of four pieces a week to twenty. Their success rested on Isaac's skill in designing at the time of the changeover from kerseys to fancy goods. He wrote in 1835; 'There was nothing for which I felt more ambitious than to bring out some new pattern which would take the lead', and he produced amongst others 'the grouse pattern . . . a right pattern brought out at the right time'. In 1836 they took Digley Mill on Digley Brook at the rent of £140 a year, and the Beardsells became some of the leading manufacturers in the Holme valley.[1]

Or take John Buckley (1754–1825), a yeoman clothier, who built two water-driven mills, one with his cousin about 1767, Lower and Upper Broadhead in the Castleshaw valley, near Delph (*see plate* 7). Two of John's five sons, Henry and Hugh, frequently journeyed abroad, one to New York and the other to Lisbon where they joined English colonies of merchants. Henry sold woollen goods and bought cotton, and Hugh sold fine quality broadcloth and remarkably beautiful printed shawls destined for Spain. In 1821 Hugh advised that canary, buff, scarlet and orange were the favourite colours, and, because there were other makers of shawls from Saddleworth, that competition was keen (*see plates* 8–9). In 1879

[1] Isaac Beardsell, 'An Historical Account of our Trade from the time of becoming a Partner in 1828', transcript of MS. lent to us by Mr Stephen Beardsell. For patterns of fancy goods see those designed by W. Etchells in the mid-nineteenth century in the Tolson Memorial Museum, Huddersfield.

members of the Buckley family moved to the better equipped Linfitts Mill on the river Tame.[1]

In passing it may be noted that life at Broadhead and Holme House was pleasant and dignified. A boarding school existed in the Castleshaw valley, and one of Hugh Buckley's sons took violin lessons which he disliked and used a string for his fishing-rod. Peter, one of the Beardsell brothers, enjoyed shooting woodcock, and whilst staying at Buxton visited Chatsworth House.

In that shawl-wearing century Saddleworth and the upper Colne valley from about 1820 were the main centres of manufacture. Little mills at Marsden and Slaith-waite made them. One built in Crimble Clough in 1832 dyed and finished silk shawls, and a maker, Shoddy Sam (Samuel Shaw), is remembered gathering wool caught on bilberry bushes on the moors. Elsewhere worsted yarn was spun for them. S. Cunliffe Lister invented a fringe-twisting machine, as did Joseph Craven of Thornton, near Bradford, a member of a firm that drew the trade in shawl cloths away from Paisley.[2] *The Yorkshire Textile Directory*, 1919, gives forty-four flannel and shawl manufacturers of whom sixteen makers are in the Saddleworth district. One of the last, James Bailey of Uppermills made travelling rugs and little shawls costing 2s. 6d. for the kaffirs in South Africa.

Morley provides examples of both a 'room and power' and a company mill. In the first category the Crank Mill is in any case famous as one of the earliest mills powered by steam; and it was built in 1790 for £1,250 by Lord Dartmouth and leased to John and Joseph Webster at £100 a year and later to others (*see drawing on page* 34). In the second category Gillroyd Mills are antedated by many, for instance Healey Mill built at Ossett in 1765, but its first committee book survives.[3]

The Gill Royds Mill Company, as it was then spelt, was started in December, 1834, by a group of twelve men (one of whom was the father of the Right Honourable H. H. Asquith, prime minister from 1908 to 1916). Over a period they subscribed £30 a share to build a public fulling and scribbling mill to which dyeing was soon added. To finish and equip the mill they borrowed money, mortgaged the premises to complete them, urged Hird, Dawson and Hardy of Low Moor to build the engine, and after two years' effort paid £4,413 for the building, five cottages and a dam, out of which the architect, Mark Holmes, received £75 4s. 1d. They then appointed from time to time a date for the 'Mill Feast', celebrated by a dinner, and

[1] Documents and shawls shown to us by Mr and Mrs G. E. Buckley.
[2] William Cudworth, *Round about Bradford*, 1876.
[3] John Goodchild, 'The Ossett Mill Company', *Textile History*, 1968–70, vol. I, No. I, pp. 47–61; MS. Committee Book, Gill Royds Mill Company, 1835–61, Archives department, Leeds Central Library.

pay day for all who had had goods processed. Over the years new buildings were added to include spinning in 1858 and weaving in 1860. A severe fire destroyed the mill in 1885, but it was built up again by the company. In time shareholders sold out and founded their own businesses, and one of them, John Hartley (1847–1919), first leased then bought the mill which was run by his descendants until 1966.

Meanwhile in mid-century the founders of the great mills of the high noon of the Yorkshire textile industry, almost all based on worsted and the new materials—alpaca, mohair and waste silk—emerged: John Crossley (1772–1837), who leased a mill at Dean Clough, Halifax, in 1802, and founded a carpet factory which a hundred years later was employing 5,000 workpeople; John Foster (1799–1878), the son of a farmer and colliery owner, who in 1835 started to build Black Dyke Mills at Queensbury between Halifax and Bradford, who was followed by William Foster, the dominant figure, and who in the 1870s were employing 3,500 workpeople; Titus Salt (1803–76), who was foremost in discovering the use of alpaca and built the mills and a model village at Saltaire; Isaac Holden (1807–97), inventor and woolcomber, who was born in Scotland and ran combing plants in France; Edward Akroyd (1810–87) of Halifax, whose family sprang from yeomen clothiers in upper Calderdale, who pioneered model housing estates in the West Riding; and Samuel Cunliffe Lister (1815–1906), inventor, discoverer of the use of waste silk and builder of Manningham Mills. All these major figures who made vast fortunes are well known and the subjects of various studies.[1]

Others rose to the fore: the Brookes at Armitage Bridge Mills, who for 'fifteen generations and through four centuries have owned and occupied a mill on the waters of the Holme'; the Firths at Heckmondwike and Brighouse building three mills, one in the United States, established a great carpet-making firm, whose ownership changed in the early years of this century to the Aykroyds; Wormalds and Walker of Dewsbury Mills started in 1811 with five corn, fulling and scribbling mills on the river Calder, which became the largest blanket-making firm in the country.[2]

Some mills and their owners dominated a village, such as the Shaws who built Brookroyd Mills, Holywell Green near Halifax, employed 1,200 people, had a

[1] R. Bretton, *The Crossleys at Dean Clough*, 1950; R. Balgarnie, *Sir Titus Salt*, 1877; E. M. Sigsworth, 'Sir Isaac Holden Bart: The First Comber in Europe' in *Textile and Economic History*, ed. N. B. Harte and K. G. Ponting, 1973; R. Bretton, 'Colonel Edward Akroyd', *Transactions of the Halifax Antiquarian Society*, 1948, pp. 61–100; Samuel Cunliffe-Lister, *Lord Masham's Inventions*, 1905; E. M. Sigsworth, *Black Dyke Mills*, 1958.

[2] W. B. Crump and G. Gorbal, *History of the Huddersfield Woollen Industry*, pp. 47, 117–20; *150th Anniversary, Flush Mills, Heckmondwike, near Leeds*, 1972; F. J. Glover, 'Dewsbury Mills, a history of Messrs Wormalds and Walker Ltd', University of Leeds, PhD. thesis, 1959.

private railway, and as a family firm finished in 1952.[1] At Gomersal in 1752 the Burnleys were yeomen clothiers living at Pollard Hall, and 100 years later Thomas Burnley bought the Cloth Hall Mill at Gomersal, now called Gomersal Mills, and ran it until 1913. These mills, now part of a combine, are notable for the scale of their operations and modern system for worsted spinning, combing and dyeing. In the Colne valley, besides other families, such as Hirst, Hoyle, Beaumont and Mallinson, the Crowthers, branching out from Lees Mill at Golcar, backed the building of large mills from Milnsbridge to Marsden. Bank Bottom and others run by John Edward Crowther (1862–1931) were said in his lifetime to be the largest privately owned mills in the world.

Amongst all these Cunliffe Lister was raised to the peerage, and others, amongst whom Sir Isaac Holden, who rising from poverty has the most unusual career, were given baronetcies and knighthoods. Some became members of parliament, founded banks, promoted railways, and started profit-sharing schemes. In varying degrees especially in the mid-century building era they contributed vast sums to erect churches, chapels, schools, almshouses, mechanics' institutes, model housing estates, and especially chapels for many were Nonconformists. Some built mansions, now turned into public buildings. A few—Fosters, Crossleys, Brookes, Crowthers and others—founded dynasties that still continue. In the later years of the century and in this others made fortunes and hurried away from their native places.

Many manufacturers faced adversity. They lived beyond their means, or were unlucky, or were defeated by new tariffs, and in an effort to extricate themselves from difficulty were involved in fraud, or mortgaged houses, or borrowed from relations and staff—a brother, a widowed mother, the foreman, the firer. Families quarrelled and members split off. Some colourful figures are fixed like flies in amber in local annals for their exploits such as backing plays on the London stage with dire financial results. Firms went bankrupt; men committed suicide, and even died of broken hearts. Except in fiction these agonies involving pride, home and family have been insufficiently stressed in studies of the textile trade.

Albeit strict disciplinarians and frequently powerful personalities, manufacturers were totally engrossed in the mill and often father-figures in their own world, especially before the advent of National Insurance and the Welfare State. The death of a large mill-owner shook a whole district. Usually salaries were modest and thrift was ingrained; earnings from trading were the hoped-for source of wealth. When in 1889 William Hanson, who had begun work as a little piecer at ten years old, formed his large firm of cotton spinners and doublers at Halifax into

[1] R. M. Shaw, 'The Shaws of Stainland', *Transactions of the Halifax Antiquarian Society*, 1965.

a limited company, his salary as managing director was £400 a year paid quarterly plus £100 for travelling expenses, the cost of the usual first-class ticket between Bradford and Manchester and an allowance for a journey to Germany. In 1907 the sons of the owner at one woollen mill had an extra 5s. a week allotted them on their thirtieth birthdays. At one important mill at luncheons for board meetings a director knelt down on his knees in order to measure the sherry in each glass so that all had exactly equal quantities. At Mallinson's old Eli, son of the founder, is remembered chiding a clerk for spilling and wasting a drop of ink.

Sons served an apprenticeship by going through the mill, working mill hours, thus establishing personal contact with their staff who addressed them as 'Mr John', 'Mr Harry' and so on. At Washpits Mill, Holmfirth, Mr Stephen Beardsell's grandfather went to work in 1865, his father in 1899, and he himself in 1926, when they were all three there together. In 1905 Mr Philip Kirk of the Crank Mill was 'fetched from school' when he was fifteen and has worked at the mill ever since. His father gave him nothing and he went to the 'tech.' at night, both usual practices. At the age of nineteen Mr Harold Walker of Holme Bank Mills lived in Aachen to work as a textile machinery overlooker and to learn German. One of the Shaw family spent two years in Shanghai, and another took a course in chemistry and dyeing at Bayer's in Elberfeld in Germany. As a young man Mr M. W. Shelton of Gomersal Mills spent some of his early years in mills in northern France, and his father, J. W. Shelton, used to travel on business from the Hook of Holland to Moscow and back via Vienna and Saxony with a few gold sovereigns in his pocket. As time went on sons were sent to public schools and university, and some eschewing trade turned into country gentlemen.

Women, who under the domestic system had played important roles, now only held office in wartime or became heads of firms in emergencies. For example Mrs P. D. Crowther following the death of her husband took on the chairmanship of Bank Bottom Mills in 1953, and Mrs E. M. Horsley, a director of her family firm, William Hanson, at Halifax, became secretary after the death of the holder of that office in 1952, and in 1964 the first woman president of a Chamber of Commerce in England.

Amidst all the 'hurry of work' there existed the hundreds of small firms: the top-makers at Bradford buying wool and having it combed on commission, the rag-sorting and shoddy-making establishments at Dewsbury and Batley, the makers of rugs of all kinds, the mending workshops, the fustian manufacturers of Hebden Bridge.

The rag and shoddy trade dates back to the invaluable discovery about 1813 that old rags could be ground up by machines to be re-cycled for use in the manufacture of cloth. Rags from all over the world were first auctioned at Dewsbury in 1845 by Henry Cullingworth; innumerable rag-sorting places run by members of families existed in every street in Batley and Dewsbury, and manufacturers of shoddy and mungo,[1] such as Henry Day and Sons, who started in 1844, were established. Here again thrift was the rule. Hephzibah Bruce, a rag merchant of Batley, remembered for having three husbands and three sons, sank her profits as was the custom in houses and shops.

Another firm started as a result of Jewish persecution in Europe. 'My grandfather, Samuel Strassburg, was a cloth manufacturer in the town of Pabianicz near Lodz in the Imperial Russian province of Poland.' In 1903 a son was sent to England to find a refuge, and by chance he learnt that Russian rags, called 'wants', were in demand at Dewsbury. He left for Russia, brought back two train loads, and the families changing their name to Stross settled as rag and cloth merchants in the West Riding.[2]

Cloth made of shoddy with cotton warps, besides clothing the poor, enjoyed a worldwide sale. Round the turn of the century Melton, a thick cloth, then priced at 6d. to 1s. a yard was sent in quantity to China, as were thousands of yards of cheap black coffin cloth, used in that country instead of coffins. Before the First World War low quality material could be sold at $2\frac{3}{4}d.$ a yard. But in a lifetime both the mills and the small rag sorters and mungo manufacturers have diminished in numbers as rags, bought up elsewhere, have become less available, and since synthetic materials have been introduced and heavy cloths, once a speciality, are no longer required in centrally heated buildings. Sixty years ago there were fifty-five manufacturing firms in Morley, in 1975 ten, and in Batley thirty-nine are reduced to five.[3] A feature of rags at the present day is their cleanliness and newness owing to the general use of washing machines and the habits of a throw-away society.

Another example of small units was to be found at Hebden Bridge where about 1840 the manufacture of fustian was established, followed, after the invention of the sewing machine, by the making-up of garments. (William Barker at Mayroyd Mill, was the first to use a power sewing machine.) It was general practice for the

---

[1] Shoddy and mungo are respectively ground up woollen and worsted rags. The unfortunate connotation of the word shoddy disguises the fact that if made from good quality wool it can be more valuable than less good pure new wool. See H. Burrows, *A History of the Rag Trade*, 1956, and *A Story of Woollen Rag Sales, 1860–1960. Centenary of Robert Thornton and Sons*, Savile Bridge, Dewsbury.

[2] MS. Notes on the Stross family of Dewsbury.

[3] Report, *Batley at Work, The Rise and Fall of a Textile Town*, 1974.

23. *Gibson or Lord Holme Mill, Hardcastle Crags, upper Calderdale, a water-powered cotton mill on Hebden Water built by Abraham Gibson about 1800. It ceased work about 1900.*

NUTCLOUGH MILL, HEBDEN BRIDGE

24. *Sewing Room with machinists (c. 1890).*   25. *Hand-finishers and Machine Room (c. 1890).*

26. *The Cutting Room (c. 1890).*

27. *Portable Exhibition Stand. Mr Sam Moore, traveller (c. 1910).*

28. *Cutting fustian. The cloth was stretched on a frame and the cutter sliced down the race with a rapier-like knife. This is now performed by a machine (date unknown).*

makers-up to buy grey cloth (undyed and uncut) from the weavers, and send it to dyers such as Moss's for dyeing and cutting. (Like velvet, the pile had to be cut to make corduroy, *see plate* 28) Some such as Sutcliffes and Redmans developed into large concerns. But even forty years ago many little firms flourished. A man cutting out garments and his wife machining could start a business. Everyone helped everyone else. Minimal distinction between employer and employed, who in any case were often related, encouraged a close-knit egalitarian society.

One of the firms, formerly at Nutclough Mill and now at the Hebden Works, was started in 1870 by about thirty men who, suffering hardship from lack of work and inspired by the co-operative movement then developing over the border in Lancashire, each subscribed 3*d.* a week to form a co-operative workshop. They rented a room, bought corduroy to cut, sent goods to local dyers, introduced the making-up of garments and founded the Hebden Bridge Fustian Manufacturing Society which in 1873, with the aid of a loan from the Wholesale Co-operative Society, bought a little mill at Nutclough. This flourished and was enlarged to the extent that by 1914 £15,600 had been paid out in bonus on wages, and in 1918 when 765 fustian looms were in operation, the concern was sold to the Wholesale Co-operative Society for £42,000. Nutclough closed down in 1968, but the same business continues at the Hebden Works.[1]

The various types of fustian—moleskin (plain, locally called mole), and corduroy (ribbed, known as cord)—together with denims, drills and woollen kersey were used up to the mid-1950s for industrial and institutional clothing interesting for its specific design. For instance pit sinkers in Durham, Yorkshire and Kent were supplied with suits made of white kersey which had knee and shoulder patches of moleskin. Mental hospitals were provided with cord trousers and derby tweed jackets and waistcoats, and for the less amenable patients moleskin garments, padded and quilted at the front and fastening down the back. The heavier weights of corduroy were once used for breeches and leggings for gamekeepers and country gentlemen, and are still made into climbing breeches. Thousands of yards of constitutional cloth, a broad ribbed corduroy whose pile had been cut, brushed and singed under gas burners so that gold adhered to it, were sent to South Africa for gold panning. This cloth is still in demand.[2]

What materials have we seen in the mills in the 1970s? Velvet and fur fabrics

---

[1] Joseph Greenwood, *The Story of the Formation of the Hebden Bridge Fustian Manufacturing Society Ltd*, 1888; *Report of the Coming of Age Celebrations of the H.B.F.M.S.*, 23rd and 26th September, 1891; *Rules of the H.B.F.M.S.*, 1908; 'The Fustian makers of Hebden Bridge', *The Wheatsheaf*, May 1919; all lent to us by Mr L. Barker.

[2] Information from Mr J. C. Atack, formerly of Cheethams.

such as imitation mink requiring special finishing processes at Manningham Mills, Bradford, fine worsted made in short runs for men's exclusive suits, much of it exported to Japan, at Newsome Mills, near Huddersfield, colourful finely-woven blazer cloths for Oxford colleges at Uppermoor Mill, Pudsey, mohair cloths at Black Dyke Mills, Queensbury (the largest factory for that material in the world), ladies' luxury coating and fine cloths made from cashmere, camelhair, mohair, angora at Batley Carr Mills, Dewsbury, and Hopton Mills, Mirfield, tweeds for the multiple tailors at the mills in the Colne valley, a cashmere blanket at Wormalds and Walker, a pattern of the carpet woven for the *Queen Elizabeth II* at Clifton Mills, Brighouse, hosiery yarn and knitting wools at Emu Wools, Keighley, striped denims and purple corduroy for the fashion trade at the Hebden Works, velours and union cloths at the Crank Mill, Morley, tartans to be made up into house coats in Denmark and thick felt cloth to protect the petrol tanks of aeroplanes at Washpits Mill, Holmfirth. 'You live out of versatility.'

We have seen chimneys being felled, mills standing idle or used for new purposes, and men of many nationalities attending the machines. The monopoly is over; other nations make cloth too. But inherited knowledge and skills still count. Textile historians trace the beginning of decline to the 1920s. In 1958 there were in the United Kingdom 1,087 firms with 170,626 employees, and in 1974 533 firms with 82,906, of whom 62,300 are in Yorkshire. Many family businesses have been caught up in the maw of large public companies. Others continue, harried by taxation, and all still suffer the booms and recessions of trade.

3 Half-timers

MAGNET-like the textile industry drew people to the West Riding from the far corners of the British Isles and from foreign countries. The influx of the Irish had started before the years of potato famine, and colonies grew in most towns. We have met the descendants of many emigrants: craftsmen overtaken by mass production, the grandson of a candle-maker at Hinderwell near Whitby, and sons and especially daughters of miners and steel workers from South Yorkshire where employment for women was scarce. A family pioneered and others followed, at first lodging with relatives. Others, attracted to the better pay, came from Derbyshire, East Anglia, Somerset to be maids, coachmen or gardeners to the manufacturers.

In the period with which we are concerned the days of child labour and inordinately long hours had passed. Factory and Education Acts had slowly given education precedence over work. None the less although gradually modified, half-time working for children lasted from 1844, when some schooling was made compulsory, until 1922. Several early mills had their own schools as at Low Mills, Addingham, and Armley Mills, Leeds. In Halifax in 1917 there were 1,057 half-timers,[1] and the last who began in this way retired from Dean Clough Mills on 4th July 1974, after fifty-six years' work.

But as late as the 1920s the bow-legged, the K-legged, the hunch-backed were not uncommon. It was said that a seventh child was marked for life. In other words large families suffered from neglect and malnutrition resulting in rickets and anaemia. Young people carried too heavy pieces in finishing departments and women worked too near the birth of a child. It is true that children deformed from birth could find light work in a mill more readily than elsewhere. Children, having nimble fingers and a soft touch and paid tiny wages, usefully performed operations in the spinning departments. Almost everyone in a mill formerly began as a little piecener or piecer, or a little doffer. The first joined broken threads between finger and thumb, and the second took off the full bobbins from mules or spinning

[1] Notes by H. W. Harwood seen at Halifax Courier Library.

frames. (Mules used for woollen spinning and frames for worsted are different: *see plates 33 and 35.*) A big and little piecer worked under a spinner, who, for instance, earned 41*s.* out of which he paid 12*s.* to them.[1] A team to mind mules in the Colne valley was a spinner, a minder, and two pieceners, a spinner and piecener in one mule gate and a minder and piecener in the other.

School log-books record the link between school and work. For instance, 8 February 1864, 'Admitted today many new children, nineteen half-timers from Drummond's Mill', and 17 September 1866, 'Six mill girls left the school to go full time'.[2] At Staincliffe, near Batley, on 14 December 1886, the master commented that he was 'greatly disappointed with the work of half-timers. They seem to forget facts almost as soon as they are taught. Either weariness or idleness seems their great characteristic'.[3]

The system frustrated teachers who had mixed classes of full- and half-time scholars. The latter suffered, although George Cooper, a half-timer in the 1880s at the age of ten, wrote that older people were helpful and sympathetic, that he worked a thirty-three hours week for 1*s.* 6½*d.* which he proudly took home, and that most never advanced beyond the fourth or fifth standards, but in reading, composition, spelling, and geography they compared favourably with the average scholar in the 1930s. An example beyond compare of a half-timer rising above circumstances is Joseph Wright (1855–1930), who started work as a doffer at Saltaire Mills at the age of seven, and eventually handed down to posterity that feat of scholarship the *English Dialect Dictionary*.

Former half-timers, whom we have met, dependent on their age, began work at from ten to thirteen. (At thirteen you became a young person with whom women were classed.) Mrs A. Tupman (b. 1882), then of Heptonstall, says that her father, William Townsend, started work at eight as a doffer, here pronounced 'dorfer', at Low Lumb Mill, on Colden Water (*see plate 6*). Up to then he had worn a dress and a pinny and was breeched to go. He earned 1*s.* 6*d.* a week rising to 2*s.* 6*d.* and when he was thirteen or fourteen made up for lack of schooling by attending classes at the mechanics' institute. He became a weaver, then a loom tackler (repairer), married and brought up a family of five boys and a girl, and, a keen bandsman and a conductor, he lived to be ninety-one.

Mrs Tupman herself began work as a half-timer when she was ten at 'Tommy Sutcliffe's' in Hebden Bridge. One week, leaving Heptonstall at 5.30 a.m. and

---

[1] E. Baines, *Yorkshire Past and Present*, 1858, vol. IV, p. 629.

[2] Log-books of St Paul's Church of England School, Manningham, seen by permission of Mrs B. Hudson and the governors.

[3] L. Kemp, *Staincliffe, near Dewsbury, Church of England School Centenary Handbook, 1869–1969.*

walking down the steep track known as the Buttress, she started work at 6 a.m
going to school in the afternoon, and the other week vice versa going to work at
1.30 p.m. until 6 p.m. and on Saturdays working until one o'clock. She learnt to
machine for eight weeks without pay, was then given 1d. a week pocket money
and earned 2s. 6d. rising to 5s. a week when she was thirteen. After that it was
usual to go on piecework and earn what you could, at the most £1 a week. After
marriage she left and did not return.

Only a week younger than Mrs Tupman, Mrs A. Walton of Heptonstall (b. 2
January 1883), because of intervening legislation could not go to work until she
was eleven. She too was a machinist. The girls sat on either side of a long table,
which had gas lights down the centre (for comparison *see plate* 24). They 'worked
through', that is, made complete garments such as 'riders' (riding breeches), cord
leggings for 3d., a boy's vest (waistcoat), jacket and trousers for 9d. Piecework
prices were reckoned down to eighths of a penny. Mrs Walton's sister, Miss E.
Akroyd, continued at work for sixty years.

Mrs A. Ashworth, whose early life follows a similar pattern, lived as a child at
Lily Hall near Heptonstall. The three-storied house was divided into four dwellings including a farmhouse on the ground floor, and her family occupied the
middle part at the back—a kitchen and two bedrooms. She was one of seventeen
children, only five of whom survived. She began half-time work at the age of
eleven, and earned 2s. 6d. a week given to her by the woman who taught her to
machine. When she married, she remembers, 'You could put 10s. on t'top o'
t'sideboard and buy a week's food'. Another industrial clothing worker, Mr H.
Barrett (b. 1885) of Heptonstall, began as a half-timer and eventually worked at
Nutclough Mill for forty-five years. He said, 'There's not a man in Hebden Bridge
as has been a band-knife cutter as long as what I have. . . . If I had mi time over
again I'd go to t'Nutclough. Never a wrong word.'

Take Mrs M. A. Collins' story. She was always called a 'Feast child' because
she was born on the Whit Sunday before Adwalton Feast in 1878. Her father, a
mine manager, was killed at work in America at the same time as his brother died
in a pit accident at Bruntcliffe Pit, Morley. The telegrams bringing the news
crossed on the water. The mother took her five children to live with her father at
Drighlington and returned to the mill to weave, whilst another sister looked after
the home; a third, a dressmaker, made their clothes and the other grandfather, a
shoemaker, their boots. 'We were poor enough, but we managed.' A clever child,
she won a scholarship to the grammar school, but her mother could not afford to
let her go.

Instead, at the age of ten she went as a half-timer to Bower's Mill, where one of her aunts taught her to cap spin. Her mother retired from weaving at forty, and she took her loom at Bulrush Mill, Batley, where her sister and other members of the family worked. This meant leaving home at 5 a.m. and crossing Adwalton Moor. A party of them were once coming home in a snowstorm, and Ned, the only man, cried, 'Follow mi stick and mi coat'. Leading them in single file, he fell into a hole in the moor, Sally Dick's pond, and 'one after another we all fell in after him. We always laughed about it afterwards'. 'The owners of Bulrush were very kind, real Christians. On a wet morning they'd say, "Now lasses get into t'tentering place, and get warm before beginning work". At Christmas we'd put up mistletoe, and one of the girls had to kiss the boss. My first year it was me. Aye they were right good bosses. I wouldn't care if it was coming all ovver again.'

Another half-timer, Mr Alfred Brown, began as a doffer aged twelve at Saltaire Mills. His mother had asked if he could go and he had the required labour certificate from the education office stating the number of his school attendances. Going to the Gatehouse, he was sent to a room 'where the overlooker told you to take your coat off and you were in'. He earned 9s. 9d. a week with a rise of 3d. weekly until he started full time at 18s. 9d. 'If you could get in at Salt's, you'd accomplished something. There was always competition between Salt's and Lister's.' It was in fact generally conceded that Salt's, Lister's and Foster's were the most prestigious places to work at. In any case to get into a good mill you had to put your name down. 'Weavers were waiting to come in.'

Or consider Mr H. Johnson who came from Haworth over seventy years ago 'on a flitting'. As a half-timer, aged eleven, he began as a doffer earning 2s. a week. There were 144 spindles on a spinning frame and a set of five or six doffers with a gaffer sharing them out. A doffer started at one end of the room by taking off and replacing bobbins as the frames stopped one after another all the way down. The one who was last most times in a week had to put on knee pads and with a big piece of oily cotton rub down the alleyway. If you became a jobber lad putting on the bands to run the spindles, you earned 6d. extra. In some mills a form was provided for the doffers and when the overlooker whistled they ran, and the last was given a swipe with the alleydasher (a cleaning implement, a piece of leather attached to a picking stick which when waved created a draught which swept up fluff). In well-kept mills you could eat off the floors which were 'polished like ballrooms'.

When Mr Robert Dennis of Churwell began as a little piecer apprenticed to a spinner (but not a half-timer), one of the mules was steam driven one way and pushed by hand the other. 'Some of the old spinners directing operations sat in an armchair in the mule gate, and paid us what they thought we were worth. The more they could earn by telling us what to do the more they could pay us.' Mr Dennis doffed and put on bobbins. 'It was marvellous how you could fasten about fifty bobbins in the crook of your arm, and go right down the mule hitting about 500 spindles every time like lightning.'

The family of Mr H. Ambler at Queensbury illustrates the tradition of families following on in the same mill generation after generation. This was expected, and in any case if they occupied a mill house or cottage it was obligatory. Mr Ambler (b. 1898) worked half-time for a year in the spinning department, known as t' slave 'oile at Black Dyke Mills, moved on to learn the trade of mechanic, and has been in the mill for sixty-four years. Seven out of eight of his brothers and sisters worked there totalling 304 years in all in the mill. Until they grew up and had learnt their trade, the oldest in the family drew the wages for all.

We met several retired workers from Lock Hill Mills, Sowerby Bridge in Calderdale, formerly W. and R. K. Lee engaged in cotton spinning and doubling (*see plate* 34). Two friends, Mrs N. Broadbent and Mrs M. Shaw, worked as a pair at reeling, that is taking off and tieing up finished hanks, a top job. 'You had to work very swiftly at the same speed. May was quick at starting then slowed up; I was the other way round. They were the happiest hours of my life. We were always laughing.'

Mrs Vera Gaukrodger met her husband who was the boiler firer at Lock Hill. She worked for a year half-time as a setter putting bobbins on, 190 at one side and four sides to set. In her third year she qualified as a doffer. There were fifty-seven machines in one large room, with twenty-five doffers of whom four and a setter each had a 'share', making five shares in all. 'It was marvellous when I got to top doffing, and was given a ticket to say how many machines had to be doffed.' At sixteen, following her sister, she became a fully fledged ring doubler and 'that was really something'. Each doubler patrolled a pair of frames to join any broken threads with a 'dog' knot. (Many practised making these at home.) A doubler was never without a knife or a stone for sharpening, although many stone window-sills in mills were in use as whetstones. The knife, used for cutting off the ends of the knots neatly, wore hooves on the hand. 'I earned about 37s a week, a lot of money. I'd take it home to my mother and I'd say, "How much spending money am I going to have?" and she'd reply, "Half a crown". I used to save half of it every week.'

However undesirable the half-time system was, no one has grumbled. It was taken for granted. Others were going and you went too. For young men there were apprenticeships and night classes, whether at mechanics' institutes or 'techs.', leading to the first rungs of the ladder that led to promotion. For young women a ladder barely existed, only a better wage earned by efficiency on piece-work. Further education had often to be denied them. In 1935 the training rate for a welfare officer was 18s. A spinster, and there were many after the First World War, worked not by any means always unhappily, at the same job for fifty or sixty years. 'I had two lives, my mill life and my home life.' On the other hand marriage, usually but not always, ended a woman's career in the mill.

Many life stories illustrate success from small beginnings. It was possible by ability, hard work and good luck for men to rise to be directors. Others became heads of departments. In 1915 Mr F. Alderson began half-time work in the mill as an errand boy earning 7s. 2d. one week and 4s. 10d. the next. Two years later he moved to Manningham Mills, and by the 1930s was in charge of the finishing department. Times were so bad for about five years that to avoid sacking anyone he kept an alphabetical list of names and shared out the short-time work.

When he was twelve Mr J. Greenough went to Gomersal Mills half-time as a bobbin lad, earning 3s. a week and became cashier. His father had worked in the warehouse there for three months short of seventy years, and in his day the wages were paid in gold. Mr Greenough used to make up the wages, wrapped in pound notes placed on a rack, so that they could be paid out to about 1,000 workpeople in some twenty minutes.

Or take Mr W. Horton's career at Bank Bottom Mills, Marsden. In the bad times of the early 1920s he had gone for a job as a flour boy at the local co-opera-tive stores, but there was a queue of boys waiting there already. He did not dare go home without work, so he went as a piecener to Crimble Mills, Slaithwaite. Moving to Bank Bottom in 1921, he proceeded from piecener, to spinner, to warper, to weaver, to finish percher, to greasy percher, to foreman mender with fifty menders and five men under him.[1] 'I liked to see everything correct and proper and the customer satisfied.'

Consider Mr W. Spink who worked at Gomersal Mills from 1911 when he went as a half-timer for twelve months, to 1965 when he was given a gold watch on retirement. He progressed from a little doffer earning 5s. 3d. one week and 2s. 9d. the next to a jobber lad (oiling round and so on), to mule spinner, to a stint in the territorial army, to card jobber, to night overlooker, to day overlooker, to manager in the carding and wool scouring. An overlooker's wage when he married was about £3 16s. a week, but a manager was salaried. In the carding he had about ninety people under him, half working day and half night. He had charge of both shifts and was often called out 'if owt had gone wrong'. Sometimes they dis-

---

[1] A warper prepares the warp for a loom. A finish percher examines the cloth for faults after it has been washed and scoured. A greasy percher examines it straight from the loom.

mantled the huge carding machines weighing ten tons, and moved them to another room.

The women tell a different story. Weaving was sought after for the better pay, and in spite of the noise and having to stand for hours on end, it was rewarding and companionable (as for that matter was other work in the mill). Formerly one weaver looked after one loom, and did not welcome anyone else using it. She kept it clean, sometimes coming early and providing her own brushes and even emery paper. In some work if dust penetrated the material 'buttoned'. Sometimes looms were set on fire by a spark falling on fluff. Standing in a *gate* (the passageway between the looms) the weaver could talk to her gate mate by lip-reading and shouting. 'You get very close to your mate' and an equable temper helped. In those days fines were levied for bad work, but if anything was missed, the weaver nearly cried. The best ones were given the best work, weaving the most valuable pieces. When she had finished she 'felled out'.

Weavers wore aprons and mill skirts, long and voluminous, and made of harden that washed as white as snow, and if the work were dirty a belly patch, a piece of leather about two feet square, was worn where the belly pressed against the loom (*see plates 52 and 54*). Aprons and skirts were utilized to carry full bobbins from the piecers in the spinning department to the looms. For twenty or thirty bobbins the apron served, but for a full doffing of 450 bobbins, six inches long full of weft, they were worked round and packed tightly into a skirt held up high with hands crossed towards the neck, and carried perhaps up four flights of steps. On Monday mornings John Hartley of Gillroyd Mills used to stand at the top of the mill yard, and if any weavers came in dirty bobbin skirts he sent them home.

'The nicest people I ever met in the mill', says Mr R. Dennis, 'were the old weavers. They'd do anything for you. They'd rush out and deliver a baby, and they'd come back and they'd weave. These were the real people. The ladies in the mill. There was a camaraderie about it that's missing today.'

Miss L. Speddings (b. 1889), whose family came from Sheffield, worked at Listers, Manningham Mills, for fifty-seven years, for the last twelve part-time. After starting in the combing, and washing and teazing raw silk, she went into the Beamsley Shed, spending three weeks being taught to weave. Her family and the mill paid the weaver, and she herself received a small sum. She often used to go home and cry, but her teacher said, '"She'll never leave. She's too interested." And I never did. When I came out I could weave anything. I taught a lot to weave. You had to work hard to get any wage.'

Miss A. E. Britton, beginning as a half-timer at Manningham Mills at the age of fifteen earning 2s. 7d. one week and 3s. 5d. the next, continued at work for forty-eight years. She first put labels on silk reels, then on skeins for embroidery, and at the age of seventeen to earn more money went on to weaving and eventually wove the crimson velvet for the Coronation robes. Listers also made the thick white fur fabric, on to which tails were sewn, for the ermine capes. Another weaver had woven thousands of yard of moquette for the Canadian Pacific Railway, and a third had worked at Manningham for fifty-five years, forty-five of them in the seam finishing, and 'enjoyed every minute of it'.

Mrs Annie Marlow's story differs slightly. Her father, a farmer at Drighlington, died on a Wednesday in March 1915, and on the following Monday when she was thirteen, armed with her labour certificate, she started work first as a piecer earning 5s. rising by 1s. a week to 12s. She then went to Keighley and Moorhouse at Bruntcliffe Mill and was taught to weave standing by the weaver for three or four weeks. 'When you got on and the tuner gave you a loom and you started earning, you gave the weaver your first week's wage. Talk about the good old days. I don't want them back.'

Similarly in 1910 Miss Agnes Morton, whose family originally came from Birkenhead, was taught to weave at Manningham Mills when she was sixteen. She progressed from a single plush loom, earning on average 17s. a week, to a velvet loom, to a double shuttle loom when the wage increased to 19s. Her sister died leaving five children and a baby. Her husband was out of work, so her mother, a widow, took the baby. There was then no chance of marriage, 'whoever had married me would have had three to keep'. 'What if you were sick?' we asked, 'Sick? You couldn't be sick. You had to work it off. You got 12s. a week and nothing for the first three days.'

Miss Olive Booth of Batley went to work for her grandfather who employed about thirty girls pegging rugs which were sold in colliery districts. After three or four weeks she could not see, and her mother put 'a teea leeave poultice on mi eyes. They talk about folk today as if they were made of china'. So at thirteen she learnt to weave in three days on an old fashioned slow loom. 'I've never worked so hard in my life.' She continued as a weaver for fifty years. 'I wore a shawl a long time. Mi mother said I'd worn it to ribbins because I thowt I were picturesque wi' a shawl thrown over mi shoulder. But they weren't as warm as coats. . . . Wages were small, but we'd some fun. The worse conditions were the more fun we had. You may not believe that, but it's true. I tell you when I read Osbert Sitwell, I were sorry for t'Sitwells, they'd a sorry time.'

Other jobs for women were whipping blankets and fringeing rugs and shawls (see plate 47). In the shawl-making districts of the upper Colne valley and Saddle-worth fringeing shawls was undertaken either in the mill or in the home. Men used to carry away over their shoulders an 'end of twisting' which made fifteen shawls for their wives to fringe at night, or many boys had barrows in which to take them after school from the mill to the house. Money earned by fringeing or tazzling was invariably saved, and two well-built cottages at Slack Cote near Delph, nicknamed Twisters' Rest, were paid for in this way.[1]

Mending and burling because it was quiet clean work was much sought after. Burling, a simple task picking out knots and lumps in a piece with a burling iron, was in early days undertaken by married women to pay the rent. Mending on the other hand is skilled work, especially in worsteds, requiring training, so that menders always regarded themselves as superior. Their job, tiring for the eyes, is to repair faults—a pick or an end out—in the pieces of cloth which had been examined and marked (*see plate* 46). It used to be said that if it took a week to weave badly it would take a month to repair it. W. B. Crump records that the mending room at Bean Ing 'was the most impressive spectacle in industrial Leeds'.

We met Miss Mary Lee at Batley Carr Mills who has been a mender for fifty-nine years, and as head of the department has trained two lots of girls. When she 'got a board the forewoman had a stick and gave you a rap if you weren't doing well'. Mrs L. Addy (b. 1880) says, 'They were very particular then who they took in as menders'. Her father was horseman for Hudson Sykes and Bousfield, Springfield Mills, Morley. When she was thirteen he took her down to the mill and 'they wanted to know if we knew anybody what was a mender, and of course we did. That's how you got in. Whilst learning, we had to go for a month for nothing, then for another month for 5s. a week'. The price paid per piece varied according to its quality, and earnings came to about £1 a week. Mrs Addy worked at the mill, except for intervals (her husband died and her father was ill), all her life. 'Oh, we'd some happy times. You see we could talk when we were mending.'

[1] Mrs M. A. Gartside, Delph, Mr E. Schofield, Diggle, and Mr J. Whitehead, Delph.

4 In the Mills

THE majority of the workers lived within walking distance of the mill, or near any other job for that matter, in rows of houses built for them at 't'back o' t'mill', houses mostly now pulled down, although some of them were 'little palaces'. At the heads of the Pennine valleys where people passed through woods or over rough ground, it was customary going to work on early winter mornings to carry lighted candles in jam jars, so that, like Swaledale in the lead-mining days, a little string of lights might be seen moving along the hillsides. At Marsden in the Colne valley many came by train from Lancashire and Saddleworth, and called at the Railway Inn for a rum and coffee, formerly a popular drink costing 2*d*. or 3*d*.

It was the father's task to waken the family by shouting their names. Or some people rapped on their neighbour's adjoining wall. Or knockers-up toured set streets wakening occupants of specific houses and charging 2*d*. or 3*d*. a week. Elderly Mrs Griffiths at Manningham rattled the spikes of an old umbrella tied to a long clothes prop on bedroom windows, and called out the name of the person, the state of the weather and the time of day. Or another had a long bamboo cane with three wires with corks on the ends and took his dog for protection. A third in Leeds shouted 'Right-O' when heard and was paid 6*d*. a week.

In general workers were summoned to and let out of work originally by horns, then bells, and when steam engines were installed by buzzers or whistles, sometimes called 'Whews'. Bell turrets may be seen for instance at Batley Carr Mills and Brookroyd Mills, Holywell Green. In *A Spring-time Saunter* Whiteley Turner records that he heard one of the last of the factory bells ringing in 1913. Within recollection the different notes of the buzzers made a familiar cacophony of sound.

Women wore clogs, fringed woollen shawls and black stockings. Shawls were not an innovation, but had been standard wear for all women. Dress or Sunday shawls, made of silk or cashmere, were complementary to those worn during the week. For going to work in they were large for winter and small for summer, and were fastened with a safety-pin under the chin or thrown over the shoulder (*see plates* 56, 78, 81, 83). 'You didn't need gloves in a shawl.' Woven in checks or in plain colours, red was popular at Queensbury, and black in a honeycomb design was worn at Heptonstall 100 years ago. Sold at drapers and co-operative stores, they were advertised at a yearly clearance sale at Heckmondwike in 1897 at 2s. 11d. to 8s. 9d. each.

Those coming from a distance took their packets of food, called *jock* in Calderdale and the Colne valley and *snap* in the Leeds district, tied in a red and white spotted or flowered handkerchief often carried under the arm. Sometimes the handkerchief held a basin with a saucer on top and another basin on top of that containing the pudding. Others used baskets, not popular with younger people, or stuffed newspaper packages into their pockets. In many places tin or enamelled billy cans, of which the lid served as a cup, were taken filled with tea, and at night, well scoured, they were hung on nails outside houses to sweeten them. Or a small oval tin canister with two compartments held tea and sugar or a mixture of the two for mashing tea at the mill. Mrs Tupman remembers, 'My mother put up breakfast and dinner (bread for breakfast and teacake sandwiches for dinner) the night before all arranged round a table for the different members of the family, and my father made us a hot drink before we set out.' She carried her jock in a red flannelette bag. When all her family were working, Mrs Marlow buttered twenty-six slices of bread every morning and was often stuck fast as to what to put in. Dripping, especially 'mucky' fat, was a general favourite.

Although some firms started dining-rooms much earlier, in general canteens followed on statutory requirements in the Second World War. (A dining-room was provided by the Akroyds at Copley in 1840 and by the Hadwens at Kebroyd Mills in the Ryburn valley in the late 1880s.) Mostly food was eaten at the loom gate, or on the floor leaning against the spinning mules, or sitting on a woolsorter's board. 'Our canteen was where we worked.' Places variously called 'snap 'oiles', 'scalding 'oiles', or the 'kettle house' contained a jacketed tank of hot water heated by steam from the engine and with a steam oven on top or near by, and often a large stone sink, usually choked with tea leaves. The billy cans could be hung in the tank to heat them, or otherwise tea was scalded in pint pots (mugs). Many retired mill workers continue the pint pot habit. Tea they think tastes better that way and also they have become accustomed to and like it half cold. Eggs for breakfast were boiled under running hot water taps. Fish and chip shops supplied mill orders (a ha'porth of each thirty times) perhaps fetched by the bobbin ligger, or a tasty fry might be bought for 3d. Meat and potato pies were favourites, and heated in the oven were sometimes marked to indicate whose they were. It is related at one mill that a greedy man often claimed the best pie regardless of the ownership. One of his mates asked his wife to bake 'a right nice mouse pie', and placed it in a prominent position in the oven. The man took it, ate it, and when he was told, 'it cured him'.

In many cases, perhaps every other day, children took their parents a hot meal in their dinner hour. When she was eleven or twelve Mrs L. Addy of Morley, who lived a good mile from where her father worked, had winter and summer to come home from school at m dday when she was given something to eat to put her on, carry her father's meal in a basket over her arm to the mill, eat her own dinner, and return to school for half past one. Sometimes snow lay deep on the ground. 'We did run i' them days. Children are too pampered today.'

The penny 'oile already mentioned preceded the time office, and took its name from the fine imposed on late-comers. Is the first record of this custom in *Shirley*? 'Mr Moore made him pay his penny down ere he entered.' 'You were pennied' is the remembered expression. The office was often occupied by a dour character, perhaps an old soldier, who fifty or more years ago not only 'pennied' but shut the gates five minutes after 6 a.m., so that late-comers were left standing outside until after breakfast time thus losing part of their wages. At Gomersal Mills, the penny 'oile is remembered presided over by George Crabtree, a little man who wore a checker brat down to his feet, and at Black Dyke Mills by Dan Cullen who wore a uniform and finished about 1920. Here the gates were shut and late-comers had to enter at the door of the penny 'oile and go out by another door which Cullen could bolt and unbolt from inside. He then wrote your name on a slate, sent it to the office and the money was taken off your wage. When it was realized that the employers were losing good labour penny 'oiles were dispensed with, and in any case the breakfast half hour disappeared with a shorter working week.

At the end of the day the mill *looses*, and if it is not working during holidays or strikes, or if on short time, it is standing and the staff are playing or *laiking*. 'I haven't played many Saturdays.' There were 5,000 people at Manningham Mills and when the mill loosed, 'You couldn't walk against the crowd. Folk on holiday came to look.' A football team which trained at night was once walking home in their white clothes over Crosland Moor, and a woman who saw them shouted, 'Hey, by gum, t'cemetery's looised'.

At Gillroyd Mills one Saturday in August, 1859, the engine was stopped 'to allow the workers an afternoon for a trip to Halifax'. In the 1860s in the Colne valley jollifications in the New Year were always arranged either on mill premises or at the inns, and usually consisted of tea for the women and a 'substantial' supper for the men, followed by singing and a ball. One such event took place in the tentering room. The coffee had been too well laced with rum, and the dancers lurching against the tenter hooks tore their clothes disastrously. In more modern

WOOL AND WOOL COMBING

29. The comb setting department at Hardings, Tower Works, Leeds. There are 50,000 pins in the large rings for Noble combs. Here the operatives are setting the pins, a highly skilled job, by placing a small steel tube over the pin and straightening if necessary. It takes three weeks to complete one ring (1950).

30. Wool-sorters at Manningham Mills, Bradford. They wear full-length blue and white checker brats fastened with a back button and a tape half way down, and formerly leggings, like over-trousers, also of checked cotton to button on to the trousers (early 1950s).

31. *A Lister comb used for long hair wool, in this case mohair, at Black Dyke Mills, Queensbury.*

32. *Noble combs combing tops at Thomas Burnleys, Gomersal Mills (1950s).*

33. A doffer (the boy) and a piecener (the girl) at a flyer spinning frame for worsted yarn at William Fisons, Greenholme Mills, Burley-in-Wharfedale. The piecener has stopped the flyer with her left thumb and is about to piecen with her right hand (c. 1907).

34. *Cotton spinners at Lock Hill Mills, Sowerby Bridge, in the Stop Motion or Cheese Winding Room,
which is decorated for the Coronation of King George VI (1937).*

35. *Self-acting mules for spinning woollen yarn at Gillroyd Mills, Morley. The machines move
backwards and forwards on the rails drawing out and twisting the condensed slivers (from the carding
machines), seen on the spools on the right, on to the bobbins in front of the women (1930s).*

36. *Weaving silk at Manningham Mills, Bradford (1918).*

37. *The many pattern looms at Taylor and Littlewoods, Newsome Mills, near Huddersfield, makers of fine worsted. Only two are in use now. The dressing frame in the foreground was for dressing the warp with size (1892).*

FULLING, DYEING AND TENTERING

38. Fulling stocks installed at Armitage Bridge Mills on the river Holme, near Huddersfield, in 1813. The two sets of wooden stamps were lifted a certain distance, and when they fell they milled the cloth which was in a rounded trough below the sloping iron supports (1936).

39. Mr W. T. Birks at Slaithwaite Dyeworks. He is stirring loose wool in the dye-pan with a stang. Note the mushroom in the centre out of which the dye was forced and sprayed (1940s).

40. Blankets drying on tenters in the tenter fields at Wormalds and Walker, Dewsbury Mills, Thornhill. Tenters continued in use for blankets much later than for cloth, and these held five miles of blankets. The men on the right show the height (1920s).

times outings first by train, then by charabanc, later coach, to Blackpool, Morecambe, Scarborough were arranged, either subscribed to or paid for by the owners
to celebrate a special occasion. For instance the firm of Hirst and Mallinson in the
Colne valley sent all their operatives on a monster excursion to the British Empire
Exhibition at Wembley. Rooms in the mills were decorated for Christmas or for
Coronations or for visits of royalty. Clubs or raffles were run to help save for
holidays or Christmas fare. Life in the mill is said to have been more friendly than
now. You worked and still do not at such and such a mill but for Rhodes, Jarmains,
Sykes, Roberts, Priestmans, Martins or Murgatroyds.

Many of the tasks already referred to have been either modified or made obsolete. Weavers, now often men, look after three or four looms, or up to sixteen when
automatic. Spinners do their own doffing, and they and doublers use a machine to
tie knots and wear a plastic ring containing a razor blade to cut the ends. Nor are there
many engine tenters and firers left, or those such as Strap Alf at Bank Bottom Mills,
who attended to the belting connecting the machines with the shafting and the engine.

Two now obsolete jobs were those of velvet and cord cutting. (Velvet is a cut
warp and corduroy a cut weft pile fabric; for the latter *see plate* 26.) In 1894 at Low
Mills, Addingham, then and now run by Lister's, there were fifty-five hand-
cutters of velvet, a number which four years later had dwindled to one owing to
the introduction of the double velvet loom incorporating a mechanical cutting
knife in the loom's action. The last cutter, Robert Hustwick, lived to be over
ninety and remembered the care taken with the cutting of silk velvet for Queen
Victoria. When the velvet left the looms it was stiffened on the back with boiled
sago, stretched on a frame, and with special scissors the cutter sliced the row or
race with a deft sure motion.

Another job that has gone was that of the *seeak* 'oile man. Briefly seeak was a by-
product of scouring. A thick soapy liquid was run off from the scouring machines
into tanks, cracked with acid, and the fatty scum run on to ash beds, dug up like
thick porridge, and wrapped in sacking parcels about 18 inches square. Pressed
steam was blown through the parcels which were squeezed to produce crude oil
which was barrelled up for sale, and the cake residue was sold for manure often to
hop fields. A dirty job, it blackened and *stalkened* (stiffened) trousers enough for
them to stand up on their own. 'Wearing them was like having a treacle tin round
your legs.' At Washpits Mill, Holmfirth, Sam Fattycake was in charge of the seeak
'oile, and we have met Mr Tom Godfrey (b. 1879) who was the seeak 'oile man for
twenty-six of his fifty years at Crimble Mill, Slaithwaite. He remembers a dog, and
others remember a hen and even the seeak 'oile man himself, falling into the tank
with fearful results.

The process of dyeing, totally modernized and scientifically conducted, is also remembered as a dirty, wet, smelly job, cold and draughty in winter and hot in summer. The dyepans, now stainless steel, were square wooden boxes with a mushroom in the centre out of which dye was forced and sprayed out, and the dyer stirred the loose wool with a stang, a process called stanging (*see plate* 39). Dyers could be swung off their feet with the weights being lifted. When new stangs were bought they were tested and the heavy ones left to the last. Powdered dye was mixed with hot water in buckets, and after about half an hour of boiling material in the dyepan, a sample was taken. If it was too pale extra dye was added, called *cobbling*, a process if necessary repeated five or six times. Or if too dark the wool might be stripped with a stripping agent. Mr Hilton Sykes, a dyer's labourer for fifty-two years at Slaithwaite Dyeworks, was 'on black for a start and that's shocking stuff. After a week's holiday in August I'd just about got my hands clean.' He wore overalls, a plain navy blue smock and dyers' clogs which had uppers.

Even the wool buyer, that most important member of the staff on whom the prosperity of a mill may depend, has no longer to rely solely on his own judgment by the handle and appearance of the wool to decide the percentage of top, noil, grease and sand. Instead quality control specialists take a sample and report. A well-known verse runs:

> The men who go to the London sales
> And see the fleeces packed in bales . . .
> They make a slight miscalculation,
> Then seek another situation.[1]

In Yorkshire the Bradford Wool Exchange was until the 1960s an important mart for the wool-users of the world.[2]

At Thongsbridge in the Holme valley the firm of Wood and Burtt kept on their books some 800 farmers in the Pennine dales. Their buyer visited markets such as Leyburn and Richmond, and handling 400,000 lb. of wool a year, bought on a handshake. This kind of sales organization ceased with the Second World War.

On the other hand the job of designer, again crucial to the success of a firm, has in essence hardly changed. In well-lit quiet rooms men sit matching bunches of yarn, or show you with pride pattern books, out of which if a few are winners, even one, they will be pleased. Designers at carpet firms, engaged on large-scale stylized paintings, rely on inspiration from stone, lichen, flower heads, a Chinese

[1] Otto Mombert, *Rhymes of the Wool Market* (undated).
[2] Marie Hartley and Joan Ingilby, *The Wonders of Yorkshire*, p. 76.

vase. At Crossley's Mr T. Marchetti once produced a design which proved a best-seller derived from a piece of used blotting paper. At Firth's a popular pattern came from a micro-photo of a bar of steel. Here, none of the forty people under a well-remembered head designer were allowed to leave until he had tapped his desk twice with a pencil. In the 1920s carpets were made for as little as 2s. 11d. a yard, 3s. 4d. laid from the shop.

Nor has the job of wool sorter changed. Formerly some of the best paid of men, they used to go to work in top hats and only worked in daylight so that in mid-winter the hours were from 9 a.m. to 3 p.m. In the upper floors of mills men still work at grease-encrusted boards in front of a north light with a stand for the bales on their left and a series of skeps on their right (*see plate* 30).

In 1920 when he was sixteen Mr W. S. Barnes began an apprenticeship of five years at a Bradford works as a sorter at 12s. 6d. a week. At first he picked up bits of wool from the floor and scraped and swept it twice a day, for it was always said that 'wool was dearer than sugar'. In some places they even had a man scratching slivers off the workers' clothes as they went out of the door. As he progressed he stood by a sorter looking at the skeps and their contents. 'You think you'll never pick it up, but suddenly you've got it.' After a year, perhaps two, the apprentice is promoted to a stand. Each man adjusts to the correct height by raising himself up on extra boards. A visitor once remarked, 'What a fine set of men you've got!' The boss shouted, 'Hey lads', and when they jumped down, they were all different heights.

The sorter might deal with Australian cross-bred and Merino or English wool, but if the type were changed he singed the skeps with a roll of lighted paper. To sort he uses both touch and eyesight. Low quality is harsh and vice versa. 'Your eyes are looking for the serrations in the fibre. Light is shining on the wool, and a shadow is cast between the serrations. The finer qualities have them very near together so they are all shadow and look dull. You tear the wool off.'

When a skep is full of one quality, the sorter takes it to a square trap in the floor where the taker-off checks that it is in order. Occasionally he might bear a grudge and return it for no reason, or even in the past be open to bribery such as a bottle of beer in the skep. The wool is then tipped down into the packing floor below, put into wool sheets slung up from the roof, then skewered by using a *jerry*, a double pronged lever and in former days a *soldier*, a V-shaped tool of which one end stuck in the floor and the V supported the pack. Then it was sent, in this case, to the combers.

Lastly, two important posts in a mill—the overlookers and the managers. Much depended on the former. (It was they in the early days who had the power to ill-treat children and who wielded the alleydasher.) In charge of sections of machinery, they were important enough to be listed under their occupation in directories. Fifty years ago they ran outings and arranged cricket matches. In weaving departments they are called overlookers in Bradford, tuners in the Huddersfield and heavy woollen districts and tacklers in the region bordering on Lancashire. Tuners at Morley wore navy blue smocks, and at Heptonstall tacklers some eighty years ago white cord trousers and white cord vests, which were laid on the floor to be scrubbed clean. 'They don't know what work is today.' At Hebden Bridge Cheethams made tacklers' trousers of bluette and blue drill, also sleeved vests, with fronts of bluette and sleeves of black twilled cotton; individual tacklers sometimes requested up to a dozen pockets for their spanners.

A man in charge of women could and did give easy work to favourites, or be so popular that if he moved to another mill the women followed him. A Catholic overlooker might have all Catholics under him. Good tuners with vile tempers had to be tolerated, 'If he tunes thy loom, thou'll have nowt to do wi' his temper'. Or they conducted Christmas sings in the dinner hour.

At Gomersal Mills Mr Hartley Brook starting as an overlooker under his father, the mill manager, was told, 'Now think on your job's to see that the machinery is cleaned, greased, and that the premises you occupy are in perfect condition—no bread left about, no rats, no mice. We want none o' that. If you can't get them as works for you to do it, I shall force you to do it.'

Mr J. H. Gill of Haworth (b. 1894), who started as a half-timer at a spinning mill at the age of twelve, served a five-year apprenticeship, being paid 5s. or 6s. a week, at Hattersleys, the loom-makers at Keighley, and then worked for fifty years for a large part of the time as a weaving overlooker at Merralls, Ebor Mills, Haworth. When he began there, all were narrow looms, 55 to 60 inches wide, and a warp with four cuts (to make four pieces) was an advance. In his lifetime looms were increased in size, and warps instead of having to be changed every week or ten days were lengthened to eight or ten cuts lasting a month; and improvements such as the dobby, which controlled the movement of the heald shafts, and four boxes for shuttles at each end of the loom allowed for the weaving of different colours in the weft. Thus fancy patterns, such as tartans, could be woven as well as plain whites for piece-dyeing. He looked after twenty to twenty-four plain looms and made sure for example that cloths were of the right weight by changing the number of picks to the inch by fitting a different wheel with more, or less, teeth. Here the overlooker wore corduroy trousers and a short white smock (clean on every week), with a pocket for a red handkerchief, whilst the weaving manager in charge of the loom shed wore a longer smock.

Mr and Mrs R. J. Atwell, both born in 1892, both worked at Manningham Mills, she as a velvet weaver, he as a foreman overlooker. As Mrs Atwell said, 'It was there that I met mi fate'. In 1914 after apprenticeship he became an overlooker with a share of twenty-one looms earning 30s. to 32s. a week, and after the war took charge of a shed with 150 weavers, men and women, and thirteen other overlookers and velvet cutters. He was responsible for allotting the work, deciding which quality should go into which loom, and interviewing prospective staff. If her mother had been good, it was likely that a daughter would take after her. Women with fine delicate hands were chosen. Sweaty hands damaged light coloured velvets, and a little bag of French chalk in which to dip the fingers used to be kept at the side of the loom. He decided bonus payments (4s. a month for good work), or was told of a 'trap', a serious mistake, so that all the ends had to be taken up and even a hole might be made in the piece. To remedy this disaster other weavers often rallied round. The fine for bad work was 2d. Everything had to be perfect. '"Go fetch Bob" they would say. I knew every name. It was one happy family.'

Lastly the mill manager. It is remembered at one mill that a Scotsman who overworked the weavers had been appointed manager. One day the owner returned from lunch to find the yard full of five or six hundred of them, all threatening to throw the man in the dam. Knowing that he could not swim, there was no option but to sack him. At Gomersal Mills Mr Hartley Brook told us that he wanted to be a farmer, but his father argued him out of it, and he eventually took over as manager. 'I was brought up to make sure that when you go home, you've earned your day's wage. I've loved working at Burnley's; it's been a pleasure. I've been seeing improvements for the benefit of the workpeople, not for the boss all the time. Nobody knows what hard work's been put into this mill.'

The last sentiment echoes down the years. Changes have been immense, in hours and conditions of work, in wages, and in the machinery, so that less skill is required resulting some would say in less interest. On the other hand there is more professionalism and less loyalty. What has struck us in those to whom we have talked is pride—pride in the mill they worked in, pride in the family who owned it, pride in their own work, and pride in themselves and the way they won through.

TEAZLES

41. (Above) Teazles growing in Somerset for use in Yorkshire mills. Mrs D. J. Maddick harvesting teazles at Fivehead, near Taunton.

42. (Above right) Mr D. J. Maddick has slotted the bundles on to a pole, and carries a lug of teazles to the gallows (more correctly two uprights and a crossbar) for drying.

43. (Left) The old method of packing teazles for sale. A Somerset grower with a completed stav containing twenty fan-shaped bundles each with twenty-five teazles, in all 500. Forty stavs made up a pack (date unknown).

44. *Mr Norman Dawson, who has been a journeyman teazle man for fifty years, uses a setting iron to fill a rod with teazles for a raising gig at Henry Wheatleys, Hopton Mills, Mirfield.*

45. *Mr Arthur Binns, overlooker, who has been at Hopton Mills for forty years, with one of the six raising gigs there.*

46. E. Lofthouse mending William Fisons, Greenholme Mills, Burley- in-Wharfedale (c. 1907).

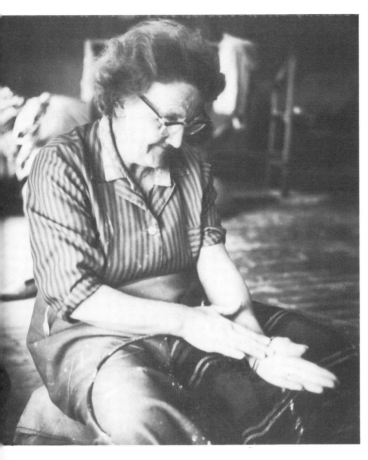

47. *Mrs J. Frain fringeing travel rugs at Joshua Ellis's, Batley Carr Mills. She twists the fringes by rubbing them up her arm, and uses whiting to assist.*

48. *(Below) Finish perching at George Akeds, Vicar Lane, Bradford (early 1950s).*

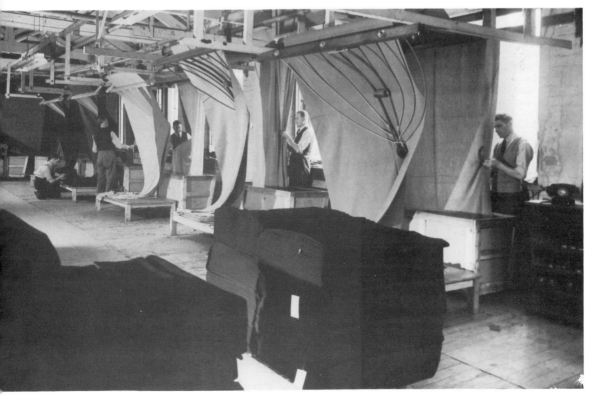

RAGS

49. Rag sorting at J. R. Burrows, Carlinghow Mills, Batley. The operatives mostly work at riddles, and an innovation was the conveyor belt on the right (early 1930s).

50. A rag sale at Henry Cullingworth and Sons, South Street, Dewsbury. This was the last sale of a firm of rag merchants which began in 1845. The auctioneer is Mr A. Summers. Cullingworth Summers continue to conduct rag sales at Batley (1974).

51. Rag grinding machine made by George Thornes and Sons, Batley, now made by Knowles Wilson and Sons, Heckmondwike. The merchant using this machine dyes its products —shoddy and mungo—to match simple patterns (date unknown).

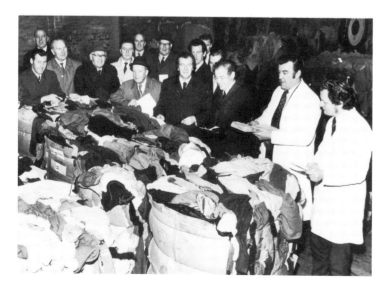

52. *Weavers at Keighley and Moorhouses, Bruntcliffe Mill, Morley, wearing voluminous mill skirts made of harden, and the bibs which were separate. Mill skirts held up to 500 bobbins of weft (1916).*

53. *Workers at Albert Mills, Morley (c. 1902).*

54. Work people at Bank Bottom Mills, Marsden, leaving the mill at Saturday dinner time. Some carry their mill skirts to be washed in readiness for Monday morning (1880s).

5 Textile Machinery

THE great diversity of large and small family businesses in textile manufacture is echoed in the making of textile machinery. In the last century the many machine-makers catered for the needs of their particular districts, and were aided by the supply of iron from Low Moor and other iron works, by castings from local forges such as the old established Kirkstall Forge, and by a host of individual craftsmen who made special parts. Some were originally blacksmiths, some clock-makers, and some were linked with Lancashire, the birthplace of invention. All were engaged in improving and perfecting already established principles of construction often behind locked doors.

At the series of great exhibitions started in 1851 (for instance the London Exhibition of 1862 and that at Roubaix in France in 1911), firms won prizes bringing their inventions to the fore. Up to the Second World War machines and parts, and the men to set them up, were sent all over the world, in particular to India and Russia, but since then competition from Europe has made inroads into the former monopoly of a pioneering nation.

As we have seen early motive power was supplied by water-wheels, but of the very few *in situ* in textile mills in our area, for example that at Lumb Mill, Wain-stalls, near Halifax, none are in working order.[1] There were formerly great wheels at Rishworth Mill in the Ryburn valley ($57\frac{1}{2}$ feet in diameter and 12 feet broad), at Diggle New Mill, Saddleworth (64 feet 8 inches in diameter and 7 feet wide), and at Mytholm Mill, upper Calderdale (52 feet in diameter and 9 feet 6 inches wide). Sixty years ago the latter used to be heard 'dreaming' as with water trickling in from the buckets it was just turning over. It has been passed down that young people working in the mills rejoiced when after heavy rain water backed up the tail goit so that the wheel was stopped and work ceased.

Horse gins, another form of early motive power, worked rotary carding machines and slubbing billies, especially from 1780 to 1790 round Rawdon and

[1] G. Binns, 'Water Wheels in the Upper Calder Valley', *Halifax Antiquarian Society*, 1972; W. Pickles, 'Water Mills around Leeds', the *Dalesman*, vol. 24, 1962, pp. 435–40.

CARDING MACHINES

55. *Casting cylinders for carding machines in the iron foundry at John Haigh and Sons, Priestroyd Ironworks, Huddersfield (1935).*

56. *The erecting shop at John Haighs. Note the size and length of the machine more than 70 feet long. The set includes the scribbler, carder and tape condenser (1935).*

57. *Carding machine minders or feeders wearing black Italian pinafores, at Joshua Ellis and Co., Batley Carr Mills. They looked after four sets putting raw material into hoppers by hand at one end and doffing the bobbins of slubbings at the other (c. 1926).*

Yeadon.[1] Water-wheels continued in use after the invention of steam engines, for although unreliable, money had been put into them and they cost less to run. Many early steam engines were utilized to throw the water back on to the wheel. However, coal already used for heating dyepans and in the finishing processes was at hand, sometimes so near that it could be barrowed from day-hole to mill boiler. The age of the steam engine began.

Early engines with a crank motion were installed at the Crank Mill, Morley in 1790, Low Bridge, Damsdale and Hope Mills, Keighley,[2] the first St Peg Mill, Cleckheaton, built about 1803, and no doubt at others (*see drawing on page 34*). The engine at the Crank, replaced in 1872, antedated by three years that at Bean Ing, Leeds, a 30 to 40 h.p. Boulton and Watt rotative engine. By 1850 the changeover from water to steam power was almost complete.[3]

In 1822, besides sixteen machine-makers, there were three firms making steam engines in Leeds, of whom Fenton, Murray and Co. were the early locomotive engineers.[4] The ironworks at Low Moor, Bowling and Shelf, all made engines, and other makers started up elsewhere. At Sowerby Bridge Timothy Bates, founded in 1786, was followed by Pollitt and Wigzell, responsible for many engines in Calderdale. Mr Pollitt is remembered visiting mills every three or four years, and if his engine was well kept giving the engine tenter £1. This firm was taken over about 1933 by Cole, Marchent and Morley, founded in 1848 and still flourishing at Bradford, who made their last engine about 1926, and are the last of the long line of steam engine makers in the West Riding.

At Ready Carr, Marsden, a foundry developed from the blacksmith's shop of Enoch and James Taylor, the two brothers famous as makers of the cropping frames attacked by the Luddites, and this continued first as Taylor and Hirst, and then as Robert Taylor and Sons (Robert, 1787–1868, was their nephew) making steam engines and Lancashire boilers.[5] About 300 men and boys were employed. Mr Joe France's father worked there marking out end plates, fire boxes, water gauges and so on, and he travelled all over England, to Scotland and even France seating boilers. These monster cylinders, 30 feet long by 8 or 9 feet in diameter, were taken up the steep road to Marsden station pulled with ropes by every available man, and by twenty or thirty horses hired from local farmers. Steam traction engines next came into use for transporting and manœuvring them into

[1] P. Slater, *The Ancient Parish of Guiseley*, 1880.

[2] I. Dewhirst, *A History of Keighley*, 1974.

[3] W. B. Crump and G. Ghorbal, *History of the Huddersfield Woollen Industry*, p. 74–80.

[4] E. Baines, *History, Directory and Gazetteer of the County of York*, 1822, vol. 1, *West Riding*, p. 125.

[5] L. B. Whitehead, *Bygone Marsden*, 1942.

position in the boiler houses in mill yards—a task fraught with danger and difficulty.

As the need for more power arose, old engines were scrapped and often two or more put in to drive different parts of the mill. The engine man or tenter, keeping his charge clean and polished 'like furniture', was the king pin of the mill, and his boiler firer, who often lived in the mill yard to be at hand for stoking in the early morning, was trained to take over if the engine man was ill. Steam power from the boilers heated the premises and kept the tenter house going. Mills in the West Riding worked on Good Fridays because of the economics of maintaining the boiler fires. Every room was connected to the engine either by noisy gear wheels and shafts or by ropes and pulleys and had a danger bell which rang in the engine house. Boiler explosions, owing to faulty construction or the incompetence or even drunkenness of the engine tenter, caused deaths and were frequent enough to concern eminent engineers. On 9 June 1869 an explosion at a bobbin turners at Bingley killed thirteen people. On the other hand at Bowers Mill, in the Blackburn valley, Ben Jackson slowed down his engine to indicate mealtimes; at Gomersal Mills the engine is said to have worked the mill clock, and at Elmfield Mill, Bramley, when the engine started a fountain began to play in the owner's grounds.

Mr Arnold Townsend (b. 1883) graduated from plumber's and fitter's apprentice to millwright, to assistant engineer, and at twenty-four to engineer in charge of the five engines at Dean Clough Mills, Halifax. One was a 1,200 h.p. horizontal compound made by Pollitt and Wigzell, and another provided power for the grinding of flour to make paste to mix with colours for putting patterns on carpets. The twenty-seven boilers reduced over the years to eight consumed between 70 to 90 tons of coal a day. Arnold Townsend recollects as an apprentice crawling up narrow pipes to seal joints and inside a boiler to help lift out the bars, and working a whole week with little sleep to repair two faulty engines. Stoking was then all by hand (hopper feeds came in some sixty years ago), and the firer shovelling coal and raking off the ashes and clinkers with a huge rake streamed with perspiration.

Engines were replaced by gas engines, steam turbines, and eventually by individual electric motors on each machine, a process accelerated from the early 1930s to the 1950s. W. and E. Crowther, Crimble Mill, Slaithwaite, installed a Brush-Ljungström turbine in 1917 to replace two steam engines and were one of the first to go all-electric. A few engines, however, remain *in situ*, some silent, some working with their hovering tenter wearing a cap and holding an oily rag in the lofty precincts of the engine house.[1] One, which makes electricity at Dearnside

[1] According to a list prepared by the Industrial Section of the Bradford Archaeology Group there were eighteen engines in working order in mills in the West Riding in 1972.

Mills, Denby Dale, was built from parts by W. H. Kenyon, the present owner's grandfather, and James Lumb, engineer of Elland, in 1900. This vertical cross compound engine and its flywheel, a magnificent sight, feeds itself with oil, and seldom breaks down except when Mr Eric Kenyon goes away 'so that he takes care never to tell it'.

All engines were christened at ceremonies appropriate to the living creatures which they appeared to be, usually with the name or names of the owner's wife. 'John and Mary' at the Haggases at Oakworth included those of both husband and wife, whilst for obvious reasons some were called 'Gladstone' as at Black Rock Mills, Linthwaite, or 'Thomas Hughes' and 'Unity' as at Nutclough Mills.

The numerous extant early inventories of machinery are not matched by existing examples of the machinery itself.[1] One of these, the carding engine or card as it was formerly called, has developed in the woollen industry from a pair of small hand cards, used for teasing wool ready for spinning, to the largest machine in the mill, up to 75 feet long and with as many as eighty rotating rollers, a marvel of invention and engineering. The principle and use are still the same, that is wire teeth inserted in a foundation, once leather, now wire teeth on sheets or fillets on different bases, clothing the rollers. (Machines for carding cotton are small.) The construction of a carding machine requires three main contributors: the engineers who make the machines; the card-makers, now card clothing firms; and the card nailers, now the card mounters, who affix and renew the clothing on the rollers.

An old established firm still in the same family, John Haigh and Sons, Priestroyd Ironworks, Huddersfield, now amalgamated with Chadwicks of Cleckheaton, has since it was founded in 1835 supplied the mills in the West Riding and those in industrial towns all over the world with woollen and worsted carding machines, once costing a few hundred, now tens of thousands of pounds. Skilled craftsmen, serving apprenticeships, make the cylinders, formerly of well-seasoned mahogany, still occasionally used, then iron, now steel and aluminium. On these the card clothing is fixed not in the workshop lest it be damaged, but after installation of the machine in the mill (*see plates* 55–6).

Card-makers, plying their ancient and essential trade, were concentrated round Halifax, Huddersfield, Brighouse and Heckmondwike, where there were 116 in 1822. As an example, John Sykes, apprenticed to a card-maker at Elland, started a business in 1809 at Dearn House, Lindley, near Huddersfield, tanning leather, probably drawing wire, and using two machines, one called the Bendigo to cut and

---

[1] Early machines may be seen in Yorkshire at Cliffe Castle, Keighley, Bankfield Museum, Halifax, Tolson Memorial Museum, Huddersfield, Saddleworth Museum, Uppermill, Bradford Industrial Museum, Moorside Mills, Bradford, and Museum of Industry and Science, Armley Mills, Leeds.

bend the teeth and another to prick holes in the leather. Then in the card-maker's workshop or in 'setting schools', or often sitting on the doorsteps of their cottages, women and children were engaged in inserting teeth into leather straps, repeating nominies to count by and to encourage each other 'one o' me rody, two o' me rody' or naming people round the village. The tedious ill-paid work, comparable with the hand-knitting industry in organization and monotony, ceased altogether about 1870 as new machines were invented.[1]

In 1833 Charlotte Sykes, the widow of John and mother of six sons and five daughters, built Acre Mills, Lindley, and with her sons continued the business which, passed on from generation to generation, and expanding significantly from 1889 to 1912, became the largest manufacturer of card clothing for cotton in the world (*see plate* 18). In 1897 the firm joined three other old established companies (all be it noted in proximity to the source of iron at Low Moor), Samuel Law of Cleckheaton, John Whiteley and Sons of Halifax, and Wilson and Ingham of Mirfield, to form the now international English Card Clothing Company. These and other firms, such as James Holdsworth at Mirfield, employ skilled card-setters who each attend to a set of eleven or twelve machines making card clothing (*see plates* 60–2).

For his part the card nailer provided the tacks only and nailed on the leather based clothing. Metal cylinders had little wooden pegs let in for the nails, and card clothing, once made in fillets, and sheets 72, 66, 60 inches long by 6½ inches wide, is now mostly in fillets. Usually self-employed, the nailer ordered tacks by the half ton, once walked miles carrying heavy tools on his back, and charged so much a sheet or so much a cylinder.

Mr Lupton Bamforth of Marsden, a third generation of card nailers and thus employed for over fifty years, recollects: 'When you nailed a cylinder fifty inches in diameter with thirty sheets, with 240 tacks in a sheet, you get round to 7,000 tacks, 6 lb. in a cylinder, and all put in at once by hand half an inch to three quarters of an inch apart. You'd stretch the sheets with card pliers and with your foot operate a treadle to get your tension.' Now all is different. The card mounter wraps the clothing in fillets, 1½ to 2 inches wide, now often on a cotton, linen or cushion-rubber foundation instead of leather, round the cylinder in one length guided by a tension machine operated by another man.

To equip a mill the manufacturer had no need to go far afield. Take for instance Underbank Mill, which installed the machinery about 1920, in the Holme valley; the

---

[1] S. J. S. Walker, *The History of Joseph Sykes Brothers*, 1939; H. Ling Roth, 'Hand Card Making', *Bankfield Museum Notes*, No. XI; Malcolm Speirs, *A History of the Card Setting Machine Tenters' Society*, 1972.

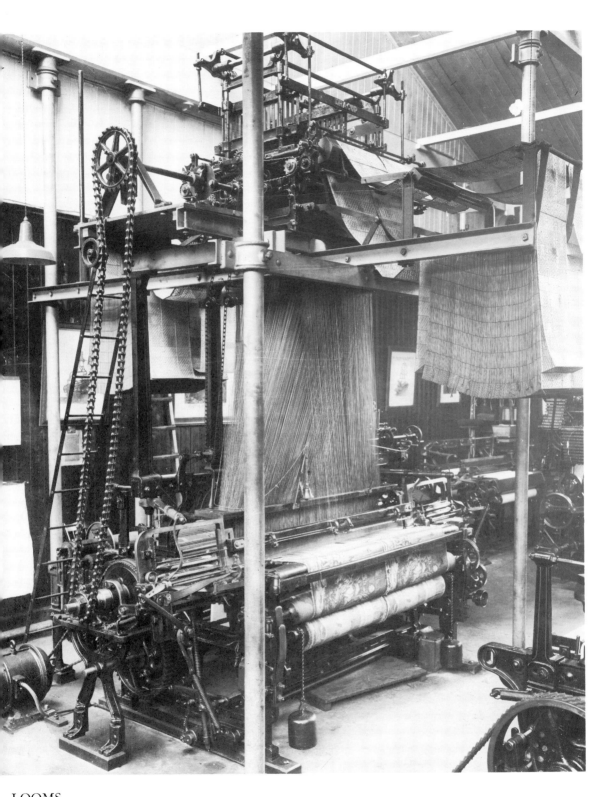

LOOMS

58. Tapestry loom built in 1908 by George Hattersley and Sons, Keighley. It was shown in operation at the Franco-British Exhibition in Paris in that year, and was awarded the Grand Prix. The tapestry being woven is of 'Bolton Abbey in the Olden Time' by Landseer owned by the Duke of Devonshire. For the production of this panel two Jacquard machines, made by S. Dracup and Co., Bradford, were used.

59. Mr Reggie Bird weaving carpet on a 27-inch Gripper Axminster loom made by David Crabtree and Son, Bradford, at Firth Carpets, Clifton Mills, Brighouse. The Jacquard cards above control the design and the yarns of the pile may be seen coming from the numerous bobbins on the creel (1948).

spinning mules came from William Whiteley and Sons of Lockwood in the Colne valley, the scouring machines from France and Lodge of Honley, the looms from Hutchinson and Hollingworth, Dobcross Loom Works, Saddleworth, and the finishing plant from Sellers and Co., Folly Hall, Huddersfield, all not more than from four to ten miles away.

Keighley, perhaps from its proximity to Lancashire, early established itself as a centre for textile engineering.[1] Small family firms began as makers of parts—rollers, flyers and spindles—for early spinning frames called throstles. William Smith, who started in this way as early as 1795 in two cottages, founded a family firm which developed into Prince-Smith & Son, later Prince-Smith and Stells as others were taken over. In 1912 they employed 12,000 men and produced machinery for all the processes of worsted manufacture, exporting to many countries. In 1960 they were said to be the largest works in the world solely engaged in the production of wool combing and worsted spinning plant. The firm was itself taken over by the great Lancashire firm of Platt International in 1970.

George Hattersley and Sons of Keighley, together with Dobcross, Northrop, Platt and others such as George Hodgson of Frizinghall, Bradford, Lee and Crabtree and David Sowden of Shipley, and Briggs of Gomersal, supplied the West Riding and the world with looms. Dobcross looms, made by Hutchinson and Hollingworth at Diggle, Saddleworth, from 1861 to 1970, rivalled Hattersleys, and Hodgsons won many gold medals at international exhibitions. Also a few large manufacturers—Listers, Fosters, Crossleys, Firths and Merralls of Haworth—formerly had their own engineering shops in which looms were made. For years Joseph Reixach, a Spaniard and the son of the inventor of the velvet loom, the patent for which had been bought by Cunliffe Lister, worked for Listers. About 1918 the firm employed some eighty mechanics making annually thirty to forty single and double shuttle looms in a secret department which was closed down in the late 1950s.

Richard Hattersley (1761–1829) had come from Eccleshall, near Sheffield, in 1789 to Keighley where he started as a whitesmith, and it was his son, George (1789–1869) who in 1834 began to make looms for the worsted trade. In 1856 the firm invented the first revolving box loom which allowed colour to be used in the weft and which supplanted many of those made locally. Further patents followed, for instance the dobby in 1867, and looms were ordered by the hundred. Fitters and tuners lived and settled abroad, especially in Germany. In the early part of this century one man spent years in France starting tapestry looms for the weaving of tapestries for the walls of French châteaux (see plate 58).

[1] John Hodgson, *Textile Manufacture, and other Industries, in Keighley*, 1879.

After the First World War new methods allowed for much finer construction, and a new Standard model loom was introduced and exported to France, and also to Italy, Japan, China, Australia and South Africa. For delivery near at hand or in Lancashire the firm once kept thirty-two horses and sent looms ready erected. It was said in loom-making that two good years were followed by five bad. Looms sold very cheaply—in 1905 at £7 10s., a price which rose to £75 in 1914, six years later to £310, in the slump of the early 1920s £150, and in 1951 £450. Hattersley's invented a domestic foot-pedal type loom first developed for the Balkans, and later sent these and still do to the islands of Lewis, Harris and Skye for the manufacture of hand woven Harris tweed. They took over Hodgson, Sowden, and Hutchinson and Hollingworth in amalgamations only too frequent amongst the makers of textile machines.[1]

There are in fact only three loom-makers of the fifteen existing in about 1911 left in the West Riding: Hattersleys, David Crabtree & Son, Laisterdyke, Bradford, and Wilson and Longbottom at Barnsley, the two last making carpet looms required to supply carpets to an affluent society. Crabtrees, founded in 1853, then Lee and Crabtree, provided plain looms for the mills in the Heavy Woollen District for 100 years. In 1926 they perfected and made their first Gripper Axminster loom of which they are the sole makers (*see plate* 59). This huge machine, of which some twenty-six are made in a year, takes four months to construct, cost in 1975 approximately £80,000, and is supplied all over the world.[2]

The many parts needed for a loom—Jacquards, sleys, reeds, healds, temples, shuttles, bobbins and pickers, of which the last three are slowly disappearing —illustrate the number and diversity of ancillary firms and craftsmen needed. Consider the Jacquard, a French invention for making figured materials, and a fascinating mechanism whereby a design is converted into perforations on cards, which by means of a harness working the healds produces the design (*see plate* 59). At the present day three firms, one in Manchester, and J. T. Hardaker and Samuel Dracup in Bradford, make them, of which Hardakers work in close association with Crabtrees.

Dracups was founded in 1825 by Samuel, son of Nathaniel Dracup, a shuttle-maker of Great Horton, Bradford, and is still in the same family. Formerly Jacquards were all wood (birch), but they are now mostly metal and steel. The harness is varnished linen thread or Terylene and the cards thick cardboard or plastic. Craftsmen still straighten the needles (which connect the threads with the

---

[1] Information from Colonel F. L. Smith, Mr R. L. Smith of Hattersleys and Mr T. E. Horsfall, retired Technical Manager.
[2] Information from Mr G. E. Phelon, Managing Director, David Crabtree & Son.

60. *Wet drawing card wire at Joseph Sykes Bros, Acre Mills, Lindley, Huddersfield, the largest firm of fine wire drawers in the United Kingdom and a member of the English Card Clothing Company. These machines made on the premises were in use from 1906 to 1960/65 (c. 1950).*

61. *A card setting machine tenter, Mr John Gledhill, at James Holdsworths, South Brook Mills, Mirfield. He runs twelve filleting machines that each put in 300 teeth a minute. The fillets 'clothe' the cylinders of the carding machine.*

62. *Mrs Irene Magee sets any missing teeth at South Brook Mills.*

ANCILLARY TRADES

63. The making department at the British Picker Company, Sandholme Mills, Todmorden. Pickers of water buffalo hide are made by folding, pressing and boring, and every one is made by weight (late 1940s).

64. Mr G. S. Hirst of Roberts and Hirst, Cote Hill, Halifax, bobbin turners, makes ring spinning bobbins.

65. Mr Cecil Fearnside, shuttle and loom accessories manufacturer, Park Works, Oakworth, near Keighley (1970).

MILL TRANSPORT

66. Despatch of a loom from George Hattersleys, Keighley. This particular loom and its attendants may have been going to join a pageant. The firm had at one time thirty-two horses (date unknown).

67. Bogies, Ford lorries, steam waggons, and large lorries at Manningham Mills, Bradford (1920s).

68. Early lorry belonging to Tom Liversedge and Sons, Canal Bank Dyeworks, Huddersfield (1909).

healds) by hand as has been the practice for 150 years. Jacquards, of which some forty types are made, may be used for designs in the finest silk, for carpets, or, one of the smallest, for weaving the name of a firm or its trademark down the selvedges of the cloth. They cost from £350 to £10,000. At Dracups we were shown a portrait of Queen Elizabeth II, a Coronation tapestry, and other remarkably fine work woven on Jacquard looms.

As for the shuttle-makers, there were thirty-four in 1849 in the West Riding, a few combined with bobbin turning and picker-making. Now there are three or four and a few in Lancashire. Shuttles ranged in size from 22 inches for blanket looms to 12 inches for silk. In the past they were made of boxwood or perhaps apple, and an apprentice knocked in the metal bushes on the ends, shaped with clogger's knives, and sand-papered the inside. There were shuttle boddiers and shuttle finishers; and a man might make a shuttle throughout, whereas now he tends one lathe and one machine fashioning one stage in the manufacture.

At Oakworth, near Keighley, shuttles have been made since the beginning of the last century in the usual three-storied building with the former living quarters on the ground floor. Built by Thomas Burwin, whose name is inscribed over a door, it formerly had a water-wheel and a beam engine, and is now run by a distant connection of the Burwins, Mr C. Fearnside. Shuttles, usually sold in pairs, one for weaving and one to be filled ready for use, are made to order. Just before the First World War they sold at 6d. or 1s. and now, made of persimmon or cornel wood imported from America, or plastics, or manufactured woods, they each sell for several pounds.

Similarly bobbin-makers, once scattered about the country especially in the Lake District, and often utilizing the water-wheels of old corn mills for power, have contracted in numbers from thousands employed in the trade to a few hundreds. Like shuttle-making bobbin-making reached a peak of demand about 1870 and flourished until the end of the Second World War. A cluster of buildings at Cote Hill, Halifax—a works, a small dam, a mill house, a chimney, and once cottages for workers, now demolished—developed from the bobbin-making begun there in 1798. Mary Bancroft, the maker in 1829, sold slubbing bobbins, mill nuts, and bobbin *broaches* (spindles). The steam engine has gone, but with complicated machines made by Fell's, the wood-working machinery firm of Kendal, and actuated by hydraulic and pneumatic power, Roberts and Hirst make large ring spinning bobbins of which the flange is sycamore and the barrel Danish beech (*see plate* 64).

So, too, sleys, reeds, healds, temples and pickers for looms require specialist knowledge for their construction. The making of pickers, the buffer which projects the shuttle every time it crosses the warp, centred round Todmorden on the Yorkshire-Lancashire border, where there were ten or twelve small firms engaged in this work. Originally they were made of wood, then leather, now water buffalo hide, and more recently plastics. All sizes and varieties for different looms are made by the British Picker Co., an amalgamation of several firms, at Todmorden (*see plate* 63).

At Leeds three firms, pioneers in the field of textile machinery, require mention: Taylor Wordsworth, amalgamated with Prince-Smith of Keighley, were the first makers of the Noble comb. Fairbairn, Lawson, Combe and Barbour made and exported the whole range of machinery for processing flax, jute and similar fibres, machine tools and other products, and now as Fairbairn Lawson exports many engineering products.

The third, Hardings, is one of the few firms of any size in the world making pins for all types of combing machines, teeth for carding and rag grinding machines and castings for Noble combs (*see plate* 29). Thomas Harding, who was born in Cambridgeshire, the son of a wool merchant, learnt the craft of making combing pins for the flax trade in Lille in France, and in 1859 founded a firm in Leeds, then the centre of that trade. Five years later he built the present works in Globe Road, with a chimney, based in design on the Lamberti Tower at Verona in northern Italy, to make a flue for the steam engine and to create a draught for an extraction plant essential to carry away the fine steel dust caused by the grinding of the steel pins. When three firms joined together and the works were enlarged in 1899 the Giotto Tower, based on the design of the famous one in Florence, took over the function of the Verona Tower. The dust, conveyed away in a complex system of underground flues, is sold to make fireworks.

Lastly, the machines used in the finishing processes, the tentering, cropping (now called cutting) machines, the latter known locally as Jerries, and the teazle raising gig, of which the last two were the cause of the Luddite Riots. The first two, although crude machines, were developed early, and they were made by William Whiteley and Sons of Lockwood, already mentioned, an important firm which no longer exists. The teazle gig consists of a revolving drum or cylinder covered with rods or spindles filled with teazle heads whose tough hooked bracts raise the nap of cloth, and is also made in the Colne valley at the present day by James Bailey, textile engineers of Slaithwaite.

Up to about 1915 teazles (*Dipsacus fullonum*) were grown in Yorkshire round Selby and Sherburn-in-Elmet where the heavy rich soil suited their cultivation, also formerly in Kent, Wiltshire, Essex and Gloucestershire. Once they were exported from Yorkshire, but instead they are imported from France and Spain to augment the small quantity still grown east of Taunton in Somerset, the only teazle growing district left in England.[1]

Taking seventeen months to grow, harvested by hand, and carefully dried on poles and in shelters (*see plates* 41-2), they then keep indefinitely. In the winter they were formerly sorted and arranged in bunches of twenty-five, called *fans* in Somerset, and bunches of ten, called *glens* (gleanings) in Yorkshire. Thirty glens were then put on a *stav* (a hazel stick 3 feet to 4 feet long, split half-way down) and sealed at the top with a willow ring (*see plate* 43). 'In the barn the stavs in rosettes looked like waxworks.' The Somerset stavs (once shipped from Bristol) were reared upright in railway box vans for despatch to Yorkshire. A grower might have had ninety packs, 1,800,000 teazles for sale. In Yorkshire 13,500 counted as a pack. Formerly dealers were both growers and merchants, such as James Bortoft of South Milford who had warehouses in Leeds. Now two remain—Edmund Taylor of Huddersfield and Sloman and Smith of Leeds who, sending pack sheets for teazles, buy in and grade them for sale. In the 1920s the price slumped to £4 a pack, rose to £18 after the Second World War, and is now nearer to £50.

In the past most mills had teazle gigs, whereas today they are only used for some knitwear, some blankets, and for cloths with a drawn finish such as quality worsted, velours and mohair, cashmere, camelhair and billiard cloths. Few firms employ a full-time teazle man, and most engage a journeyman for half a day a week or for longer as required. Skill and experience judge the strength of the teazles to be used and how long to leave the cloth, which is damped, in the gig, perhaps half an hour to two days. To keep their effect even, four or five rods out of the twenty-four on a drum are changed at one time, and the rods are also turned over (*see plates* 44-5). 350,000 teazles may be employed in one gig in a year. Wire machines have been invented, but nothing man-made quite replaces the teazles which reach to the base of the cloth and part the fibres.

Baines wrote in 1858: 'The increased speed with which everything connected

Arthur Young found 'tassels' grown as a profitable crop at Stillingfleet, near Selby, in 1771, and *White's Directory*, 1837, states that many teazle growers from Somersetshire and various parts of Yorkshire attended several inns in Leeds. See also 'A Yorkshire Plant: The Teazle', *Leeds Mercury Supplement Notes and Queries*, 1889-90; J. Billingsley, *General View of the agriculture of the County of Somerset*, 1797, pp. 110-12; *Journal of the Bath and West and Southern Counties Society*, 6th series, vol. XII, 1937-9, pp. 34-40. Also information from Mr C. George of Edmund Taylor, Huddersfield, Mr D. J. Maddick and Mr F. Brunt of Somerset, 1973. Also Mr R. A. McMillan at the Tolson Memorial Museum, Huddersfield, has kindly shown us details of teazle growing in Yorkshire given to him in the same year by Mr William Bradley of South Milford, then aged ninety.

with the [textile] trade is transacted is startling to men who remember the old times and ways.' How much more startled they would have been today by the sophisticated machines resulting from scientific research, precision engineering, and the invention of man-made fibres, all going faster and faster, taking larger packages, and lessening both the numbers of operations and labour force.

The small Bendigo machine formerly used for making teeth for card clothing.

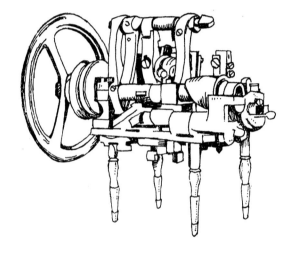

6 Paved with Gold

THE abundant natural resources of the West Riding are nowhere more in evidence than in the mineral wealth of sandstone and coal found above the millstone grit. During the last century excellent stone was at hand everywhere for the great surge of the building of houses, mills, warehouses, town halls, offices, art galleries, for pavements and for roads, not only in the West Riding but in London and elsewhere. Masterpieces in stone such as the centre of the city of Bradford (now largely rebuilt) rose on every hand.

Quarrying was formerly undertaken by farmers getting stone on their own fields, then by small men leasing a thousand or more square yards from the owners of the freehold for shallow *delphs* (quarries). Later some of these employed delvers and became stone merchants. *Huggers*, men wearing leather saddles on their backs, carrying huge slabs up ladders with broad rungs and liable to accidents, were replaced by gins and hand-cranes, which in turn were superseded by steam cranes and in the 1920s by electricity. Picks and wedges to cut stone then gave way to the plug and feather method using pneumatic drills.

In the second half of the last century new quarry owners—Armitages, Aspinalls, Briggs, Brookes, Farrars, Freemans, Marshalls, Vints and others—turned the industry into big business. Huge deep quarries were excavated, derricks pierced many skylines, and thousands of men were employed as barers, delvers, hewers, fettlers and banker masons. Although since about 1914 the numbers of quarries, many filled in, have greatly diminished, one-man quarries run in the old style remain at Spring Hall, Greetland, and Blake Hill End, in the Shibden valley (*see plate* 69), and a number of large concerns flourish.

In general two types of stone were hewn, ashlar, a sandstone with no visible grain, won in beds up to 10 feet thick, used for buildings, and the famous Elland Edge Flagrock, a stone that splits, usually called freestone, which runs along the hilltops from Huddersfield to Leeds, used for wall stones, paving, kerbstones, landings (large slabs), setts for roads, platform coping and roofing slates. Hard

York stone became and is famous especially when used for fine smooth-faced flagstones, that is paving stones.

Stone from Bramley Fall and other quarries was used for building Leeds Town Hall, that from Crosland Hill above the Colne valley for the buildings in Huddersfield, fine quality ashlar from Ringby Quarry for Halifax Town Hall, and from Bolton Woods, Bradford, stone was supplied for Manningham Mills. Colour was important and had to be matched. 'They knew a great deal about stone in London.' Stone was despatched by rail, by canal and by boat to London, America, Germany, Australia and many other countries.

At the beginning of this century on the hilltops of the Ribbleden valley near Holmfirth, a district pitted with small abandoned quarries, the Gee family lived at the Rising Sun public house combining quarrying with inn-keeping in the traditional manner. Mr Joe Gee, who was born in 1909, remembers helping in one way and another as a child, milking the cows before going to school, and that his father and grandfather before him had Longley Edge Quarry on Scholes Moor as well as Hillhouse Edge on Cartworth Moor which he and his brother worked until their retirement in 1967. From the soft rough grit at Longley Edge ridge stones for roofs and troughs for watering horses on roadsides were hewn. The troughs were hollowed out with a pick and the sides scrappled smooth and square from great blocks of stone, the largest 8 feet long, 3 feet 6 inches wide and 2 feet 9 inches deep. Similarly at other quarries huge dyepans and brewing vats were formerly hacked out by hand.

Hillhouse Edge was 'as nice a quarry as you could wish to have' and the stone 'good to work'. They employed about sixteen men including banker hands, and were equipped with steam cranes, a blacksmith's shop, two saws, a polishing machine and two horses and waggons. Men were strong in those days. A man could carry a stone slab weighing 7 cwt on his back in the old style. In the 1920s stone was delivered in the district at 2s. 6d. a super yard, whereas in 1975 it may well cost £7 or £8. At Longley Edge trade diminished about 1910, but at Hillhouse Edge it continues vigorously.

Landings, 4 to 6 inches thick, were large stone slabs used for steps, the ceilings of cellars, for pavements (when a square or a round hole might be cut in them down which coal was shot) and were despatched to London packed in straw in railway trucks. They were in constant demand for the base of memorials on graves in Christian, Jewish and municipal cemeteries. Up to about 1939 William Knight and Co., masonry contractors and stone merchants of London, used to have a standing order to deliver sixteen landings every Monday morning to the Islington and St Pancras cemeteries at Finchley. Those only 6 feet 6 inches by 2 feet 6 inches

69. Blake Hill End Quarry and Hollin Grove Farm in the Shibden valley, near Halifax, run by the Pulmans combining quarrying and farming in the old style. Note the judd walls to the left of the farmhouse.

70. *The so-called Walls of Jericho near Egypt, north of Thornton, near Bradford. They were built as retaining walls for quarry debris.*

71. *Mr Ronnie Porter, banker mason, using a slating hammer to dress a stone roofing slate on a slate banker at the quarries and works of S. Marshall and Sons, Southowram, near Halifax.*

and 4 inches thick were called ledgers, and the landings up to 9 feet by 6 feet 6 inches and 6 inches thick were used for the more elaborate monuments. Both were replaced by concrete in the 1930s.

Between Huddersfield and Halifax quarries surrounded the town of Elland, which gave its name to the stone used in particular from about 1800 onwards for the pavements of the expanding cities and towns. Up to the First World War a special tendering practice prevailed to prevent delays caused by late deliveries. A price was fixed for thousands of square yards of flags and kerbstones, but if a certain quantity, 200 to 300 square yards, was undelivered within twenty-four to forty-eight hours of the order being placed, the local authority concerned had the right to buy from a merchant and charge the firm tendering the difference in price.

At Lightcliffe, near Halifax, Joseph Brooke and Sons, a family firm founded in 1842, worked some twelve quarries, and pioneered the production of a crushed stone aggregate, patented in 1898 and marketed as 'Non-Slip stone', used for railway platforms, the pavements of London boroughs, and of towns from one end of England to the other. They also had quarries in Guernsey, Wales and Scandinavia. From the latter granite for dock works and monuments was shipped to Aberdeen and from there sent by rail to Halifax. The works, described in 1930 as the largest for roadway and building materials in the world, were closed down in the 1960s.[1]

Similarly at Southowram, near Halifax, the whole neighbourhood has been given over to quarrying, and is now the headquarters of Marshalls, a firm founded here by Solomon Marshall in 1891. A group of companies, one making rock drilling equipment for roadstone quarries and water boring tools, they employ 700 men. Marshalls took over Brookes and still supply York stone flags to paving contractors to the corporation of London, in recent years used for the new London Bridge, the Guildhall extension, the Houses of Parliament, and many other works. It used to be said that London's streets were paved with gold and at today's prices the saying has a more prosaic meaning. In 1937 Marshalls began to manufacture a prefabricated stone, Marshalite, very widely used for building, paving, and for garden layouts, and they are the largest manufacturers of hydraulically pressed concrete in the world.

It is a sobering thought that the best stone has been taken, and that in spite of easier methods of removing the overburden, sometimes 50 feet to 100 feet thick, quarries are almost finished. It is common practice and worth while to take up

[1] S. A. Leleux, *Brookes' Industrial Railways*, 1972.

kerbstones and re-dress, re-joint and re-use them. In the 1880s Welsh blue and Cumberland green slates began to replace the traditional stone slates as the roofing material for the rows and rows of houses in the cities and towns of the West Riding. Houses may thus be dated by their roofs.

Stone slates were formerly riven or split from the lifts of stone, left to dry for a few weeks, and then split off by the slate striker. Next they were to trim off on a slate banker with a slate hammer (*see plate* 71), and have the scale shelled off with an adze, a job often undertaken by Irishmen. Dick Marsden, who died in 1948, worked at Marshalls as a slate striker from the age of eight for sixty-seven years. Now suitable stone for riven slates is not there, even if they could be afforded. Their scarcity and value may be judged by their once being sold by the 100 of six score, then by the score, and now, if available at all, at so much apiece.

Behind Thornton, near Bradford, the extent of quarrying is commemorated by the judd walls, the so-called Walls of Jericho, built as in other places for example in the Shibden valley to retain quarry waste and so form a level field (*see plates* 69–70). A hundred years ago these enclaves of quarrymen were practically illiterate, and dependent for education on Sunday schools held in remote chapels. Often they relied on one of their number with a gift for figures to reckon up their piecework earnings. In severe winters they and their families endured great hardship, and enlightened employers found their men work or opened soup kitchens. From Thornton huge slabs of stone, varying in size and up to 6 feet 6 inches long and 1 foot 4 inches thick, for making steam engine beds, were transported by waggon and horses to Bradford station. Many of these were supplied from Yorkshire quarries to Lancashire mills.

At Haworth as many as eight quarries were once worked on the moors. The Jaggers, who moved from Ringby to Bankfield Quarry, Haworth, about 1928, employed at one time 100 men getting stone for new buildings in Halifax and elsewhere. Rough tough horses pulled the narrow block waggons with heavy wheels. Mr W. Jagger remembers the skill of one little man putting on the slipper brake, fastening the wheels with a chain, and driving his three horses pulling a waggon load weighing 10 tons down Haworth's steep Main Street.

Sandstone setts, the customary and once familiar paving material for streets, have been gradually replaced by tarmac. In a price-list for 1901 they ranged in size and quality from 6 inches at 48s. a rood to 'Best Yorkshire Nell Setts' 10 inches by 7 inches by 8 inches at 80s. Until the early part of this century setts were measured for sale in roods of 14 square yards, stacked in eight rows, each 5 feet 3 inches in length and 3 feet high.

Haworth Main Street, a splendid example of stone paving, was relaid in the

1930s. The Jaggers supplied 6-inch setts of stone 'as good and hard as you could find'. Setts were not laid on the bed, but edgeways to prevent weathering, and were bedded in tar and ashes from mill boilers. Ashes were once used for mixing with lime for plaster, and alone to improve early roads, and 6*d*. a load was paid to anyone who carted them away.

7 Miners Look Back

LIKE stone, coal was everywhere at hand for the expanding industries and influenced their siting and development. Mines and mills formerly occupied the same territory. Coal outcrops near the Elland Road football ground at Leeds, and within a three-miles radius of Dewsbury there were once forty-two working collieries. These were small and shallow such as the seven or eight at Batley, where it is said you could shout down the shaft to the men at the bottom. The historic Middleton Colliery and Waterloo Main were in or near to Leeds, and Gomersal Colliery in the very centre of our area only closed down in 1973. As pits were worked out mining moved from this, the western exposed coal-field, to the concealed field of the south-east.

None the less remembered scenes are of rows of colliers squatting on their haunches at popular meeting-places in the villages, walls against which they leant appearing as if polished with black lead, and black-faced men with black-rimmed eyes clattering home in clogs. In those early days owing to lack of experience in safety measures and regulations, terrible disasters occurred involving great loss of life, such as those at Morley Main Colliery in 1872 and Combs Colliery, Thornhill, in 1893. 'My grandfather and two of his brothers were killed in the Morley explosion. They took the bodies in coal carts to the Royal Hotel.' The strikes and lockouts, too, which punctuate the history of mining, affected not only the lives of the miners themselves but those dependent on coal for work and warmth.

Between Rothwell and Wakefield, only four or five miles south of Leeds, coal-mining began in earnest in the early part of the last century, and mining families grew out of old established communities of people with varied occupations. Batty in his *History of Rothwell* records the diminishing longevity of the inhabitants as mining developed. None the less a way of life emerged in which boys automatically followed their fathers' employment. Here, worked by fewer than twenty men, were many family pits in which strangers had no part. If a man left, his place was taken by a younger brother, a son or nephew. Lads gained their 'pit eyesight' starting with haulage in the pit bottom, and then joined their relations at the coal face.

The colliery officials and miners with whom we have talked, dedicated men, who spent their lives in coal-mining, worked both under private ownership and since 1947 under nationalization. Mr Syd Thompson of Rothwell started his mining career in north-west Durham against the wishes of his parents who did not want him to go underground, 'I ran away from school with a pal one Friday in January, 1921, when I was fourteen, and we were set on as pony drivers at 11s. a week. It seemed like a fortune. On the Monday morning at 9 a.m. along with other men and lads we just walked into the hillside down a day-hole or drift mine. I can smell the tang of the air yet, of timber, ponies, men, coal and powder reek, burning candles and the smoke from the naked lights of the oil *midgies*. It was a new world. You were moved to safety lamp seams later, a sinister tang all its own. There was great comradeship—to belong meant something—and the discipline was very strict.'

Influenced by his schoolmaster and like so many more lads throughout the mining industry at that period, he combined earning a living with attendance at night school, undertaking every type of job in the pit including 'sweating it out on your side with a hand pick in very low coal in the dim light of a safety lamp'. At technical college he first passed as a shot-firer and a deputy. 'During 1933 when I was fore-overman in charge of the shift and of mechanizing part of the pit, I had to be the first man down on the cage every morning at 3 a.m. with 350 men and lads to check and deploy. It was gruelling, with office work at night. I hardly saw my wife and kids. But there was a great spirit among us. We spent some happy times.' Finally he obtained the first- and second-class certificates of competency under the Coal Mines Acts of 1911 and 1920 which qualified him for the exacting job of under-manager or manager. Some men obtained degrees in mining engineering. This was the pattern in the 1920s and up to 1940. Today it can still obtain, but the selection is more keen, partly because of the diminished labour force, and partly because of the comprehensive facilities for education in mining now provided.

In 1940 when war had broken out Syd Thompson came from Durham to the Old Silkstone Collieries, Yorkshire, and after a short time was appointed manager of their Silkstone mine. He found the coal and wages in Yorkshire better, but the men's and the officials' attitudes very different. 'You had to live with the fellows and get to know them, and they had to get to know you before you could work together.'

Four years later he moved to Rothwell Collieries owned by J. and J. Charlesworth, a complex of eight mine shafts, employing 1,400 men, and listed as a necessitous undertaking. Here the famous Silkstone and Beeston seams were exhausted; the pit was threatened with closure, and the less attractive and thinner seams were being worked mainly for the war effort. The trade unionists, at first demanding this, that and the other, proved very difficult, until made aware of the true position and that their jobs were at stake. Within a short period production improved steadily each month, vying ultimately with those of its neighbours. After nationalization in 1947 and following the timely opening of the Skelton Grange Power Station which used the class of coal mined, the pit has been completely modernized and it still flourishes.

Mr Thompson, as the representative of the National Association of Colliery Managers, visited and assisted at several single and multiple fatalities, fires and one or two explosions, all of which mercifully lessen in numbers as safety regulations are constantly enforced and lessons learnt. Extraordinary chaos results in the roadways from an explosion. His work, too, has involved him in the closure of mines in West Yorkshire, each one a sad and chilling experience. Here, for 100 years or more a pit has employed hundreds of local men, whose work cannot easily be replaced by other forms of employment. After the removal of useful material, supplies and machinery and the clearing of the site, the shafts are filled in until no trace of the pit remains.[1]

Formerly in West Yorkshire if a man was killed, everyone came out and sacrificed their earnings. Only those who carried the dead man were paid. If a man was badly injured, it was customary too, although there existed a Miners' Sickness and Aid Fund, to take a collection for him. 'An injured miner was never well off.' Miners had snap tins the shape of a loaf, in two parts which slotted together, carried by a crank lever on the belt, and in the workings hung up on girders away from any mice or rats which came into the mine with the ponies' fodder. (In the 1924–38 period there were 2,480 horses and ponies in the 116 mines in West Yorkshire.) Glass bottles for water were replaced for safety by tin then enamel, and now by Dudley bottles which hold four to six pints all of which are welcome in the deep hot pits. Hard hats and safety helmets made their appearance before the Second World War.

Mr Maurice Westmoreland (1896–1975) was a member of one of the few old families at Rothwell engaged in mining since about 1800, and was a collier (that is a man working at the coal face) for nearly forty years until his hand was trapped in a roof fall. He started when he was thirteen at the pit bottom at Belle Isle (a pit which tapped the Beeston seam at 220 yards), pushing tubs into a cage and knock-

---

[1] Mines that have gone in the area in the last thirty years are Allerton Main, Whitwood, West Riding, Snydale, Middleton, Shaw Cross, Thornhill, Roundwood, Waterloo Main, St Johns, East Ardsley, Water Haigh, Primrose Hill and Gomersal.

72. *A collier getting coal with a pick at Eastwood Colliery, Nottinghamshire (1912).*

73. *During the coal strike of 1912 women look for combustible material on a dump left by an old chemical works or an industrial process at Cowrakes Lane, Lindley, near Huddersfield.*

ing the empty ones out for 10*d*. a day for eight and a half hours for five days and six and a half on Saturdays. His mother gave him 6*d*. a week pocket money.

Next he drove ponies, of which there were over seventy in the pit, for 1*s*. 1*d*. a day, and then as was customary joined his father in a team of three at the coal face. 'You couldn't have a better way of seeing to a fellow's welfare.' At first he filled the then small tubs, holding about 6 cwt, and in about six months was earning equal wages with his father, about £1 a day. He changed from his boots into clogs at the pit head, and worked in *bannakers* (long shorts), knelt on rubber pads, and leant his shoulder on a low buffet. Knees were calloused and cut, and Beat knee (fluid on the knee) was a common complaint. They were paid by the ton and won the best coal by *baring* (undercutting a large seam) and using chocks to hold it up. When these were removed enough coal fell down to fill five or six tubs. In this way round (large) coal, sold at a good price, was obtained without explosives.

A collier was paid for the amount of coal he got, and each tub full was distinguished by a *motty*, a numbered metal disc. When he started a miner was given a number. 'Mine was eighteen. I've never forgotten it. A motty is a symbol to a miner.' *Mottying*, cutting someone else's off and substituting their own, an occasional happening, was regarded as a heinous offence and the man was blacklisted. The master's weighman and the check-weighman, representing the miners, sat in the same office and weighed the tubs, 10 to 15 cwt. 2 to 4 lb. picks were supplied, and they used 10 lb. hammers for knocking timbers and wedges in for the supports, and two shovels, a round muck shovel and a square filling shovel. Picks were sharpened each day by the pick sharpener, and although they were numbered, some men buried their tools so that they were certain to keep their own.

When he moved to Methley Pit, Maurice rose at 4 a.m., walked a mile and three-quarters, caught a bus at 5 a.m., changed to a second, and riding to the face in tubs, was at work by 6 a.m. In some mines without riding facilities the men had to walk two to three miles and in these cases were allowed walking time. Nevertheless in a seven-hour shift this meant only five at the face to make a living. When Maurice's hand was damaged, all too common a happening, his compensation was then £4 a week dole and £4 from the pit.

'You couldn't save much to be married, but we'd plenty of coal, and the rent was 3*s*. 4*d*. a week. We went many a time to Leeds to shop or look round or to the theatre, and on Saturdays to a Rugby match. We'd three shows that day, the Empire for 6*d*., the Royal for 9*d*. and 9*d*. for the Rugby match. We'd to walk home many a time [five miles].' Maurice was, as so many miners are, blessed with green fingers and took immense pride in his garden and greenhouse (*see plate* 144).

By the time Mr George Garfit of Rothwell left school about 1920, boys could not go into the pit until they were fourteen, so he worked for a twelve-month at an engineering works in Leeds. Like the other lads, he too began tramming tubs in the pit bottom, which was then lit by tallow candles—in his case at Beeston Pit— and after a year learning from his brother, he became a fitter. In those days providing their own tools, he and his brother maintained the pumps and condensing engines. Later when diesel engines replaced ponies and coal shearers and conveyor belts were introduced as many as fifty maintenance men were necessary, and the colliers had only to reset supports and shovel coal from the face corners.

'You never could get shut of coal dust. My mother always had to put the fireside boiler on for Dad's bath. It was hard work for mothers before pit baths came.' When first married he earned two guineas a week. His wife was always relieved when he arrived home. For holidays they travelled all over England on a motor-bicycle and sidecar, and in retirement both share the hobby of making model railway engines.

Mr Jack Priest of Ossett also at the age of fourteen at 6 a.m. on 9 April 1929 followed his father who was a deputy down the pit at Gomersal. 'When me and mi Dad were oppening t' pit out [it had been closed and was re-opened], ther'd be big grown-up men kneeling down in front of him begging for a job at 6s. a day to get a bit better for their families. . . . An official were more like a sergeant major. If he said "Jump", they'd to jump. The hand-getting colliers were proud of their skill, and worked on contract at so much a yard or ton [it was for this that a deputy formerly carried a stick, a yardstick]. When you went to your work, if you wanted bantams, poultry, pigeons, flowers or cabbage plants somebody somewhere kept 'em, and they'd be there i' t' lamp room next day. You'd ask "How much do you want for 'em?" and the answer might be a couple o' bob or nowt.'

'Mi father, me and mi brother went home and had us dinner before we got weshed. Up to us leaving school we had to stand at table for us meals. If us belly went agen t'table or if we reached for us bun before us bread, knife used to come down at back of us hands. When we started working we got a chair. We used to get us dinner about a quarter to three; then mi Dad had a nap, and I used to go to t'set pot with a *piggin* [lading can] and take two piggins of watter and fill an enamel bowl in a stone sink at side, and take two cold ens back. You used ter take yer shirt off and wesh behind yer ears and arms and chest. Yer were black breet, then mi mother used to come and wesh yer back. She used to buy harden sugar bags and boil 'em for towels and dry your back. Ooooooh! There were always notches all down yer back like. Then you'd take yer pants off and your stockings and roll yer football breeches up and put a leg in t'bowl. If you went to t'pit wi' mucky legs, you used to get some hammer. A lot of 'em, men up to thirty year old, i' them days used to be in their pit muck till nine o'clock at neet, laiking football or piggy or cricket. In t' pit rows they used to be sat on t' doorsteps i' summer time, telling t' tale i' their shirt sleeves. It's gone is that. Culture's all gone. I don't talk broad as I used to do.' Jack Priest also has his hobbies, keeping canaries and collecting pit lamps and other bygones.

The oldest of the remarkable ninety-year-olds we have met is Mr John Chapman Fox, aged ninety-seven, a surface worker in the mines for most of his life, a keen cyclist, a great fisherman, and gifted with a memory for dates and statistics. He remembers the rioting at Featherstone in 1903 when soldiers were brought in, and that it was a hot day on 30 April 1896, when sixty-three men were killed in the Micklefield Colliery disaster, and that drunkenness and fighting on Saturday nights were commonplace.

John Chapman Fox was one of a family of two girls and five boys, all over 6 feet tall, of whom all the boys went into the pits. He himself suffered from slight claustrophobia which explains his mixed career, for earnings on surface work were half the pay of those underground. In 1887 his father, a miner, who had been left money, set up as a rope and twine spinner, and here at the age of ten John began work. However, following an eleven-week-long strike at the colliery which supplied the coal for the steam engine, the enterprise failed. By 1902 when he married he had had three jobs, of which one involved walking to Hunslet four miles there and four miles back each day for five years.

Then through his parents who knew the manager at Rose Pit, Rothwell, he was given the job of stoking the nine boilers for the winding, haulage and pumping engines. Two men worked the day shift and one the night. In the first two years, often having to work a shift and a half, he lost two stones in weight and earned only 27s. a week plus overtime. After nine years he moved to more congenial work, looking after the engine which ran the machines of the repair shop for the pit. But he displeased the bosses by canvassing for a Labour candidate and was sent back to his old job, which he shortly left.

John, then thirty-six, went as a collier to Methley Junction Pit. But this meant cycling four miles, walking two more to the coal face, six miles in all before starting the day's shift. It was too much. After three days back at home his old boss offered him work at Beeston Pit where he was employed at different jobs on the surface for thirty years until the pit closed down, after which he alternated between the dole and good jobs for a few years until his retirement.

At the present day mining presents a totally different picture from the above accounts. Such is modernization within the last forty years that the miner is now a trained skilled operative using expensive and sophisticated machinery. There are no longer either colliers or trammers, and miners are not readily recognized on their way to and from work. New mining villages have replaced old stable communities. Many men have drifted or been sent to Yorkshire from other fields where pits have closed. This is now a cosmopolitan mining area.

8 Steam and Speed

THE two converging strands of opportunity and tradition meet in the development of the numerous industries other than textiles. Opportunity for work for the many and for advancement for the gifted few attracted people to cities and towns, where stimulated by the proximity of coal, the age of steam advanced. At Leeds the basis of work changed from the manufacture of cloth to engineering which drew to it a large work force of men and the clothing industry which employed a large work force of women.

Tradition is epitomized by the Kirkstall Forge, which follows the bloomeries worked on the site from about 1600. Its recent history concerns the Butler family, who at first with the Beecrofts, rented a forge and a farm near by in 1779, and manufactured goods—shovels, spades, hammers, axes and domestic ironmongery such as patten rings—and by the middle of the next century following on the invention and installation of new forging hammers made cranes, bridges, steam boilers, railway waggon wheels and axles, of which axles for motor transport became in time a prime product.

Kirkstall Forge, like Armley Mills both on the river Aire, retains industrial relics on interesting and historic sites. Two helve hammers and a collection of trade pieces are preserved (*see plate* 75). The latter were made by applicants for work, who, given iron, were asked to make an article as proof of their proficiency. In 1974 a descendant of one family who started at the forge in the 1770s still worked there.[1]

Within a few miles of Bradford other ironworks of importance to West Riding development were started at Birkenshaw in 1762, Bowling in 1788, Low Moor in 1789, Shelf in 1794 and Bierley in 1810, all of which eventually ceased. Low Moor Iron Works mined their own ironstone and coal, for which they had at one time seventy pits, and about 1870 employed 3,700 men. They built stationary steam

---

[1] R. A. Mott, 'Kirkstall Forge and Monkish Iron-making', Misc. vol. 15, Thoresby Society, vol. LIII, p. 154, 1973; R. Butler, *The History of Kirkstall Forge*, 1954; *The History of Kirkstall Forge through seven centuries 1200–1954*, reprinted 1954. Also information from Mr J. Northrop.

engines, made plates and forgings for iron ships, armaments, supplied parts for Brunel's steamship *The Great Eastern*, suffered a serious explosion in 1914, and closed down in 1928.

On the opposite side of Leeds from Kirkstall, Hunslet Road and Jack Lane became the seat of many of the great engineering plants in West Yorkshire, plants that burgeoned into full stature in the last century, and like the iron foundries many faded away in this. Just as Matthew Murray (1765–1826) gravitated to Leeds from the North-East because of the opportunities presented there, so talented men joined him at the Round Foundry in Holbeck, and leaving, founded other works in adjoining Hunslet, such as the Airedale Foundry, which under the Kitsons became the largest of the locomotive works there.

John Fowler, who was born in Wiltshire, by his inventive genius laid the foundation of the vast works next to the Airedale Foundry in Hunslet Road. Here were made draining and ploughing equipment, steam traction engines, road rollers, locomotives, pit-head gear and winding machines, electric generators, and tanks in time of war. In its heyday 2,000 men were employed. The works in Leeds closed down in 1973. They may be said in a sense to have been supplanted in Yorkshire in so far as agricultural machinery is concerned by David Browns, a firm making gears in 1860, now employing some 4,000 people at Meltham, near Huddersfield and elsewhere, to build farm tractors exported all over the world.

Three firms in Jack Lane, Hunslet, that have gone are J. and H. McLaren, builders of steam waggons, Manning Wardle at the Boyne Engine Works, and Hudswell Clarke at the Railway Foundry. Three still in being, only the last in Jack Lane, but all connected with steam are Thomas Green whose chairman in the 1930s, Robert Blackburn, founded the Blackburn Aeroplane company, and Greenwood and Batley who made the first bandsaw for John Barran, the founder of the first of the wholesale clothing firms in Leeds, and the Hunslet Engine Company which has acquired much of the land of the Airedale, the Boyne and the Railway Foundries.[1]

The Hunslet Engine Company, started in 1864 by J. T. Leather with seven men, was the last of the great locomotive engineering firms to be founded in Leeds, and managed by three generations of Campbells and three of Alcocks, it is the one

[1] For further reading see: *Matthew Murray*, ed. E. Kilburn Scott, 1928; E. Kitson Clark, *Kitsons of Leeds 1837–1937*, 1938; R. N. Redman, *The Railway Foundry, Leeds, 1839–1969*, 1972; L. T. C. Rolt, *A Hunslet Hundred*, 1964; D. R. Bomford, 'John Fowler Memorial Lecture', Institution of British Agricultural Engineers, 1956; *Steaming*, Journal of the National Traction Engine Club, vol. 9, No. I; Alf Pepper, *Retrospect of over Fifty Years with John Fowler and Co. (Leeds) Ltd*, 1946. Records of John Fowler and Company are at the Museum of English Rural Life, University of Reading.

74. *The pit head at Walterclough Colliery, near Brighouse, worked by Joseph Brooke and Sons. The colliery was 100 yards deep, and fireclay and some coal were mined. The clay was ground and sieved to make bricks (1906).*

75. *One of the two helve hammers at the Kirkstall Forge, Leeds. The complex was built in 1686, but the water-wheel shown dates from 1740. With each revolution of the wheel, the hammer struck four blows. It ceased to be worked about 1919.*

COAL AND CLAY

76. *The Mortons (the potters) and others getting outcrop coal at Jagger Green, near Elland, during the 1921 coal strike. The seam was 2 feet thick below 2 feet of clay. Robert Morton on the left and Walker Morton, second from right, were throwers in the pottery. Albert Morton on the right was in charge (1921).*

77. *Mr L. Boothman making a Bradford Windguard chimney-pot at the works of W. T. Knowles, Elland.*

ENGINEERS

78. John Fowler operating his improved 4-furrow balance plough and using a Kitson and Hewitson chaindriven engine (1861).

79. Dom Carlos I built for the Benguela Railway, Angola, Portuguese West Africa, and staff at the Hunslet Engine Works, Leeds. It was built, tested, dismantled and packed for shipment in twenty-one days—thought to be a record in engine building (1905).

survivor. It owes its success to Mr Edgar Alcock, who came as works manager in 1912, and had the foresight to plan the change from steam to diesel. In 1927 his son, Mr John F. Alcock, then entering the works, was granted £5,000 to build a diesel locomotive, and assembling together a small team, he succeeded. He also began the practice of making a world tour twice a year, not only to obtain orders at once but to prepare the ground for many placed years later.

In those days up to the Second World War the head offices of the railways of the world were in London, with India as the chief customer and Germany the chief rival. As with textile machinery and mills, when engines were ordered, men went out with them, whilst others, often rising to be general managers, ran the railways themselves. For a variety of reasons, of which one is the early age of marriage, families nowadays have little wish to live abroad for a long period. Men also rose up from the shop floor as did Mr Edgar Alcock himself. Success is exemplified for example in the career of Mr W. Morrell. He started at the works at the age of fourteen in 1914, and by learning every job and attending trade school at the mechanics' institute at night, as was not unusual, he became at the age of twenty-three senior draughtsman with special responsibility for gear design—progress that would not be easy today when university trained men expect to enter at a high level. The company, which has for long encouraged apprentices, now takes in about twenty-five a year, including one or two girls.

In the drawing office when a steam locomotive was being designed a team of draughtsmen under a general supervisor took charge of the different sections—the boiler, the motion, the frame. Engines, modified for different gauges of rails, heights of tunnels and power required, were mostly individual in design, and built to exact specifications down to the paintwork, which for example might have 'to stand and look well in a hot climate after a long voyage'. When eventually one was finished, a particular whistle was blown and all available men, perhaps 200 of them, with long ropes hauled it into the yard for testing. The whole work force, having contributed to it, gained satisfaction from its completion.

In the 1920s when the first diesel was being built, hand work with simple tools was the rule. Then there were a dozen men capable of filing up a big diameter as perfectly as if it had been ground, and in the smithy others bent angle-irons, now almost a lost art. Today's skills are machine ones, and as old craftsmen retire, old skills, no longer required, are forgotten—a development echoed in many spheres.

Also in Hunslet three different firms illustrate success by supplying needs and they also demonstrate the interlinked nature of progress. Procter Brothers, wire-works, is the oldest firm in Leeds founded in Jack Lane in 1740. Noted for making the Little Nipper Mouse Trap, invented by a Herbert Atkinson, but now only a small part of their business, they manufacture for example wire-guards for all types of machinery. The second, Fawcetts, founded by two brothers Thomas Constantine and John Dawson Fawcett, came from Hull and invented brick-making machinery, now made in a factory in Hunslet Road and exported all over the world.

The third, T. F. and J. H. Braime, was also founded by two brothers, Thomas Fletcher Braime (1864–1955) and James Henry Braime (1868–1930), both gifted with remarkable inventive talents, whose success sprang from the invention of the oil-can. T. F. Braime, who had been apprenticed to J. and H. McLaren, never forgot the terrifying journey lasting half an hour driving a steam traction engine across a wooden trestle bridge high above the Rhône.

In the 1880s they began production of the oil-can, again in Hunslet Road, in a two-storied building rented at 7s. 6d. a week with the ground floor let off to a tanner for 5s. Eventually short of capital they advertised in the *Yorkshire Post* for a loan. It was answered by a clergyman who offered them his life savings, £500 (later repaid many times over). Thomas Fletcher then designed and built large power presses whilst James Henry invented dies and processes for the manufacture of large metal pressings. In the First World War when their inventive talents were turned to munitions they employed 1,250 men and women. The firm, run by their descendants, still makes and exports oil-cans, but its main products are deep-drawn pressings for many different industries, manufactured in workshops on the same site as the original building but now occupying six acres.

Again the adaptation of the bandsaw, to cut several layers of cloth at once, by Greenwood and Batley points to the same co-operation of different firms. The invention of the sewing machine in America and the use of the bandsaw set off the clothing concerns in Leeds, of which Hepworths, Montagu Burtons and Prices are examples and of which Prices represents their phenomenal growth.

Henry Price, the son of a Methodist minister, left school when he was twelve, and started work in a readymade clothing shop at 2s. 6d. a week. At nineteen he became manager of the Grand Clothing Hall in Keighley, whilst his wife sold men's collars, ties and socks displayed in the window of their cottage. In 1907 he opened a tailor's shop in Silsden near Keighley. The shop prospered, another was opened in Keighley and a third in Leeds, where an old building was taken as a clothing factory, During the Christmas week a heavy snowstorm caused the roof to cave in, a disaster that almost finished the whole project.

By 1930 Prices had opened thirty-five branches and the name Fifty-Shilling Tailors was well known. Under a property controller with a team of twenty-six architects, entirely engaged in designing shop fronts, new shops were opened at the rate of two or three a week on sites chosen in the best possible positions, on the best sides of the main shopping streets. Cloth had to be bought from large firms such as John Crowthers and Mallinsons in the Colne valley and Bairstows at Silsden, and Henry Price bargained down to one eighth of a penny a yard. Sir Henry, as he became, never removed his account from the Keighley branch of the Midland Bank, although his takings of tens of pounds a week rose to thousands. When in the 1950s the business was taken over by John Collier, it had 285 shops.

The experiences of John Verity (1890–1975), born in Leeds in a street behind the Infirmary, illustrate aspects of the clothing industry formerly peculiar to it. His father was the wine steward at the Queen's Hotel, and his mother, the youngest of a family of thirteen, had worked as a child of eight or nine as a half-timer in the 'line garret' at Marshall's flax-spinning mills. When his father died following an accident, John Verity had to leave the grammar school to which he had won a scholarship, and after one or two other jobs he went in 1911 to David Littles, bespoke tailors of men's and boys' clothes, then employing some 350 to 400 people, and eventually becoming an order clerk in the Special Measure Department, he stayed there until retirement in 1952.

In his early days working hours lasted from 8 a.m. to 6.30 p.m. with an hour off for lunch eaten in the basement where there was a slow oven, a geyser for brewing tea and a trestle table. Trade fluctuated throughout the year, largely because men's suits were most in demand at Easter and boys' at Whitsuntide, so that from Christmas to Whitsuntide everyone worked late until 9.30 p.m. three nights a week. (This was allowed for up to thirty nights a year.) John himself in busy times often worked until midnight and sometimes until 4 a.m., but he had ten days' holiday with pay.

In the first decade of the century girls, almost always engaged on piecework, earned about 30s. a week, and during the summer after the spring rush had little to do. In the same period youngsters straight from school at thirteen began by soaping seams at 3s. a week of forty-five to forty-seven hours, and with overtime at 1d. a night could earn 3s. 5d. Because cloths were heavier than nowadays seams were then soaped and soaked, before opening out and ironing so that they lay flat. (In 1975 learners earned about £15 a week.)

Patterns of cloth changed very little, for example schoolboys' suits were made of grey herringbone, and men's suits of good quality blue serge, some of the best manufactured by W. E. Yates of Bramley. Serge, dyed khaki, was made up into army uniform during the First World War. Sometimes work was sent out to small firms, often Jewish, in North Street, Leeds, where perhaps a few relatives and neighbours worked in a bedroom, or an attic or a hayloft, using treadle machines, and with the women hand-buttonholing, finishing off and buttoning. Buttonholing machines, constantly being improved, were in fact introduced at Littles between the wars.

It was usual in those days for an order which reached them on Wednesday at noon to be completed and sent away on Friday. Once, about 1913, a tailor at Bentham, some fifty miles from Leeds, missed the post with a funeral order, so he sent it in a cardboard box by the milk train the following morning. The lid with the label blew off, and it was by chance that the order reached Littles at 9.20 a.m. With different sections sewn by different girls, the suit was finished and put on the Morecambe train to reach Bentham in time for the tailor to deliver it that afternoon.

Caps, those important items of men's and schoolboys' wear, make a postscript to the clothing industry. When suits cost 50s., caps sold at 1s. or 1s. 6d., and Henry Price refused to sell them saying that it took as long to sell a cap as a much more expensive suit. The demand for caps has been lessened by miners wearing safety helmets and by the general trend of wearing no headgear at all.

None the less four firms of cap-makers in Leeds and about twenty all over the country flourish. The firm of J. W. Myers was founded by the present owner's grandfather in Leeds in 1889. At that early date they made for example 'Polos', a roundcap resembling a bus conductor's out of corduroy or Donegal tweed, and a Tam o'Shanter with gold braid, worn by children with their sailor suits and sold to merchants who supplied shops such as Harrods and Swan and Edgar. When Mr J. W. Myers joined the firm in the period before the First World War, the heyday of the trade, if they sold less than 1,000 dozen caps a week, retailed at 1s. 6d each, it was considered disappointing. Caps, small in Edwardian times, increased in size and were made of eight pieces, then changed in style to a one-piece flat top or were varied with stitched fronts. In 1974 mock fur caps and 'Poms' in brightly coloured cloths, worn by golfers and others, were high fashion. Many caps go to Scotland, and instead of 2s. 6d. sell for £2 to £3, even £4, still small sums for the work and the material involved.

Lastly, a firm founded on a chance meeting of two men in a foreign country, the British Belting and Asbestos Company, whose headquarters is at Cleckheaton in the Spen valley. In 1878 William Fenton, a Scotsman, born in Perthshire, was working as a foreman in a cotton mill in Sweden, and W. W. Cobbett, a Londoner, was travelling there on business. The two men met and made friends. Fenton invented a solid-weave cotton belt, showed it to his friend, and encouraged by him returned to Scotland to manufacture it there. Cobbett undertook the marketing under the trade name of Scandinavia Belting. In 1901 the works, then at Lanark, were transferred to Cleckheaton, where 3,000 are now employed. With other modern factories in other parts of Yorkshire and England BBA make brake linings, clutch facings, general asbestos and glass fibre products, conveyor belting, and much else. At Cleckheaton, besides playing fields for various sports, a sea of cars belonging to the staff surrounds the factory.

So, too, at the Hunslet Engine Works the car park has had to be enlarged many times. No longer is there 'a tide of cloth caps' in Jack Lane as the many works loosed, nor, close up to them, built at all angles on every available plot of land, the rows of back-to-back houses to which the men were returning. Houses and many large works, such as Fowlers, have been razed to the ground, replaced by new roads, new factories and new housing estates.

9 Houses

IN contrast with a rural district the long application to industry has defined the shape of settlement in West Yorkshire. The very few mansions of the gentry, such as Temple Newsam, the sixteenth- and seventeenth-century halls of the yeomen-clothiers round Halifax, the houses of merchants, and clusters of old cottages, have been inundated by waves of building in the last century—the factories, the Victorian houses of all sizes, mostly in terraces forming ranks of streets and squeezed into a small compass for the unrestrained tide of people surging into towns and villages in search of work. To picture the country for instance between Leeds and Wakefield as 'very beautiful' as Arthur Young described it in about 1770 requires a feat of the imagination.

In the 1870s it was said of Leeds that on elevated ground north-west of the town 'wealthy merchants and tradesmen have thrown out a thick fringe of luxurious mansions and country seats'. As noise and smoke had increased, the exodus from centres had begun. In course of time houses in residential squares were abandoned for use as offices, and those in the old yards and courts became derelict. As new suburbs engulfed more and more countryside round the towns, a process continuing into the twentieth century, immigrants occupied the older districts and themselves moved on to be replaced by new groups.

A comfortable home is remembered by Mrs M. A. Hare (b. 1891) in Lambert's Yard, Lower Briggate, Leeds, where her father had a bill posting business. Near by were watch repairers, Bagshaw's the silver-platers, a woman feather curler re-curling ostrich feathers, Skelton's the saddlers in Queen's Court, Reynolds and Branson, pharmaceutical works and Goodall and Backhouse, makers of Yorkshire Relish, in Wormald's Yard, and premises elsewhere. In the early nineteenth century Mrs Robert Goodall, whose home-made sauce inspired the production of Yorkshire Relish shipped all over the world, lived in one of the Georgian houses in Park Place, now no longer residential, and her husband and Henry Backhouse then had a chemist's shop next to Trinity Church.

On the outskirts of most towns and villages the houses of the well-to-do, grouped in exclusive suburbs or secluded in their own grounds, range from the large semi-detached to the vast piles such as Cliffe Castle, Keighley (now a museum). Well built of stone, the larger ones have stables, conservatories, sometimes orchid houses; and were formerly guarded by a yard dog, often an Airedale. Inside are large lofty rooms, one for billiards or music, handsome staircases and elaborate mahogany woodwork enclosing fireplaces or framing oil paintings of Highland cattle. They have backstairs from the kitchens to servants' bedrooms in the attics, splendid cellars sometimes white-tiled throughout, and formerly wooden-slatted Venetian blinds (a penance to clean) for the windows, and furniture made by local cabinet-makers.

Life in these well-ordered homes followed a routine prescribed by the arrival of husbands returning home from work and by the employment of servants, varying in number, and for large houses, gardeners and coachmen.

Dr Phyllis Bentley, Halifax, believes that this orderly framework made life much easier and less uncertain than present-day easy-going habits, and that 'It is inaccurate to think of the bourgeoisie as lazy. Everybody worked very hard indeed. All the laundry and baking were done at home. My mother and a tailoress made all our clothes even the boys' sailor suits. For a middle-class girl it was not quite the thing to work for a living. I strongly disagreed.' Mrs H. Mitchell, too, whose father was the first Lord Mayor of Bradford and who herself was a sitting magistrate for thirty years, says, 'It was argued that you would be taking a job from somebody else who needed it more than you. We enjoyed a pleasant social life of balls and concerts [attended at St George's Hall in full evening dress]—very snobby. I had plenty of charitable work to do.'

In 1916 Miss C. E. Hepworth of Morley, one of three daughters, took the unusual step, barely tolerated by her mother, of entering her father's mill eventually to become cashier. 'My father had three interests—mill, chapel, and town hall.' When he retired she continued with the firm that bought the business, but no concessions were made at home to a new time-table, and her health broke down. It was not until 1948 after her father had died, aged ninety, that she was able to take up public work in earnest, and to become a magistrate, chairman of committees, and the first woman mayor of Morley. This convention of no work for the girls of better-off families often resulted in much the same frustrations and lack of fulfilment suffered by girls from poor families short of money for further education.

In these circles At Home days, set days once a fortnight or month, when mothers and daughters, at home to friends, provided afternoon tea, were customary. Ladies on arrival placed one of their own printed cards and two of their husband's on a silver salver on the hall table. 'My mother hated At Homes,' said Mrs Mitchell. 'Lady Tree who was acting in Bradford once came bringing a huge dog, which ate all the food off one of those three-tiered cake stands. I knew nothing about cooking. I couldn't even boil an egg. You weren't very welcome in the kitchen. If we entertained we had dinner at night, but usually we had high tea.'

High teas for special occasions, with salmon, chicken or Dover sole as the main courses, are remembered as delicious even sumptuous repasts. Holiday venues ranged from the Yorkshire dales, Scarborough, the Lake District, Blackpool, the Isle of Man, to Anglesey and the South of France, and were spent in rooms or for the rich at what we should now call second homes.

None the less thrift guided household management, and the rhyme beginning 'Waste not. Want not' was an oft-repeated warning to children. Nor did apparent means ensure immunity from disaster either personal or financial (*see Chapter* 2). From these Victorian houses some remember riding to work on horseback and throwing halfpennies to children turning cartwheels along the pavements in Hunslet Road. When many of these same people, the leaders and the better educated, moved still farther out into the country or sometimes migrated to southern England, the cities and towns were the poorer.

Besides these, and by far the largest group, were the vast array of houses of more modest size, often in terraces, occupied by people of a wide range of income, at the top end of the scale merging with the previous group. Possibly nowhere in England were there more of the middle-middle classes, because of the proliferation of independent units of work, than in the West Riding. At the bottom end of the scale came the slums in cities, towns and villages crammed with houses, at their best made the most of, and at their worst an affront to human dignity. Incredible as it seems now, they were disregarded by almost all except those who for one reason or another had occasion to visit them.

Before and during the period under review a series of housing, health and improvement Acts had brought some order into the chaos caused by too rapid an influx of people, and had ameliorated the indescribably insanitary conditions that had bred cholera outbreaks and prolonged epidemics of typhus and diarrhoea. No longer could parts of Leeds, Bradford and Halifax be described as 'a slimy bog' filled with 'sickening smells', nor everywhere even in villages were there so many back-to-back houses, tenements in yards, crowded lodging-houses, and the terrible cellar dwellings, the latter often occupied by old people for 1s. 3d. a week. Before the slum clearance campaigns of the 1930s there were 74,805 back-to-backs in Leeds and in 1955 30,000 in Bradford.[1]

[1] P. E. Razzell and R. W. Wainwright, *The Victorian Working Class. Selections from the 'Morning Chronicle', 1849*, 1973; J. Mayhall, *Annals of Yorkshire*, vol. III, see 10 February 1866; J. N. Radcliffe, *The Sanitary State of Leeds, c.* 1870; A. Ravetz, *Model Estate, Planned at Quarry Hill, Leeds*, 1974.

Model village: Saltaire, built by Sir Titus Salt between 1854 and 1872. There were then 45 almshouses and 850 houses, of which those facing Albert Road were larger than the others. The streets were named after his wife and children and Lockwood and Mawson, the architects. The mill is at the top on the right. Each house had a parlour, kitchen and three bedrooms.

Former slums at Camp Field, Leeds, close to the city centre, demolished about 1900. They originally consisted of four unbroken rows of back-to-back houses. Between the rows the spaces had been filled in with other back-to-backs, trough closets and ashpits.

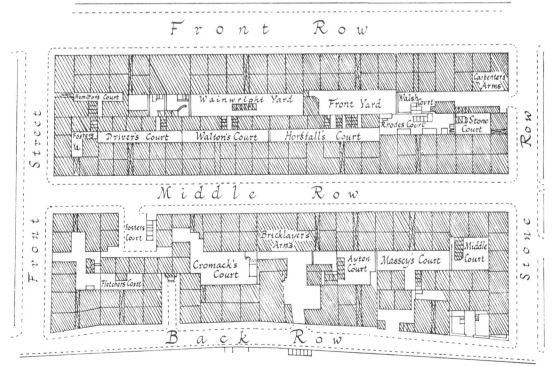

At Midgley, a village in Calderdale, 'When first we were married we lived in a one up and a one down in a cellar. I put up his jock in a red handkerchief on the sideboard overnight, and next morning rats had eaten t'jock and t' handkerchief.' [1] Remembered as particularly vile were Middle Row, Back Row and Front Row in Camp Field, Leeds, within a few minutes' walk of City Square, a ghetto of fifty-nine houses demolished after the 1890 Housing Act. 'People wouldn't go near them.' In 1904 complaints were made of the awful smell down Heaton Road, Bradford, where the fever van was often seen, and at Churwell, near Leeds, in the 1930s local councillors visiting houses in order to condemn them were sprayed with disinfectant.

Old houses everywhere, not only in city slums, were infested with bugs, and in consequence smelt like rotten apples. People stuck tarred paper on to walls to prevent them from penetrating from house to house. They stood bed legs in round glass cups filled with paraffin, speared them with pins at Gildersome, sizzled them on walls with a lighted candle at Holbeck. It was a heart-breaking experience for a newly married couple moving into a clean house to find bugs crawling in from adjoining ones. On the other hand in 1962 one old man who had moved from a slum area of Bradford into a new house, dogged by ill luck, returned to the old house before it was demolished, and collected some bugs in a matchbox which he kept in his pocket as a charm. They were the luck of the house. [2] Undertakers and upholsterers of necessity took precautions against fleas. The introduction of DDT was a godsend.

From 1907 a few Octavia Hill-trained lady social workers and housing managers were employed in Leeds. Mrs A. Maitland, formerly Brenda Hall of Leeds, remembers, 'In the 1930s old Quarry Hill was as verminous as anything I saw in London. The best way to look for bugs was to peel off the wallpaper by the fire-place. Layers and layers of paper on one wall I remember went back to a news-paper dated 1832. They were terrible houses, one room up, one down, back-to-back, long streets of them, and every so often two knocked down and a row of filthy lavatories in their place.'

'I would be given a block of forty to 100 houses and told that they were due for demolition in say six months. I collected the rents myself each week (3s. 6d. to 7s. or 7s. 6d. with debts of £4, £5, £6) as a means of getting to know the people, their families, places of work, and where they wished to be re-housed, and then gradu-ally moved them into new houses which were handed over in batches every week

[1] Tape recording, 15th January 1956, Institute of Dialect and Folk Studies, University of Leeds.
[2] Anecdote from D. McKelvie, 'Some Aspects of Oral, Social and Material Tradition in an Industrial Urban Area', University of Leeds, PhD. thesis, 1963.

80. Raising the bell 'Big Matthew William' (named after the then mayor of Bradford, Matthew William Thompson) for the town hall clock at Bradford. The bell, weighing 4½ tons, is the hour bell of a peal of thirteen bells forming the carillon (1873).

81. North Bridge, Halifax, soon after midday. The book-seller and printers on the left was also a Post Office. Across the road on the right was the Grand Theatre (1903).

*82. Main Street, Haworth.
Groups of men and children
probably waiting for the
procession on the occasion of
the Co-operative Society
Gala held in June (c. 1903).*

83. *Women at the well, Heptonstall. In common with other places all water had to be fetched from wells (1890s).*

84. *Bell Street, Leeds (c. 1901).*

*85. The interior of a typical working-class home of the early 1900s.
The house in Hanover Street, Boothroyd Lane, Dewsbury, was back-to-back,
one up and one down, and with an attic. Mrs Annie Eleanor Pickles sits
crocheting and was photographed by her husband, a miner.*

86. *The interior of a middle-class home. The drawing-room of High-cliffe,
Eccleshill, a house built by Christopher Pratt, the founder of the firm of
cabinet-makers and house furnishers of Bradford in the 1860s. The house had
sliding doors opening up two rooms, a form of central heating and a bath with
water laid on, features unusual in those days (1890s).*

by the builders. The council did the move, collecting all furniture, clothes, belongings in the morning and delivering everything fumigated to the new home later in the same day. Coals in the bath were common. But almost all without exception wanted to get out of the slums.'

'Many were old. One woman shouting and swearing used to terrify me. Another, an old evil-looking woman with a deeply lined face, had living with her a slightly mental granddaughter, who was always having illegitimate children. They mostly disappeared, but the police were never able to trace where they had gone. An old couple, both nearly stone-deaf, possessed two old and mangy dogs and a parrot, not allowed in the new houses, and did not want to leave. I persuaded them to have the dogs put down and the housing manager to let them take the parrot. That parrot was the saving of them. Neighbours and children came to see it, so that they were never lonely.'

Thousands of terrace houses had been built before the 1840s and many in the 1890s. They are remembered costing £30, £40, £60 and £100 each, put up by speculative builders or mill-owners or by private individuals who built a row and lived in one. In a few cases five or six people joined together, and built a short row calling them Club Houses, to be seen for instance at Illingworth, near Halifax, and at Old Town above Hebden Bridge.

The demand for houses was such that it was commonplace to buy a key for £1 from the landlord (and for that matter to pay £50 for one for a council house). Most had a cellar, a living-room about 12 feet by 14 feet, with in one corner a staircase leading to a small and a larger bedroom, and outside a shared privy. 'If you had a scullery house you were posh.' A cupboard recess on the window side of the fireplace held a tap and a sink and shelves for crockery. Many houses have attics. In Blackman Lane, Leeds, the back-to-backs have individual toilets in small back yards. But this was once a district for the better-off, who sometimes built a stable and coach-house in the garden.

From 1865 scavenging was carried out in parts of Leeds by the corporation, and tons of filth were taken to a depot by the river to be transported by boat or by railway trucks from luggage stations to farming districts. Night soil and midden men with horses and carts mostly worked during the night. An Act of Parliament in 1907 led to outside privies being converted to water-closets, but still families shared. 'You had a door with a key; there were eight of us and six next door, so— fourteen to a toilet. In winter the water froze.' At Hebden Bridge some tipplers still operate, a method whereby sink water is collected in a pan which when full tips over and flushes.

'They were all poor people living together in poor conditions, but they were happy. Old Hunslet had a spirit like the war; the conditions drew people together.'[1] 'As a child I lived in Domestic Street, Holbeck. Someone who came to live there brought a gramophone, and on a summer's night (and we used to have summers then) they opened their windows and people sat on the steps listening. Mother got a gramophone for us when we started work.'[2] 'I lived as a boy about 1922 in Hargreaves Square, Shipley. There were 171 back-to-back houses built by Hargreaves, a worsted spinner, and folk who lived there were known as Square-ites. Children ran about without boots and with their breeches' backsides hanging out. It was rugged—with women often fighting and shouting and a lot of drink. Yet I look back on it with happiness.'[3] 'At Hunslet the tingalary came on a Friday night after everyone had cleaned up. We flocked out and danced to the jazzy tunes. Local fellows borrowed them from Italians, Tomasso's, off the York Road. They paid so much and kept what they made over' (see plate 95).[4]

'When I was a boy we lived on Health Street down Commercial Road, Halifax, and the houses were back-to-back—one room up one down. My mother had to do everything in the one room, cooking, baking, washing, drying the clothes. We had our meals in that room, washed in it, lived in it and on Friday nights we had the old zinc bath up from the cellar to bath in it. [Some houses had set pots in which the water was heated.] In the house we had a good coal fire which was banked up at night with coal slack so that when we came down in the morning one jab with the poker and fire would be burning up. On one side was a small boiler and on the other a small oven, and the rule was that if you took any water out of the boiler you put some more in. My mother used to make all the bread we ate. On baking day the room had the smell of the bread—small flat cakes, large flat cakes, small loaves all laid out were a welcome sight when you arrived home from school on a winter's day.'[5] 'Everyone in Drighlington had huge roaring fires and kept the door open. My grandfather used to say "Oppen t' door. Oppen t' door". Coal was cheap. There were no indoors then. The neighbours all knew each other.'[6] 'We thought people were very poor if they didn't have a fire.'[7]

As the main bread-winners, fathers demanded full respect. A story, prevalent in more than one quarter, tells how when a son reached the age of twenty-one he came home and said, 'Now then we've got another prop in t'house'. But the father stood up and felled him saying, 'There's only one prop i' this house', or 'Thou sees t' house is still standing'. Whenever possible heads of households were

[1] Mr T. Sinclair, Hunslet.   [2] Mrs E. Hardisty, Leeds.
[3] Mr D. Larvin, Shipley.   [4] Mr T. Sinclair, Hunslet.
[5] Mr W. Gaunt, Sowerby Bridge.   [6] Mrs M. A. Collins, Drighlington.
[7] Mrs I. Humphreys, Gomersal.

indulged their favourite foods. 'My father used to go into the market every Friday after work, and bring home a bass full of fish and conger eel. He liked conger eel, and steaked it and picked out a few pieces for his tea next day.'[1]

The death of a man or his having an accident or absconding for one reason or another or his addiction to drink caused ripples of suffering which were of course not the prerogative of the poor. School careers and further training were time and time again the main casualties, and the youthful disappointments of the elderly have often been sublimated today in children's and grandchildren's success in their careers. Sometimes the overwhelming disaster of both parents dying left children homeless. Sixty years ago when this happened in a street in Morley, the neighbours each took one of the five orphans and brought them up as their own, so that they all stayed in the same street. 'It wouldn't happen now.'[2]

Mothers besides cleaning, washing and baking managed the money and mostly kept discipline. They were the recipients of wages, the dispensers of pocket money (1*d*. or ½*d*. a week), and 'smacked and leathered us'. 'Mrs Wilkinson, of Armley, had three sons, a daughter and her husband all working. They came in and put their wages on the table. She had a jar and they had to put 2*s*. 6*d*. in for saving. She was very strict and wouldn't let her sons marry until they were about thirty.' On the other hand some managed less well. One woman with three or four grown-up sons all working went every Monday morning with a bundle of clothes to pawn and redeemed them every Friday.

'All women, your mothers and grandmothers, looked old. I can't remember many without shawls fifty years ago. We respected age and feared the law. If a lady come on a tram we were made to get up, and if a bobby come, we run. We did the same as these lads do, pulled trees down, pinched apples, and *chumped* for bonfires but we were frightened of the law. I won a scholarship when I was ten, but was not allowed to go to High School, because mi mother couldn't afford it. You'd to provide a uniform, which was only a blazer and a cap and 7*s*. 6*d*. for your books. She wanted me to work when I was fourteen. So when you left school, you'd no chance to get in anywhere. I was always a good figure man and school came easy. Father was a checker in the railway goods yard and liked a drink.'

'Usually the married women didn't work except by taking in washing. When I was about ten my mother started earning a little bit of money, and we moved to a bigger house. Mi mother was terrible for moving—always Armley way. She used to sing in clubs and pubs, and earned 10*s*. to 15*s*. a night. She took the *News of the World* because it printed popular songs, and she went to Woolworths for a 6*d*.

[1] Mrs E. Nolan, Leeds.
[2] Miss C. E. Hepworth Morley.

record, pasted the words on brown paper and learnt them. There was a residential pianist and the customers joined in the choruses. [At the bottom of Call Lane, Leeds, was a pub called the George, kept by Mrs Simpson, where all the good vocalists of Leeds used to practise.]

'My mother always lit the oven on a Sunday night. I used to go for a pennyworth of gunpowder. Dad put this in its little paper bag, with the *News of the World* packed round it, and stuffed it right well under the oven. We all got behind the couch while he lit it. A terrific bang went off. Then mother lit the fire, and the heat was drawn under the oven.

'Even if you were poor nobody liked "Boots for the Bairns" because there were two big holes in the top and people knew where they were from. Free school meals were the same. Nobody wanted to go. Up to the age of eleven or twelve you never had a toothbrush, only a bit of rag used sometimes with soap or Sutton's Salt. Everybody was wearing cast-offs. The only time you were decent were once a year when everybody, choose how, however poor they were always had something new for Whit Sunday. If you'd nowt new, you stopped in. My father had a free pass on the railway, and we used to go for a day to Cleethorpes.

'As you got older, you had walks like up to the park looking for girls, and when you got one you walked them round. Before proposing you always asked your father, and you bought a cheap ring for 13*s*. or so. You'd to do your courting outside. Your mother couldn't afford to feed anyone extra for tea, and it was always could she manage the tea for a wedding. There were no houses and if there were, you couldn't afford the rent. Times were hard, but you were happy. There was always some fun.

'In Grannie's days they couldn't afford insurance, but I've two policies now mi mother took out when I was born for funeral expenses. I still pay it. Mi mother lived to be eighty and still sang to the last. She left sixty quid and a note which said, "This is to put me away nice."' [1]

Deaths cast gloom over the whole street. All blinds and curtains were drawn and children had to whisper until the funeral was over. Paying for this was not easy. Even in the early 1960s when a mentally defective daughter, one of a family of thirteen, had died in hospital, the father, who had worked as long as he could, drew £15 from the Rechabites. But it didn't cover the ham tea, two cars and the undertaker's fees, which the mother had arranged, costing £35, and expecting help from social security she waited indoors for four months until her plight was discovered.

The housing of the corpse, too, posed a severe problem. 'I [Mrs C. Greaves,

[1] Mr H. Bradford, Armley.

Halifax] was ten years old in 1912 when my mother died. We had only two bedrooms and the body was laid out on the bed in the best bedroom in snow-white
sheets and a handkerchief put corner ways over the face. We had to pass through
every night to go to bed—five of us in one room for a week. Next day the visitors
began to arrive and I was sent up with them to "view the body", lifting the handkerchief for them to gaze on the face quite a while. This went on for five days. On
the funeral day relatives and friends wore deep mourning, but I being a child was
allowed a white dress with a broad black crêpe armband, black hat, shoes, and
gloves and coat. One hymn was sung: "Peace, perfect peace". We had a terrible
week.'

At the present day whole districts of cities and towns have been demolished,
and high-rise flats built. Two comments show the dichotomy of opinions. 'In 1974
I went back to look at the old streets. I got lost. They have all been pulled down
and not before time.' 'When t'old square went summot else went wi' it that all t'
posh tahn centres in t'world can't fetch back.'

10 Communities

IN the period under review local life was circumscribed. Cities were and are up to a point a series of villages, and towns a string of hamlets with their own identities. Towns with populations of 10,000 and even more are still referred to as villages. You were either a Top Ender or a Bottom Ender at Pudsey, and in the Pennine valleys, where in any case nicknames were essential to distinguish the ramifications of the indigenous families, you might be a Cragger in Cragg Vale or a Slowiter or a Marsdener in the Colne valley. Everyone knew everybody in their own little orbit, and others were outsiders. At the beginning of this century in remote places such as Heptonstall they threw sods at strangers shouting '*Scutch* up rotten pockets', a demand for pennies; and signalled their arrival by knocking from house to house on the backs of fireplaces.

Apart from work life revolved round chapel, church and home. Each community supported its own schools, clubs, newspapers, shops, hawkers and village idiots, and spoke slightly differing local dialect readily distinguished by a keen ear. In spite of the worldwide connections of its industries, life for most people was provincial.

Nor is the country usually far off. Many mourn the loss of the green woods and fields of their childhood, destroyed and covered by housing estates. 'We used to pick bluebells in Middleton Woods [near Leeds].' But blackberries may still be gathered for instance in Shibden Dale, nor are the freedom and enjoyment of the moors diminished. 'I've never heard larks sing like those on Haworth moors.' On fine summer days generations of people have walked up to the Ladstone, a millstone grit outcrop on Norland Moor above Sowerby Bridge. 'My grandfather used to take me to play on the moor. He always brought a tiny miniature mug, and put it on the springs which bubbled up like boiling water. They lifted it up. It was a delight to me.' [1]

Developing from the seventeenth-century Independents, Nonconformity had taken root in the Pennine valleys, and in the nineteenth century in the great

[1] Mrs S. E. Grayshan, Norland.

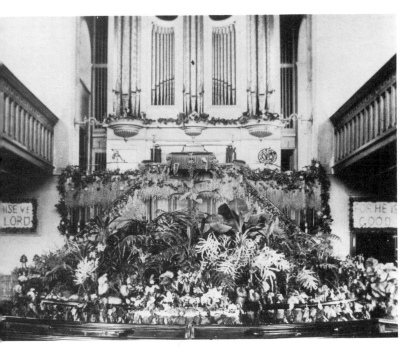

87. *West Lane (now Trinity) Methodist Church, Gomersal, decorated for the harvest festival, built by Edward Brooke in 1827. The hothouse plants are mostly from the conservatory at West House, the Brookes' family home (1890).*

88. *The Upper Independent Church, Heckmondwike (Congregational), built in 1890, architect Arthur A. Scott, Heckmondwike. It cost £10,976 8s. 11d., and followed other chapels built since the first in 1674.*

89. *All Souls Church, Haley Hill, Akroydon, Halifax, designed by Sir G. Gilbert Scott, built 1856–1859. The statue is of Sir Edward Akroyd.*

90. *Whit Monday walk at Heptonstall. The children carry flags, a custom later abandoned and replaced by men carrying a banner (1890s).*

91. *Sunday School Feast of Hinchliffe Mill Wesleyan chapel in the Holme valley, or a united sing with Hinchliffe Mill chapel, Holmbridge Church of England and Hall's School, Holmbridge, held about 1900.*

building era of the 1860s and 1870s a few churches and many chapels of all de-
nominations rose on every hand.[1] Huge edifices with lofty classical porticos in
cities and towns and small plain structures perched on Pennine heights were built
by the better-off who gave their thousands and the many who contributed their
mites in single-minded endeavour. Some individuals even built and ran their own
chapels and gospel halls. Remote situations such as that of Pole Moor chapel above
the Colne valley were sometimes dictated by the refusal of landowners to give or
sell land elsewhere. The names Brunswick, Eastbrook, Ebenezer, Square,
Providence, Zion, Mount Tabor, Upper Independent are as familiar to the elderly
in the West Riding as are the names of pop-stars to the young. Many, too, were
simply known by the name of the family connected with them, such as Henry
Brooke's chapel, Gomersal, or Pawson's at Morley, or the Primitive Methodist
Rigg's chapel at Rawdon. The latter was built in 1866 by Thomas Rigg, a butcher,
who collected money from the townspeople, and who when it was opened had his
ten children baptized there.

Except in cities where a majority did not attend places of worship, almost all
social life and popular culture centred round them. Nor was it uncommon for
attendance to be obligatory for employment. Men and women gave lifelong
service, and held simple beliefs. 'My father was organist at Norland for thirty-four
years morning and afternoon and only missed three times.' At Heptonstall Slack
Baptist church one old man prayed: 'We thank Thee, O Lord, that in heaven we
shall have crowns that need no fettling.' It is fashionable now to regard this great
religious climax as a panacea for then current social evils, yet it bred generations of
people of sterling worth and transparent honesty.

Famous preachers and ministers drew packed congregations, for example
Bertram Smith and Francis Wrigley, who in 1891, coming straight from college,
stayed until 1928 in a dual pastorate at Salem chapel (Congregational), Hunslet
Lane, Leeds, a chapel then deprived of its supporters by the exodus to the suburbs.
Amongst many innovations they started Men's Brotherhood meetings attended by
well over 1,000 men on Sunday afternoons, and At Homes for women whose
children were looked after whilst they enjoyed talk, music and a cup of tea. Here,
hymns sung in the streets on Sunday afternoons were accompanied by exhorta-
tions to 'Come to the chapel, dear brother and sister'.

Regular meetings filled every night and often afternoons: choir practice,
Christian Endeavour, Band of Hope, Bible Study, At Homes, sewing meetings for

[1] See for example, *Memorabilia in the History of Lydgate Chapel*, 1945; Upper Independent Church,
Heckmondwike, Historical Sketch, 1674–1924; *The Heptonstall Octagon*, 1764–1964; H. W.
Harwood, *History of Methodism in Midgley*, 1933.

bazaars, Girls' Friendly Societies, Young Men's Improvement classes. Less frequent events—anniversaries, socials and bazaars—involved special efforts. Bazaars were sometimes gargantuan affairs lasting three days, perhaps called the Egyptian, Sunrise or the Blue Bird, culminating in lavish teas and raising thousands of pounds. In many cases cricket, tennis, billiards and football clubs were church and chapel organizations, and provided venues at which young people often met their future husbands or wives.

Eagerly anticipated, especially by music-lovers, were the concerts and performances of oratorios in chapels and churches. 'After long hours at work we used to get washed and dressed and go to rehearsals, always arranged on moonlight nights.' Singers, instrumentalists, choir masters, organists, all were recruited locally. Famous soloists, also native—Mrs Sunderland, Walter Widdop, Norman Allin, Edna Thornton, for example—and an augmented choir performed *Judas Maccabeus*, *Elijah*, Haydn's *Creation*, and above all *Messiah*, often with readings interspersed between the choruses. 'I was a violinist in the King Cross Methodist Church orchestra for twenty years. At Christmas people came for miles and were sitting on the pulpit steps and up the staircases.'[1] Who can now conceive of the communal enjoyment, the pitch of excitement, the euphoria of these occasions, perhaps still experienced but more sedately at the Christmas performances of *Messiah* given in town halls by the great choirs.

Sunday schools, important on any count for their early role in education, filled a large part of Sundays. 'I went before I was ten. We started about 9.30 a.m. and had to say our collects, then we went to church. We had three marks for that, two for going in the afternoon and one for good conduct. Then I started teaching, taking a class alternate Sundays.'[2] 'At St Chad's, Hunslet, we used to go to Penny Romps in the autumn to raise funds for the Sunday school. We played singing games, "Bobby Bingo", "How Green the Grasses Grow", and "Mocking Bird" in which we sang loud and soft as a child searched for an object.'[3] 'We practised Whitsuntide hymns five or six weeks beforehand.'

Hymn practices heralded Whit Monday walks. 'Yes, Whit Monday, we looked for Whit Monday.' The first description of this annual event must surely be in the chapter entitled 'The School-Feast' in *Shirley*. These began early in the last century as treats to follow examinations then held in Sunday schools, and when they ceased after the foundation of Board schools, the walks continued as a reward for good

[1] Miss Pattie Smith, Halifax.
[2] Mrs I. Humphreys, Gomersal.
[3] Mrs A. Morrell, recalling Hunslet.

attendance and behaviour until superseded by coach trips.[1] In and near the Holme valley one or two walks still continue.

For the event printers prepared hymn sheets free of charge, dressmakers and tailors worked overtime making dresses and blue serge suits, farmers and coal merchants and others cleaned and decorated waggons and horses for the transport of children or pianos or harmoniums, and on the day Sunday school teachers assembled early to fill clothes baskets with long buns packed in paper bags. With local variations the programme followed the same patterm. A procession wound up and down and round streets and lanes, and stopped at pre-arranged points such as the town hall, big houses or those where someone was ill. At Gomersal 'My father was a Sunday school superintendent, so I always had to walk, trailing along feeling hot and uncomfortable.' Here, a small place but with several chapels, 'we never collided' as they did in *Shirley* with comical results.

The highlight was undoubtedly the tea, followed by sports and games. After the home-brewed ale era, tea or occasionally coffee 'laced with an egg dashed in at the last minute' or milk were provided together with buns, sometimes sandwiches, oranges and perhaps bags of nuts. In the Holme valley a bell was rung when it was time for the children to collect their buns, here called schoolcakes. At Hebden Bridge sweets were scutched, that is, thrown in the grass for children to scramble for. (In the 1860s scrambles for nuts were a customary treat at the ends of school terms.)

These rich tea-cake buns are well remembered all over and may still be bought here and there. A recipe used by the Dobsons, confectioners, of Elland for 'Whitsuntide Buns' made in 1884 gives: 24 lb. flour, 5 lb. butter, 5 lb. lard, 8 lb. sugar, 8 oz. salt, 20 eggs, 13 qts milk, 2 lb. yeast, 20 lb. currants, 5 lb. peel which made 180 10 oz. buns or 450 4 oz.

One Whit Monday at Drighlington Mrs M. A. Collins (b. 1878) remembers winning 3d. in a race at the sports, and on her way home she saw a pork pie in a shop window and bought it to give to her mother. But as she walked along, she thought, 'I'll try a bit, and then a bit and then a bit. My mother greeted me, "I reckon you've won t' race. What have you got?" I said, "3d. and I bought you a pie." "Where is it then?" I had to confess, but she only laughed.'

These Sunday school events burgeoned into the Jubilee Sings first held in the quadrangle of the Halifax Piece Hall on 14 September 1831, at the time of the

---

[1] Information from Mrs E. V. Chapman. Minute in 1818 from records of Birchcliffe Baptist Chapel, Hebden Bridge: 'On Whitmonday the children shall be examined in Reading the Scriptures, writing, and the Catechism, for a period not exceeding two hours, after which they shall be turned loose in Murgatroyd's field and given buns and milk with ale for the teachers.'

jubilee celebrations for Robert Raikes, the founder of Sunday schools. Tens of thousands of people flocked there to hear local choirs and bands led by well-known conductors rendering popular hymns, the 'Hallelujah Chorus' and other items. In all fourteen were held in the last century, that in May 1890 was attended by 29,897 people. A few other Sings followed up to the Second World War.

People speak with zest of childhood games and amusements. So little depended on money: pins, buttons, stones, bits of pot formed a ready currency if any were needed. Infrequent horse traffic menaced no one. 'The street was our playground', and the flagged pavements provided plenty of scope. Children *tilluped* (a hop then a stride) lightheartedly along them, or went 'hop a dock' with one foot on and one in the gutter. Chalk marks for hopscotch covered them, and children cried 'In a nick, out of the nick', as they sped along avoiding the cracks. On hot summer days globules of tar exuded between the stone setts of the roads, and when covered with fine dust and rolled into small balls they made temporary playthings.

In winter boys warmed their fingers on home-made hand-warmers, old cocoa tins with holes pierced with a nail at either end, filled at Hunslet with oily waste begged from railway engine drivers, or at Gomersal with cotton-band, round woven band used on spinning machines, which like the waste smouldered when lit. The cotton-band, called slow- or wheely-band, was wrapped in paper by youths to make foul tasting cigarettes, and a red-hot end of it was an essential accessory to November the Fifth celebrations for lighting fireworks.

At Shrovetide whips and tops, shuttlecocks and battledores, and marbles appeared everywhere. Peg and whip tops, called giant and monkey in Hunslet, could be whipped and bounced all over up and down the pavements. At Gomersal 'We drew circles with coloured chalks on them, so that when they spun round it was a lovely blur of colour'. For shuttlecock and battledore the girls at Heptonstall, for this was a girls' game, started with wooden *braids* (bats), advanced to drum braids made of vellum, and later 'if we got a racquet wi' string on, it were wonderful'.

Taws (marbles) take precedence over all street games, and although mostly for boys, they were played by girls. Different versions abound: 'Knicks', 'Chivvy up', 'Three Oily', 'Bobby Longy' and others, and the actual marbles included plain glass ones from pop bottles, *stogs* made at local potteries, the large *dobbies* and beautiful coloured glass *alleys*. Pockets which mothers emptied at night bulged with them, or toffee tins or special home-made bags held them. A hole cut in an earth floor or a suitably broken flag made pitches. Allied to taws checkstones, called checks or checkers, was a girls' game, played with four or five checks (pot cubes) and a large marble or small ball. This consisted of picking up the checks whilst the ball was thrown up or bounced and caught with the other hand. Jacks or Five Stones played with small stones caught in some versions on the back of the hand was comparable.

The ringing sound of *bowls* (hoops) being propelled along the pavements echoes yet in the ears of the elderly. In the evening boys raced with iron hoops, guided by a *shirl* (an iron stick with a hook on the end), for miles across towns and cities. But girls, unless they borrowed from brothers, had wooden ones laboriously bowled along with a wooden stick, and felt this piece of sex discrimination keenly. Variations of skipping games, mostly but not necessarily for girls, became the craze in high summer. Duck Racing involved two girls who, perhaps living on either side of a street, each stood in their gateways winding the rope. A dozen or more girls and boys, even young women, dived in turn into the rope and skipped first once, then twice, and upwards to thirty or more. If you missed you were out. Often children skipped in bare feet to save their shoes.

'We played Diabolo, pillar box jumping, gas lamp swinging, stilt walking, train spotting, cricket with a home-made bat, and hide and seek on dark winter nights.' The latter played with a tin can in a chalked circle was variously called 'Tin Can Hiddy' (Shipley), 'Squat Can' (Batley), 'Kick Can' (Oakworth), and 'Kick Can and Hook it' (Halifax). Or children hid in all the best hiding-places like the yards where the dustbins stood near the outside toilets crying 'Relievo! Relievo!'. Or at Heptonstall the girls played a kind of 'Follow my Leader' round and round the village singing as they went, 'Through the long lobby we go, we go'. 'Buck Buck' or 'Ships', a wall game, 'Statues', pize-ball, similar to rounders, kite flying, and games with cigarette or football cards all filled leisure hours.[1]

Indoor round games included the well known 'Here we come Looby Loo', 'The trees are all covered', 'King William was King George's son', 'Poor Mary sits a-weeping', and many others. Less common are 'The big ship sails on the alley alley O', and a rhyme from Gomersal for a 'Drop the Handkerchief' game,

> I have a pigeon in my pocket
> If I haven't lost it
> Peeps in peeps out
> Peeps through the dish-clout.

At Rawdon they played a kissing game 'Here come three jolly jolly sailor boys/ Who've just returned to shore', for which the boys stood in a circle surrounding girls sitting on chairs. Three boys with handkerchiefs tossed over their shoulders,

[1] See for comparative descriptions of 'Tin Can Hiddy', 'Statues', 'Buck Buck', 'Drop the Handkerchief', etc. Iona and Peter Opie, *Children's Games in Street and Playground*, 1969.

walked round singing until they knelt on the handkerchiefs in front of the girls of their choice and kissed. They then linked arms. The girls proceeded to do the same and so on until all having chosen partners they paraded round the room.

A favourite forfeits game at Morley and in the Spen valley went:

> Here I come as stiff as a stump,
> Selling mi blacking a penny a lump.
> You must neither laugh nor cry
> But say 'I will'.

Miming an old woman leaning on a stick, the person in the centre of a ring addressed a catch question to a boy or girl sitting round, and if not answered adequately he or she had to take their place. Girls made a simple peepshow and recited 'Pin-a-sight, a sat a-sight, a pin to look in', or stuck cut-out pictures in a book and charged a pin a prick. If you pricked a picture it was yours.

For little children, sitting on a parent's knee, fathers used to recite:

> Hob shoe fellow fine
> Will you shoe this lad/lass of mine?
> Yes, sir, that I can
> As well as any other man
> Here's a nail, here's a prod,
> This shoe's well shod, shod, shod.

On the last line the parent patted the shoe sole.

In the congested streets of cities and towns, hawkers sold their wares—'Long strong pins a penny' called a blind woman in Ivegate, Bradford. Most followed their particular rounds often on specific days. Moses Harrison sold 'wet yist' and skim milk on baking days round Thornton, near Bradford, and at Heptonstall William Hey brought round hardware—donkey stone, yellow stones, soap, block salt, pots and pans. The oatcake baker called once a week. They mostly came on foot, sometimes with a donkey or horse and cart. 'Grey peas all hot' were carried in a heated oval bucket or Pay Lionel at Gomersal brought them in a hand-cart. Dispensed with a mug, these were brown or pigeon peas eaten with vinegar. There were Pot Joe at Slaithwaite, Pie Sammy and Pie Tom at Hebden Bridge and Bradford. Pie and peas, this time dried green peas, was and still is a cheap satisfying dish (*see plate* 93). Up to 1914 good quality coal, sold at 9*d.* a cwt, was hawked and weighed on scales hanging at the back of the cart. Best coal rose from 11*s.* 4*d.* a ton in 1870 to 47*s.* in 1939.

At Heptonstall, Blacking Ab sold two pennyworth of blacking in a bit of paper. 'You put it in water and brushed it on boots and clogs.' In the Spen valley and

STREET PERSONALITIES

92. *John Mort, known as Johnny Lonkey, scissor grinder and umbrella repairer, who lived at Northgate, Heckmondwike. He performed many feats of endurance, for instance walking 1,000 miles treadling his grinding machine in 1,000 consecutive hours (c. 1880).*

93. *Seller of hot peas in Westgate, Keighley. One such Keighley vendor who had a wooden leg was said to stir his peas with it (1890s).*

94. *John Christopher Kennedy of Bramley delivered 5,000 copies of the (Bramley) 'Weekly Advertiser' every week in two days. He never missed from 1916 to 1940.*

95. *Luigi Tomasso at Bowman Lane, Leeds, with one of the barrel organs which he made from start to finish. In the 1920s these were hired out at 2s. a day (1930s).*

elsewhere the old nettle woman came in the early spring with baskets of young nettles, bought for making beer, and porridge, called nettle cole, made with oatmeal. The hop ale man carted round brown stone bottles holding half a gallon of ale, made by one of the several botanical brewers. 'When the bottles were empty we used them as hot water bottles.' At Keighley railway station Freddie Gramophone played a tinny gramophone and held out a cap, and there were Joe Pumpwater and Sally Matchbox. Dancing bears with their attendants, organ grinders with monkeys, and German bands every now and again paraded the streets. In the 1920s in the spring in Briggate, Leeds, boxes and boxes of mimosa were sold at 3*d*. or 4*d*. a bunch. Gypsies and potters selling pegs and artificial chrysanthemums were occasional visitants to houses, as were elderly women or old soldiers after the First World War hawking bootlaces, elastic and reels of cotton from trays covered with black oilcloth.

More pathetic were the characters who were daily pottering round the streets. Many at Halifax remember Bull Pratt, a very strong man who went about barefoot, never worked, and who although harmless alarmed people, and also Grunter who grunted and Tabby Oggie who picked up cigarette tabs. At Morley they had Silly Edith and Silly Clifford, of whom the latter always dangled a piece of string, and at Gomersal Edwin Twe Twa and Little Jinny, who carried a doll dressed as a baby round the village.

The rag-and-bone man, the tatters, found fruitful pickings in the whole area, and still a fairly familiar sight, was important as a collector of rags for the shoddy trade. The experiences of one man, Mr Fred Bloomfield, now of Churwell, who was born at Diss in Norfolk, illustrate the life. Hearing that there was better pay in the north, he had come as a boy to live with an uncle in Morley, and eventually started with a horse and a flat cart collecting rags, bones, jam and pickle jars and scrap metal. He bought clippings from dressmakers, remnants from tailors, rags from housewives, and selling them to rag merchants at Batley at 1 cwt. for £1, could live on that for a week. At Christmas time when the women were making rugs from clips the supply dropped off. Since those days man-made fibres have confused the trade, and he sells four or five tons of rags for flocking, cloth, and cleaning rags (wipers) now important. Bones, often mixed up in the household rag bag, were sold at 3*s*. a cwt. Sometimes people concealed heavy weights such as cog wheels amongst the rags.

Scrap metal—pewter teapots, brass and copper kettles, brass candlesticks and fire-irons—were bought from midden and dustbin men, and he smashed up grandfather clocks for firewood and sold the faces as brass. Jam jars, wine bottles, pickle jars and broken glass, all could be sold at a profit to the respective factories or merchants. Sometimes he unwittingly bought coats with money or betting slips in the pockets, and people came running demanding them back. Fred Bloomfield has only had three ponies in a lifetime, and regrets the old days. 'I wish I could have one Friday, just one Friday before the war. . . . All rag men are not rogues.'

Lastly, what of the speech of these people? An easy answer would be broad, but it also has that 'comforting and coaxing inflection peculiar to Yorkshire folk'. When dialect faded, word-conscious families, who failed to find equally expressive words in current English, used: *tew* (to struggle), *thoil* (cannot bear), *moithered* (confused), *brussen* (bursting with self-importance), *nesh* (delicate), *peff* (a little cough), *chuff* (pleased with oneself) *minnin '-on* (a snack between meals), *frummety-sweat* (a state of trepidation or excitement), *soot wisel* (hanging spider's thread with soot on the end). They savoured phrases like 'Tha talks and says nowt' or 'I'm hearing through a foxglove' (muffled sound), or, said of a mean person, 'If she had a mouth full of gumboils she wouldn't give me one'.

One word, *'oile* (hole), perhaps epitomizes it all. There were and are face 'oiles (nostrils), snap 'oile (eating place), carring 'oile (place where men squatted gossiping on their haunches), best 'oile (sitting-room), Morley 'Oile (place-name), chip 'oile (fish-and-chip shop), a nice bit o' honeycomb (tripe) wi' vinegar i' every 'oile. 'Oiles describe all parts of a mill from scouring 'oile to tentering 'oile. A constituent visiting London in the last century managed to find his M.P. and, having been shown round the House of Commons, asked if he could see t' other 'oile.

11 Individuals

THE chronic lack of ready money for so many people was exacerbated by coal strikes and the desperate slump of the early 1920s which was worse in effect than that of the 1930s. During a coal strike 'We would meet during the day and arrange to go scratting. We went with barrows or sacks up to Middleton pit or tip-hills and dug into the slag and got out bits of coal. Scores of people would go in gangs. "Let's go scratting", they'd say' (*see plate* 73).[1]

'I started as a teacher in 1926, right in the middle of the General Strike, at Rye Hill, a colliery area, with huge classes of sixty pupils. The children, whose parents raised money for them by band playing and other means, had meals at school. Kippers and bacon and egg for breakfast was reduced as money became short to long buns and margarine.'[2]

'I was born in 1902 one of a family of thirteen. We lived in a house with a stone floor, one room downstairs, and one bedroom and a boxroom. We slept six in a bed. I always wore clogs; the only time I had boots was when I joined the army. In the slump of the 1920s I'd been out of work for a long time and was at my wits' end, for we were so very poor. On my daily travels looking for a job, I came across a lot of men standing by a wall outside an engineering works, and a man walking along was picking men out for jobs. I was only small, 5 feet 1 inch, so I found two bricks and stood on them at the back with the other men in front of me. Up came the works man and he says, "That big man behind. You can start in the morning." And from that day I was never out of a job until I was sixty-five. I still have one of my wonderful bricks, but I have had it gold-plated. In those days you were a millionaire if only you had a job.'[3]

'In 1922 my husband was out of work, and was told that the 19s. 4d. I was earning was enough to live on. After paying 6s. each week for rent it didn't leave anything for luxuries. We often dined on mashed turnips and dry bread with an

[1] Mr T. Sinclair.
[2] Mr C. Armitage, Batley.
[3] Mr Luke Crawshaw, Lightcliffe, Halifax.

occasional 1*d*. herring as a treat.'¹ 'In the 1920s I was wrapping 600 toffees by hand on piecework for 1½*d*. Your fingers bled, so you put alum on to harden them. When I was a girl my mother, a widow with no pension, got 7*s*. 6*d*. parish pay and earned about the same. She used to make a dinner for 2*d*. for five of us: a halfpenny worth of damaged potatoes, the same of savoury duck from the pork butcher's, with gravy if you took a basin, together with potatoes and water made a hash, which was followed by a halfpennyworth of bruised apples stewed.'² 'We had an old fitter [in Holbeck, Leeds] who had five or six sons who were sent down the street to get their suppers from other people's dustbins.'³ At morning roll-calls schoolmasters looked out for children who might faint from lack of food, and 'many children had such poor foot-gear that they could not attend school in snowy weather'.⁴

'As a lad mi father used to go window tapping and all that sort of thing. They went up to Windy Top (near Thornton, Bradford) and in the middle house was a little old chap that lived by hissen. He were praying to the Lord to send him some bread. These lads listened for a bit and mi father ran home, got a loaf, wrapped it i' paper and tied it up wi' band, and they got on top of this little low cot and dropped it darn t'chimney. It made a din when it dropped on t'floor. He jumped up, oppened it out and "Praise the Lord! Praise the Lord!", he says, "I've gotten a loaf." He didn't know where it had come from.'

'My father was a quarryman and I'm seventh of a family of twelve. One week mi father told me he had to laike for fifteen week o' frost and got to t'bottom. "We went to bed," he said, "did me and yer mother. We hadn't a crust in t'house. We knelt at bedside and prayed, and at eight o'clock next morning when we got up, there were a horse and cart outside our door, and a chap brought a stone o' flour, a pund o' lard, sugar, tea, yeast, and ivverything we needed. After a fair while I picked it out mi brother had sent it." '⁵

In country districts poverty also struck the unfortunate. In the Holme valley 'We'd only a poor home, the walls were whitewashed, sand was on the floor, and we'd a long scrubbed table and a high-backed langsettle under the window. My father was once six weeks and never a stroke of work. I remember two or three of us sharing an egg plastered on a teacake, and we ate lumpy flour porridge with skim milk. My father came home drunk many a time. They'd nawt else to do. At

---

¹ Mrs S. Farnell, Halifax.
² Mrs D. Begley, Ovenden, Halifax.
³ Mr H. S. Sykes, Leeds.
⁴ Log-book, 23rd February 1923, St Paul's Church of England School, Manningham.
⁵ Tape recording, May 1957, Institute of Dialect and Folk Studies, University of Leeds.

one time we owed a shop £20, and were taken to court and had to pay 1s. a week. As a lad [in the 1890s] I walked every Monday to Holmfirth court with a shilling.' [1]

Another story illustrates the problem of drink. In the Colne valley there were and are Wellhouse, Scarhouse, Ridings and Hoylehouse Cots, indistinguishable from ordinary houses. They are run by a secretary, a committee and a landlord, who formerly bought in barrels of beer. They had a coal fire and a bed upstairs for 'them as couldn't go home'. 'My father used to go on a Friday night and come back home on Monday mornings for his overalls.' [2]

Mr G. W. Atkinson of Morley recollects: 'Mi father was out of work, and he and my mother and three boys we'd lived on lard and bread for four days. I was nine. I heard mi mother weeping and saying to mi father, "We'll go and see our Walter tomorrow." Uncle Walter operated the first electric coal cutter, and in those days of twenty and twenty-six bob a week he earned £14 (probably paying about £4 to a mate). He was a millionaire. We set off for Castleford, some fourteen miles away, where he lived. My father borrowed 7d. which got us to Leeds on a tram, and from there pushing the younger ones in a little Tan Sad [make of push-chair] we walked to Oulton. A fellow came along with an old solid-tyred lorry and gave us a lift. He said to me, "Half a mile farther on, I shall slow down, don't make any mistake, shake hard because I shan't stop." Soon after I saw all these apples. Henry and me both jumped. We got thirty-four apples. My mother quite rightly said, "Two each and no more." Then we reached this old shop at Methley, and an old lady made us a pot of tea and gave us sandwiches with home-made potted meat in. My mother promised to come back to Methley to pay her, but the old lady said, "To see t' barns happy is my reward". And we walked from there to Castleford and got a wonderful meal with a tin of salmon at Uncle Walter's. I've eaten some expensive meals since, but none have tasted as good as that tin of salmon. He gave my mother £2 and sent us home by train which was terribly exciting.'

'In 1922 I worked in a bakery at Peel Street, Morley, making food for 100 impoverished children. Shepherd's pie was made of left-overs, corned beef, bits of tongue, ham, ham fat with plenty of potatoes, glossed over with fifty-six yolks of egg out of a tin at one go on top. We also took a huge container full of cocoa. When we went back to get the empties, one of the little tenpence halfpenny to t' shilling lads waited at the corner, and winter and summer ate all that was left of the shepherd's pie. Then we turned over the cocoa thing which was on wheels, and he lay on the floor and drank all that was left as I tipped it into his mouth.'

Children earned small sums in various ways: running errands, carrying and

[1] Tape recording lent by Mr Frank Burley, Mr W. Coldwell, Holme valley.
[2] Mr M. Taylor, Golcar.

minding babies, scrubbing shared lavatory seats, taking food to work, delivering newspapers on a paper round, always avoiding fights with other boys. Boys might buy bicycles out of their earnings. One girl at Sowerby Bridge, who was temporarily away from school, earned 5s. a week as a penny runner taking out telegrams for the Post Office. Favoured children took a mixture of oatmeal and sugar to school, so coveted by the hungry that it could be bartered say for a dozen taws.

On the other hand life on the farms, proceeding alongside and interrelated with industry, was less subject to fluctuating fortunes. In the Pennine valleys workers in the mills lived on smallholdings; manufacturers kept horses for transport and poultry for home consumption, and often owned farms as a hobby.

Many West Riding people living in towns look back on the idyllic days of childhood visiting farming relatives. Mrs Doris Rhodes used to go up to Crawstone Hall, near Elland, almost every weekend and every holiday. 'My grandfather went every day delivering milk and had a big cream round. How we loved haymaking time! When it was done we still had the fields to play in. We filled a milk can with blackberries, and took them to my auntie who made lovely pies. I used to sleep in a big bedroom. We used to take a candle up in a candlestick, and I can still remember the roses on the jug and bowl on the washstand. My other grandma lived alone on Norland Moor. When she was forty-two she was left a widow with eight sons to bring up. One was my father. They nearly all used to visit her on Sundays. I can see them now sat round her big fire. She was the most contented person you ever met.'

Farming on the Pennine hillsides resembled that in the rural Yorkshire dales; pasture and meadow rather than arable land predominated. It differed in that a larger population and a ready market was at hand to absorb dairy produce.

Mrs M. Murgatroyd lived as a child at Upper Hanroyd, near Midgley in the Calder valley. This was a farm of about thirty acres adjoining the moor and supporting some thirty cows and 100 hens, run by her father, Henry Fisher, with the help of an Irishman in hay-time and her tireless mother who helped to milk the cows, made 30 lb. of butter a week, cleaned, washed, cooked, sewed and knitted for a family of seven girls and a boy. The butter, made up into round pounds with a pattern of a sheaf of corn printed on it, together with eggs, was delivered to regular customers and sold at 2s. 6d. a lb. and 12d. a dozen respectively. 'We had a big vegetable garden with apple trees and gooseberries, raspberries, and blackcurrant bushes. We always killed two pigs for winter and made blood puddings and cured the hams.' In the spring dock pudding, fried in bacon fat, was a favourite dish eaten mostly at teatime, and pounds of bilberries gathered in the summer holidays were made into bilberry and apple jam. 'We were well fed.'

Clogs were polished every night ready for school next day. At one time five of the children, taking teacake sandwiches, went to Midgley school together, well over half an hour's walk. Chapel provided the chief entertainment. 'Eight from our house and twelve from a neighbour's attended Sunday school, more from what we call Midgley Heights than go there altogether now.'

The story of a farm dog comes from the Colne valley, told by Mrs G. E. Buckley of Delph. Her father, William Sharpe of Orchard Hey Farm, Marsden, used to buy stock from Carmarthen, and wherever he went so did his dog, Bowser. One day in 1921 returning home by rail, he found at Marsden station that the dog had been left on the train. He asked that a message be sent to the porter at Diggle, the next station, to put Bowser on the road facing Marsden, and as he had often driven cattle along it, he would find his way home. But the porter only put the dog on the platform, and he set off through Standedge tunnel. An express train coming through cut off his tail and damaged his rear legs, and workmen, finding and recognizing him, wrapped him up and took him home. He was nursed and nursed, and lived to be fifteen.

A ninety-five-year-old friend has a different story to tell. In the 1880s her father, earning 30s. a week, was the manager of a busy co-operative stores in Cragg Vale. The shop sold groceries, meat, crockery, drapery, corn, and employed a shoemaker, a clogger with an assistant, and a dressmaker, for in those days eight cotton mills (formerly ten) flourished in the valley. The mills paid wages fortnightly, one group one week and the other the next, some on Wednesdays and some on Thursdays. On these nights her father and two or three assistants were occupied serving customers, who sat awaiting their turn on benches, until 11 p.m. The family lived at the back and above the store, and the child wearing a pinafore, shawl and clogs, went to Cragg Vale School.

'When I was ten, my father told me that I was appointed a monitor with a salary of 8s. 4d. a month. I was very excited.' Out of this her mother allowed her 3d. or 4d. a week, and she no longer wore clogs. Besides ability the reason for her appointment was that the other children were leaving to go as half-timers, and there was little for her to do. She was given homework and the teachers helped her, especially a newly appointed young headmaster who came at 8 a.m. and coached her with 'a respectable woman' present for an hour. 'Children really learnt then.' At fourteen she graduated as a pupil teacher earning 10s.

When she was eighteen her father had died. But her mother, determined that she should not go to the mill, encouraged her to take a Queen's Scholarship examination for the Stockwell Training College in south-west London. She passed number 816 out of 1,600, and set out on a first long journey for an interview. Lest she be overcharged she was warned to enquire the fare from King's Cross by hansom cab, and she returned to the station by horse bus, changing once and thus saving money. She was at college two years from 1898 to 1900, took London Matriculation, and could have taken a degree. But she had already cost her mother £100, 'all of which I paid back'. After training she taught at Hebden Bridge School, walking the three miles there and back daily, earning £70 a year. Fifteen years later when she left to be married, her testimonial stated, 'Never absent. Never late'.

Mrs L. Wardman (b. 1889), of Birkenshaw near Bradford, came of a family of four boys and three girls. 'We'd only three bedrooms, two girls slept in one, I slept in another, the boys in the third and my parents in a shut-up bed downstairs. Mother put up their meals in a red handkerchief tied on top, and I used to take two of 'em their dinners to Bottoms Mill twice a week and another of 'em their tea at Broadbent's Mill, Gomersal. When my mother fell ill I followed mi own folk and washed and baked for nine of us—4½ stone of bread and sixty teacakes, thirty currant and thirty plain. I answered an advertisement to sing at Tong Parish Church, twice on Sunday, morning and afternoon, and was paid 10s. a month. I enjoyed it. I always had a day off. I used to walk across the fields to mi uncle's at Cleckheaton and sing all t' way home. Men called out, "Good night lass"; and there was no fear. We were a lot happier then, and a lot freer. Life were different when neighbours helped each other. You don't get it now.'

'I had learnt to weave, and when I was twenty I returned to the mill. I went on after I were married and had 15s. a week on two narrow looms, and mi husband had 19s. 11d. Eggs were 1s. a dozen, mi milk were 1s., with a pint over on Sunday, rent was 2s. 3d. and rates 1s., and I paid 1s. to t'co-op for mi coal club. You could get a joint of meat for hef a crown. I could save 5s. to 6s. a week. My home cost me £44 for furniture, upstairs, downstairs, overmantel, and bed and fire-irons. It's all here barring that china cabinet. My husband had a rolling pin, a baking spittle, a baking board and summat else given him from Farnells [a saw-mill where he was employed]. Eventually he went to t' pit, but was off work wi' blood poisoning for thirty-two week. I never owed nobody nowt. You can't pay old debts wi' new money.'

Her husband became a lamplighter attending to gas lamps which from October to March were left on until 7 a.m. and the rest of the year put out at midnight. 'He had to put his head through a ladder and go round and wash 'em, and when he lit 'em and died 'em out his wage was 37s. 6d. a week.' She herself left weaving for charring and continued at this for forty-five years. 'I went to wash for some new people and was told to go to get mi dinner in the kitchen. I carved myself some meat, then saw a nice custard and ate that too.' But the family had company and had to say to their guests, 'We're sorry to tell you the washerwoman has eaten the custard'. She also took in three washings a week, and providing her own soap and using a charcoal iron she charged 2s. 6d. for washing 'and taking 'em back ready for t' drawer'. Her husband helped with putting the clothes through *nets* (clean waters). Some of her employers never forget her birthday and one or two take her for drives.

Now living comfortably but alone, she remarks that she has all her life given 10 per cent of her income to the chapel, and she looks philosophically back on the loss of one of her sons who was given a good education and had just passed his accountancy examinations when he was killed in the Second World War. 'I've had a long life, a hard life, but a happy life.'

Lastly, a romantic success story told us by Mrs V. Gaukrodger of Sowerby Bridge. 'My husband never played or signed on a day. I met him at work. As I was coming in at the entrance of the mill yard, he was filling the bunkers up with coal [for the boiler furnaces at Lock Hill Mills, Sowerby Bridge], and he used to wink at me. He wore a neb cap, and I used to think, "Oh heck, I wonder who he is". One Friday afternoon he brought me a bunch of green grapes on to my machine you know. I lived right up Norland and I thought no boy would want to walk me home all that way. Anyhow he came, and we were courting and saving up four and a half years. The first thing I had for my bottom drawer was some ebony for the dressing table. First I got the tray, then the brushes, then the candlesticks, and then the ringstand. I paid £48 for a bedroom suite. People used to say, "If you don't get a bedroom suite when you marry you'll never get one." Nobody was going to do me out of a bedroom suite.

'We got married in 1928, and lived on Pickwood Scar. I always used to look across as I came down at a hen pen on Sunny Bank, and after our little girl was three years old we heard that they were going to build thirty houses there. We put £5 down for one and watched it going up brick by brick. It was a middle house much warmer than an end one. Then we paid £50 and the house was ours. But the full price was £388, and we paid it off at £2 0s. 4d. a month. It took us fifteen years. We retired in 1966. John had forty-five years' work and I had forty-eight but out of that I had had eleven years off when the children were small.' They still live on Sunny Bank and since retirement they have been four times to visit relations in America.

12 Food

ALTHOUGH the regional dishes of the West Riding vary from district to district, from town to country and from class to class, a staple food was formerly oatmeal, eaten either as oatcake or porridge. By and large the same type of thin oatcake baked in the same way was made from the Saddleworth district adjoining Lancashire, northwards across the Pennines to the far boundaries of upper Wharfedale. 'The manufacturing parts of West Yorkshire', wrote Marshall in *Rural Economy* (1788), 'use principally oaten bread', and he adds that new oats making a good price were imported from the Vale of Pickering. Stiff porridge eaten twice a day was the diet in bad times, and up to about 1900 the chief breakfast food. The decline in the growing of oats locally began as early as 1800 when difficulty in ripening the crop seems to have been experienced.[1] Later, as the population increased oats were imported from Scotland, Ireland and elsewhere.

Oatcake was baked on three forms of bakestone—stone, iron and clay—of which the latter, a mudstone, quarried throughout the centuries in the Castleshaw valley near Delph in Saddleworth, is interesting for its antiquity.[2] To make the clay bakestones a huge block, euphemistically called a fly wing, was dislodged, immersed in the Hull Mill stream near the quarry, and the same day or within a day or two it was split with wedges into leaves half an inch to three-quarters of an inch thick. The under surface was chiselled and the upper surface scraped smooth (*see plate* 96). The bakestones, about 22 inches square, or made in sizes to fit specific ovens, were left in the stream, and after a few weeks stacked with the chiselled side inwards, and baked round a wood fire in an oblong pit in a small hut (*see plate* 97).

Crying 'Havercake bakst'ns' the maker hawked his wares in Yorkshire over the moors to the Colne valley and Calderdale. Two dozen formed a load, balanced on

[1] P. E. Razzell and R. W. Wainwright, *The Victorian Working Class, Selections from the Morning Chronicle*, 1849, 1973.

[2] Johannes Bakestoman appears under Quick (Saddleworth) in the West Riding Poll Tax, 1379, for which the returns were published by the Yorkshire Archaeological and Topographical Association in 1882.

96. James (Nipper) Mills shaping bakestones with a length of scythe blade near the quarry at Delph. Many finished bakestones are hardening off in the water of the Hull Mill stream. The men had a hut and grindstone, but most of their work was undertaken out of doors (1910).

97. *Arthur Schofield and James Mills firing bakestones in the hut or kiln at the bake-stone quarry at Delph. Inside the hut was a pit in which wood or anything available was burnt, and the bakestones were reared up round it. Schofield and Mills are given as bakestone-makers in 1838 (1910).*

either side of a horse or donkey or later carried by a horse and trap. They were sold by bargaining or barter, latterly at about 3s. 6d. each. For more than 100 years the Schofields of Grange, a hamlet above the quarry, were connected with the trade. It has been handed down that Tom Schofield, travelling with his wares during a cattle plague (rinderpest) in the 1860s, threw a sack over a *boskin* (partition) in the byre at the inn where he lodged and thus brought the disease back to Grange where some forty cattle were infected and died. Abraham Schofield, Ab o' Chit's, made the last about 1928.[1]

In the home the portable bakestones were placed over the fire for baking oatcake. When ovens were introduced, in the Saddleworth district they were put in the bottom for baking oven bottom cakes, made of bread dough, here called 'mowfins', and were said to make them sweeter. Also, wrapped up in blankets, they served as bed-warmers. On the other hand Sally o' Ben's using a built-in bakestone is remembered baking oatcake in an outhouse at Crow Trees, Marsden, in the 1890s.[2]

In 1883 Easther wrote that 'Oatcake is seldom made by any but public bakers'[3] and already by about the middle of the last century Joseph Wright, ironfounder of Shipley, had invented a complete cast-iron bakestone, some of which had inscribed on the fronts in raised letters 'Evil be to him that evil thinks'. One, formerly at the Feathers' bakery at Haworth now at Cliffe Castle Museum, Keighley, was heated with coal, has two plates, one when in use hotter than the other, and measures 7 feet in length. Beginning by charging customers so much for baking a stone of meal, commercial oatcake bakers, usually small family concerns, started up in every town and village, and the occupation only completely ceased in the West Riding in 1968.

Basically the same method of making was employed as that in the home, except that in the bakery the batter was placed on and propelled by a tram, a mechanical roller on rails, fixed at one end of the bakestone (*see plate* 99). It was usual, too, to make muffins, *pikelets* (crumpets) and milk cakes for sale to shops or to hawk them with the oatcakes to regular customers. The flavour was all important, hence the demand for new oats which made the best.

[1] Information from Mrs A. Lawton and Mrs M. H. Gartside, Delph, Mr E. Schofield, Diggle. See also Ammon Wrigley, *Songs of a Moorland Parish*, 1912; E. Baines, *Directory and Gazetteer of the County of York*, 1822, Vol. 1. p. 270, gives 'Schofields and Co. Bakestone delf, near Delph.' A good example of a bakestone may be seen at the Saddleworth Museum, Uppermill.

[2] Mr Joe France, Marsden.

[3] A. Easther, *A Glossary of the Dialect of Almondbury and Huddersfield*, 1883, describes the process of making oatcake. See also Marie Hartley and Joan Ingilby, *Life and Tradition in the Yorkshire Dales*, 1969, and Miriam Lord, *The Yorkshire Havercake*, 1961.

As oatcake bakers are not listed as such in directories it is difficult to be precise as to numbers. There were said to be forty in Bradford. Like cloggers they are remembered by name in every locality, where they travelled on their rounds with the oatcakes in baskets, covered with white cloths, slung over each arm or balanced on their heads. Mr and Mrs L. Feather, the last bakers in Yorkshire, to whom we are indebted for information, retired in 1968 (*see plates* 98–102). Hird Lord (1860–1950), an early Christian Socialist, worked almost up to his death in his bakery at Worthington Street, off City Road, Bradford. He bought meal from Scotland, used milk for mixing to improve the flavour, and gave misshapen cakes away to poor children. At Highburton, near Huddersfield, five Oldroyd brothers ran an oatcake and bakery business combined with a smallholding from about 1920 to 1941. They kept three horses and carts for delivery to surrounding villages. When they retired, the recipe, in all cases always a secret, went too. When his niece asked for it, Alfred Oldroyd replied, 'Aye, it cost me a lot o' brass to learn that. I'm not telling thee for nowt.'

Asa Nicholson of Thornton, near Bradford, then a quarryman, took up baking after the rigours of the winter of 1898. He bought a second-hand iron bakestone with a tram for £2.10s., and learnt how to make oatcake from a baker in Mount Street, Halifax, who charged him £5 for the tuition plus ¼d. for every cake he spoilt. The ¼d. fine was not unreasonable, as throwing the batter from the tram by cranking a lever requires considerable practice. He soon bought a Galloway, a spring cart, two hawking baskets, and medium oatmeal from Ireland. In 1918 when his son, Mr J. C. Nicholson, joined him, they delivered far afield. Oatcake ceased to be made by them in 1939, but a bakery flourishes at Denholme Gate.

The cost of meal regulated the size of oatcakes so that comparisons of prices do not hold good. However, in 1814 they were sold at 1d. each, in the early part of the century at 4½d. a dozen or four for ½d., and in 1966 at 3½d. each. Innkeepers served them with stew as 'Stew and Hard'. They were linked with a traditional riddle: 'What is edged all round and not a stitch in it?' At Outlane Billy Breead Hawker's old horse, which had 'three pot legs and a wood un', was said to have a gait like 'hard breead running on a bakestone'.

Two practices shared in common by most classes were high tea, eaten about five o'clock and deriving its importance and timing from the return home at the end of the day of the workers of a family, and home-baking undertaken by the mother during the day, by the working wife at night after a day's work, or by servants in middle-class households. 'My mother thought they were sluts if they bought bread.' 'We never had anything out of a tin.' Thursday or Friday was baking day, followed the next day by cleaning-up operations.

In consequence flour was a much needed commodity. Every Friday morning Miss A. Jones, shopkeeper, at Delph End, Pudsey, used to weigh out forty stones of flour into stones, half stones, quarters and pounds for Yorkshire pudding-making. At the Akroydon Cash Stores, Halifax, Miss Pattie Smith, then a child, helped her mother weigh up three types of flour, Best Snowflake at 1s. 1d. a stone and two cheaper kinds, all milled at Raventhorpe Mill, near Felixkirk. People fetched flour in white cotton bags which they carried away in big blue or check handkerchiefs or sometimes balanced them on their heads.

In households where workers needed packed-up meals teacakes which were readily cut for sandwiches took pride of place. Some housewives to earn a little extra money made them for sale, and others were baking them all day with one or two loaves for week-end consumption. A delicacy for those who liked caraway were seed teacakes, which split and well buttered were warmed through in the oven and eaten for tea (Morley). 'My mother baked on Thursdays ten loaves and about twelve teacakes, a sweet cake of some kind, either madeira or currant, and always a thin cake which we ate with bacon for tea. The bread was stored in a big crock, glazed outside but not at the top' (Mirfield). At Thorpe, near Wakefield, Mrs G. M. Brears baked gingerbread almost every week throughout the year in a tin 12 by 9 by 2 inches. Here and there we have heard gingerbread called *moggy*. Parkin, a different form of ginger cake, was always in some homes cut with a fork, and baked for November the Fifth.

The thin cake—variously called thin, flat, new, oven or oven bottom cake—already referred to, was made in all households. At the end of the kneading of dough for bread, a piece was set aside, rolled out round and flat, a hole made in the centre, and baked in the bottom of the oven, turned after ten minutes with a baking spittle. They were then leant to cool against the doors of houses on well-scoured doorsteps to be ready for tea. 'You could look down the street and see them at nearly every door.' 'When new cakes were there kids congregated on the doorsteps. A place called Simpsons sold fish and chips, $\frac{1}{2}d$. for each, and children sat on the pavement edge or on the doorsteps eating this with new cake.'[1] The cakes, never cut, were riven into triangular pieces and split into two for buttering. Many took oven cakes to work for snap with the favourite 'mucky' fat spread inside. Or in the early years of the century delicious 'skull-draggers', a hot steak placed inside a small oven cake which soaked up the juices, could be bought in Leeds.[2]

[1] Mr G. W. Atkinson and Mr R. Dennis, Morley; Mrs E. Nolan, formerly of Holbeck, near Leeds; Mr T. Sinclair, Hunslet.
[2] John H. Wilkinson, *Leeds Dialect Glossary and Lore*, 1924.

Yorkshire pudding scarcely needs elaboration. Suffice to say that traditionally it was made not in small individual tins but in large ones and then cut up, and it was served with a thickened gravy as a separate course before the meat. Seasoned pudding, similarly baked in a large tin, and made of oatmeal, white bread-crumbs, onion, egg and herbs, was served before pork, duck or goose. In upper Calderdale suet cakes, a dough with currants or sultanas and sugar, were eaten warm for breakfast or after dinner 'to finish off with'. Fritters, resembling small oval thick pancakes with currants added, were eaten on Ash Wednesday.

Some foods had their origin in the country, where as seen in Chapter 11 farming families benefited from having their own produce. But formerly pigs were kept by many even in the slums. In upper Calderdale the tradition of making dock pudding, so called from the main ingredient, *Polygonum bistorta*, picked in the fields, continues. The similar Westmorland Easter pudding differs only in that barley meal is used instead of oatmeal, and in Littondale, off Wharfedale, the local name for the Bistort, 'pashdocken' with its reference to Easter, the time when it is picked, suggests that once the pudding was made there.

At Mytholmroyd, Midgley, Hebden Bridge, Heptonstall and thereabouts the young leaves are gathered in early spring. A recipe, which may vary from family to family, consists of 2 lb. fresh dock leaves, 2 large onions or 2 bunches of spring onions, a knob of butter, $\frac{1}{2}$ lb. nettles, a handful of oatmeal or more if required, salt and pepper. The onions are chopped small, the leaves well washed, the stalks removed, and all boiled with seasoning until tender. With oatmeal added the mixture is then boiled for some twenty minutes, strained and stored in a jar. Usually it is eaten for breakfast, fried with bacon, but many enjoy it at any meal.

A very different food is rhubarb, grown on the lowland farms within an eight-mile radius of Leeds, chiefly between Leeds and Wakefield, where 95 per cent of the forced rhubarb grown in Europe is produced. It is a strange concentration in a once beautiful countryside despoiled by man. The land, too, is man-made, for in the past thousands of tons of night soil from privies and middens, as well as sewage and shoddy waste, have enriched it. This and the once cheap coal near at hand to heat the forcing sheds to 50 to 60 degrees, and a clay soil cold in late October and November when the dormant roots are brought in from the fields, make ideal conditions for cultivation. Started 100 to 150 years ago, this has grown from small men, often colliers, and their families planting and later splitting a few roots in back gardens and allotments, building a shed for forcing, acquiring land and building more sheds, to the 110 growers of the present day, half the number of fifty years ago, combining with rhubarb the growing of sprouts, peas and broccoli to give a rotation of crops.

OATCAKE AND MUFFINS

98. Mr L. Feather in his bakery at Haworth pours a ladleful of batter on to the scored bakboard which is made of mahogany, and has been sprinkled with semolina (1965).

99. Having transferred the batter on to the cloth of the tram he pulls a lever which jerks the tram forward to throw the batter on to the bakestone.

100. He turns the oatcake with a bent knife, after which it is transferred to the cooler end of the bakestone shown on the left. Mr and Mrs Feather working together made eight dozen cakes in an hour.

101. Mrs Feather weighs out the dough for muffins and Mr Feather kneads it.

102. The dough is dropped into a ring on the hot bakestone.

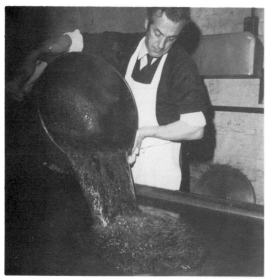

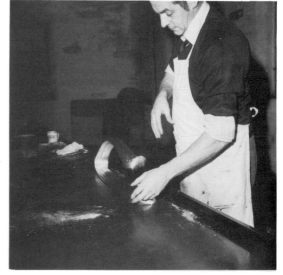

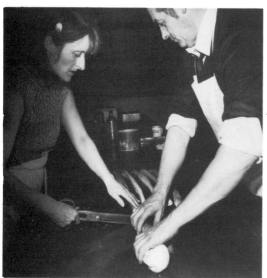

SWEETS

103. Mr R. Berry at Joseph Dobsons, Elland, making boiled sweets. He pours the boiling mixture on to an oiled steel plate which has a cold water jacket below.

104. A length has been cut off with scissors, and is being pulled first one way and then another until it appears white from the many air bubbles.

105. Mrs J. Whalley and Mr R. Berry striping humbugs by cutting lengths of candy and laying them across a main lump.

106. A length is put through a roller with dies which press on the right shape of the sweets. It comes out in narrow strips of thirty-two sweets, which when cold are easily broken up into individual sweets.

107. The various rollers which are used to shape the sweets—round, fish-shaped, oblong, pear-shaped, square, ridged and so on.

A thousand roots produce thirty-seven cwt of rhubarb, and in the dark sheds—dark to preserve the cerise colour of the sticks—it grows audibly, to those attuned to hear it, at the rate of an inch a day. W. G. Smith & Sons of Thorpe Lane Farm, near Wakefield, grow ninety tons a year and send it to London, South Wales, the Midlands, Glasgow and Edinburgh; and the women of the family, competing with others, formerly made jam and rhubarb pies for local shows. The Asquiths, based on Brandycarr Farm, Kirkhamgate, near Wakefield, have seven farms, and eleven sheds 200 feet long and 10 feet high to the ridge, each holding 5,500 roots, which each are groomed to produce six *fangs* (sticks).[1] Several days old forced rhubarb compares unfavourably with that freshly picked obtainable in Yorkshire. Soaked in sugar overnight, gently stewed, and eaten with a runny egg custard, it is a delicious Yorkshire sweet.

Either cooked or uncooked onions were relished. Raw onion sliced up in vinegar, with if available a little cucumber on top, was an accompaniment to cold meat, and offered in the past at fairs with roast beef sandwiches. At Delph oven cake was 'best eaten with raw onion'. Onion and potato pasty, with the filling sliced up raw between the pastry, then baked, made a tasty winter's tea. At one time in Methodist circles at Sowerby Bridge it was tantamount to a declaration if a boy bought a girl a present of onion pasty.

Tripe, sheep's heads, frozen Australian rabbits without heads and Egyptian eggs at twenty-four for 1s. provided cheap meals. Both honeycomb and seam tripe were popular—the former in a thick white sauce for high tea. 'I used to go night after night for my father's supper, and was told to say, "A quarter of thick seam for someone who's poorly." He never had a day's illness in his life.' Because easily digested, tripe was in fact given to invalids, as were *pobbies*, a bed-time food for both children and adults, made from cubes of white bread covered with boiling milk, with a dab of butter and seasoning added. Brown peas, as already described, were sold by hawkers and made a satisfying dinner boiled with a ham shank. Cockles and mussels, more of a treat, were sold by greengrocers at so much a pint, and boiled in large iron pans ready for supper. 'In the 1890s my father used to have a dozen oysters, brown bread and butter, and a pint of stout for 1s.'

Fish and chip shops, fish 'oiles, abounded and still do, although diminished in numbers. At Hebden Bridge twelve are remembered (now three), and at Queensbury six (now four). In some streets there might be three in 100 yards. Many fish friers started in wooden huts, of which a few still function. Prices varied according to the quality of the fish. At Hebden Bridge fifty years ago they were 2d. for fish,

[1] Information from Mr N. Asquith. 5,000 tons of forced rhubarb was produced in 1970, see R. A. Giles, *Forced Rhubarb in the West Riding of Yorkshire*, University of Leeds, 1970.

1*d*. for chips with perhaps a few scraps on top for nothing, 1*d*. for a 'bit' (a child's portion), 1*d*. for a steak or collop (three or four slices of raw potato fried in batter), and 1*d*. for cakes or sandwiches (little pieces of fish cooked between a potato cut in half). Other recollections give 1*d*. for fish and ½*d*. for chips. Formerly too brown peas were on sale with them in canisters standing on gas rings, and were taken away in pint or quart pots. 'If you were really poor you could just order chips with pea gravy.' Fish friers cooked special batches of fish and chips for husbands returning home late to take as peace offerings to their wives.

Although fish and chips were cheap, they cost 2*s*. for a family of eight—'a lot of money'. 'When father got his money on a Friday we all got fish and chips for Saturday dinner.' 'For mill orders we used to pack them in cartons, with salt in a paper and vinegar in a pop bottle. Those were the days. They were fish and chips then.' Harry Ramsden led the move away from the solely take-away shops, when he abandoned his wooden hut for a large restaurant started in 1931 at White Cross, Guiseley. Now open six days a week, twelve hours a day, and run by a staff of between 150 and 160, it is nationally, even internationally, famous.

The grocers, greengrocers, butchers, pork butchers, confectioners and sweet shops, individual to each town and with individuals as proprietors, are remembered vividly. Grocers were noted for their tea, cheeses, hams and bacon, and now banished to the suburbs, were a feature of the centres of towns. At Ellins, grocers, down by the Kirkgate market, Leeds, people were allowed to sample the huge mounds of butter and huge cheeses on show all round the shop by nipping a bit out with a 6*d*. Maypole shops, now gone, are remembered for their sawdust on the floor, and a continuous sound of Scotch hands slapping pounds of butter into shape. Corner shops whose proprietors knew the characters and finances of their customers gave 'tick', as did Thrift Stores in Leeds up to Friday. Greengrocers sold slices of raw coconut, liquorice root to chew, locusts (the sweet pods of the carob tree) and pomegranates in the autumn.

Pie shops were well known such as Gosnay's in Wakefield and Roberts' with its outsize imitation steaming meat pie in the shop window in Godwin Street, Bradford. 'When we were children we used to go with my father to Bradford market. It was a red letter day. We ate pie and peas, or *trunnel* pie with peas on top, stood up at a stall. You helped yourself to mint sauce. My father used to have warm black pudding, and there was a big dish of mustard to put on it.' Trunnel pie, eaten hot, had boiled chopped-up tripe as a filling.[1]

On the other hand there were the pork butchers. 'We always had brawn and a big stand pie for Christmas from Etheringtons at Birstall.' 'As a boy I reckoned to

[1] Mrs A. Marlow, Gildersome.

get $\frac{1}{2}d$. change out of a tanner—5 Woodbines for $2d$., a gill of beer for $2d$., and a pork pie for $1\frac{1}{2}d$.' Craps, the rendered down pieces of fat from pig *leaf* (inner layer of fat), eaten with mustard sauce, made occasional teas, and slices of hot pork in gravy, fetched in basins, were bought for dinners. About the middle of the last century German pork butchers settled in many towns, for instance the Zieglers, Gebherds and Hoffmans at Wakefield. F. M. Keitel, who came to Colne in 1879 as a boy of sixteen, when he married bought a shop in Rothwell, with a slaughter-house and a building for cooking in the yard behind. In the First World War they encountered hostility; some left, and others anglicized their names.

Confectioners, too, ran special lines, such as Parrots of Batley, who advertised malt bread and made penny parkins. Gregson's ecclescakes and Miss Smith's cream cakes at Dewsbury were 'out of this world'. Collinsons at Halifax was founded in 1834 as a tea and coffee business by Thomas Collinson, a Westmorland Quaker. It is related that he used to ask an assistant to turn off the coffee grinder, so that he could hear the German bands in the street. His sons opened cafés in Leeds, Halifax and Huddersfield, and his grandson, Edward, started Beech's chocolates. The cafés have now closed and the business has been taken over.[1] Woods, confectioners, with a café above the shop, in Commercial Street, Leeds, and presided over by Mrs Wood, was known far and wide for sausages and first-class confectionery, whilst the foreign confectioners who came to Bradford at the end of the last century made 'wonderful cream cakes'. Bought cakes were in fact a treat.

Hundreds of sweet shops flourished in this sweet-loving county, and local sweet factories, often begun on a small scale in houses, were numerous. The Smiths in their shop at Akroydon always sold boiled sweets especially mint drops from Bottomleys of Keighley, and toffee from Turner and Wainwright of Brighouse before Mackintoshes had made their name. In the last decade of the last century there were four sweet manufacturers in Halifax—Binns, Moore, Bancroft and Mackintosh. As a means of advertising, one used to scutch sweets from his front door to passing school children on Fridays. Mr Arnold Townsend (b. 1882) remembers John Mackintosh, not to be outdone, asking him to scutch a box of sweets for him from his pastrycook's shop where he was then beginning to make toffee in 1890.

Joseph Dobson and Sons, founded in 1850, still a family firm, make boiled sweets at Elland (*see plates* 103–7). They hailed from York, where they were connected by marriage with Bayldon and Berry, a firm from which Terrys developed. They, too, started as bakers, and were famous for their sponge cakes. An undated recipe book shows that amongst other confectionery they made common

[1] Mrs E. Hyde-Welch, née Collinson.

peppercake, brandy snap, bride cakes, moggy and various lozenges such as opium for curing tickling coughs.

Nowadays horehound, cassia and oil of cloves are some of the ingredients in the cough candy, which together with voice tablets, were invented by Thomas Dobson, Joseph's youngest son. Joseph made conversation lozenges which had phrases like 'I love you', 'Be mine', and 'Will you be my sweetheart' on them. They have a shop in Elland and stalls in Halifax and Huddersfield markets. Formerly the boiled sweets were taken to the markets in 28-lb. cans by horse and flat cart and tipped on to the long sloping counters, from which they were served with a shovel and scoop at 1 lb. a time for about 2½d. Yorkshire Mixtures, for which they are famous, contain about twenty varieties.

Children only spent their Saturday pennies or halfpennies after considerable thought. 'For a halfpenny you could buy a kali sucker, which consisted of a paper with kali [sherbet] in it, with a piece of liquorice telephone wire stuck in it.' Lucky packets or bags, too, about 2 inches in diameter, sometimes triangular, contained sweets, a trinket such as a tin brooch or ring or a small toy, and cost 1d. or ½d. It was said that some had a 3d. piece in the bottom, but this was never found. There were coconut chips or aniseed balls at so many a halfpenny, and lamb, green peas and potatoes, little red, green and white sugar sweets. At Heptonstall Palm Sunday Fair Roseanna actually rolled rock in sugar on a little table in the street. Tiger nuts (*Cyperus esculentus*) were bought and chewed for their juice, and all types of liquorice confections—pomfret cakes, telephone wires, boot-laces and shoe leather (squares) were ever popular. Chopped up black liquorice sticks bought from chemists, shaken up with water in medicine bottles, made 'Spanish', a pleasant childish drink.

One of the biscuit firms of Yorkshire, Fox's Biscuits at Batley, now a public company, originated from the sale of brandysnap to stallholders at fairs. The firm began with Michael Spedding, who in 1853 having started a small confectionery business launched out into the making of brandysnap then curled by hand. In 1882 F. E. Fox joined him as a boy, and in 1897, having married the daughter, took over the business. Even up to the 1930s all the family worked overnight at fair times. Orders were sent on a postcard, and canisters of brandysnap delivered to fairgrounds by horse and cart. It was always heaped up on the stall, never laid out neatly, because people preferred to buy it from a pile. Modernization and expansion, begun after the First World War, continued, with the introduction of new machinery including a brandysnap curler. Sixty types of biscuits, many of them sold at 6d. a lb. up to the Second World War, are supplied all over the world, for people are prepared to pay high prices for British biscuits which are the best.

However disparate the food of the better and the less well-off may have been, all shared an appreciation of flavour—of the taste of new home-baked bread, ham, oatcake, chicken, rabbit pies—flavours that to some of us seem to have gone for ever. Home-baking largely ceased during and after the Second World War owing to a combination of the need to supplement rations by the purchase of confectionery, increasing affluence that enabled people to buy the more expensive cooked and baked products, and of women of all classes going out to work.

13 Shops

AFTER the Industrial Revolution, when quantities of goods became available, shopkeepers entered a golden age. They were then, like Swiss hoteliers, individuals providing individual service and before the Shop Hours Acts were passed open early and late. Shops were of their era, and often only lasted the lifetime of their owners. Small- and medium-sized shops with narrow frontages of different designs and with goods massed against the glass of the windows were the rule. The last century saw the building of those early pedestrian precincts—arcades, covered markets and department stores, as this has seen the spread of the chain store, the multiple tailor, the supermarket and the hypermarket. Shops were and are both a necessity and an entertainment.

Consider the Grand Pygmalion, the first department store in Leeds, established by Alexander Monteith, a Scotsman, in Boar Lane, a main shopping street. In March 1888 he bought a building with a 90-feet frontage, framed large windows in ornamental brasswork, built a new staircase with flights off to right and left, made two entrances, and in three weeks' time was partially open. The departments included women's and children's clothing, dress goods, lace, millinery, upholstery, haberdashery, dressmaking, carpets, furniture and later toys. Two features were that the ground floor sloped upwards from Boar Lane, and that cash was sent in wooden balls and change returned on an overhead railway, working by gravity, to and from a cash desk high up like a 'floating gondola'. Monteith was joined by his brother-in-law, Andrew Hamilton, and by his son, and became Monteith, Hamilton and Monteith.

The store was both in advance of and of its time. The merchandise could be handled and purchases could be exchanged or the money refunded. But in the old style the fourth floor was entirely devoted to staff quarters, with dining- and living-rooms and mostly separate bedrooms for fifty of the 100, later the 200 employed, and superintended by a housekeeper and a housemaster who doubled as floor walker. Employees stayed for years. The sales ladies wore black dresses even in summer, and high collars stiffened with little whalebones. The head of the toy department, T. B. Duncan, the first Labour Lord Mayor of Leeds, not only acted as buyer but mended anything including the eyes of dolls which refused to shut. To people who remember them there never have been such toys nor such Christmas toy shows.

For Christmas 1892 before an electricity supply existed, the Pygmalion and a few other shops were lit by electric light from a John Fowler engine stationed in a side street working a generator. The Pygmalion lasted only thirty-nine years, yet it impressed itself permanently on the memories of the adults and children of those years. Following the slump of the 1920s and the deaths of the two elder partners, the shop was sold to C. and A. Modes in 1927.

In Leeds Schofields, at the present day the only family controlled store in the city, attracts shoppers living in times of more widespread affluence. It was founded by Snowden Schofield (1870–1949) who was born in Bradford, where he was apprenticed at the department store of Brown, Muff's. After working in London and Liverpool, he had saved £300, and with a view to starting on his own, he visited Blackburn where it snowed and Leeds where the sun shone, so that he plumped for Leeds, and for £50 a year rented a two-windowed corner shop in the newly built Victoria Arcade, in what was Upperhead Row not then the main shopping area (*see plate* 111).

He opened as a fancy draper and milliner, with two full-time assistants earning 10*s*. a week and others part-time, on a beautiful spring morning in May 1901. On that day he took £62 3*s*. 4½*d*., £43 10*s*. of it in gold. By 1910 he had built up the nucleus of a store by renting shops as they became vacant in the arcade, and he gradually acquired buildings near by including the Red Hall, one of the old halls of Leeds, the Leeds Hippodrome which had closed, and in 1946 the entire arcade of twenty-four shops on either side for £250,000. Meanwhile the Headrow, the first major rebuilding project in Leeds, had advantageously brought a new main shopping street past his door. When Snowden Schofield died in 1949 the staff numbered 700. Never forgetting a face, he cared for them all, and had introduced a welfare service, a house journal, annual garden parties and outings. He had also pioneered in Leeds advertising on the front pages of newspapers—the first was for nappa (capeskin leather) gloves sold at 1*s*. ¾*d*. a pair, on which he made ¾*d*.

Schofields was carried on by his son Ronald who supervised the complete rebuilding of the store between 1956 and 1962. Part of this included the old Theatre Royal which was alongside the Hippodrome in Lands Lane. Ronald died in 1971 and was succeeded by Mr Peter Schofield. In recent years the store has added a multi-storey car park, an out of town warehouse, and in 1972 another family business, Cockaynes of Sheffield.

One of the most remarkable of success stories which, as it originated in Leeds, must be mentioned in passing is Marks and Spencers, for it was here that Michael Marks came from Poland in 1882. In the Leeds covered market he first sold goods for a penny, from which developed a chain of Penny Bazaars, and out of these eventually came the chain of superstores. The trademark, St Michael, was registered in 1928.

Whilst in Leeds, let us look at a shop specializing in china, pottery and glass: Doyles, the story of which has been told to us by Mrs Maggie Doyle. In 1842 James Alfred Doyle had opened a little shop on Leeds Bridge, where he sold domestic ware made by the Castleford Pottery. When in the 1870s Leeds Bridge was rebuilt, he moved to a shop in Boar Lane, and stocked it with a more varied class of goods. James Alfred, a handsome autocrat, thought that women engaged in trade were not only out of place but immoral, and when he died he left the business to his son, Sydney, and the premises to his three daughters. Maggie Doyle, who had married Sydney, was shortly left a widow, with two children, no pension, a small insurance and total ignorance of the shop business.

However, she was invited to Staffordshire by Major Frank Wedgwood, the head of that famous firm and an old friend of her husband's, and encouraged by him she decided to take over the running of the business. But first at Wedgwood's invitation she returned to Staffordshire and toured all the important potteries including Minton, Coalport, Doulton and Stewart's Glass Works. At the shop, the chief assistant left, and eventually her husband's sisters gave notice that they wished to sell the premises. This was not altogether disastrous, as they were on five floors, so that when anything was sold a whistle was blown, the order whispered, and it came down on a lift on a pulley. In 1937 she moved to Albion Street, and as an attraction had early morning tea-sets wrapped up ready to give away to the first customers. But the opening coincided with the Abdication and no one claimed a set.

This inauspicious beginning only served to emphasize later success. Amongst her many customers she particularly remembers the gypsies, always women, who, carrying baskets of pegs and bringing children with them, ordered goods worth £50, £60, even £100. They had catalogues and knew exactly what they wanted, and the prices. Often these, Crown Derby or Worcester ornaments, plates and so on had to be ordered and sent on, and were not paid for. Instead they deposited jewellery in her safe, until they came round again and had saved sufficient money to pay. When Maggie Doyle retired in 1963, she was presented with specially made gifts from all the potteries.

Two shops in Bradford, Brown, Muff's and Lingards, illustrate how different

108. Halifax Market.

109. Mrs E. Stanley and helpers in her café, a booth in the old Kirkgate Market, Bradford.

110. A corner of Dewsbury Market.

111. *Schofield, Milliner and Fancy Draper. A postcard captioned 'One of the sights in Victoria Arcade, Leeds' Schofields has developed from this one shop to a huge department store (c. 1905).*

112. *In 1822 Manoah Rhodes walked to Bradford from Morley and took work with John Allott, a watch- and clock-maker, and there in 1836 set up his own business which became one of the best known gold- and silversmith's establishments in Yorkshire (date unknown).*

113. McKitrick Bros, Huddersfield, a present-day firm founded by Abel Hellewell, brazier and tinner, in 1819. It was taken over in 1855 by C. W. McKitrick, then aged eighteen, later joined by his brother (1890s).

shops developed under the personal imprint of their owners. Brown, Muff's has a long and distinguished history, for it was founded in 1814 by Mrs Elizabeth Brown who opened a small draper's and outfitter's shop in what was later to become Market Street, Bradford, selling underclothes and fustian goods. Her son, Henry, joining her, ran a circulating library and bookshop, and he married a cabinet-maker's daughter, Betsy Muff, whose brother Thomas eventually came into the firm. In 1845 the two men, described as woollen drapers and tailors, entered into partnership as Brown and Muff. As Henry Brown had only one child, who died, the connection with that family ceased, and Thomas's sons became partners—as their descendants are today.

In 1871 they opened a fine new store near Mrs Brown's first little shop when they were described as drapers, silk mercers, tailors and outfitters. A boy's suit then cost £1 3s. and two pairs of blankets £2 16s. About six apprentices used to live in. Milliners, tailoresses and men tailors were employed as well as carpet fitters and mattress-makers. Bridal dresses were a speciality. In those days when lino was required a roll was taken to the house by horse and cart, laid out in the street, cut, fitted, and the rest of the roll carried back.

Brown, Muff's opened a restaurant in 1923, an innovation comparable with developments in London and other stores, and like them they also had a small orchestra. Formerly, the high quality goods for which they are renowned catered only for 'carriage folk'—a distinction that has not applied since the Second World War. A separate furnishing store near by, warehouse and service departments have been added, and large new stores opened in Skipton in 1963 and in Doncaster in 1975.

Another Bradford draper's shop, Lingards, was founded by Henry Lingard (1839–1903) after he had prospered as a stall-holder, at first in the open market, then in Kirkgate market when it was built, and as a warehouseman selling *fents* (short lengths of cloth or remnants sold cheap). A pioneer in the fent trade, still prominent in local markets, he was one of the first to realize the potential of the business, and it is said that he once climbed over a gate into a field to cut up his long lengths and so did better trade.

Built in 1875, the shop was intended to resemble a market, and was without display windows on to the street. Two large wide entrances led to the ground floor open to a glass-domed roof, with two tiers of balconies, so that sitting in the café on the first floor shoppers could look down into the shop. Averse to ostentation, Henry Lingard neither advertised nor held clearance sales. His employees eventually numbered some 200. About 1920 his eldest son, Asa (1872–1956), built a modern store with windows which for some ten years more were painted over, and he flourished like his father. The shop was sold to the United Drapery Stores in 1938, bombed in 1940, rebuilt on a different site in Westgate, and still continues.

By and large the big family drapery stores were the exception. There were the first-class outfitters and dress shops such as John Holmes in Manningham Lane, Bradford, where children going to boarding school were fitted out, also Madame Neil who, like Madame Arthur of Bond Street, Leeds, supplied the well-off with model dresses. We should not forget the branches of Marshall and Snelgrove at Leeds and Bradford whose very name spelt high-class clothes. Nor must men's shops be omitted—the tailors, shirtmakers and hat shops flourishing before the arrival of the multiple tailors and chain stores—Hardy, Bissington, John Wales Smith in Leeds, all individualistic.

Every town had its modest but well-stocked drapers, such as Manchester House, Elland, founded in 1900 by Thomas Forrest and so-called because goods were regularly bought from Manchester wholesale warehouses, and in 1975 still run by Miss D. Forrest. Or Waterloo House, which has gone, at Holmfirth, owned by John Beardsell, who employed eight girls as tailoresses and milliners living in a dormitory with a housekeeper to look after them.

Or consider Mrs E. Barrett (1869–1965) who because her husband was delicate (he died in 1918) rented a shop in Thwaitegate, Hunslet, in 1916, and started with a stock of drapery bought on a month's credit from a wholesale trader's warehouse, where a brother-in-law who could vouch for her worked. Later she went regularly to Leeds to buy material, carrying it home on the tram. She made ladies' and children's underclothes, dresses and men's shirts on a sewing machine in the back room, and at Whitsuntide worked all night long. Her daughter, too, with a second-hand machine provided for her, helped for many years sewing up to eight, nine or ten o'clock.

Emma Barrett lived in a poor district and was 'right soft' so that many people owed her money, paying part off, then owing more again. To help she ran a club to which people paid 3*d.* a week and after so many weeks had saved enough to have a garment made. Eventually she joined the well-known Provident Clothing Club for which she paid a collector a commission. He called weekly on householders who paid 1*s.* a week for twenty weeks and a further 1*s.* for the cheque, which presented to shopkeepers such as Mrs Barrett purchased goods. The cheque was sent to headquarters where a percentage was deducted and paid out at the month's end. In 1933 moving to a better shop, eventually run by a daughter and son-in-law, she still served behind the counter when she was ninety.

Various systems, of which one is club cheques, have evolved especially in the poorer districts of cities and towns to obviate the shortage of ready money. One group is the travelling draper or credit trader, originating from the old packman, Scotsman or tallyman who kept accounts on his stick. Usually dealing in drapery, clothing, furniture, sometimes hardware, they range from one person running a club to a nationwide firm such as the Provident Clothing and Supply Company started in Bradford in 1880 by Sir Joshua K. Waddilove, who was a deacon at the Wesleyan Methodist church in Carlisle Road, Bradford, and wished to help the poor to obtain much needed goods on credit.

The small individual credit trader may have a shop and employ collector sales-men. Both he, members of his family and the paid collectors spend their time 'doing the round', calling at houses delivering goods, collecting the weekly shillings, maybe more, showing samples and taking further orders. He charges fifty per cent profit on the goods for the credit. He and the customer both keep a book. Many are proud of this, 'a picture with not a payment missing', but some irresistibly fall into debt, and a few 'pay nowt nor nobody'. A trader makes discreet enquiries before taking anyone on, for unlike hire purchase he cannot reclaim goods for non-payment. He may buy a book of 'deadeyes' (debts) at 15s. or more in the £1, which gives him an inroad into a district, and by fair trading, recommendation, a personal approach and a 'gift of the gab', builds up a connec-tion. On his rounds, undertaken in all weathers, he meets other collectors: rent, club, bad debts, even of doctors' accounts, all of whom share a mutual fellowship.

Besides these, the other main group are the many catalogue agents acting for the big mail order firms such as Grattan Warehouse or Empire Stores, both based on Bradford, which differ from the above by issuing huge catalogues and themselves carry a very large stock of branded goods. Club agents for one scheme and another, perhaps more than one in a street, in the mills and in other works still abound.

A chain of shops, already referred to from time to time, are the Co-operative Stores, started in the hard times of the first half of the last century, and returning profits to the customers in the form of dividends. The bald statement disguises the determined effort and selfless devotion behind the movement. For instance at Honley the first shop was begun by twelve men who walked to Huddersfield, brought back cheese and sold it at a profit of 1d. a pound. That at Slaithwaite in the Colne valley was opened in 1858 in a remodelled cottage rented for 2s. a week. As at other places they transferred to new enlarged premises, opened department after department, ran libraries, provided services such as coal deliveries, under-taking and life assurance, and organized outings, and concerts in the winter months. By 1908 Slaithwaite had five branches and by 1922 ten.

Another type of shop, the pawnshop with its distinctive sign, has greatly diminished in numbers. Between Hunslet and the centre of Leeds sixteen might once be counted, now two, and at Huddersfield fourteen, now one. Before the days of social security they played a vital role in society. Traditionally they have two entrances, one at the front leading to the counter selling new goods, and the other at the side or the back for pawnbroking.

New goods form a large part of the trade. In 1900 Horatius Lloyd, who had run a pawnshop in the Quarry Hill slum area of Leeds for fifty years, had advertised throughout that period, and made the most profit from sales of jewellery. Jewellery, especially wedding rings and watches, were traditional stock, as may still be seen in the window of Claude Hill's pawnshop in Huddersfield. In the past mostly shawls and cord trousers for men were the new goods stocked, and heald rugs, already mentioned. List rugs, hanging up outside, may still be bought at Beethams in Mabgate and Hunslet, Leeds.

In the past almost anything was pawned: men's suits, overcoats, boots, freshly washed and ironed bedding bundles, silver Albert watches and chains, all kinds of musical instruments, even a piano to pay for a family holiday. About 1911 at Beethams a concertina in a box was brought in each week and each week redeemed, so that from familiarity they did not trouble to check it. One week it was not redeemed, and they found that the box was empty. At one time people even brought in a tin or earthenware bowl full of dough. In the 1930s slump a queue fifty yards long and six people deep waited outside, and so many parcels were strewn all over that they had to walk on them. Eventually they were sent unseen to auction with their tickets still attached.

Nowadays Tuesday rather than Monday is a busy day, and some of the commonest articles 'shoved up the spout' are typewriters, radios, electrical goods and men's wear. In 1973, rather than lack of money, the usual troubles were mismanagement, compulsive gambling, stealing, drug-taking, or the buying of jewellery beyond the purchaser's means. A pawnbroker must be ready for anything. A man came into a shop not long ago, wanting to buy a bag and a suitcase for very little money and leaning over the counter said, 'We've got guns now'.

Again catering for the enormous influx of people various patent medicines were manufactured at considerable profit to their promoters in the West Riding. Zambuk was made by Frank H. Fulford, a Canadian who came to Leeds in the early part of the century, and Teasdale's Chlorodyne mixture for coughs and colds by George Teasdale at Bramley and sold all over the world. They operated against a background of self-medication, stemming from poverty, and the habits of country people flocking to the towns who were used to folk medicine. Herbalists, too, supplied this need, and the early exponents 'Dr' D. I. Coffin, an American, and

John Skelton, herbalists, made Leeds a centre for their itinerant practices and the publication of literature.

The original J. W. Clapham of the herbalist's shop of that name in Vicar Lane, Leeds, founded in 1859, was an American. Mr W. Rutter who came to live with his aunt over the shop in the 1920s describes those days. Then, pickers with hand carts explored the surrounding countryside, reported on their finds, and if the herbs were required, brought them in. Paid by the pound, they collected for example elder flowers, which had to be picked in dry weather, ragwort, used for bathing, burdock, a blood purifier, eyebright, for eyes. If a mandrake with its huge roots were found, it was displayed on the counter before being sliced up and sold as good for black eyes, bruises and rheumatism. After Christmas Claphams bought cheap any mistletoe left over, whose leaves and stalks were good for the nerves.

The herbs were dried on dated hand-made trays, then, with the thick stalks removed, they were chopped into small pieces in a chopping machine, weighed out and sold. The buyer scalded the soft herbs and boiled the hard ones. They also made pills, powders and herb extracts. The ingredients of, for instance, stomach and liver pills were mixed, kneaded, put through a worming machine, then a pill machine, cut and coated with simple liquorice powder. They also made Slippery Elm food mixed in a long narrow trough, and a bath and poultice powder, made from mustard, bran, ginger and cayenne, which when scalded was used for bathing the feet and to keep the temperature down. Today, regulations control what may be made and sold. Herbs are imported from abroad, and pills, especially for indigestion, literally bought by the ton for sale.

14 Craftsmen

WHETHER craftsmen lived in town or country, they found their jobs usurped by machines and their ranks depleted by economic pressures. A few were engaged in rare occupations. In the 1930s Tom Riley, as his father and grandfather had done before him, carved rocking horses at a toy-makers, Whiley Bros in Camp Road, Leeds. Matthew Henry Sunderland's life's work until retirement in the 1940s was the making of thimbles at Charles Horner's, gold- and silversmiths at Halifax. Horners in 1884 had obtained a patent for what were to become their Dorcas thimbles, constructed with a sandwich of steel between two layers of silver so that they did not easily puncture.

In 1822 Leeds supported sixty-five cabinet-makers by which time Thomas Chippendale, born at Otley, had been dead forty-three years. One of the Leeds makers, John Kendell and Company of Mill Hill, established in 1760, was bought by a partnership, Marsh and Jones, later Marsh Jones and Cribb, whilst another, Josiah Teale and Son, established in 1789, first in Lowerhead Row and later in Upperhead Row, Leeds, worked continuously until the 1920s.[1]

Chippendale represents the London cabinet-maker furnishing the great country houses; Marsh Jones the provincial firm catering for magnates such as the Salts; and Teales the local craftsmen supplying well-designed furniture to the less wealthy. In other towns, too, many cabinet-makers of good standing flourished such as Simpsons of Halifax, Eldwicks of Wakefield, and Pratts of Bradford who still function.

The Pratt family hailed from Gunnerside in Swaledale, and moved in 1830 to the then growing town of Bradford where Christopher Pratt (1819–1903) was apprenticed to Joseph Nutter, a cabinet-maker. After his marriage he started in business on his own, and in 1850 after Nutter's retirement he leased, with another craftsman, his house, workshop and showroom, now part of the present premises in North Parade, Bradford. These were extended in 1874 to house piece masters,

---

[1] *Furniture made in Yorkshire, 1750–1900*, Temple Newsam, Leeds, 1974; L. O. Boynton, 'High Victorian Furniture: The Example of Marsh and Jones', *Furniture History*, vol. III, 1967.

specialist craftsmen who, employing journeymen, were provided with timber and other materials—an individualistic system which worked well, but ceased about 1914 owing to trade union opposition.

At the turn of the century, the firm's heyday as cabinet-makers, they were employing 200 men, and providing a complete furnishing and decorating service for houses, town halls, banks and churches. Like others they signed their furniture by affixing paper labels on each piece, after 1913 replacing them with brass plates. In this era when trifling sums were allotted to the equipment of kitchens and servants' bedrooms, a seven-bedroomed house could be well furnished for between £175 and £200. Pratts is still a family business offering a comprehensive service and making fitment furniture, with workshops and a design studio attached to their extensive modern showrooms.[1]

Clock-makers add up to a far smaller body of craftsmen. One firm flourishing as cities, towns and transport expanded was Potts of Leeds, famous all over the north of England for their public clocks. The family originated from Berwick-on-Tweed, and via Darlington were drawn to the West Riding to settle at Pudsey in 1832. By 1840 they were making turret clocks, and about 1862 William Potts (1809–86) moved to Leeds, where three of his sons joined the business of clock-makers and jewellers.

In the last half of the century they made roundhead wall clocks for the stations of the Great Northern, Midland and other railway companies. Apart from the dials, cases and springs, these were all hand work and finished to perfection. They made and supplied floral clocks, ones for schools and offices and above all turret clocks for town halls, works, cathedrals and churches. Potts are thought to have been the first in the field to illuminate dials. They also installed the two mechanical clocks, with moving life-size figures, in Thornton's and the Grand Arcades, Leeds. In 1907 a staff of forty-seven were employed, ten of them engaged on small clocks, fifteen including a foreman, a tuner and labourers on turret, and two as a blacksmith and a striker.

They also repaired old church clocks, often after difficult journeys having to mount rickety ladders leading to belfries deep in bird droppings and with mechanisms covered with flies. They contracted for the winding of clocks, no mean task when for instance all the clocks in Leeds Infirmary were wound by hand. For this job the winder took a boy to hold the ladder steady on polished floors. Latterly

---

[1] L. W. Pratt, *Yesterday Our Ancestry*, 1929, reprinted 1969; Christopher Pratt & Sons, *Small Hints on Furnishing*, 1893; Day books and Catalogues; *Victorian and Edwardian Furniture by Pratts of Bradford*, exhibition catalogue 1970, Bradford City Art Gallery and Museums. All lent to us by Mr C. B. Pratt.

Potts installed automatic electric winding for and fitted cut-out apparatus to the striking mechanisms of many public clocks, for example that on Leeds Town Hall. In the 1930s the old name and the firm were sold to John Smith, clock-makers of Derby. Charles, grandson of William, started on his own account, and in 1964 Cecil, the last of the Potts family of clock-makers, retired and this business was sold to a London firm.[1]

A still more rare occupation and one totally unmechanized, dependent on touch and eyesight, is that of organ builder, engaged especially in the Victorian era in putting organs in the many newly built churches and chapels. Formerly firms were to be found in several West Riding towns, added to by apprentices who having served their time set up in a small way as pipe-makers or voicers, the two trades that together with the fabrication of the consoles and chests go to the completion of an organ. Every part was made except the keys, a specialist's job. Apprentices earned 6¾d. a week. Workmen and journeymen were constantly on the move, travelling from workshop to workshop, or to distant places to assess the acoustics of a building, to enquire what type of music was required, and eventually to put the organ in, perhaps a three-weeks' task for two men. 'When you built an organ you put up a memorial to yourself.' Now the decline in religious observance has lessened demand.

The works of Peter Conacher and Company, a firm founded in 1854 at Spring-wood, Huddersfield, were purpose-built after a fire in 1910, and resembling a vast chapel, was one of the largest organ factories in England. When Mr Brian Hirst, who showed us round, came here in the early 1930s a constant flow of whole new organs was leaving the works. Many were sent to Ireland and many more to the chapels in the Welsh valleys. Then followed the demand for cinema organs, rush jobs which sixty or eighty men, including twelve engineers, laboured night and day to complete. Formerly a steam engine running all day drove the wood-working machinery. Now the firm is part of a group under Henry Willis, organ builders of Petersfield, and the four or five men employed were in 1974 engaged in rebuilding the organ for the city hall in Johannesburg. Mr Farrar was voicing and Mr Gillhouley making components for the consoles. Mr Hirst engaged in soldering pipes, was attuned, as we were not, to hearing the cry of tin, made by solder with a high tin content (see plate 116).

At Bramley an enclave of pipe-makers has sprung up in the wake of the now defunct but formerly well-known firm of J. and J. Binns, organ builders, established here about 1881. In 1974 Fittons, Rogers and Booths were to be found there engaged in their skilful and delicate task of pipe-making and voicing. Mr

[1] Information supplied by Mr W. A. Potts, son of Charles H. Potts.

CRAFTS

114. (Above left) Mr Bill Clarke and Mr Charles Lofthouse from Potts of Leeds repairing Leeds Town Hall clock (1956).

115. (Above right) Mr J. Gledhill and Mr W. Cook, apprentice, outside the printing works, in Town Street, Beeston, Leeds. They published the 'Beeston Gazette' (1910).

116. *Mr B. Hirst of Peter Conacher and Co., Huddersfield soldering an organ pipe, a skilled and delicate operation.*

117. *Mr Norman Fitton of Bramley voicing an organ pipe.*

CRAFTS

118. Mr Albert Smith, a cooper's apprentice, at the Melbourne Brewery, Leeds, undergoes the custom of 'trussing out' at the end of his apprenticeship. He is covered with wood shavings, rubbish and a bucket of water, then rolled round the yard (1960).

119. Mr H. Beckett shaping a cricket bat with a draw knife at the works of International Sports Co., Horbury Bridge. Bats have been made in these works for many Yorkshire cricketers.

120. The rope-walk at Coates and Sons, St Ann's Ropery, Nottingham. A branch of the Coates family came to Carlton, Wakefield, in 1929, and took over a ropery established in 1812. The figures in the foreground are William Coates, George Coates and another William. From left to right operations being performed are twisting, spinning by hand, polishing, balling and twisting. The rope-walk at Carlton closed down in 1954 when machines were substituted (1860s).

Norman Fitton, whose father, William, was linked with Binns and apprenticed to Conachers, and who made complete organs, now has a workshop adjoining his home which was once a clothier's house with a blocked up 'takin'-in' door. By the time he was eighteen he had travelled all over the British Isles putting in organs.

Fittons used to buy their pipes from Rogers, a firm founded in 1897, now run by the Buckle family, who employ six or seven men, and who in 1974 were engaged in making 5,000 pipes for an organ in Ghana. Small organs may have from about 300 to 1,500 pipes which are made of alloys, usually of lead or tin, with zinc in large ones, and copper for display pipes, all cast in the works by melting the metal in a crucible, transferring it to a skillet and pouring it on to a special casting bench. The higher the tin content the better the ring, and the more lead the sweeter the note. Pipes are shaped round mandrels, planed up, sized inside, turned and knocked down even, and then soldered down the joint using tallow as a flux and solder with a slightly higher tin content than the metal of the pipe.

The voicer needs to have perfect pitch. (People who cannot sing in tune are said in the trade to have cloth ears.) Like a human being a pipe has a body, foot, ears, toe and mouth with a top and bottom lip, and is said to speak, and there are two kinds, reed and flue, in the proportion of one reed to ten flues. A stop of reed pipes, sixty-one, may be voiced in three days. By enlarging the mouth, paring, nicking the languid in the mouth of the flue pipe, blowing and trying it out on a small organ, the voicer slowly attains his note (*see plate* 117). We were told that reed voicers used to have a pint of ale on the bench.

Another craft, printing, with its long and distinguished history, was established in the last century in every town. Men set up on a small scale, sometimes beginning in an attic or a cellar with a hand-fed machine and a case of type. They printed the yearly almanac, the weekly advertiser, church, chapel and school magazines, posters, invoices, hymn sheets, show catalogues and so on.

One such firm was founded by William Witts (1838–1914), the son of a Gloucestershire weaver who came north and found employment in Leeds as an overlooker at Gott's mill at Bean Ing. After apprenticeship to a printer Witts came to Bramley where in time a descendant, Mr William Murgatroyd, first ran then bought the business, now continued by his son. He remembers learning his case, soaking and stretching paper, the Columbia Press in use, and that ten or twelve posters, occasionally huge ones made up of six or seven pasted together, were usually printed every week.

In 1896 Mr C. Roberts's father started the *Colne Valley Guardian* (now taken over by the *Huddersfield Examiner*) a four-page paper sold at ½d., and composed with loose type, used, washed, cleaned and replaced to use again. He had settled at Slaithwaite because no other printer was there.

On the other hand when in 1885 Mr A. Charlesworth began his printing works and shop at Holmfirth two others had started at much the same time. In addition to the usual work the Charlesworths ran a circulating library, and sold decorative greeting cards with photographs for which the printer's own young family acted as models. His son, Mr N. J. Charlesworth, remembers that as a boy he delivered handbills as far as six miles on a wheelbarrow. Barrows, hand carts and horses and carts for the quick delivery of orders were in fact usual transport for the rush jobs so frequently associated with the printers' trade, even for the despatch of paper by merchants.

Mr W. Cook, whose parents left Middlesbrough for Leeds in 1910, was apprenticed to a small printer, J. Gledhill, in Beeston, Leeds, for 3s. a week, and developing a flair for composition fell in love with the craft. He attended classes at the then Leeds Printing School, where he was later to teach and examine for the City and Guilds candidates in machine work, and moved about to gain experience. Although it was said that if you could set and print a parish magazine, you could do the same for the Bible, some men were kept for years at composing nothing but railway time-tables or hymn sheets. In 1927 he started on his own, and in time entered into partnership in the firm of Whitehead-Miller, formerly known for chess publications and music printing, but now for general work and colour.

In a long lifetime printing has been transformed and the demand for it increased a hundredfold. Gone are the days of hand-setting, treadling, the Eagle presses, even of the Wharfedale Presses, once made at Otley and worldwide in use, or of the one ink manufacturer in Leeds, who made the ink while you waited and asked for cash on the spot. From small one-man firms large ones have grown such as Alf Cookes, E. J. Arnold and Son, and Waddingtons, Leeds, specializing in particular spheres—packaging, educational publications, playing cards and games. At Bradford Lund Humphries are world famous for high grade work and Sharps for their greeting cards, and at Idle, near Bradford, Watmoughs, beginning by publishing sporting magazines, now work round the clock printing huge fully coloured mail-order catalogues.

One after another almost every craft has been transformed by new machinery, new developments, fashion and other factors—none more so than tanning. About 1840 Thomas Smith, tanner, of Ouzlewell Green, Rothwell, employed several tailors and supplied local people with tough leather suits and the army with leather breeches. Other tanneries existed and still do in other parts of West Yorkshire. In 1822 Leeds had one tanner, but by the latter half of the century it was the tanning centre of the country with twenty firms situated on the Meanwood Beck, a tributary of the river Aire running through Leeds. About the turn of the century the trade gradually began to drift away southwards to settle near the then expanding boot and shoe factories of the Midlands and elsewhere, until now only four firms remain.

Of the original twenty, Harold Nickols, the best known, supplied hides for upholstering motor cars, railway carriages and so on; William Paul made the well-known Beaver leather stuffed with grease for country boots; J. Bateson and Sons dressed sheepskins for lining women's shoes; E. B. Balmforth made golf club and tennis racquet grips, Thomas Wright leather for book-binding and jewel cases. W. H. Ingle and Sons, a large firm which moved to Churwell, has only recently closed down, and W. and H. Miers, still very active, were amongst the first of the chrome tanners of calf.

One of the remaining firms, Charles F. Stead and Company, was established in 1823 by Wilson Walker, who built the present tannery at Sheepscar in 1863. Charles Stead, who began as a traveller with Thomas Wright, a firm on the Meanwood Beck, invented the use of East Indian Persians (the fine skin of hair sheep from Southern India) in the construction of gas meters, and flourishing on his own account, he bought the Sheepscar tannery in 1904 and formed a company. When his son, Mr Philip K. Stead, joined the firm, machines were still simple, tan pits filled the yard, and sumac but not oak bark was being used. Also at that time tanners employed *puer* (dogs' droppings) in the bating process to make the leather flexible. Selling this was a huntsman's perk, and people collected it for sale in buckets in the streets. Calf and ox hides were British, and large quantities of goat and other skins were imported mostly from India. Glazed kid, made from goat skin and used for women's shoes, is now too costly to produce.

Instead of men laboriously scraping the skins with knives over a beam, machines quickly remove the flesh; synthetic materials, not puer, aid the curing; mineral tanning with chromium salts has replaced oak bark in pits, and dyeing has become so sophisticated that the once basic five or six colours have increased to as many fashionable shades as in textiles. The large companies still operating produce as much leather as did all the original small firms, and one such as Steads makes 10,000,000 square feet a year, an amount unheard of in the past. They run a laboratory for research and development and make chrome tanned leather for shoes, for clothing, especially suede, and for industrial gloves.

Although in the early days they were to be found in cities and towns, rope-makers, because of the flat farmland available and the proximity to growing centres of population, came to be concentrated in and near Wakefield, where twenty-seven flourished in 1838. The first Ordnance Survey map of this area shows rope-walks running alongside hedgerows which gave shelter for work then undertaken in the open and dependent on the vagaries of the weather. Wells, too, were sunk for washing the yarn and for sizing. In 1822 there were four rope and twine spinners at Carlton, near Wakefield, one of them, John Dobson. It was this business that the Coates family, which originated in Nottingham and had moved first to Shipley, bought in 1929.

Mr Eric Coates recollects that when they came there had been a heckling shop where hemp was dressed with oil, beaten and straightened on steel pins, and that his father, so as not to waste it, spun half a ton of hemp in the old way by tying it round his waist, walking backwards paying it out by finger and thumb, whilst a boy wound a wheel at the other end to twist it (*see plate* 120). Men were employed for rope-making and drum polishing, and women for twisting and balling. They had a covered rope-walk until the 1950s, and made packing twine for baling, loom cords, waggon ropes, plough lines, halters, whipcords and gaskins for soil pipes. Clothes cords, too, were sold to Woolworths in competition with Calverts, another rope-making firm at Potovens, near Wakefield. Now, different types of twisting and balling machinery, some made by Fairbairn Lawson, have replaced hand work, and the firm, sold to H. Barnett and Company of London in 1951, make twine for butchers and the furniture trade.

Lastly the ancient craft of coopering, once a closely guarded secret and for apprentices after they had served their time culminating in a trussing-out ceremony (*see plate* 118). At Joshua Tetley and Son, Leeds, they employed thirty-six coopers in 1919, fifteen or sixteen in 1948. In the early 1960s they ceased to make new casks, and in 1974 had three coopers engaged in repair work.

Here, too, in the vicinity of Tetleys, were the premises of William Waide and Son, a firm noted for its dairy equipment. William Waide, a farmer, lived in a Leeds surrounded by farmland where bees swarmed and crops grew, and in February 1840 he wrote down in his 'Working Book' the length of staves and the dimensions and prices of spirit and wine casks, peggy tubs, piggins, tub and barrel churns. In the 1860s he began to specialize in dairy equipment and from the 1880s onwards in churns, in particular the Victoria Churn, which had an end-over-end action and of which Waide's were the inventors and sole makers. Gold medals and prizes were awarded them at the great dairy shows held both in England and on the Continent. In the late nineteenth century they were selling 6,000 to 7,000 a year. Many went to Ireland where William's son, Richard Waide, went round for orders in a jaunting car. They had agents in Germany and Japan, and before the First World War sent fifty to sixty churns at a time to Russia, some huge ones to the Siberian salt mines, with instructions in Russian. Later trade moved to East, West and South Africa, Egypt, and India where churns were used for making ghee. Waides exhibited at agricultural shows from 1860 up to the end, and with their churns dairymaids competed in making the most butter in the shortest time. The winner often bought the churn. If kept washed, this could last for sixty years.

When English oak, at one time grown and sold from the Bolton Abbey estate, became scarce, Memel oak from Russia was shipped to Goole and brought up the Aire and Calder canal. Later oak was imported from America, Poland and Persia. When Mr D. G. Waide was apprenticed to his father in 1927, some eighty men were employed. If he was satisfied with the finished barrel, and only then, did a cooper put his initials on the bottom. The firm closed down in 1966.

15 Pottery Chimney-Pots and Clay Pipes

WHEN considering so richly endowed a Riding, clay must be added to stone, coal and water. Clay, fireclay in particular, found in conjunction with the coal seams of the exposed coal-field, especially in the Leeds and Halifax districts, led to the establishment of important potteries, the making of chimney-pots, bricks and sanitary ware and of clay tobacco pipes.

Although they had existed long before, potteries come into focus in the mid-eighteenth century. From then onwards and throughout the nineteenth century a widely stratified society created a demand for pots, fine and coarse, ornamental and useful. At one end of the scale were the potteries using white clay suitable for fine quality pots, and at the other end clay, which because of its iron content turned terracotta when fired, for coarser wares.

Amongst the makers of fine earthenware several were grouped in or near Hunslet, Leeds. Of these the Leeds Pottery, formerly in Jack Lane, was not only the earliest and the best but its creamware, noted for quality and beauty of design, now ranks with the products of other notable eighteenth-century potters. Its best pieces were made when it was Hartley Greens during the last twenty years of the eighteenth century, and it virtually ceased in 1878.[1]

Two potteries in a different class, one at Wibsey and another at Eccleshill, near Bradford, of which the first was founded in 1770, and the second lasted until 1867, when it became a brick works, made well-moulded figures and good examples of salt-glazed brown stoneware. The co-called Eccleshill jug at Bolling Hall is so large that it may well have been made to celebrate the marriage of Queen Victoria and Prince Albert in 1840 (*see drawing on page* 137). Burmantofts at Leeds, flourishing as a pottery from 1862 to 1904, entered an altogether more modern era

[1] For further reading see J. and F. Kidson, *Leeds Old Pottery*, 1892; 'Pottery' by Maud Sellers, *The Victorian History of the County of York*, vol. 2, 1912; Donald Towner, *The Leeds Pottery*, 1963. The Leeds museums contain excellent examples.

POTTERIES

121. Mr Harold Morton and his sister, Mrs Ethel Lockwood, *making plant pots at Lindley Moor Pottery, Salendine Nook (1946).*

122. Isaac Button, *the last potter at Soil Hill Pottery, Ogden, between Halifax and Keighley, standing by the kiln, ready for one of the last firings (1964).*

123. Slipping a mixing bowl—coating the inside with light-coloured clay (1961).

CLAY PIPE MAKING

124. Mr Samson Strong, Leeds, making clay pipes. The first process—rolling with the hand board (1938).

125. The shanks were pierced with a wire.

126. The rolled clay has been put into a cast-iron mould and pressed in the gin-head (on the right). This operation also hollows out the bowl, and was called stopping down.

127. Trimming off the clay which had oozed over the seams in the moulding process.

making art pottery and architectural tiles, and in its day employed a host of people, some mining clay and iron on the spot, others engaged in design and manufacture.

The redware-makers rooted in tradition and aesthetically on a different level, provided households of all walks of life with pots for domestic and horticultural use, such as baking bowls and plant pots. They also made ornamental wares, usually decorated with slip, which appealed to the unaffected taste of humble folk. Amongst the salt kits, tea caddies, frog mugs, tobacco, money and knife boxes, were cradles and two-handled loving cups given as significant presents for christenings and betrothals, and puzzle jugs, which had been made in Tudor times and which puzzled because it was apparently impossible to drink without spilling from the numerous spouts (*see drawing on page* 137).

These potteries, some again near Leeds, were early grouped on the hillsides north and south of Halifax at for instance Blackley, Woodman House and Ainley Top near Elland, and at Ovenden, Ogden and Denholme between Halifax and Keighley. Almost twenty might be counted flourishing at one time or another. The oldest, Howcans, near Ovenden, although not always precisely on the same site, was run by the Halliday family from the mid-seventeenth century until 1889.

Often family concerns, the potteries frequently occupied a small farm which had mineral rights for the coal and clay on its land and space for kilns, clay mills and drying sheds. Brothers, sisters, cousins, aunts and uncles, as well as hired help contributed—the skilful as throwers, others as labourers, and often the women as decorators.[1]

At Salendine Nook, south of Elland, Lindley Moor Potteries were also long established, founded in the seventeenth century by the Mortons, a Scottish family of potters who fled here from religious persecution. In 1739 Joseph Morton gave land for the first Baptist chapel there, described a few years later as at Pot Oven. About 1834 the family split into two firms, Joseph Morton and Son and Enos Morton and Sons, housed in adjacent buildings. It is related that Joseph in busy times waylaid labourers at Enos's and offered them 6*d.* more to work for him. In 1887 he was making bowls of all sizes, cream pots, stew pots, pie dishes, plain and fancy tree-pots, and rhubarb and seakale forcing jars.

Although on a greatly diminished scale, Mr Harold Morton, a descendant of Enos, was making some pottery at Salendine Nook in 1973. Fifty years ago this was a busy place. Thirty-three workers, including six or seven members of the

[1] For further reading see Oxley Grabham, *Yorkshire Pots and Potters*, 1915, reprinted 1971; P. C. D. Brears, *The English Country Pottery: its History and Techniques*, 1971. Examples of the work of the country potteries may be seen at the Yorkshire Museum, York, Shibden Hall Museum, Halifax, Cliffe Castle Museum, Keighley, and Bolling Hall Museum, Bradford.

family, were employed. They had an 8-h.p. steam engine, known as 'Whoa Emma' because to start it Aunt Emma used to have to put her foot on the flywheel and quickly release it. This ran clay mills, four potters' wheels, and a hay chopper for horses' fodder. Horses and carts, with chain horses for the steep hills, fetched clay from Holywell Green three miles away. Coal and clay was dug from day-holes with a 22 feet drop to reach the Halifax Hard and Soft beds (*see plate* 76).

To prepare the clay they stacked it, poured water on it, and trod it wearing clogs until they knew by the feel of the suction that it was the right consistency. After this it went through the pug mill to mix the clay to a plastic form. The clay was then moulded into balls the correct weight for the goods to be made. The largest, bowls 20 inches in diameter, were thrown in two parts. The kiln, which had seven fires and took thirty-five to forty-eight hours to heat, held 7,000 large and small plant pots, and as each fire took three or four hodsfull, by the time a man had gone round and recovered his breath it was time to start again. Harold Morton began stoking when he was thirteen and a half, and if a factory inspector came round, he hid under the flue. After a good firing they used to say 'What a gloss they have on!' but if 600 to 700 pots fired badly 'We could be weeping'.

They kept horses and carts to carry pots, packed in straw, to Lancashire and Yorkshire towns, sometimes returning at two o'clock in the morning, and Harold Morton's father travelled as far as Scotland, always taking orders written down in dozens. Many people came to the pottery to buy, including gypsies who wanted seconds. It is remembered of these that they once put a tiny child in straw in a bread pot to keep it warm on the journey back to Bradford.

In those days 3½-inch plant pots sold at 2s. 9d. for sixty (*see plate* 121). They despatched them to Bermuda, South Africa and the Bahamas, insuring them for breakages. An unusual line was gilders' pipkins, made in three sizes, and sent to middlemen in London who sold them to firms in Ireland, France and Belgium. Sometimes they made cheap marbles, stogs, sold at schools at sixteen for 1d.

Another potter, Jonathan Catherall (1740–1807), had migrated from North Wales, and eventually established near Ogden Soil Hill Pottery taking its name

1 Puzzle jug, Howcans Pottery. 2 Rustic log basket, Lindley Moor Pottery. 3 Flask, Eccleshill Pottery. 4 Vase, Wibsey Pottery. 5 The Eccleshill Jug. 6 Money box (1846), snail horn ware, Howcans. 7 Teapot, Denholme Pottery. 8 Cradle, Howcans. 9 Tea caddy, Howcans. 10 Cup (1907), Woodman House Pottery. 11. Knife box (1853), Denholme. 12 Rocking chair, Denholme. 13 Flower pot (1868), Soil Hill Pottery.
1, 2, 3, 8, 13, Yorkshire Museum, York; 4, 5, 10, 11, Bolling Hall Museum, Bradford; 6, 7, 9, 12, Shibden Hall Museum, Halifax.

from the hill behind it, 1,320 feet above sea level. It continued in the family's hands until the 1880s when the Button family who came from Roberttown near Heckmondwike took it on. The Catheralls sometimes fired the kiln with bracken, and Jonathan of the third generation used a hand wheel turned by his grandson. As late as 1939 thirteen men worked at Soil Hill, but latterly Isaac Button, the last member of two generations of large families, ran the pottery alone until 1964, when it closed. The largest vessels in regular production were brine pans that took 70 lb. of clay. Isaac could throw a huge vase on a wheel in about six minutes, and make a ton of clay into pots in a day (*see plates* 122–3). Both the Catheralls' and Buttons' houses and the pottery building that the Buttons built may be seen on a scarred hillside.

The last pottery to be started was at Pepper Hill, near Shelf three miles over the tops from Soil Hill, begun by John Pickles Sunderland and from 1926 run by Sam Bradley (1890–1964), who had been apprenticed to Arthur Button, Isaac's brother, at Soil Hill, and had worked for Eliot and Rhoda Morton, Joseph's descendants, at Salendine Nook. In their heyday in the late 1930s the Bradleys, then making mostly domestic earthenware, had three throwers and employed three labourers. A donkey engine ran the potters' wheels, a blunger (a machine with revolving knives), and a pug mill; but coal had to be bought at 18s. to 19s. a ton. The kiln held 8,000 3- to 4-inch plant pots, and they once fired thirteen times in thirteen weeks. Sixty 3-inch pots sold for 3s.

People visiting Pepper Hill bought mugs with their names put on in white slip. Sometimes a rhyme was scratched on a square of the slip on puzzle jugs, for example:

> From mother earth I claim my birth
> I'm made a joke by man
> So now I'm filled with good cheer
> Come taste me if you can.

They also made clay pigeons, and pot knurs for the game of knur and spell. Delivering to a few places in Yorkshire, they sent small lots of goods up and down the country. The pottery closed in 1958.

These men and women formed a community of craftsmen whose passing may be deplored. Some of them were buried in the graveyards of the Nonconformist chapels on the moorland heights. Local potteries had been dealt mortal blows by cheap wares imported from Staffordshire, by the cessation of home-baking, and finally by the change from clay to plastic plant pots.

Potteries and brick works were interlinked. Men turned to making what was needed. When Gillroyd Mills, Morley, was being extended in 1845, notices were put up at the Waggon and Horses, Holbeck and the Green Man, Hunslet, 'for a person to make two hundred thousand bricks'. The Buttons made their own for their new pottery buildings, and Joseph Morton ran a brick and tile works at Cinder Hills, Siddal, near Halifax. On the other hand large firms developed round Leeds, Wakefield and Halifax.

The Elland hillsides on both banks of the river Calder have been torn by brick and sanitary and drainage pipe works. On the one side Wilkinson's clay works cover up the sites of some of the old potteries such as Kitsons and Woodman House, and on the other W. T. Knowles and Sons mine a six-foot seam of clay half a mile into a hillside honeycombed with workings, meeting up with the Marshalls' quarries at Southowram.

Knowles employ skilled hand-moulders who with the aid of moulds used to make the intricate chimney-pots of the West Riding, fashioned to break the wind and to forestall downdraughts. Every corporation or borough favoured a different pattern. There are the Bradford and Halifax Windguards, the Carlisle Blow Down, the Hooded Leeds, and others named after the chessmen they resemble: Little Bishop and Long Knight, as well as Tulip Top Tall Boy. Especially after a severe gale many would be ordered, in the old days sent by horse and cart and a *teamer*. Now the two or three hand-moulders left chiefly make gullies of clay ground up as at the potteries but on a huge scale, and fired in kilns so large that the pipes and gullies can be barrowed in.

Whereas clay mines and makers of chimney-pots and the like operated on a large scale and were not numerous, in the last century every city, town and even the occasional village supported one or more clay tobacco-pipe-makers. In the seventeenth century a few existed at Hull, York, Wakefield and Halifax. The Gill family flourished in the two last places from 1709 to the mid-nineteenth century. Thoresby says that the craft was introduced to Leeds about 1700. By 1837 there were for instance six in Bradford and sixteen in Leeds, but when in 1950 the last maker in Yorkshire, Samson Strong (1873–1953) of Leeds retired, his nearest rivals were in Manchester and Edinburgh. By then cigarettes had become fashionable and briar pipes had superseded the clay.[1]

As we have seen in other crafts families passed on their skills from one generation to the next. Both sides of Samson's family were clay tobacco-pipe-makers: his

[1] Thomas Sheppard, 'Early Hull Tobacco Pipes and their Makers', *Hull Museum Publications*, No. 6, 1912; Simon Lawrence, 'Clay Tobacco Pipe-Makers in West Yorkshire', *Yorkshire Archaeological Journal*, vol. 45, 1973; W. White, *History Gazetteer and Directory of the West Riding of Yorkshire*, vol. 1, 1837; *Slater's Directory of Yorkshire and Lincolnshire*, 1849.

grandfather, another Samson, in Derby, and his mother's people, the Pickles, in York. His father, Frederick Strong (1832–95) had moved to Leeds to work for his wife's sister, Jane Wilson, née Pickles. Later Frederick and Angelina his wife buying moulds and equipment started up in Cottage Street, Leeds, where the one-storied workshop continued in use to the end. They had eight children, of whom Samson was apprenticed to his father in 1884. From 1895 when he took over, aunts, sisters and cousins all worked under him, and the youngest brother, John Frederick (b. 1892), remembers that times were hard. About 1900 when they had three kilns in use, fifteen people were employed, and in 1920 about ten.

Clay was not obtained locally as in Thoresby's day. China clay from Cornwall came by sea to Hull, and at Leeds was stacked in balls up to the ceiling in the clay store, one of six places into which the building was divided. The others contained the kiln, the packing, drying and moulding rooms, and a bottom place where the clay was prepared. For this the balls were broken up with a hammer on a block with a $\frac{1}{2}$-inch thick steel top, then left in water in a big steel tub for two days. The clay was thrown back on to the block and belaboured from side to side with a heavy wooden beating hammer, chopped into pieces by hand, rolled, patted and put on the bench with wet sacks round it. If a little dry, Samson took a mouthful of water and sprayed it.

'Grip your clay! Grip your clay' he used to exhort his helpers as they took a nip the correct size and weight to make two pipes. This was rolled on a rolling board, broken in two, doubled again, so that a nip of clay was in either hand. Each was then rolled by hand, making it as long as required and tapering at one end, and put side by side the two were rolled with the hand board (*see plate* 124).

The rolls, placed on dozening boards which held sixteen to allow for breakages, were put on drying racks to await moulding for which a gin-head and cast-iron moulds, which were greased with a mixture of paraffin and sweet oil, were employed. First the roll was ducked in water two or three times, then pierced with a wire which had a small twisted end, called a button, and the end of the roll was bent, fitted into the mould and slipped into a slot in the gin-head. The handle was brought down, called stopping down. After this the wire was removed, and if it came out with a little plop they knew that the hole was clear. Finally the pipes were trimmed with an iron smoother, and dried on racks all over the workshop, even on the roof of the building, or on orange boxes in the street.

The kiln held 150 gross, with the shanks arranged uppermost round three inverted bowls one above the other. Fourteen to sixteen pipes were handed to Samson at a time until he had potted up. Stoked with best coal in three fire-holes, the kiln took sixteen hours to fire, and a day and a half later they emptied it, taking out six pipes at a time. If a lot of churchwardens came out soft, called 'pink', it was a catastrophe.[1]

For years a little old man, Jack Hayes, came in at 7 p.m. to make Dandies, and was gone by morning. Another, a big Irishman, called Tom Doyle, who lived in lodgings and moved on with his belongings tied up in a muffler, was asked to make say a dozen gross of Acorns and stayed until he had finished them. Another, Benjamin Wilson, one of the cousins, taught by Samson, was always the first to use new moulds which, bought from Turpins of Macclesfield, had to be handled carefully. A good worker could make about forty-eight pipes an hour, some 3,000 in a week, and in 1900 the total weekly output was about 36,000.

They made Cutties: Thorn, Basket, Ship and Anchor, Soldiers, Auld Lang Syne, Acorns, the ribbed Cutty, with no heel, and the plain, the cheapest and smallest. The Miner with sloping head was sold in Durham. Footballers had a heel in the shape of a foot kicking a football, and Kitcheners had the Field Marshal's head on them. The last to be made were bubble pipes for children, sold at $\frac{1}{2}d$.

Sometimes when the kiln was being burnt, Samson started off with the horse, Tommy, and a cart-load of pipes packed in boxes, and travelled from town to town in North Yorkshire. Or he took pipes round to local inns, where they were given free with a pint of beer, so that he used to say, 'You couldn't expect a big price when they were given away'. The price was 2s. 6d. a gross, even 1d. each. Trade boomed during and after the First World War, but after that came the slump and trade gradually faded away.

---

[1] The equipment is to be seen at Kirkstall Abbey Museum, Leeds and the Castle Museum, York. Mrs E. Hope, Samson Strong's daughter and Mr J. F. Strong, his brother, have described the processes for us.

16 Clogs

CLOGS, associated with industry, are none the less an ancient form of footwear for long in use on farms. First worn by mill-workers in Lancashire at least by the early nineteenth century, they rapidly commended themselves to operatives elsewhere in mills, breweries, quarries, pits, potteries and foundries, for they were cheap, warm and waterproof. But in this century they began to be looked down on as a sign of poverty and were frowned on by school teachers for the noise they made. These factors, and the introduction of Wellington boots, the wearing of silk stockings, and the diminishing number of agricultural labourers, all conspired to a decline in their use.

In the first half of the last century cloggers (clog-makers) often combined their craft with patten-making. The similes 'As elate as any midden cock on pattens' and 'As bad as a cat in pattens' perpetuate the memory of their use. Early in the century the numbers of cloggers, although never so great as that of boot- and shoemakers, increased until every village had one or more, towns between ten and twenty, and co-operative stores clog-making departments.

Formerly to obtain the wooden soles the maker himself felled suitable trees (alders), or gypsies and other family groups camping in woods partially prepared and dried them in stacks. However, in the latter half of the century, as a result of invention and improvements to machinery, the Maude family in upper Calderdale developed a clog sole-making business which together with a firm at Snaith in Yorkshire near Goole supplied the needs of a wide area.

About 1870 James (1844-1919), the son of John Maude, a wood-turner, at Jerusalem Farm, Luddenden, began to make clog soles at Hawksclough near Hebden Bridge, and ten years later he erected there a purpose-built mill, subsequently enlarged, between the Rochdale canal and the river Calder. Later James's son, John R. Maude (1875-1964), bought a small engineering works across the river where machinery was made.

Up to 1900 they bought logs cheaply from southern Ireland, and then ran a sawmill on the Duke of Devonshire's estate at Lismore in Co. Waterford, where wood was cut up and roughly band-sawed into shape. But when freight charges doubled after the First World War, they erected a mill with an 80-h.p. engine at Raybeck on the Raby Castle estate near Barnard Castle, where T. Place & Sons, timber merchants of Northallerton, felled and delivered trees. Here, under James R. Maude, grandson of the first James, forty people were employed, and machines—roughers, side cutters, shankers—partially shaped the soles, which were then dried in brick steam-heated chests which each held 300 dozen pairs. They were despatched to Hebden Bridge where a similar number of employees were engaged in finishing them.

Until the First World War a dozen to fifteen hand-makers using stock knives were kept busy, each known for their own particular shape of soles. For hand-making alder was used, but beech 'kind to machinery' and some sycamore replaced it. Up to 1954 a steam engine ran the machines which were simple but numerous, at least six, each performing a different stage in the shaping of the sole.

Soles were air dried for about two months, then stacked in racks containing the different sizes—the smallest, size two, 5 inches long, and the largest, size fourteen, 13½ inches. (Clog sizes are three sizes larger than shoes.) They were then matched up in pairs. These in the early 1920s sold at 10d. a pair, a sum corresponding roughly to the hourly wage of a man, and as many as 50,000 dozen pairs might be kept in stock. Eventually customers who had once asked for 100 dozen pairs of one size alone reduced their orders to a gross in all (*see plates* 128–9).

Usually clog soles were sold to grindery merchants, such as Greens of Silsden, near Keighley, or Horsfields of Bradford, who stocked leather for uppers, also tacks, clasps, toe-plates, clog welting and irons, of which the latter were sold in pairs in two parts, fronts and heels. At Silsden a nail-making industry, started there in the middle of the eighteenth century, led to the making of clog irons, and both crafts continued side by side from about 1850 to 1919. Ill-paid jobs, they suited the independent way of life of farmers and hand-loom weavers who needed supplementary employment.

About 1850 it was a nail-maker who gave impetus to the making of irons by developing a series of mechanical processes and at the turn of the century there were four clog iron smithies at Silsden. They are remembered as hot and dirty but companionable places where men brought their books and pets, and discussed theology and current affairs.

Thomas Greens, founded about 1874, had at one time sixteen to twenty hearths in use making ten to fifteen gross a week. They specialized in Colne irons, a pattern introduced from Colne with flat sections on the fronts. Formerly mild steel rods, 12 feet long, were bought in Birmingham, but after 1918 these were obtained more cheaply from Belgium. The iron was worked red-hot in all the processes. In the 1920s a man on piecework earned 18s. to 28s. a week, and boys often put in two or three years at primary tasks before going on to mills or engineering works (*see plate* 130). The Greens, by then the only makers in Silsden, made their last Colne iron on 2 August 1950, and Mr C. T. Green gave the tools to Cliffe Castle Museum, Keighley, where they may be seen.

Horsfields, who at one time employed 100 men and issued catalogues, not only supplied Yorkshire, Lancashire and Cheshire clog-makers, but sent goods as far north as Dumfries and to London and Wales. Founded by James Horsfield in 1867, this business too succeeded because of the invention of machines manufactured on the premises and perfected by James's son, Walter (1868–1950), who had trained as an engineer. After 1914, when trade had declined, they turned to the making of clog uppers, usually in two patterns, Derby and Balmoral, made from waxed splits, which were split hides of which the flesh side was used, tanned again, waxed and blacked. In 1919 Horsfield's output of clog irons was 300 gross sets a week, that is 300 times 288 heels and the same number of fronts, sold at 23s. a gross. When the firm closed in 1962 it had dropped to a tenth of that amount.

Acquiring the necessary parts from the grindery merchants, the cloggers in different districts supplied different styles, chiefly based on the shape of the sole. The many shapes included common, mostly worn in Yorkshire, wide common, round duck, peculiar to Lancashire, London which had a wide square toe and was favoured by brewers, a Leeds and a Halifax shape which were variations on the duck, and spear points used for Sunday clogs. Besides these there were three strengths in each—strong, medium and light.

Formerly the clogger used mostly black leather with some brown for clogs worn at night. George A. Wilde, who had come from Lancashire to be manager of the clogging department of the Slaithwaite Co-operative Stores, advertised himself as the only maker of the Lancashire one-piece clog. This, with one-piece uppers sewn down the back and spear-pointed soles, had designs of birds or flowers scored on the leather. These clogs, highly polished and with brass nails, clasps and toe-plates, were worn on Sundays, and cost 10s. a pair in the late 1920s. Women's and children's had brass tacks, clasps and toe-plates, whereas men's usually had steel tacks and sheet-iron plates.

All cloggers employed a square clog size-stick for measuring the foot, with a gauge for clogs on one side and for shoes on the other, and they also hollowed out the soles for deformities, hence the continuing popularity of clogs with some orthopaedic surgeons. Based on Lancashire, the Amalgamated Society of Master Cloggers published a series of tables setting out wages and prices, just as the makers

CLOGS

128. *Mr Leonard Sharp
stacking clog soles in drying
racks at Maudes, Clog Sole
Works, Hebden Bridge. They
are left for some two months,
whilst warm air circulates
above and below (1962).*

129. *Mr Willie Moss at
Maudes, hand shaping
a clog sole with a stock knife
(1960).*

130. Clog iron makers at Thomas Greens, Silsden. The man with the beard is Frank S. Green, son of Thomas and head of the firm. Three of them eventually completed over sixty years' service, others were musical. Note the white smocks and fustian trousers (1897).

131. Mr H. Schofield, Walton Bros, Halifax, is fixing a steel toe-cap to a safety-clog (1961).

of clog-irons had a society with offices at Birmingham. In the 1920s a pair of child's clogs cost 2*s.* and good men's, said to be double the price of the uppers, 6*s.* 6*d.* Cheapness was the prime object. 'It was a right poverty job.' 'If clog soles went up 1*d.* a pair it was the end of the world.'

Many children had, besides their clogs, only one pair of shoes to their name. At Heptonstall school each morning they toed a chalk line to have their well-blacked clogs examined. At Queensbury the children owed Fred Firth 'who had the co-op clogging, many a penny' for putting on irons. Boys revelled in striking sparks on setts and pavements with their clog-irons, or in winter sliding on the ice. In time children wearing them were shouted at by their school fellows. 'They called me Cloggy Dick and I went home and cried.' Clog fights disfigured feast and other events. Each contestant stood on opposite sides of a fixed horizontal bar, and held it whilst kicking each other until an opponent was brought down.

Two family firms, Waltons of Halifax, established in 1910, and Walkleys of Huddersfield, started in 1946, still make a variety of industrial and safety clogs in standardized shapes. When Mr W. Walton (b. 1888) came out of his apprenticeship to a bespoke boot-maker in 1909, mass production had taken over. However, after starting at Siddal, near Halifax, in a small way he bought with his savings a shop in North Parade, Halifax, for £30, and developed a wholesale trade in clogs. At this time, although uppers cost 1*s.* 10*d.*, soles 10*d.*, irons, nails and tins 4*d.*, laces 1½*d.*, and the employee's pay 7½*d.*, they sold at 3*s.* 9*d.* a pair. He also made 'old top' clogs, always in great demand, by knocking the soles off old boots, adding a wooden sole and oiling them. Or he bought old boots from a repairer in the East End of London at 3*d.* a pair, and could sell clogs made of these for 3*s.* Increasing trade, buying shops and inventing the trademark, 'Walco', Waltons had in 1974 forty-four retail shops for all kinds of footwear and leather goods in Lancashire and Yorkshire.

Mr F. Walkley, who started with a small repair shop and remembers travelling round with sample clogs on a bicycle, has adopted the trademark 'Eliminax', and employing about twelve people at Huddersfield makes some 40,000 pairs a year. In 1972 he bought the Maude's mill at Hawksclough and there installed new lathes.

When shoes were rationed during and after the Second World War, clogs enjoyed a revival. But now the sources of supply for toe-plates and tacks are reduced to one firm. Clasps as fasteners and clog hoops for protecting the backs of clogs have gone. Clogs are laced, and moulders' clogs with quick release patent fasteners are worn in foundries and a Wellington wooden-soled boot in fish docks. They are sent to Wales for the steel industry, to Cornwall for the China Clay Works, even sometimes to Singapore. Enquiries come for clog-dancing and Morris dancing clogs. Now as expensive as boots, they may cost from over £4 to over £8.

17 Recreations

'ALL their dearest associations cling round their own hillsides', wrote Mary Jagger of the people of Honley, near Huddersfield, a sentiment applicable only to old communities. The thousands who came to settle in the West Riding brought their own habits and traditions, but they were also assimilated into a vigorous life already there. Perhaps the textile industry forged the strong continuous link. Formerly all the manifold activities of the leisure hours of the peoples revolved round the age-old seasonal events, as time went on added to by new departures such as brass band contests and carnivals in aid of local hospitals.

Those once indispensable gatherings—fairs—included the ancient events of Wibsey Fair, Bradford, Lee Gap Fair, near Morley, and Adwalton Horse Fair, near Drighlington, between Bradford and Wakefield, the first two still held in a very minor way. Some were primarily horse fairs, some marts for cattle brought down the drove roads from Scotland and for merchandise of all descriptions. Within memory Atherton or Adwalton Fair took place on the Friday of feast week, the week after Whitsuntide, when horses for farmers and dray horses showed their paces up and down the main road, and every gateway and open space held stalls selling brandysnap, nuts and sweets. Accompanied by a pleasure fair, it was and had been for centuries 'together with all other fairs' the occasion for reunions of families and friends who were regaled with vast quantities of food, usually cold beef and pickles.[1]

Sixty years ago at Haworth Tide the streets and lanes were filled with pens for sheep, some being driven down to Derbyshire for the winter, gypsies trotting horses, geese and crates of pullets from Ireland.[2] Feasts, wakes or tides, the holidays originally based on the feast days of the saints' days of churches, still signify the holiday weeks, as do rushes and thumps, derived respectively from rush

[1] Mrs M. A. Collins, Drighlington.
[2] Mr J. H. Gill, Haworth.

132. *Heckmondwike Fair, held on the green the first week-end in May, was typical of the fairs and feasts of every town. B. Powell's Swiss Mountain High Flyers on the right are worked by a steam engine, and a marionette exhibition and other side-shows are on the left (1889).*

CUSTOMS

133. *A rushcart in Oliver Lane, off Garfield Place, Marsden in the Colne valley. They were built there by the firm of Pinder's. A man is sitting astride the top, but instead of the traditional boughs a decorated triangle has been substituted. Men hold up the stangs with which it was drawn (c. 1903).*

134. The Pace Egg play being performed at Luddenden by the boys of Calder Valley High School on Good Friday, 1973.

135. Hepworth Silver Prize Band playing at Holmfirth Band Contest in Victoria Park, Holmfirth. Although they had uniforms, it was not then the custom to wear them at band contests, only at School Feasts, galas and park engagements (May 1923).

136. Morley Parrock Nook Band. One of the several comic bands which performed at fêtes, sports and so on (1907).

OUTINGS TO THE DALES

137. Choir trip from Rehoboth Chapel, Morley. The members halt for refreshment part way up Ingleborough. It was a very hot day and they did not reach the top (c. 1910).

138. Shop trip from Pratts of Bradford to Bolton Abbey in 1876. The picture includes—middle row: far left, the yard foreman, fourth from left the cabinet foreman, fourth from right the polisher foreman. Front row: second from left the designer draughtsman. Others are a carpet planner, a wood turner, an upholsterer, eleven cabinet-makers and, top centre, the errand boy who had stowed away.

bearings, always occurring at feast times, and thumps literally from people thumping each other.[1]

Those chiefly remembered today are the pleasure fairs with, in the past, travelling theatres, such as that erected at Halifax Fair, the huge Parish's Temple of Thespis, which had a lofty proscenium arch with classical columns and a pediment, an apron stage and open auditorium. In 1897 William Scruton complained that the fair at Bradford had altered for the worse with the coming of pea saloons, shooting galleries and fat women.

In the Leeds district Woodhouse and Holbeck feasts were so large that 'they were as good as Christmas week for the shopkeepers'. At Churwell Feast or 'Churrill Thump' a string of lads swinging great sods tied to cotton bands snaked in and out of the crowd. Gomersal Fair, held in March, was 'the next event to look forward to after Christmas'. Here Harry Ashington's marionettes performed such barnstormers as *Maria Martin or The Murder in the Red Barn*. At all of them were helter skelters, Shamrock and Columbine swing boats, roundabouts, cake walks, coconut shies, hoop-la and brandysnap stalls, pie and pea stalls with monkeys running up and down poles, and the bursts of gay music and the dazzling lights of the steam organs.

Rush bearing, when fresh rushes were strewn on the earth floors of churches at the time of feasts, developed in the eighteenth and nineteenth centuries into an elaborate ceremonial of the building of rushcarts in Cheshire, Lancashire, and the south-westernmost corner of the West Riding. Originating in rivalry between villages, they consisted of pyramids of bolts of rushes skilfully built up in the manner of thatching on a cart, then hung with sheets on which were fixed flowers, paper rosettes, ribbons, tinsel, even silverware. They were topped by boughs astride of which sat one or two men. These extraordinarily decorated vehicles, at times up to seven or eight of them, were drawn to churches by men holding stangs attached to the cart, accompanied by musicians, and sometimes Morris dancers.[2]

How far the custom penetrated into Yorkshire is not easy to ascertain. They were certainly made for Almondbury and Brighouse Rushes and in the Holme valley.[3] At Uppermill, Saddleworth, the ceremony continued to about 1890, and

[1] *The English Dialect Dictionary*, vol. VI, 1905, ed. Joseph Wright.

[2] A. Burton, *Rush-Bearing*, 1891; Ammon Wrigley, *Annals of Saddleworth*, 1905; 'Rush Carts of the north-west of England', Alex Helm, *Folk Life*. vol. VIII, p. 20, 1970.

[3] A. Easther, *A Glossary of the Dialect of Almondbury and Huddersfield*, 1883; Horsfall Turner, 'Brighouse Feast', *Leeds Mercury Supplement Local Notes and Queries*, May 1889–Sept. 1890; H. J. Moorhouse, *History and Topography of the Parish of Kirkburton*, 1861.

at Marsden over the hills in the Colne valley the last was built in 1903 (*see plate* 133). Having lost all meaning the whole procedure deteriorated and faded away. In recent years a rushcart has been made for the Saddleworth Festival.

The Pace Egg play, performed every Good Friday in the neighbourhood since 1949 by the senior boys of the Calder Valley High School, enacts a revival of a version of a play deriving from age-old celebrations of the renewal of life with its roots in antiquity. Although the words and characters are now an accretion and a jumble of folk memory, they none the less illustrate renewal, and listening to it stirs deep memories. The play was once performed all over England, and in Yorkshire a text of the words then extant was printed in Otley in 1840. It owes its revival in Calderdale to H. W. Harwood and F. H. Marsden, who collected the words and details of costume from old people, resulting in the boys of Midgley school playing it in the 1930s.

The characters are the Fool, St George, Bold Slasher, the Doctor, the Black Prince of Paradine, the King of Egypt, Hector, and Toss Pot, of whom five carry swords and are attired in brightly coloured clothes and exuberantly conceived headgear (*see plate* 134). The play begins with the Fool ringing a bell, walking round and exhorting the crowd to remember that ''tis Pace-Egging time', and the plot turns on the exploits of St George who wounds Slasher, kills the Black Prince and wounds Hector, all of whom are revived. The verse, remembered elsewhere in Yorkshire,

> Here come I Little Devil Dout
> If you don't give me money
> I'll sweep you all out

is not part of the Midgley version, nor is the character of Beelzebub, found in other similar mummers' plays. Instead of him is Toss Pot who collects money (once eggs) from the audience.

As the play was forgotten, the custom turned into mumming or guising on Old Year's Night (now New Year's Eve) when boys and girls dressed up or disguised went round singing carols. Collop Monday, before the start of Lent, was an occasion for children to beg for collops, slices of raw bacon, saying 'Pray, dame, give me a collop'. A multitude of local rhymes attached themselves to November the Fifth but not the making of a guy, and on Boxing Day married children and their families came back 'to the homestead'.

It was a matter of pride for those who could afford it to go for holidays in feast weeks to Blackpool, Morecambe or Scarborough. Morecambe at one time was known as Bradford-by-the-Sea. For the less well-off bedrooms only were booked in advance, and every item of food—joints of meat, eggs, bacon, bread, butter and so on—was packed into a tin trunk and handed to the landlady on arrival.

On the other hand by means of the then fully operative and cheap railway system marathon days' outings, often for educational purposes, were possible. For example round the turn of the century the Sowerby Bridge Flour Society and the Hebden Bridge Manufacturing Society in co-operation with the Lancashire and Yorkshire Railway Company ran annual excursions from upper Calderdale in July to Chester and Llandudno, Scarborough, Liverpool, Southport, Bridlington, Windermere, Grimsby and Cleethorpes, Lincoln, Boston and Skegness, Lancaster and Morecambe, Redcar and Saltburn. The train left the first station at 4 a.m. and was timed to start back about 6.30 or 8.55 p.m. The fare varied from 5s. 6d. to 10s. 6d., and the comprehensive descriptions in the handbills listed the points of interest, the walks, brake drives or steamer excursions.[1]

Nearer at home members of choirs, groups from shops, works or mills set off for the day to the Yorkshire dales to see the Strid on the river Wharfe, Aysgarth Falls on the river Ure, or even to climb Ingleborough (*see plate* 137). Many aimed for the Tennant Arms or the Anglers Hotel at Kilnsey (*see plate* 138). In the 1890s the proprietress of the latter, Mrs Horner, catered for the annual foremen's excursion from Hattersleys at Keighley, led by the head of the firm, Alfred Smith, on Boxing Day, 1898. Taking the train to Skipton, they then proceeded by open wagonettes to Kilnsey, and on this occasion went on to Hawkswick in Littondale. Breakfast cost 2s., 'a very good substantial dinner' 2s. 6d., cigars and a good deal of beer were consumed, and they left Skipton at 10.25 p.m.

Simpler outings on foot sometimes started with a short train or tram ride. On Whit Tuesday, 1900, a beautiful day, up to 20,000 people, some having arrived by train, cycle or wagonette, walked to Hardcastle Crags at the head of Calderdale. Huddersfield people came similarly to Marsden, and set off for the moors, to the inns, Nont Sarah's and the Isle of Skye for ham and egg teas at 1s. 3d. For a special treat Leeds families went by train to Weeton and explored Almscliffe Crag, Cockers Dale and Howley ruins, near Morley, Gildersome, and Gomersal. Shipley Glen, and Shibden Dale, near Halifax, drew people into the country, in some cases to cottages or tea gardens for tea.

Walking, although a pastime in itself, was inevitable for those who attended some of the innumerable activities—the lanternist for instance who at lectures operated the magic lantern. This, together with the cylinders of oxygen and hydrogen necessary for the limelight, was often transported by milk float. Societies, many fostered by the mechanics' institutes, ranged from 'Lit. and Phils.' with

Posters lent by Mr L. Barker, Co-operative Wholesale Society, Hebden Bridge.

their own libraries and distinguished lecturers, to naturalists'. The Heckmond-wike lecture, founded in 1761, still functions as an occasion in the calendar of the Spen valley. There are the dramatic societies, the Bradford Civic, the Halifax, and the Huddersfield Thespians and others, some with their own theatres, which as well as entertaining foster talent for the professional stage. Or take the Ovenden (near Halifax) Naturalists' Society whose annual subscription in 1944 was 2s. 6d. and who organized twenty outdoor meetings and seven indoor with subjects such as Mendelism and Microscopy. Occasionally a few of the members of these groups, the less privileged so far as education was concerned, have made important contributions to knowledge on rare subjects.

Arising from the early spade husbandry and land societies started in times of stress, grew the many allotment associations, a movement accelerated in the 1890s. We met an elderly allotment holder in Leeds, who by selling produce and bunches of flowers had in ten years saved £250, enough to buy a house which he eventually sold for £4,500. Other groups still flourishing specialize in chrysanthemums, auriculas or tulips. The development of the Leeds Paxton Society points to social change. It was founded in 1886 to exhibit chrysanthemums by professional gardeners then employed by the wealthy Leeds families, and is now supported by amateur gardeners, women as well as men, with small gardens and allotments.

Or consider the Wakefield and North of England Tulip Society whose members since the first society, with a different title, was formed at Wakefield in 1836 have always been working men supported by the better-off as patrons. At their spring show, although classes for other tulips have been introduced, the real interest lies in the different types of Old English Tulips, the Bizarres, the Roses and the Bybloemens, the species seen in Dutch flower paintings. Traditionally they were shown in salt-glazed stoneware containers made by local potteries, but as these have been broken or lost they are now exhibited individually in small beer bottles (*see plate* 142).

Indoor hobbies are different again, and here the attics of the terrace houses serve a useful function containing many likely and unlikely collections. One of the suppliers of collectors' items is Bamforths at Holmfirth, publishers of calendars, views and comic seaside postcards. The firm originated when in 1870 James Bamforth started making lantern slides to illustrate lectures, stories and songs using local people as actors posing against backcloths painted by himelf. From this cinematograph films developed, some of the first to be made in England, employing local talent in the same way, taken on location in streets, shops, banks and railway stations. When the craze for collecting picture postcards developed, sentimental cards were printed from negatives copied from the lantern slides, and

139. The children of West Lane chapel, Gomersal, in their decorated waggon at the celebrations for the Coronation of George V (1911).

140. Playing billets near Scout Road, Mytholmroyd (c. 1919).

*141. Early picture house (cinema). The Royal Electric
Theatre at Hebden Bridge (1913).*

142. Mr J. Akers judging Old English Tulips at the spring show of the North of England Tulip Society at Wakefield. Mr H. V. Calvert, secretary, is in the centre.

143. Bowls. A veterans' match, Hebden Bridge v. Mytholmroyd at Mytholmroyd.

144. Mr Maurice Westmoreland, retired miner, in his greenhouse at Rothwell.

following these Edwin Bamforth, James's son, conceived the idea of the comic card, vulgar, funny and topical, drawn by special artists. Again these are a commentary on the times, for more outré jokes than formerly are admissible nowadays.

Often comic, too, with Buster Keaton, Fatty Arbuckle and Charlie Chaplin featuring, were the early silent films, at first shown in makeshift buildings (*see plate* 141), then in newly built picture houses sometimes with frontages faintly resembling the white marble façades of Italian cathedrals. Mr H. Ambler remembers the first moving pictures coming to Queensbury, and that the apparatus was brought by tram and pushed on a wheelbarrow to the Hall of Freedom. Mr J. E. Hardy of Morley, an early cinema manager, recollects that he took the tickets, ran upstairs to tear them in two, dashed back to put through the film and played the piano in the interval. He was the first in the neighbourhood to show the early cliff-hangers featuring Pearl White.

Week by week children from the slums, paying 1*d.* each, flocked to the Saturday matinées, and although the advertisements on the safety curtain as well as the films (always breaking down) were an attraction, extra inducements were gifts of sticks of rock, an orange or a lucky packet. At Armley some used to wait for a huge woman to arrive to be swept in unseen under her voluminous skirts.

Different theatres catered for all tastes. Touring companies visited the Leeds Grand and the Bradford Alhambra where many people first saw *Peter Pan*, Sir Frank Benson and his company in Shakespeare's plays, Sir Martin Harvey and his company in *The Only Way*, seasons of Shaw plays, Gilbert and Sullivan, and the British National Opera Company conducted by Sir Thomas Beecham, as later generations see similar and different programmes performed by a new breed of artistes. One ninety-year-old lady of our acquaintance remembered that she was allowed to go and see Wilson Barrett at the Leeds Grand in *The Sign of the Cross* only because of the play's religious content. At or around Christmas most families went to the pantomime, at Leeds weighing up the reported merits of those at the Grand and the Royal. Few saw both. Mr H. Ambler at Queensbury, near Bradford, one of eight children, says that his family only afforded to send one child a year, and still remembers his two visits with delight.

Music was above all the great outlet for joyful expression developing from singing to bands, to orchestras, to musical festivals, such as that at Leeds founded in 1858. It cost nothing to sing; people clubbed together to buy scores; inns served as meeting-places as they did for many hobbies; church and chapel choirs trained by their organists acted as forcing houses, and enthusiastic audiences filled the assembly rooms, and mechanics' institutes, churches and chapels and later concert rooms of town halls. Even children knew the arias of oratorios from hearing their elders practising. On 29 September 1818, Thomas Cook of Dewsbury Mills wrote in his diary, 'At Wakefield this day at our Oratorio in the Church, the Messiah much gratifying.' Over the years *Messiah* has become associated with Christmas, and is performed annually by the many choral societies, the Halifax, the Huddersfield, the Bradford, the Holmfirth, the Leeds Philharmonic and others.

The Colne valley may be taken as a focal point of musical fervour. There were glee and madrigal societies, a string band attached to the Slaithwaite Mechanics' Institute, the Crosland Moor United Handbell Ringers, who in 1912 toured Australia and New Zealand. The Slaithwaite Philharmonic Society was founded in 1891 to form a band, as early orchestras were often called, and after struggles and poor attendances at concerts was transformed by its conductor, Arthur Armitage, into a fine orchestra continuing at the present day. There was the Longwood Philharmonic conducted by the village cobbler, Eli Brearley, which played all the Beethoven symphonies including the Choral. Although not precisely in the Colne valley but not to be omitted because it is the oldest is the Huddersfield Philharmonic orchestra which celebrated its centenary in 1971. Many professional players of one instrument and another, born in the area, have made their names elsewhere. Seven silver bands are still in being, and the Colne Valley Male Voice Choir, founded in 1922 and conducted for forty-four years by George E. Stead, has won innumerable prizes and trophies at festivals and eisteddfods including the 'Mrs Sunderland' competitions.

It was at Longwood on the north side of the Colne valley that the Sings (not to be confused with the sings connected with Sunday schools), for which the whole neighbourhood became famous, were started in 1873. They grew from small groups of friends and relations gathered together to make music in particular in the garden of Oliver Ainley, a violinist, at Longwood (*see plate* 145). When Nab End Tower was built near by and an open air theatre made, the Tower Sings began on Thump Sunday, and from these arose many others taking place annually on Sundays in different villages. To Longwood people flocked from far and wide walking or arriving in wagonettes; even famous professional singers returned home for it.[1] Choirs, bands and orchestras sang and played hymn tunes or excerpts from oratorios, and collections for charity, often hospitals, were substantial. Sings began to dwindle in the 1950s, but that at Longwood has celebrated its centenary and still continues.

As well as these, brass bands, most later to become silver bands, were everywhere being formed. In the early half of the century some such as Silsden, Saddle-

[1] Information from Mr George E. Crowther, formerly of Huddersfield.

145. *The local reading-room and the garden of the family of Oliver Ainley, seen here, were meeting-places for sing-songs which developed into the Thump Sings held at Nab End Tower, Longwood. They were the first of the Sings (c. 1880).*

146. *The Heckmondwike English Concertina Band playing on the occasion of a royal visit to Heckmondwike on 10 July 1912.*

147. Young members of the Black Dyke Mills Band in practice, with the professional conductor, Major Peter Parkes, in the band room at Black Dyke Mills, Queensbury.

worth and Cleckheaton started as reed or reed and pipe bands. There were town, village, mill, works and colliery bands which competed in local contests and at the public competitions at Belle Vue, Manchester, and the Crystal Palace. They played on every conceivable occasion from Whitsuntide walks to musical festivals, gave concerts in local parks, in town halls, and recently have taken part at the Proms. Some were disrupted and not re-formed after one or other of the two World Wars, and several were affected by the coming first of radio and then television.

In the Holme valley five bands still flourish: Hepworth, Holme, Hade Edge, Hinchliffe Mill and Honley, and an annual contest is held, as one is at Dobcross, Saddleworth, staged in different villages. Some bands are household names: Black Dyke Mills, Brighouse and Rastrick, Grimethorpe Colliery and Hammonds Sauce Works bands.

Black Dyke Mills Band, winner of world and national championships, was founded in 1835 by John Foster, himself a player of the French horn, who converted the Queenshead (later Queensbury) reed and brass band into all brass. In those days, although not obligatory now, all members had to be employees of the mill, and it used to be said that 'half came out of the machine shop and the other half out of the wool-sorters'. One man, a collier, migrated from Rotherham to Queensbury in order to work in the mill and join the band, and his son, Mr E. Keaton, followed on and played the E Flat bass in it for fifty years.

It was and is a way of life. After performances far afield bandsmen thought nothing of arriving home in the early hours of the morning, and although if very late they were allowed the day off, one is said to have reached Queensbury at 5 a.m. and to have been at work an hour later. They may at times be away for weeks, and when in 1972 they visited Canada for six months, they started by each putting down £50 and finally broke even. In the old bandroom, still used, framed photographs hang on the walls of bandmasters with the dates of their years of service and the money prizes won—Phineas Bower, a euphonium player, bandmaster for twenty years, and the famous Arthur O. Pearce, for thirty-seven—as well as the blue banners awarded to the champion band of Great Britain.

Coming on to the scene later were several concertina bands which also competed in local and national contests playing test pieces: 'La donna è mobile', Handel's Largo, waltzes and the 'Hallelujah Chorus'. Amongst them the Heckmondwike English Concertina Prize Band founded in 1902 won more prizes than any others at contests at Shrewsbury, Belle Vue, Manchester and the Crystal Palace. Fred Tyne, a miner, took a leading part, and his daughter, Mrs N. Power, who plays the concertina herself, tells us that neighbours used to sit on their doorsteps listening to practices. A tour of America had to be cancelled in 1914, and the band finished at the beginning of the Second World War.

Comic bands, too, flourishing in the early part of the century and into the 1920s, consisted of groups of men dressed up and with painted faces who made their own fantastic instruments out of cardboard and thin sheet tin incorporating tommy talkers down which they blew the tune. (The tommy talker acted on the principle of a comb and tissue paper.) They too entered contests and played at carnivals and charitable functions. The Morley Parrock Nook Band included one performer on a hobby horse with a donkey's head harking back to Morris dancers (*see plate* 136). We may picture the members of the Hunslet band, called either the Wiffum Wuffam Band or the Nanny Goat Lancers, as was usual standing up in a waggon, playing *The Death of Nelson* (composed by John Braham) and one by one falling down in turn and disappearing into the bottom of the waggon. In one of the last contests the Jungle Band at Holbeck won with this piece not because they were better musicians but 'because their conductor deed better'.

Hunting in the Pennines, especially on the hills round Halifax, the Colne valley and the Saddleworth district, has accumulated as much lore—poems, and stories of hunts and huntsmen—as in other places more generally associated with hunting. When he died, Ab o' Chit's, the Delph bakestone-maker, was buried in full hunting regalia with cartridges in his coat pockets and a gun in his coffin.

Another sport, racing pigeons, also had and has its devotees. In 1852 it was said to have become a nuisance in the Huddersfield district where 'swarms of children from six to twenty years of age gather to test the powers of their pigeons'. In the last century in the Colne valley rival fanciers arranged matches called 'Cote to Cote and Run'. They employed their own runners and threw up the pigeon at their antagonist's cote. It flew to its own cote where it was caught and put in a bag, and the runner ran with it to a halfway mark between the two cotes. The one to arrive first was the winner.[1] 'It used to be quite a gala day did that.'

Until budgerigars ousted them from favour many people kept or bred canaries, of which there is a particular Yorkshire variety. Again in *Shirley* is the description of twenty cages containing as many canaries hung above the tables at the school feast 'whose piercing song . . . amidst confusion of tongues . . . always caroled loudest'. Fred Tyne's wife, distracted by the constant trilling of her husband's canaries, once opened all the cage doors and the windows and set them free.

Sixty or so years ago arrow throwing matches were a pastime at Gomersal and in the colliery districts as were the games of piggy, billets and knur and spell, all venues for betting. The arrow, 30 inches long, was loosely attached with a length

[1] Mr Joe France, Colne valley.

of string to the finger of the contestant who ran to a mark and threw it with the string still attached.

Knur and Spell enjoyed its zenith in West and South Yorkshire in the last decades of the last century and was still played in the 1930s when it lost its appeal until revived in a minor way in the 1960s. Champion players used to be as revered as many a present-day sportsman, and crowds followed the two participants, taking bets and eagerly marking where the knur fell. It was not unknown for someone deliberately to tread a knur into the ground. At Greetland on the hills above Halifax, Mr Tom Ellis still makes *pummels*, the sticks and their heads, and speaks of the participants at knur and spell as *laikers*. Each player is followed by a *baumer*, a kind of caddy, and a knur sent farther than an opponent's is a *cut*. How old, we wonder, are these terms in the life and traditions of the West Riding?[1]

[1] F. Atkinson, 'Knur and Spell and Allied Games', *Folk Life*, 1963.

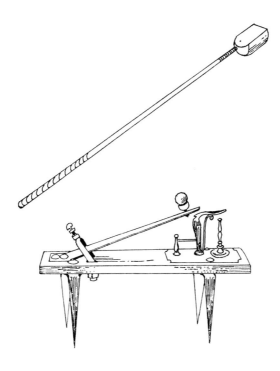

The
HEALTH OF
NATIONS

prepared by the U205 Course Team

THE OPEN UNIVERSITY
Health and Disease   U205   Book III
A Second Level Course

THE OPEN UNIVERSITY PRESS

The U205 Course Team

U205 is a course whose writing and production has been the joint effort of many hands, a 'core course team', and colleagues who have written on specific aspects of the course but have not been involved throughout; together with editors, designers, and the BBC team.

Core course team

The following people have written or commented extensively on the whole course, been involved in all phases of its production and accept collective responsibility for its overall academic and teaching content.

Steven Rose (neurobiologist; course team chair; academic editor; Book VI coordinator)

Nick Black (community physician; Book IV coordinator)

Basiro Davey (immunologist; course manager; Book V coordinator)

Alastair Gray (health economist; Book III coordinator)

Kevin McConway (statistician; Book I coordinator)

Jennie Popay (social policy analyst; Book VIII coordinator)

Jacqueline Stewart (managing editor)

Phil Strong (medical sociologist; academic editor; Book II coordinator)

Other authors

The following authors have contributed to the overall development of the course and have taken responsibility for writing specific sections of it.

Lynda Birke (ethologist; author, Book V)

Eric Bowers (parasitologist; staff tutor)

David Boswell (sociologist; author, Book II; Book VII coordinator)

Eva Chapman (psychotherapist; author, Book V)

Andrew Learmonth (geographer; course team chair 1983; author, Book III)

Rosemary Lennard (medical practitioner; author, Books IV and V)

Jim Moore (historian of science; author, Book II)

Sean Murphy (neurobiologist; author, Book VI)

Rob Ransom (developmental biologist; author, Book IV)

George Watts (historian; author, Book II)

The following people have assisted with particular aspects or parts of the course.

Sylvia Bentley (course secretary)

Steve Best (illustrator)

Sheila Constantinou (BBC production assistant)

Ann Hall (indexer)

Rachel Hardman (designer)

Mark Kesby (illustrator)

Liz Lane (editor)

Vic Lockwood (BBC producer)

Laurie Melton (librarian)

Sue Walker (editor)

Peter Wright (editor)

External consultants

Richard J. Hayes (medical statistician) Tropical Epidemiology Unit, London School of Hygiene and Tropical Medicine.

Betty R. Kirkwood (medical statistician) Tropical Epidemiology Unit, London School of Hygiene and Tropical Medicine.

Tom. F.De.C. Marshall (medical statistician) Tropical Epidemiology Unit, London School of Hygiene and Tropical Medicine.

Peter G. Smith (epidemiologist) Tropical Epidemiology Unit, London School of Hygiene and Tropical Medicine.

John P.W. Rivers (nutritionist) Department of Human Nutrition, London School of Hygiene and Tropical Medicine.

External assessors

Course assessor

Alwyn Smith President, Faculty of Community Medicine of the Royal Colleges of Physicians; Professor of Epidemiology and Social Oncology, University of Manchester.

Book III assessors

Brian Abel-Smith Professor of Social Administration, The London School of Economics and Political Science.

Michael J. Goldacre Lecturer in Clinical Medicine, Department of Community Medicine and General Practice, University of Oxford.

Christopher Robbins Director of the Coronary Prevention Group, Central Middlesex Hospital, London.

The Open University Press, Walton Hall, Milton Keynes MK7 6AA.

First published 1985. Copyright © 1985 The Open University.

Designed by the Graphic Design Group of the Open University.

Typeset and Printed by the Pindar Group of Companies, Scarborough, North Yorkshire.

ISBN 0 335 15052 7

This book forms part of an Open University course. The complete list of books in the course appears on the back cover.

For general availability of supporting material referred to in this book please write to: Open University Educational Enterprises Limited, 12 Cofferidge Close, Stony Stratford, Milton Keynes, MK11 1BY, Great Britain.

Further information on Open University courses may be obtained from the Admissions Office, The Open University, P.O. Box 48, Walton Hall, Milton Keynes, MK7 6AB.

About this book

A note for the general reader

The Health of Nations is the third of a series of books on the subject of health and disease. The book is designed so that it can be read on its own, like any other textbook, or studied as part of U205 *Health and Disease*, a second level course for Open University students. As well as the eight textbooks and a Course Reader, *Health and Disease: A Reader**, the course consists of eleven TV programmes and five audiocassettes plus various supplementary materials.

Open University students will receive an *Introduction and Guide* to the course, which sets out a study plan for the year's work. This is supplemented where appropriate in the text by more detailed directions for OU students; these study comments at the beginning of chapters are boxed for ease of reference. Also, in the text you will find instructions to refer to the Course Reader. It is quite possible to follow the argument without reading the articles referred to, although your understanding will be enriched if you do so. Major learning objectives are listed at the end of each chapter along with questions that allow students to assess how well they are achieving those objectives. The index includes key words in bold type (printed in italic in the text) which can be looked up easily as an aid to revision as the course proceeds. There is also a further reading list for those who wish to pursue certain aspects of study beyond the limits of this book.

A guide for OU students

In this book we examine contemporary and historical patterns of health and disease in the UK and the rest of the world. The emphasis of the book is on the interrelationship of epidemiology, biology and social science as descriptive and explanatory accounts of the world. We therefore draw on a number of the methods of studying health and disease discussed earlier in the course, and provide some empirical foundations for later books.

The book contains twelve chapters which can be grouped around the following broad themes. After the introductory Chapter 1, Chapters 2 to 4 provide an epidemiological and demographic survey of the contemporary world, discussing population trends and structures, birth and mortality rates and causes of death in different parts of the world, and recent trends in life expectancy. In Chapter 4 we sketch the way in which these patterns manifest themselves in the life of a Bengal village.

Chapters 5 to 7 continue the focus on the world as a whole, but switch to a social and economic perspective. In these chapters we examine the extent to which world patterns of health and disease can only be properly understood if placed within a social and economic context.

The focus then changes to one country — the United Kingdom — and we examine in more detail the nature and causes of health and disease patterns *within* a nation. In Chapter 8 we look at changes in the patterns of health and disease in Britain from the eleventh century to the present, and at the debate over the relative effects of social change and medical intervention in improving the health of the population.

The contemporary health of people in the United Kingdom is analysed in Chapter 9 in which we look at the influence of factors such as social class, gender, ethnicity, marital status and age, and at regional and other variations. In this chapter questions are also raised about what such data mean and what interpretations can be placed on them. Chapters 10 and 11 assess the extent to which these patterns of health and disease can be related to particular social features such as housing, income, occupation, and unemployment.

The book concludes (Chapter 12) with a case study of food and health. The objective of this case study is to bring together the epidemiological, historical, and social perspectives adopted elsewhere in the book, and to show as vividly as possible the many factors that influence what we eat, and equally the complex relationship between diet, nutrition and health.

The time allowed for studying Book III is four weeks or 40 hours. The following table gives a more detailed breakdown — to help you to pace your study. You need not follow it slavishly but do not allow yourself to fall behind. If you find a section of the work difficult, do what you can at this stage, and then rework the material at the end of your study of this book.

---

* Black, Nick *et al.* (eds) 1984 *Health and Disease: A Reader*, Open University Press.

Study time for Book III (total 40 hours)

Chapter	Time/hours	Course Reader	Time/hours	TV and audiocassettes	Time/hours
1	$\frac{1}{4}$			TV programme 2	
2	$2\frac{1}{2}$				$1\frac{1}{2}$
3	$1\frac{1}{2}$			Audio sequence	
4	$1\frac{1}{4}$			TV programme 3	
5	2			*Salford. Dirty Old Town*	$1\frac{1}{2}$
6	$3\frac{3}{4}$	Engels (1844)	$\frac{3}{4}$	Audio sequence	
7	2	Sen (1981)	$\frac{3}{4}$		
8	$3\frac{1}{4}$	McKeown (1976)	$\frac{3}{4}$		
9	$4\frac{1}{2}$				
10	$4\frac{1}{4}$	{ Royal College of Physicians (1978), Harrison (1983) }	$\frac{3}{4}$		
11	2				
12	$4\frac{1}{4}$				

Assessment There is a TMA (tutor-marked assignment) associated with this book; three hours have been allowed for its completion.

Final note

This book contains many diagrams, tables and statistics. All of them are discussed in some way in the text, although you may wish to refer back to relevant parts of Book I *Studying Health and Disease* when interpreting them. However, please do not feel threatened by any need to *memorise* them: they have been included primarily to illustrate and help to explain the patterns and relationships that the text is exploring, and to give you practice in interpretation. Some will also be referred back to in later parts of the course.

Acknowledgements

The course team wishes to thank the following for their advice and contributions:

Sheila Adam (community physician) North West Thames Regional Health Authority.

John Ashton (community physician) Department of Community Health, University of Liverpool.

Louise Burghes and Chris Pond Low Pay Unit, London.

David Gee (National Health and Safety Officer) General, Municipal, Boilermakers and Associated Trade Union.

Hilary Graham (Sociologist) Department of Applied Social Studies, University of Bradford.

Kate Hunt (human scientist) Department of Community Medicine and General Practice, University of Oxford.

Maggie Pearson (social scientist and SRN) Centre for Ethnic Minorities Health Studies, Field House Teaching Centre, Bradford.

Maggie Pelling (historian) Wellcome Unit for the History of Medicine, University of Oxford.

Linnie Price (sociologist) Department of Sociology, University of Essex.

Hilary Rose (sociologist) Department of Applied Social Studies, University of Bradford.

Ron Sawyer (historian) Wellcome Unit for the History of Medicine, University of Oxford.

Alex Scott-Samuel (community physician) Liverpool Health Authority.

Contents

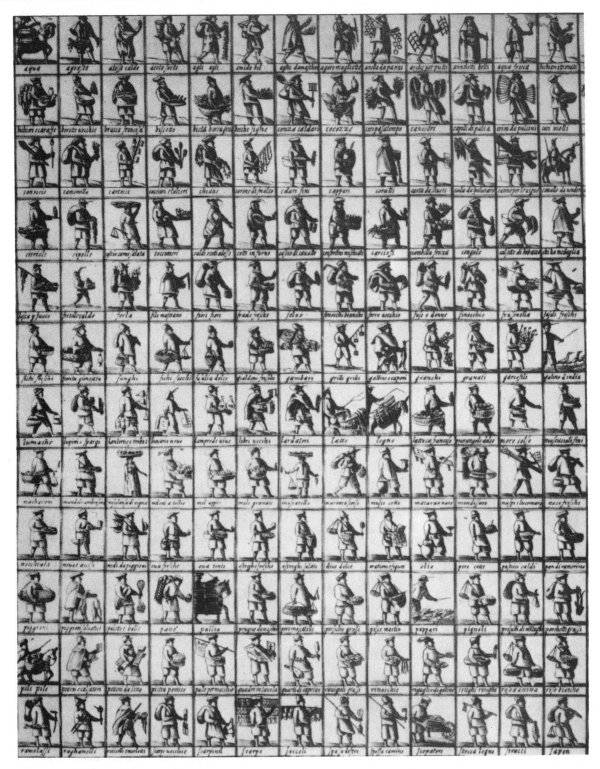

The 'full tide of human existence' on display in this extraordinary collage of the street cries of Rome. (Photo: Oscar Sario)

1

Introduction

This book is about the patterns of health and disease that exist in the United Kingdom and the rest of the world, and how they have changed over time. The first aim of the book is to describe these patterns: for example, how long people in different countries or social groups can expect to live and what they are likely to die of; or the way in which birth and mortality rates are influencing population size and demographic structures. The second aim of the book is to consider why these health and disease patterns exist, and what factors can best explain the way they have changed.

One way of attempting to explain changes in patterns of health and disease is to focus on the development of medical science, and on the people whose discoveries, skills and work helped to elevate medicine to the position of power and influence it holds today. This has been called 'triumphalist' or 'Whig' history, teeming with the names of outstanding individuals.* There is another approach, however, which emphasises the social and economic characteristics of societies, and the way in which these characteristics influence health and disease.

This is an approach in which the 'great names' of history figure hardly at all, and in which primacy is given to the conditions among much wider populations. Viewed in this way, most of the historical improvement in health in industrialised countries could be attributed to rising standards of housing, nutrition, sanitation, and general living conditions rather than to the rise of medicine.

This is the approach with which this book is largely concerned, and is present in two forms. One is the evaluation of the extent to which large-scale social and economic changes, such as the agricultural and industrial revolutions, have shaped world patterns of health and disease. The other is the assessment of the degree to which patterns of health and disease in the contemporary UK can

be related to more detailed aspects of the UK's social and economic structure, such as housing, income, occupation, or unemployment.

The book, therefore, has a number of dimensions. First, it ranges across different disciplines, drawing on material from epidemiology, history, demography, economics, social policy and geography. Second, in it we seek both to describe and to explain. Third, it demonstrates the use of a comparative method. The comparisons made are between nations, between different population groups within nations, and between different historical periods. These dimensions are regarded as complementary, but to present them all simultaneously would be highly confusing. Instead, the book has been designed gradually to build up an integrated view of health and disease patterns through a series of perspective shifts. Thus, we move from an epidemiological survey of world health and disease patterns to a social and economic analysis of world development patterns, and then onto the epidemiology and social and economic characteristics of the UK. However, at the end of the book we present a case study of nutrition and health which is intended to show how these different perspectives can be combined. In the case study we consider, for example, how our diet is affected by the way in which food is produced.

Because we shall be looking at health patterns across the world we have to use some way of grouping or classifying countries. However, there is no simple or unanimously agreed way of doing this.

☐ Note down some of the ways in which countries are frequently grouped together.
■ You might have thought of some of the following: East and West; North and South; advanced and backward; industrial and non-industrial; developed and developing; rich and poor; modern and traditional.

All such groupings tend to suffer from two big problems. First, the similarities between countries on which they are supposedly based may be less important than the differences between these same countries. Iceland and

---

* This forms an important part of *Medical Knowledge: Doubt and Certainty*, the Open University (1985) The Open University Press, (U205 *Health and Disease*, Book II).

Russia are both in the 'North', but their cultures, histories, size, politics and roles in today's world are totally different. Second, the way in which countries are grouped and the label attached to them are not neutral; these choices indicate a particular view of the world with which many might not agree. For example, to talk of the 'developing' countries is to imply that the countries referred to are undergoing progressive changes that in time will make them developed. A quite different view is implied by the word 'underdeveloped', which somehow implies that these countries are not as developed as they should be or could have been.

There is no simple solution to these difficulties. We have opted to use the terms *'Third World'* and *'industrialised' countries*, except in parts of the text where official statistics using other classifications are being discussed. The 'industrialised' countries are taken to include Europe, North America, The Soviet Union, Japan, Australia and New Zealand. These include capitalist industrialised countries (the 'First World'), and socialist industrialised countries (the 'Second World').

The 'Third World' is taken broadly to include the countries of Africa, Central and South America, Asia excluding Soviet Asia and the Pacific countries apart from Japan, Australia and New Zealand. The advantage of the term is that it is the one by which these countries tend to refer to themselves, and avoids the pejorative or value-laden content of terms such as 'backward' or 'developing'. Clearly, however, the grouping together of such a large number of countries is also fraught with difficulties. Some 'Third World' countries such as India, China, or Brazil, have substantial industrial sectors (India, for example, has a sizeable aviation industry, a space programme and is a nuclear power). Some characteristics of Third World countries are examined in Chapter 5: they tend to be poor, agricultural, rural and relatively powerless in the world economy.

Many 'Third World' countries were colonised by the now industrialised countries and have only recently ceased to be colonies. An important aim of this book is to examine the connection between these characteristics and the heavy disease burden and high mortality rates which are also characteristic of Third World populations. Chapter 2 begins that task by examining world patterns of mortality.

2
World patterns of mortality

This chapter builds on some of the basic concepts of demography introduced in Book I, *Studying Health and Disease*, particularly, the age-sex structure of a population, age distribution, age-standardised and age-specific mortality rates and the crude death rate. You may wish to refer to the explanations of these terms, using the index in Book I.

In this and the following chapter we shall be looking at the way in which levels of health and disease vary around the world, and how they have changed over time. We shall try to see if there is a general improvement in health across all societies, irrespective of their level of development, or whether 'the healthy are getting healthier and the sick are getting sicker'. We shall also be examining how disease patterns vary within countries in different population subgroups. Studying these differences will give us clues as to their causes, which in turn may help us understand why some differences persist while others are diminishing.

Measuring health

Before embarking on a comparison of the levels of health of different populations we must be quite clear what we mean by 'health' and how we are going to measure it.

☐ Think about how you would define 'health'.

■ The World Health Organization (WHO), an agency of the United Nations, in its constitution has defined *health* as 'a state of complete physical, mental and social wellbeing' (WHO, 1958, Annex 1).

It is easy to see that if we use this famous and frequently quoted definition there are going to be considerable problems in actually measuring the health of a nation or even an individual: using this definition, what proportion of your own life is 'healthy'? Most of us would have some difficulty in answering this question even though the state described seems a desirable one to strive towards.

The WHO definition has been criticised because of the difficulty of defining 'complete wellbeing' and, for practical purposes, we are forced to use other surrogate or 'proxy' measures that are closely correlated with health, in particular the use of levels of disease as a measure of the absence of health. It should be noted, however, that when the WHO defined health, they pointed out that *health* was 'not merely the absence of disease and infirmity'.

Therefore, instead of looking at world patterns of health we are forced to look at world patterns of disease. Furthermore, we shall have to use well-defined and perhaps rather rigid and limited definitions of disease — much more restricted than just the absence of health! Some aspects of disease will be neglected almost completely. This is not because they are unimportant but because reliable information is not available from enough places to allow meaningful comparisons. In general, diseases involving major physical sickness with well-defined symptoms and signs are easier to 'count' in different communities than are, for example, mental illnesses or more minor physiological disturbances.

Even if we select only certain diseases or disease states to study, there are several different measures that we might use to assess the magnitude of the disease problem in a given community. Measures that are commonly used include the disease *incidence*, *prevalence*, and *severity*.* The last is difficult to measure, sometimes being assessed by the amount of (physical) disability or discomfort caused by the disease, and at other times by the *case-fatality rate* — the proportion of all cases of the disease that die of the disease. These measures are each useful for different purposes but even these are not generally available for many countries.

The major focus of our interest is in comparing the health of populations in different countries, particularly in comparing Third World and industrialised countries, a classification of which was introduced in Chapter 1. Unfortunately, data from most Third World countries are very limited and, for many of the contrasts considered, only variation in the *mortality rates* from all causes of death combined will be examined. In doing this it must be borne in mind that there are many diseases that kill only a small proportion of the persons they afflict. Chronically disabling diseases such as polio and leprosy in Third World countries or arthritis in industrialised countries are good examples. Nevertheless, it is in general reasonable to assume that communities in which the death rate is high are those in which rates of non-fatal diseases are also high.

The quantity of disease in a community is affected by both the size and the age–sex structure** of the population. In studying the variations in disease rates between countries, neither the influence that the population structure may have on death rates nor the effect that death rates have on both population size and structure can be ignored. These, together with the birth rate, are very closely interrelated and this relationship will be explored in Chapter 3. You probably already have some idea of the large variations in mortality in different parts of the world. You do not need to have studied the statistical sources to

know that death rates are in general higher in the poorer, mainly tropical countries than in the industrialised countries in Europe and North America, or that the average length of life is correspondingly shorter. Let us now look at these variations in more detail.

Distribution of the world's population

Before looking at mortality rates, it may be helpful to begin our survey of world health and disease by reviewing how the world's population is distributed over the globe. In 1981, the total population of the world was estimated to be about 4 500 million.

Table 2.1 Estimated 1981 population by continent and region/millions

Africa	484
Western Africa	146
Eastern Africa	138
Northern Africa	112
Middle Africa	55
Southern Africa	34
America	623
Northern America	250
Tropical South America	204
Middle America (mainland)	95
Temperate South America	42
Caribbean	31
Asia	2 625
China	1 008
Japan	117
Other East Asia	65
Middle South Asia	965
Eastern South Asia	369
Western South Asia	101
Europe	485
Western Europe	153
Southern Europe	140
Eastern Europe	111
Northern Europe	82
Oceania	23
Australia and New Zealand	18
Melanesia	4
Micronesia and Polynesia	1
USSR	268
World total	4 508

(data from UN, 1981)

* These terms were discussed in, *Studying Health and Disease*, The Open University (1985), The Open University Press (U205 *Health and Disease*, Book I).
** Age–sex structure refers to the proportional distribution of the population across different age and sex groupings.

□ Before reading on, write down how you would expect this total to be divided between the continents of

Africa, America, Asia, Europe, the USSR, and the 'sixth continent' of Oceania, which includes Australia, New Zealand, and all the Pacific Islands.

■ Now compare your estimates with Table 2.1, which shows the population estimates for 1981 published by the United Nations.

Asia alone accounts for more than half the world's population. In fact over a third of all the world's people live in just two countries, China and India.

□ You saw in Chapter 1 that the Third World is usually taken to include most of Africa, the whole of South and Central America, most of Asia apart from Japan and the USSR, and Oceania apart from Australia and New Zealand. Using this classification, how many of the world's people live in the Third World?
■ Approximately 3 400 million people, or roughly 75 per cent of the world's population.

You will see in Chapter 3 that the proportion of the world's population living in these countries is going to increase during the next few decades.

In Figure 2.1 (opposite p. 10), the distribution of population is shown graphically by means of a demographic map. On this map the area of each region is proportional to the total size of its population, although the general shape of the region is retained as far as possible. The most striking feature of the map is that Asia and Europe are much larger than in conventional maps, indicating that their population densities — that is, the number of people in relation to surface area — are high, whereas Africa, America and Australia are smaller, indicating a lower population density.

Measures of mortality experience

Various measures are employed to compare the mortality experience of the populations of different countries. The *crude death rate*, *infant mortality rate* and *expectation of life at birth* are all widely used for this purpose. Table 2.2 shows estimates of these measures for a sample of countries from each continent. These countries were chosen to illustrate the range of variation in mortality both within and between continents.

Crude death rates

Consider first the crude death rates* shown in Table 2.2. Looking at the table, you will see that the highest rates among the countries listed were recorded in Malawi, Sierra Leone, Bangladesh, Bolivia and Papua New Guinea, all of which are Third World countries. The rates in these

* The crude death rate is the total number of deaths in a population in a year, expressed as a rate per 1 000 population.

Table 2.2 Estimates of crude death rate, infant mortality rate and expectation of life at birth for selected countries (most recent data)

Country	Crude death rate (per 1 000 per year)	Infant mortality rate (per 1 000 live births)	Expectation of life at birth/years males	females
Africa				
Egypt	10	110	52	54
Kenya	14	92	47	51
Sierra Leone	19	215	44	48
Malawi	25	130	41	44
America				
Bolivia	18	138	46	51
Brazil	9	82	58	61
Jamaica	6	16	63	67
USA	9	12	70	78
Asia				
Bangladesh	19	140	46	47
China	7	49	66	69
India	14	122	46	45
Japan	6	7	73	79
Sri Lanka	6	37	65	67
Europe				
England and Wales	12	12	70	76
Sweden	11	7	72	78
Yugoslavia	9	33	65	70
Oceania				
New Zealand	8	12	69	75
Papua New Guinea	16	111	50	50
USSR	10	28	64	74

(data from UN, 1981)

countries ranged from 16 to 25 per 1 000 per year. The rates in the industrialised countries were lower, generally between 7 and 12 per 1 000. You may have been surprised however, to see that the lowest rates in the table, around 6 per 1 000, were recorded in Jamaica and Sri Lanka. Neither of these is a high income country, and Sri Lanka in particular is among the poorest of the world's countries.

□ Sri Lanka has a lower crude death rate than Sweden. Do you think this necessarily means that, on average, people live longer in Sri Lanka than in Sweden?
■ Before drawing that conclusion, you would need to look at the *age distributions* of these two populations. If the age distributions differ, the use of crude death rates to compare levels of mortality is likely to be misleading. It would be preferable to calculate

age-standardised rates, or, if possible, to compare the age-specific death rates of the two countries.

A comparison of age- and sex-specific* death rates for Sri Lanka and Sweden would show that in both sexes and in almost every age group, the death rate is *higher* in Sri Lanka than in Sweden. If the population of Sri Lanka had the same age distribution as that of Sweden, the crude death rate in Sri Lanka would be 15.5 per 1 000 compared with 11.1 per 1 000 in Sweden. But because the age structure is so different, Sri Lanka's unstandardised crude death rate is *lower* than Sweden's. This comparison of *age-standardised rates* has reversed the result of the comparison of the mortality rates in the two countries.

☐ What does this information imply about the age distributions of the two countries?

■ It suggests that Sri Lanka has a younger population than Sweden. To see why, suppose we were to observe 1 000 Sri Lankans and 1 000 Swedes for one year. If more of the Swedes fell into the older age-groups, in which mortality rates are generally high, more deaths would be likely to be observed among the Swedes than among the Sri Lankans, who would be more concentrated in the younger age-groups in which mortality rates are low.

We shall be looking at the variations in the age distributions of a range of countries in Chapter 3. For the moment it is sufficient to note that these variations are substantial and that Third World countries are characterised by having populations which are, on average, considerably younger than those of industrialised countries. This is why the crude death rate is an unsatisfactory index for comparing mortality in different parts of the world.

The crude death rate is also unsatisfactory for another reason: in many countries it is estimated very inaccurately. In order to calculate the crude death rate, it is necessary to know the number of deaths occurring in a given year and the total population in the middle of that year. National censuses are conducted at regular intervals in most countries and provide a reasonable estimate of the total population (although in a small number of countries there have been no reliable censuses in recent years). Obtaining a reliable estimate of the number of deaths in a given year is much more difficult. In the majority of industrialised countries this is done by means of a national system of death registration, but in most Third World countries either such a system is lacking or else registration is very incomplete. Age-specific mortality rates are even more difficult to estimate reliably.

---

* Age-specific and sex-specific death rates refer to deaths in a particular age or sex group of a population, expressed as a rate per 1 000 people in that population group.

Infant mortality rates

You have seen that the crude death rate is an unsatisfactory index for mortality comparisons, because it is both difficult to estimate and to interpret. Another measure, the infant mortality rate (IMR), is often used as one of the key indicators of socioeconomic development. You might think it rather odd to focus on the IMR (the number of deaths in the first year of life per 1 000 live births), when we are really interested in the overall health of a community. It is, however, a very useful index of health for several reasons. First, it is relatively easy to measure. In industrialised countries it is calculated by using data on births and infant deaths collected through routine birth and death registration systems. This cannot be done in most Third World countries because of the incompleteness of registration systems, but 'indirect' methods of estimating the IMR have been developed by demographers. These methods generally rely on questioning women of reproductive age about the number of children they have had, and the number that have died. By using this information, obtained either from special surveys or from censuses, demographers have derived fairly reliable estimates of IMR for most countries.

A second strength of the infant mortality measure is that it is quite strongly correlated with adult mortality: if infant mortality is high then adult mortality is likely to be high.

Third, in countries with high mortality, policies to reduce mortality are directed principally at young children. This is because a high proportion of child deaths in such countries is due to infective and parasitic diseases that could be avoided through simple preventive or curative public health measures. When such measures are implemented, the IMR is likely to change much more dramatically than the crude death rate, making the IMR a useful indicator of the impact of health care.

☐ Return now to Table 2.2. What general conclusion can you draw about the infant mortality rates across the selected countries?

■ It is clear that, even allowing for some inaccuracy in the estimates, there are dramatic differences in the IMR between countries. An IMR in Sierra Leone of 215 per 1 000 means that more than one child in five dies before its first birthday, and this rate is over thirty times that of Sweden. The general pattern is that the IMR is below 30 in most of the industrialised countries, but considerably higher in most Third World countries. It exceeds 100 in many of the poorest countries.

It is important to note, however, that there is also substantial variation within these broad groupings, even between countries in the same region. There are also important exceptions to the general pattern, some of which will be discussed further: for example Sri Lanka has an IMR of 37 per 1 000, which is very low for a poor country.

Expectation of life

Another index of mortality is the expectation of life at birth; that is, the average length of life. This can be estimated from a 'life table' of the population. In industrialised countries, life tables are produced using age-specific mortality rates determined through censuses and death registration. Once again this approach is not possible in most Third World countries, and although indirect estimation techniques have been suggested, they are not as reliable as those used to estimate the IMR. Thus, some of the estimates of the expectation of life in Table 2.2 should be regarded as approximations only.

Like the crude death rate, the expectation of life is an index reflecting both childhood and adult mortality, but it has the advantage that its interpretation is not complicated by differences in the age structures of populations. It should be noted that this index is influenced particularly heavily by childhood mortality. To see this, consider the following simplified example:

☐ Suppose we start off with 1 000 newborn children, 20 per cent of whom die in the first 5 years of life, whereas the remaining 80 per cent survive until the age of 60 years and then die. What is the expectation of life at birth?

■ Of 1 000 newborns, 200 will die in the first 5 years, and we shall assume they live an average of 2.5 years. The remaining 800 will live exactly 60 years. So the total years of life lived by these 1 000 will be

$$(200 \times 2.5) + (800 \times 60) = 48\,500 \text{ years}$$

giving an average of $48\,500/1\,000 = 48.5$ years per person. Thus the expectation of life at birth is 48.5 years.

In the above example, the expectation of life at age 5 would be 55 years, considerably higher than the 48.5 years expectancy at birth. This increase in the expectation of life during early childhood is typical of countries with high childhood mortality. To illustrate this, Table 2.3 shows the expectation of (remaining) life at selected ages, for Bangladesh and England and Wales. Notice how in Bangladesh the expectation of life increases considerably between birth and the age of one year.

A newborn child in England and Wales can expect to live for over 70 years, about 25 years longer than its counterpart in Bangladesh. However, once childhood has been survived, the gap is much narrower. Thus an adult aged 30 years in Bangladesh can expect to live to around 65 years of age, whereas a 30 year old in England and Wales can expect to live to about 72 (30 + 42) if male and 78 (30 + 48) if female — a much smaller differential.

Turning again to Table 2.2 you can see that expectation of life at birth ranges from about 45 to 75 years in the selected countries. It is closely related to the IMR, countries with high IMRs tending to have a low expectation of life.

☐ If you wanted to examine the relationship between the IMR and expectation of life, using the information in Table 2.2, how might you display the data?

■ You could plot a scatter diagram of IMR and expectation of life.

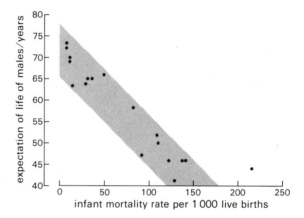

Figure 2.2 Expectation of life of males and infant mortality rates, selected countries. (Data from Table 2.2)

Figure 2.2 shows such a scatter diagram, each dot representing a country, and reveals a clear negative relationship between the IMR and expectation of life. Of course this is just what would be expected in view of the strong influence of infant mortality on expectation of life that has already been noted.

Table 2.3 Expectation of life (years) at various ages, in Bangladesh (1974) and England and Wales (1977–79)

Country	Sex	Expectation of remaining life at age					
		0	1	5	10	30	50
Bangladesh	males	45.8	53.5	54.5	50.5	35.4	20.9
	females	46.6	53.5	54.2	50.3	35.1	20.5
England and Wales	males	70.2	70.3	66.4	61.6	42.3	23.8
	females	76.4	76.3	72.4	67.5	47.9	29.1

(data from UN, 1981)

Recent changes in mortality rates

All the evidence considered so far leads to the same conclusion: mortality rates vary greatly between different parts of the world. As noted earlier, however, we are also interested in finding out whether these differences are becoming greater or smaller, and to do this we have to look at trends over time in these mortality rates. For the reasons discussed above, the infant mortality rate is a particularly useful measure for this purpose. Table 2.4 shows changes in infant mortality rates between 1950 and 1980 for selected countries. Note that the IMR is shown as an average of five-year periods. This removes some of the year-to-year fluctuations which are inevitable in such statistics.

Table 2.4 Changes in estimated infant mortality rate between 1950 and 1980 for selected countries

	Infant mortality rate (per thousand live births)		
	1950–55	1965–70	1975–80
Africa			
Egypt	183	140	110
Kenya	163	118	92
Sierra Leone	239	229	215
America			
Bolivia	176	158	138
Brazil	138	102	82
Cuba	85	48	22
Jamaica	85	47	30
USA	28	22	14
Asia			
Bangladesh	180	150	140
China	144	75	49
India	190	145	129
Japan	51	16	9
Saudi Arabia	220	154	121
Sri Lanka	91	61	48
United Arab Emirates	165	87	57
Europe			
Sweden	20	12	8
United Kingdom	24	19	14
Yugoslavia	129	61	35
Oceania			
New Zealand	26	18	14
Papua New Guinea	190	141	111
USSR	73	26	29

(data from UN, 1982, p. 43)

□ Describe the main features of Table 2.4.

■ The IMRs have decreased steadily between 1950

and 1980 for all countries except the USSR, where they appear to have increased slightly since 1965–70. The rates of decline in the countries are, however, very different. For example the IMRs of Sierra Leone and Saudi Arabia were similar in 1950–55, but by 1975–80 that of Saudi Arabia was only just over half that of Sierra Leone.

There are two ways of comparing the changes in the infant mortality rates, which will be illustrated by contrasting the IMRs of Kenya and the United Kingdom. One method is to calculate the *absolute difference*. In 1950–55 the IMR was 163 in Kenya and 24 in the United Kingdom, an absolute difference of 139 deaths per 1 000 live births. In 1975–80 this difference was 78 (92 − 14).

An alternative, and perhaps more appropriate measure is to assess the *relative risk* of an infant dying by expressing the two IMRs in the form of a *ratio*. In 1950–55 the ratio of the IMR in Kenya to that in the United Kingdom was 163 divided by 24, which equals a ratio of 6.8:1. That is, the IMR was 6.8 times higher in Kenya than in the United Kingdom. This can be compared with 1975–80, when the ratio was 6.6:1 (92/14). Although the IMRs in both countries had dropped considerably between 1950–55 and 1975–80, the *relative risk* of an infant dying stayed fairly constant.

Of particular interest is whether the differential between Third World and industrialised countries is decreasing or increasing. Figure 2.3 shows the changes in both the absolute and the relative difference between five countries and the United Kingdom. In absolute terms, the difference between the IMRs for the five selected countries and that of the United Kingdom has decreased for each country. A different picture emerges, however, from a comparison of the relative differences. There is considerable variation from country to country. For example, in 1950–55 a baby born in Bangladesh was 7.5 times more likely to die before its first birthday than one born in the United Kingdom. This difference decreased to 6.8 times in 1955–60 but has since been increasing and in 1975–80 reached 10.0. Thus in Bangladesh there was a period of relative improvement followed by a relative deterioration. In Sierra Leone the relative risk of infant mortality has increased steadily over the period while that for Brazil and Kenya remained constant and that for Jamaica has decreased steadily.

In summary, although the infant mortality rate has been steadily decreasing in almost all Third World countries, in many it has fallen at a much slower rate than in the industrialised countries; thus the relative difference has increased. Even in 50 years time the projected rates for Third World countries are predicted to be considerably higher than those currently experienced in industrialised countries.

So far you have seen that there are very substantial

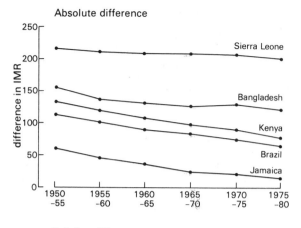

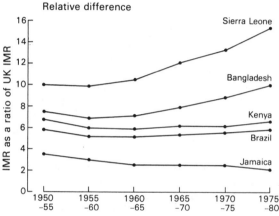

Figure 2.3 Absolute and relative differences in IMR in selected countries compared to the UK rate, 1950–1980. (Data from Table 2.2)

differences in mortality between the Third World and industrialised countries which do not appear to be decreasing in relative terms. However, there is also considerable variation within each of these groups, and some interesting exceptions to the general pattern have been noted, such as the very low mortality rate in Sri Lanka. Indeed, the Sri Lankan statistics are an excellent example of the need to avoid simplistic generalisations about health patterns, and later in the book we will briefly consider why Sri Lanka is so different from, for example, Brazil.

However, just as average statistics for groups of countries can disguise variations between countries, so mortality statistics for a country as a whole fail to tell us anything about variations that might exist *within* countries. Within Third World countries, mortality rates are strongly influenced by age, gender, place of residence, and socioeconomic status. (And, as Chapter 9 will show, the same factors are also important influences on mortality rates in an industrialised country such as the United Kingdom.)

Variations in mortality within Third World countries

You have already seen that mortality rates vary dramatically with age. This is one reason why crude death rates are so difficult to interpret. There are other factors that must also be taken into account in trying to explain the variations in mortality within Third World countries, such as gender, place of residence, socioeconomic status, and family structure.

Age

Unfortunately it is difficult to look in detail at the variation of mortality with age in many Third World countries, as reliable data are generally not available. Figure 2.4, however, brings out the main points. It shows the published age-specific mortality rates for men in Egypt compared with those in England and Wales. In both countries the mortality rate is relatively high in the first year of life, then falls to low levels which are maintained from around 5 up to 40 years of age. Mortality then begins to rise steeply, reaching high levels in those aged 70 years and over.

☐ What are the main differences between the two age-specific mortality curves?

■ The most important differences are that the rate in the first year of life is much higher in Egypt than in England and Wales, and that mortality in Egypt is still relatively high in the 1–4 year age group, falling to its lowest level only after the age of 5 years. At older ages,

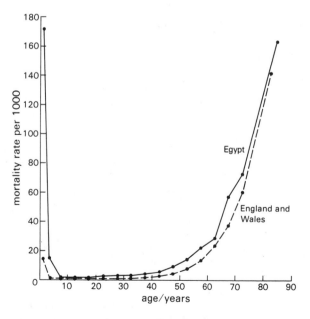

Figure 2.4 Age-specific mortality rates of males. Egypt (1976) and England and Wales (1979). (Data from UN, 1981)

the mortality rate is consistently higher in Egypt than in England and Wales, but proportionally the difference is smaller.

This 'U-shaped' curve for Egypt is typical of Third World countries, although the actual mortality levels vary considerably, as we have already seen.

Gender

□ Look back again at Table 2.2 in which the expectation of life is shown separately for men and women in different countries. Do men or women tend to live longer?

■ The expectation of life at birth is greater for females than for males in 17 out of the 19 countries in the table.

□ However, the difference between the sexes is not uniform. See if you can find any pattern in the figures shown in Table 2.2.

■ In the industrialised countries, the expectation of life is consistently higher for females by between 5 and 10 years. The differences in Third World countries are generally smaller, and in India and Papua New Guinea, males actually have a slightly greater expectation of life than females, according to the published data.

The data from industrialised countries have been taken by some to imply that, given favourable living conditions and health care, women have a 'natural' biological advantage in terms of longevity. If this interpretation is correct, the smaller differences between the sexes in some Third World countries suggest that women there are at some special disadvantage. Childbirth is one important factor. In Third World countries, women tend to experience more pregnancies than their counterparts in industrialised countries, and the risk associated with each pregnancy is considerably higher. Many of the deaths of females aged 15–49 in Third World countries are due to complications of pregnancy. In addition women may be disadvantaged by their position in society. For example a recent study in Pakistan showed that boys are more likely than girls to be taken to a clinic or hospital when ill. Of course, gender differences in access to health care, in occupational stress, in nutrition and so on, will vary substantially in different societies and cultures. However, as countries become more 'developed', the general pattern is of an increasing female advantage or male disadvantage in life expectancy. This suggests that gender roles in societies at different levels of development require closer examination. Later chapters of this book will return to this issue.

Place of residence

Though few Third World countries publish mortality data classified by place of residence, for a small number of low-income and middle-income countries there are data available on the mortality rates for urban and for rural areas.

□ Can you think of any reasons why these data should be interpreted cautiously?

■ There are several reasons. First, definitions of 'rural' and 'urban' vary from place to place. (You might like to think how you would define them. How large would a town have to be before it would be regarded as urban? What would you do about an area comprising a city surrounded by a large rural area?) Second, where rates are calculated using a death registration system, registration will often be more complete in urban than in rural areas, so in some instances the rural rates may be artificially low. Third, in some countries rural dwellers may travel to the nearest urban area to seek hospital treatment for their illness. If any die in hospital, their deaths may artificially inflate the death rate for urban areas. (This would depend on whether care is taken to record the place of *usual* residence on the death register.) Finally, it might well be that those people migrating from rural to urban areas tend to be the healthiest members of the rural population, and those staying behind are the least healthy. In this instance, the death rates for urban areas may be held down and those for rural areas pushed up.

Table 2.5 contains data on rural and urban mortality rates for a sample of countries. It is often assumed that Malawi and India are typical of the Third World, with higher mortality rates in the rural areas. There are many reasons why this might be expected. People in urban areas generally have advantages that include higher incomes, better educational opportunities and greater access to preventive and curative health services. On the other hand, some features of urban living may lead to increased mortality. Accidents and violence are often more common in urban settlements, and overcrowding may enhance the transmission of infectious diseases. In some countries, people

Table 2.5 Mortality rates classified by rural and urban residence for selected countries

Country	Year	Infant mortality rate		Crude death rate	
		rural	urban	rural	urban
Egypt	1978	64.9	85.7	11.0	9.7
El Salvador	1980	38.4	47.0	6.4	11.0
India	1978	—	—	15.3	9.3
Malawi	1977	135.1	71.0	26.3	10.6
Malaysia	1979	29.2	19.1	—	—
Sri Lanka	1978	33.8	40.7	—	—

(data from UN, 1981)

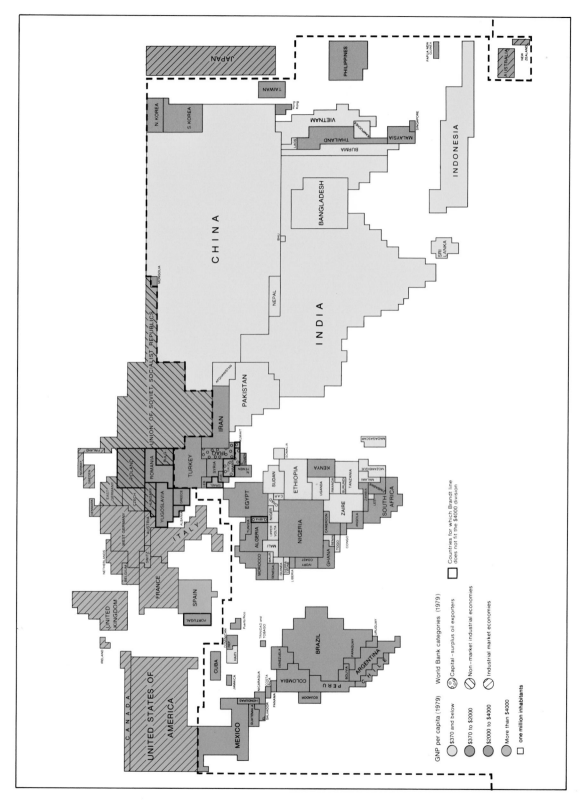

Figure 2.1 A demographic map of the world, showing size of country based on population size and Brandt's 'North-South' divide. (The Open University, 1982, p.14)

living in the slums or 'shanty towns' of the cities may be in a much worse position than peasant farmers in the countryside. The importance of all these factors will vary from country to country, and Table 2.5 may well reflect real differences in urban or rural living which do influence mortality rates.

Socioeconomic status

Social class, defined by occupation, has an important influence on patterns of health and disease, but there are many problems involved in defining, measuring and using class when analysing data*. In Third World countries, class or other socioeconomic characteristics undoubtedly have a central influence on patterns of health and disease; however, they also present some additional problems of analysis.

☐ Why might Third World countries present special problems in using such a classification?

■ There is, of course, the general problem of the availability of data that has been raised several times already in this chapter. There may be no reliable death registration system, and incomplete coverage of the population by censuses. A more fundamental problem, however, is that the whole concept of occupational-class measurement has been devised to suit industrialised countries, that is, most of these occupations and work patterns do not exist in most Third World countries. In consequence, caution is required in transferring class measures to Third World countries.

In fact, the emergence of particular forms of class stratification is an important characteristic of societies at different stages of development, and will be discussed in more detail in Chapter 6.

Bearing this in mind, what can nevertheless be said about variations in mortality rates according to socioeconomic status in the Third World? The most reliable data relate to infant and child mortality rates, and are based on the sorts of indirect estimation techniques discussed earlier in the chapter. The studies we shall examine focus on Latin American countries, and attempt to relate child mortality to 'social class' as measured by the occupation of the child's father.

Table 2.6 presents data on child mortality rates in Costa Rica, classified by the father's occupation. The social-class groups used by the researcher may not be familiar to you. Broadly, 'high and middle bourgeoisie' includes farm owners, industrial proprietors, higher executives and

Table 2.6 Probability of dying between birth and two years of age by social class, Costa Rica, 1968–1969

'Social class'	Number of deaths per 1 000 births
high and middle bourgeoisie	20
middle class	39
proletariat	80
agricultural workers	99
average	80

(data from Behm, 1979, Table 13, p. 160)

managers. 'Middle class' includes other salaried employees, technicians, teachers, and so on. The distinction between the 'proletariat' and 'agricultural workers' is that the former mainly includes wage-earning workers and labourers in manufacturing and service industries, whereas the latter are mainly small farmers and farmworkers.

☐ How might this distinction be related to place of residence, as discussed earlier in the chapter?

■ It is likely that the distinction will be in part between the rural and urban populations, as most manufacturing activity is likely to be concentrated in towns.

☐ In Table 2.6, how did the risk of death in Costa Rica vary with social class?

■ There was a dramatic relationship between mortality and social class. The risk of death in the first two years of life increased steeply from 20 per 1 000 (one child in 50) among the 'bourgeoisie', to almost 100 per 1 000 (one child in 10) among 'agricultural workers'. Mortality rates in the 'middle class' were approximately twice as high as among the 'bourgeoisie', and among the 'proletariat' they were four times as high.

The same researcher has produced data on infant mortality in Chile, and this is shown in Table 2.7.

Table 2.7 Infant mortality rate and father's occupation, Chile, 1972–1973 (per 1 000 births)

| | Father's occupation | |
	white-collar worker	blue-collar worker
neonatal	17	26
post-neonatal	13	41
infant mortality	30	67

(data from Behm, 1979, Table 11, p. 158)

Again the social-class grouping is based on the occupation of the child's father, but the classification is simply one of two groups: white-collar (non-manual) and

* Book I, *Studying Health and Disease* Chapter 10.

blue-collar (manual). The IMR among children of white-collar workers was 30, but among the children of blue-collar workers it was 67, more than twice as high.

☐ Was the excess mortality in the blue-collar group due chiefly to extra deaths in the neonatal period (the first month of life) or the post-neonatal period (the next 11 months of life)?

■ Most of the excess was due to the large number of post-neonatal deaths in the blue-collar group. The post-neonatal mortality rate was over three times larger in this group than in the white-collar group.

In Chapter 3 we shall be examining the causes of death in Third World countries in more detail, but a brief look at the causes of death of these Chilean children shows that most of the excess deaths were caused by infectious diseases, acute respiratory diseases and malnutrition, almost all of which could have been prevented by improvements in social conditions.

A basic difficulty in studying socioeconomic factors associated with mortality in Third World countries is that income, education, housing, sanitation and access to health care may all be highly correlated. Numerous studies have shown, for example, that childhood mortality is associated with the education of the mother or father. It is likely that higher levels of parental education are linked to occupations with higher incomes and hence better social conditions, making it difficult to assess the separate contribution of each of these factors to childhood mortality. Nevertheless, some Latin American studies have shown that the relationship between mortality and mother's education *remains* strong, even after allowing for the effect of income.

Family structure

Family structure is another factor that appears to be associated with childhood mortality, and the spacing of births seems to be particularly important. Short intervals between births can lead to increased child mortality for several reasons. First, a rapid succession of pregnancies puts pressure on the mother's health. This can lead to

babies with low birth weights, and these are known to be at higher risk of infant death. Second, when the new baby is born, the previous child will no longer be breast-fed, and this may lead to under-nutrition, especially in countries where supplementary foods may be contaminated or inadequate. Third, there is the obvious fact that where there are several young children, it is difficult for the mother to care for all of them adequately.

Table 2.8 shows childhood mortality in three East African communities in the early 1950s. (Notice that the rates are per 100 rather than per 1 000.)

Table 2.8 Probability of children of mothers under 40 dying between birth and 5 years of age/per cent

| Community | Average birth spacing/years | | | | |
	0–1.5	1.5–2	2–2.5	2.5–3.5	3.5+
Kisii	39	42	34	36	
Msambweni	32	29		27	24
Kasulu	43	36		18	11

(data from Brass, 1981, p. 358)

☐ Was there any relationship between birth spacing and child mortality in these communities?

■ In all of these communities, short intervals between births were associated with higher child mortality.

In this chapter you have seen that the experience of health and disease of people living in Third World countries is systematically different from that of people in industrialised countries. Death rates are higher at all ages, but particularly in the first few years of life, and expectation of life is lower. This general pattern is overlaid, however, by variations between and within Third World countries, and these variations raise many intriguing questions about the origins of such patterns of health and disease. The next step, therefore, is to examine in more detail the demographic structure of populations in Third World countries, and the main causes of death and types of disease. These are the themes of the next chapter.

Objectives for Chapter 2

When you have studied this chapter you should be able to:

2.1 Discuss the advantages and disadvantages of the following three measures of mortality: crude death rate, infant mortality rate, and expectation of life at birth.

2.2 Outline the distribution of the world's population.

2.3 Describe the main differences in the mortality experiences of industrialised and Third World countries and how these differences have changed in recent years.

2.4 Describe how mortality rates in Third World countries vary with age, and differ between males and females.

2.5 Describe the association between socioeconomic status and mortality.

Questions for Chapter 2

1 (*Objective 2.1*) Why is it more useful to use the infant mortality rate rather than the crude death rate as a measure of the health status of different parts of the world?

2 (*Objective 2.2*) The land areas of the USA and Australia are approximately the same and far in excess of that of India. What does this information, alongside Figure 2.1 tell you about the relative population densities of those countries?

3 (*Objective 2.3*) Looking at Figure 2.3, what conclusions can you draw about the change in the IMR in Sierra Leone, compared to the UK, between 1950 and 1980?

4 (*Objective 2.4*) Consider Table 2.3 and answer the following:

(a) What is the gender difference in expectation of life at birth in Bangladesh and in the UK?

(b) Does the advantage of one sex over the other persist in both countries?

5 (*Objective 2.5*) Table 2.6 shows that in Costa Rica the overall risk of dying in the first two years of life (all social classes) was 80 per 1 000, but that mortality varied between the classes. What can you deduce from this about the numbers of people in the different social classes?

World patterns of disease

Neither is the population to be reckoned only by numbers (Francis Bacon, 1561–1626)

In the previous chapter it was seen that roughly 75 per cent of the world's population live in Third World countries, and that a great gulf separates their health experience from that of the populations of industrialised countries. In this chapter we explore further these differences, by comparing the *age–sex structures of populations* in Third World and industrialised countries, and then by considering variations between countries in the causes of disease and death. The crude death rate, as Chapter 2 showed, is influenced by the age structure of a population, and to remove problems associated with the comparison of crude rates it is necessary to make use of age-standardised rates. Standardisation allows us to compare mortality rates between populations, or in different subgroups of a population, after allowing for the effect of age differences in the populations or in the groups under study.

It is important to realise, however, that the age structure of a population is closely related to age-specific death rates. The age structure is entirely defined by the rate at which people enter the population through birth, or at a later age through immigration from another population, and leave the population through death or by emigration to another population. A census gives a cross-sectional 'snap-shot' of this dynamic process at one point in time.

The population pyramid
A direct and simple way of presenting a 'photograph' of the age–sex structure of a population is by means of a *population pyramid*. A population pyramid is drawn in much the same way as a histogram. In effect, it consists of two histograms, one for each sex, arranged vertically (as opposed to the usual horizontal orientation), and set back to back. The bar areas are made proportional to the population in each age–sex group.

Figure 3.1 contains population pyramids for five countries, which show strikingly the contrast in population structure between Third World and industrialised countries. The five countries are:

Brazil: undergoing rapid industrialisation and urbanisation, but still with a large underdeveloped sector.
Malawi: predominantly rural with only a small industrial/urban sector.
Sri Lanka: a poor country undergoing rapid industrialisation, with a large rural sector and relatively well-developed health and social services.
Great Britain and Sweden: fully industrialised and have been so for a long time.

For Brazil, Malawi and Sri Lanka, the pyramids are true to their name, each with a broad base, narrowing upwards so as to give a triangular picture. The most numerous age-groups are the youngest; more than half the population are aged under 20 years in Brazil, and almost half under 15 years in Malawi. Old people are relatively few in number; the percentage of the population over 64 years was 3 per cent in Brazil, and 4 per cent in Malawi and Sri Lanka.

The picture for the two European countries is quite different. In both, the most numerous age-groups are between 15 years and 34 years. The tapering-off with advancing age, seen so strikingly with Brazil and Malawi, is confined here to age 55 years and more. The percentage under 15 years is about 20 per cent, considerably lower than in the Third World countries, while that above 64 years is higher (about 15 per cent).

☐   In most Third World countries, childhood diseases demand a high proportion of the resources given to provision of the health services. Can you give two reasons for this?
■   One reason is that the incidence of diseases is high in young children, especially infections and parasitic diseases; a second reason is that a high proportion of the population are children.

This population structure has many consequences for patterns of disease and death. In Third World countries 40 to 50 per cent of the population may be aged less than 15 years of age. In this group the toll of infectious and parasitic

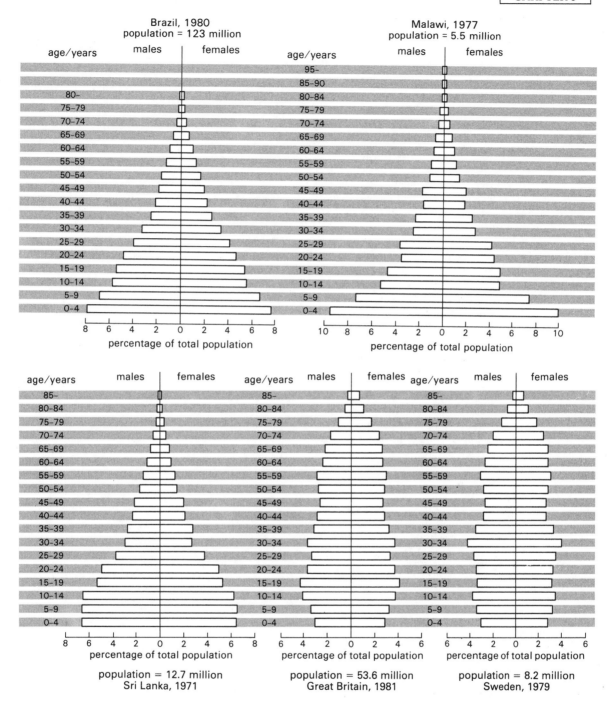

Figure 3.1 Population pyramids based on census data.

diseases is especially high, partly because the protective immunity to many diseases, which is acquired with age, has not developed. Children are thus major consumers of health services.

A population's size and structure is determined by its *past* pattern of births, deaths and migration. How do these factors interact with each other? Because we shall be thinking only in fairly general terms, we shall not be looking in detail at migration. In most, but not all, countries, migration into and out of the country has not been great in recent decades and has not had an important influence on the overall population structure. It should be noted, however, that migration has often had an important influence on differences in the population structure in different regions *within* a country.

If the birth rate of a country increases, the number of women of childbearing age will show a corresponding increase after an interval of 15 years or so, provided infant and child mortality rates have not increased at the same time. The increase in the number of women of childbearing age will, in its turn, increase the number of births still further, and the population expands as more and more children are born generation by generation. This situation can give rise to a triangular-shaped population pyramid, like those of Brazil, Malawi and Sri Lanka.

Another factor leads towards the triangular shape. If mortality rates have been high for all ages, the numbers in each age-group will tend to decrease with advancing age. For example, the broader base of the Malawi pyramid, compared with those of Sri Lanka and Brazil, suggests a higher mortality under the age of 5 years.

Generally, populations with the triangular shape have high birth rates, high mortality and substantial rates of increase in overall population size.

☐ In the population pyramids of Great Britain and Sweden, how would you interpret the low percentage of children under 5 years of age in the population?

■ They reflect a low birth rate. In fact, the larger percentages in the 5–9 and 10–14 years age groups compared to the youngest age group tell us that the numbers of births have declined over the last 10–15 years.

Another feature of the British and Swedish pyramids is the irregularity between some adjacent age groups. There is, for instance, a narrowing of the pyramid in the age interval 40–54 years. This resulted from a fall in the birth rate during the economic depression before the Second World War.

☐ In most Western countries, there was a 'baby boom' immediately after the Second World War. Can you see the effect of this in the British population pyramids?

■ This is reflected by the 'bulge' in the pyramid in the 30–34 years age-group, whose members were born in the period immediately after the war.

The irregularities in the Malawi pyramid are more difficult to interpret as in part they may reflect the difficulties in determining ages with accuracy, a problem in most Third World countries.

We have seen that a triangular pyramid is typical of the population of a Third World country. It was also typical, in the past, of the countries that are now industrialised, such as England and Wales. Figure 3.2 shows the population of the USA in 1900 and in 1970. The general resemblance of the American population structure in 1900 to, for example, that of present-day Brazil is quite striking. This has led some people to suggest that as a country

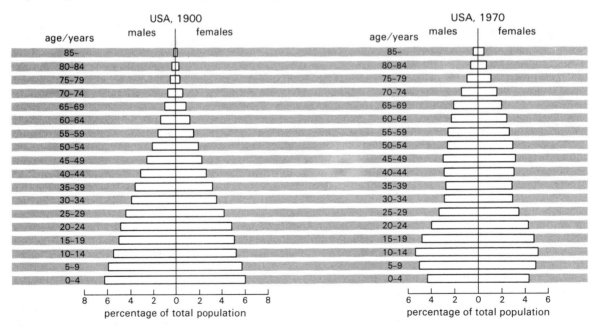

Figure 3.2 Population pyramids for USA, 1900 and 1970. (Westoff, 1974, p.114)

undergoes a transition to fully industrialised development, so the population structure also changes, and they refer to this as the 'demographic transition'. This is clearly an important concept with wide implications, and we shall return to it in Chapter 7 when we consider the process of industrialisation and development from a historical perspective.

Variations in diseases and causes of death between countries

You have seen that there are large differences in the death rates in Third World and industrialised countries, especially among children. What are the main differences in the *causes* of disease and death in the two groups of countries and what could be the reasons for these differences?

The occurrence of disease is part of a complex interaction between humans and their social and physical environment. Thus, in different environments different diseases predominate. This relationship is modified more or less successfully by social, economic and political changes that, deliberately or otherwise, affect the material conditions influencing health, and by disease-control programmes that seek to change the environment in order to reduce the burden of disease. Before we can contrast disease patterns we need to have some method of measuring the relative importance of different diseases.

☐ How might the disease patterns of different countries be compared?

■ By comparing the mortality rates for specific diseases.

There are problems, however, in comparing disease-specific mortality rates. First, there is a lack of reliable routine statistics for many Third World countries. Second, even when available, such statistics only provide information about lethal diseases, giving no indication of the morbidity (illness) and disability caused by diseases that are seldom lethal. Third, crude mortality rates for specific diseases fail to take into account the age at which a person dies. A disease that kills young adults may represent a greater social and economic burden on a country than one that causes the death of elderly people. Various modifications to mortality rates (such as calculating the years of life lost and trying to quantify the disabling effects of diseases) have therefore been used in attempts to take such problems into account and, where relevant, will be introduced in the following discussion.

The profound changes that have taken place in industrialised countries over the last century in death rates and causes of death will be discussed in some detail in Chapter 8 in the context of the United Kingdom. The most striking change has been the virtual disappearance of acute infectious diseases as major killers. In their place other diseases that were relatively unimportant in the past have become major causes of public health concern.

Some of these diseases are purely modern epidemics and their emergence has been closely related to changes in patterns of living — the epidemic of lung cancer that has followed the introduction of tobacco smoking on a widespread basis is an example of such a disease. These are the exceptions, however, and other diseases have become important not because the causes of the diseases have become more prevalent, but because the population has 'aged'. Many diseases are more common in old people, and as infectious diseases that killed children and young adults were conquered, increasing numbers of people have survived long enough to be at risk of death from the diseases of older ages, such as cancer and heart disease. Thus, for example, the *crude* death rate from cancer is much higher now than it was at the turn of the century but, if we exclude lung cancer, and compare *age-specific* rates of all other cancers combined, the differences in the rates between the two time periods are only small.

The relative importance of different diseases can be assessed by calculating for each cause the '*years of life lost*' due to death from that cause. For example, if a disease kills a person at age 50 years in a country in which they might otherwise have expected to live to 70 years, they have 'lost' 20 years of life. Thus by looking at the ages at which people die of a specific disease and their expectation of life at those ages it is possible to compute the total years of life lost by all persons dying of the disease. Diseases can then be ranked in order of importance according to the years of life that each costs the community. The pattern that emerges for Canadian males is shown in Table 3.1.

Table 3.1 Years of life lost by Canadian males between the ages of 1 and 70 years due to various groups of causes, 1967

Cause of death	percentage of total years of life lost
accidents	38.9
diseases of circulatory system	24.3
cancer	15.7
diseases of nervous system	5.2
respiratory diseases	4.2
diseases of digestive system	3.8
allergic, endocrine and blood diseases	1.8
infectious diseases	1.3
diseases of genito-urinary system	1.1
all other causes	3.7
all causes	100.00

(data from Romeder and McWhinnie, 1977, Tables 2 and 4)

Table 3.1 shows the percentage of years of life lost between the ages of 1 and 70 years. Perhaps surprisingly, accidents come out top, accounting for nearly 40 per cent of the total years of life lost. Diseases of the circulatory system (heart disease and strokes) are next, followed by cancers. Infectious diseases are near the bottom of the list.

□ Why do you think accidents have come out first when, in fact, more people die of cancer than from accidents?

■ This method of assessing disease importance gives most weight to diseases that kill at young ages and thus cause a greater loss of years of life. A person dying at the age of 1 year loses 69 years of life, whereas someone dying at 60 years loses only 10 years. Accident rates are highest in the young and thus are given greater weight than cancer deaths which usually occur at later ages.

The same pattern emerges if specific causes of death (rather than groups of causes) are considered. Motor vehicle accidents account for only 8 per cent of all deaths, but 18.2 per cent of all years of life lost, whereas coronary heart disease is responsible for 26.2 per cent of deaths and 15.1 per cent of lost years. It is notable that infectious diseases account for only about 1 per cent of all years of life lost. This is in striking contrast to the pattern in Third World countries.

As was pointed out in Chapter 2, data on death rates from all causes combined are hard to come by for many Third World countries. Data on deaths due to specific causes are even scarcer. A group in Ghana has tried to rank the disease problems in that country using methods similar to those in the Canadian example. Their methodology was not identical as they considered deaths at all ages, not just between 1 and 70 years, and they also attempted to include the effects of diseases that cause disability as well as death. Thus, for example, someone who was blinded was regarded as having lost 90 per cent of the rest of their healthy life at the age they became blind, rather than the 100 per cent that would have been lost had they died. These adjustments, however, had a relatively small effect for all but a few diseases and it would not be unreasonable to compare their data with those of the Canadian workers. Shown in Table 3.2 are the 25 diseases that were rated to be the most important causes of loss of healthy life in Ghana. Some of the causes result in deaths predominantly under the age of 1 year (these were specifically excluded from the Canadian study), including prematurity, birth injury and neonatal tetanus (lockjaw in the newborn).

□ Compare the percentage of total years of life lost in Ghana with that in Canada for the three categories:

Table 3.2 Years of healthy life lost in Ghana due to different diseases

Rank order	Disease	Percentage of total healthy life lost
1	malaria	15.4
2	prematurity	9.1
3	sickle-cell disease	6.2
4	measles	6.2
5	birth injury	6.0
6	pneumonia (child)	5.5
7	malnutrition	5.1
8	gastroenteritis	4.5
9	neonatal tetanus	3.7
10	accidents (all kinds)	2.9
11	tuberculosis	2.7
12	stroke	2.4
13	pneumonia (adult)	2.3
14	psychiatric disorders	2.2
15	neonatal respiratory disease	2.1
16	congenital malformation	1.9
17	pregnancy complications	1.6
18	cirrhosis	1.3
19	cancer	1.2
20	hypertension	1.2
21	hepatitis	1.2
22	hernia	1.1
23	schistosomiasis	1.1
24	umbilical sepsis	1.0
25	leprosy	1.0

(Ghana Health Assessment Team, 1981, Table 2)

accidents; diseases of the circulatory system (which include heart disease, strokes and hypertension); and cancer.

■ Accidents account for 2.9 per cent in Ghana and 38.9 per cent in Canada; circulatory diseases account for 3.6 per cent in Ghana and 24.3 per cent in Canada; cancers account for 1.2 per cent in Ghana and 15.7 per cent in Canada.

In contrast to the pattern of diseases in industrialised countries, *infectious diseases* are the most important category in Third World countries. Malaria is probably the most serious health problem in most parts of tropical Africa, where it has been estimated to cause over a million deaths a year. It is caused by a microorganism which invades red blood cells and it is transmitted from one person to another by certain kinds of mosquitos (*Anopheles*). Malaria used to be endemic to the United States and Europe but never represented the health problems there that it does in Africa because of less favourable environmental conditions for the transmission of the parasite. The life cycle of the malaria parasite is complex, involving passage between humans and mosquitos. Attempts to break this cycle have been successful in some parts of the world but singularly unsuccessful in most of Africa. Chapter 4 describes the impact of a malaria eradication programme in a village in India.

Sickle-cell disease is a group of genetically determined conditions (inherited rather than acquired from the environment) in which there is an abnormality in the structure of haemoglobin (the oxygen-carrying molecule in the red cells of the blood). This abnormality makes the red cells fragile and susceptible to crises in which the cells collapse and are unable to function properly. Such crises, which may be precipitated by an infection or fever, can be fatal. The most common and severe condition is sickle-cell anaemia which affects many Africans and people of African descent (about 1 in 400). However, there is also a much commoner form (1 in 10 people) of the condition (sickle-cell trait) which can only be detected by special blood tests and rarely causes any ill-effects. An interesting feature of this form is that it confers a degree of resistance to malaria. It has been assumed that the high prevalence of sickle-cell disease in African populations has come about because those with the mild form (trait) have a survival advantage in terms of resistance to malaria, compared with 'normal' people, which more than compensates for the increased risk of death among those with the serious form (sickle-cell anaemia).

It may come as a surprise to see measles so high on the list in Table 3.2. Measles is certainly not a 'tropical' disease. It is very common in the populations of industrialised countries also, where it is rarely a cause of death. Why it causes so many deaths in Africa (and other areas of the Third World) is not fully understood. Few diseases occur in isolation in children in Third World countries and it is likely that the reason that so many die of measles is that the infection hits hardest those whose defences are already weakened by malnutrition or malaria and other parasitic or infectious diseases. Another reason why measles may cause so many deaths in the Third World is that it occurs at very young ages, often before the age of one year when the body is less able to cope with such an infection. In industrialised countries, even before vaccination programmes, measles was predominantly a disease of later childhood, at least in the recent past. The probable reason for this difference is the greater contact between very young children which takes place in Third World countries, associated with the 'extended family' system. This is in contrast to the more protected and isolated environment associated with the 'nuclear family' system of industrialised countries, perhaps because contact between children does not become so widespread until school-age is reached.

Estimating the number of cases of different types of disease on a worldwide basis is a daunting task and is liable to be fraught with errors. An attempt at this ambitious undertaking for Africa, Asia and Latin America for malnutrition and the major infectious diseases is shown in Figure 3.3.

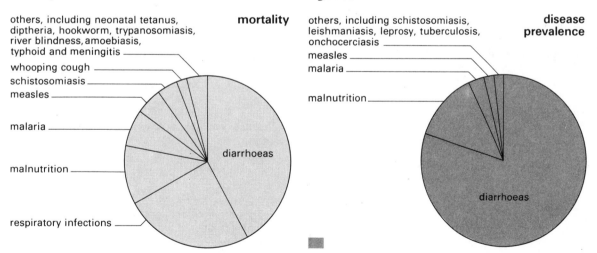

Figure 3.3 Proportions of mortality and disease prevalence* of the major infectious diseases and malnutrition of Africa, Asia and Latin America, 1977–8**

* Disease prevalence excludes respiratory diseases for which no reliable estimates exist.

** Based on estimates from the World Health Organisation and its Special Programme for Research and Training in Tropical Diseases, confirmed or modified by extrapolations from published epidemiological studies performed in well-defined populations. (Walsh and Warren, 1979, Table 1)

The most striking feature of these data is the importance of diarrhoeal diseases. There were about 500 million episodes of diarrhoea in the children of Asia, Africa and Latin America in 1975, causing 5–18 million deaths. These episodes and deaths resulted from consumption of contaminated supplies of water and food, inadequate nutrition, and dehydration. Children who are poorly nourished get diarrhoea and die from it far more often than those who are well nourished. Yet diarrhoea itself can be part of the cause of malnutrition. And if malnutrition already exists, diarrhoea rapidly makes it worse. This results in a vicious circle, in which each makes the other worse. It is important to realise that the greatest disease burden of Third World countries results from inadequate nutrition and a lack of a clean water supply, rather than from the many exotic sounding 'tropical' diseases, some of which are mentioned in Figure 3.3.

The impact of the lack of adequate sanitation and clean water can also be seen in the high prevalence of worm infestations. About a billion people have worms. Studies in Sri Lanka, Bangladesh and Venezuela found that over 90 per cent of six-year-old children were affected, the commonest being hookworm and roundworm (ascariasis). Just as most deaths from diarrhoeal disease are *not* due to exclusively 'tropical' conditions, so the same is true for respiratory infections. Respiratory disease includes pneumonia, bronchitis, whooping cough, influenza, measles, T.B. and diphtheria — in other words, the same range of conditions that occurs in industrialised countries. The difference between Third World and industrialised countries is not so much in the types of diseases that occur, but in the effect and impact they have.

Changes in mortality in Third World countries

Despite the high mortality rates experienced by Third World countries, there has been some improvement in the health of the people of those countries. Much of the fall in mortality rates that has occurred over the last few decades has been due to a decline in the number of deaths from malaria, smallpox, tuberculosis and measles. For example, Figure 3.4 shows the decline in infant mortality rates over a twenty-year period for five Third World countries.

☐ From your general knowledge, can you suggest what may have been responsible for declines in malaria and smallpox in Third World countries?

■ Much of the fall in malaria was due to mosquito control, and the decline in smallpox was partly due to vaccination programmes.

It is unwise, however, to apply these general conclusions to specific countries. There is no guarantee that what works for one country will work for another, in fact there are many examples to the contrary. It is considered that the

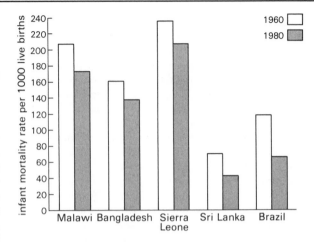

Figure 3.4 Changing infant mortality in five Third World countries. (Data from World Bank, 1982, Table 21)

malaria eradication programme was responsible in part for the rapid fall in mortality in Sri Lanka from 1945–1950, whereas a similar programme in Guatemala appeared to have little effect. In the Solomon Islands a substantial drop in mortality followed malaria eradication in the high mortality areas but there was little change in the moderate mortality areas.

Apart from the decline of the airborne and insect-borne conditions mentioned above, about one third of the fall in mortality between 1930 and 1970 is thought to have resulted from a decline in deaths from the respiratory diseases — influenza, pneumonia, and bronchitis. A smaller fall was due to a reduction in deaths from diarrhoea. In other words, the commonest cause of illness and death in Third World countries remains one of the most intractable, despite widespread recognition of the simple preventative measures necessary — improvements in sanitation and a clean water supply.

Differences between and within Third World countries

As is emphasised elsewhere in this chapter, the Third World is a very heterogeneous group of countries, and this is particularly clear with respect to patterns of disease. This results in part from the wide variety of physical environments encountered throughout the Third World. An example of how the distribution of a disease is affected by the environment has already been mentioned, that of malaria, which needs certain kinds of mosquitos, which in turn require particular conditions for their survival. Another example is schistosomiasis (also known as bilharzia), common in many tropical countries. It is a disease caused by a worm infestation of the veins of the bladder or the intestines. Eggs of the worm are excreted in urine or faeces. For the disease to be transmitted from one person to another, the parasite must first go through an 'intermediate host' — in this instance certain kinds of water snails — where parasites develop and emerge in a form that can reinfect people. Thus there must be faecal or urinary contamination of water in which people bathe, and that water must also contain certain kinds of snail. This cycle is illustrated in Figure 3.5.

If the appropriate mosquitos or snails are not present then malaria and schistosomiasis, respectively, simply cannot persist. Thus certain diseases are confined essentially to a few areas in which all elements exist for the life cycle of the parasites to continue. For example, Chagas disease, a serious parasitic infestation which often involves the muscles of the heart, is confined to South America, and sleeping sickness, transmitted by the tsetse fly, does not occur outside Africa.

Even within the same continent or country the disease patterns may be very different from one part to another. Urban dwellers may be exposed to quite different risks to those living outside towns. People living at low altitude may be exposed to diseases transmitted by mosquitos, whereas those at higher altitudes escape because mosquitos cannot exist there. Those living in close proximity to swamps and water are exposed to diseases that do not occur or are rare in drier areas.

Manuel Zuniga, a Chilean epidemiologist, examined variations in the causes of death in twenty Latin American countries in 1975. What he found was an enormous range in the mortality rates between these countries, the expectation of life at birth ranging from 48 years to 67 years. He further examined the percentage of deaths in each

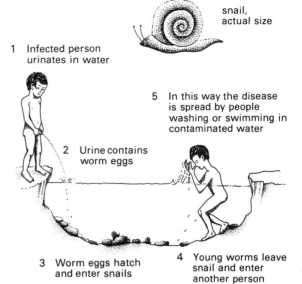

Figure 3.5 The life cycle of blood flukes (schistosomiasis, bilharzia). (Werner, 1979)

country that were due to infective or parasitic conditions. This ranged from 6.6 per cent to over 60 per cent. In this Latin American study, countries with high mortality rates (and in which a high proportion of deaths were due to infective and parasitic diseases) were those in which literacy rates were lowest and which were also least urbanised. This study again illustrates the great diversity of health problems in different Third World countries and warns of the dangers of making generalisations that are too sweeping.

Objectives for Chapter 3

When you have studied this chapter, you should be able to:

3.1 Demonstrate an understanding of how a population pyramid depicts the age–sex structure of a population, and how population structures tend to differ systematically between industrialised and Third World countries.

3.2 Describe the important causes of death in Third World and industrialised countries, and the main characteristics of these diseases.

3.3 Describe the use of the 'years of life lost' calculation as a means of comparing the relative importance of different causes of death in a country.

3.4 Describe the changes in mortality that have occurred over recent years among Third World populations, and the factors to which these changes might be attributed.

Questions for Chapter 3

1 (*Objective 3.2*) To what extent are the patterns of mortality in Third World countries a result of diseases peculiar to these countries?

2 (*Objective 3.3*) Given what has been said about cause of death in Third World and industrialised countries, why might the 'years of life lost' measure be a good way of emphasising differences in these patterns?

3 (*Objective 3.4*) To what extent has the reduction in mortality in Third World countries been limited by a lack of knowledge about effective interventions?

4 (overpage)

4 (*Objective 3.1*) Figure 3.6 shows population pyramids for two countries in the late 1960s.

(i) What are their main features, and what kind of societies do they suggest to you?

(ii) What difference might you expect to find in comparing crude death rates and age-standardised death rates for these two populations?

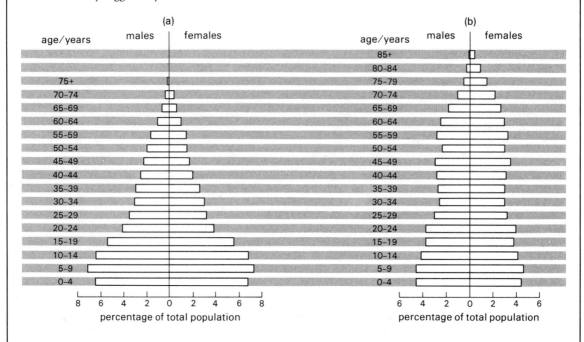

Figure 3.6 Population pyramids for two countries in the late 1960s. (The Open University, 1974, Figures 10a, 10b, p.29)

4
Village life in West Bengal

In this chapter we turn from considering comparisons between industrialised and Third World countries, to a consideration of health and disease in a village in West Bengal, India. Though India is still a Third World country in many ways, it is a peculiar one in that it also has areas of industrial development comparable to parts of the industrialised world. Data for some aspects of population, health and disease are better than in many Third World countries, so that although this chapter will use comparatively few numerical data there is a background of quantitative data underlying the discussion.

The subject of this case study, 'Kalipura', is a fictional village based on several real villages in the area. We shall be looking at some of the changes in health and social and economic conditions between 1950 and 1980.

The great snag of case studies is the temptation to overgeneralise from them, and this is obviously very great indeed when only a single case study is included. A similar description of a village in Maharashtra or in Kerala (other states in India) would differ widely from this study, and as much again from accounts of a community in Zaire, or Brazil, or Papua-New Guinea.

Kalipura community in 1950

Kalipura is situated in West Bengal in India, some 30 miles north-west of Calcutta in the western part of the Ganga (Ganges)–Brahmaputra delta (Figure 4.1 opposite p. 26). This part of the delta is sometimes called the 'dying delta', because the distributaries of the River Hooghly (a branch of the River Ganga) are less active across the surface, less liable to flood and thereby deposit fertile silt, than in the eastern delta.

The stagnation of these river channels is reflected in the complex of diseases and the general malnutrition and poor physique of the inhabitants. Stagnant water can be seen everywhere: behind carelessly constructed rail and road embankments; in ponds behind small dams across the water courses used for local irrigation in the cool season; and in the water tanks — here used mainly for ceremonial and washing purposes and often rather neglected.

Much disease is related in some way to these innumerable pools of more or less stagnant water. They all give harbourage to the mosquito larvae, and malaria is always present. Poor sanitation also contributes to other diseases, such as typhoid and intestinal diseases. Although few except the poorly regarded Hindu widow drink habitually from tank or stream, ritual cleanliness demands bathing, which invariably includes washing out the mouth, in such polluted places. Sanitary practices are extremely

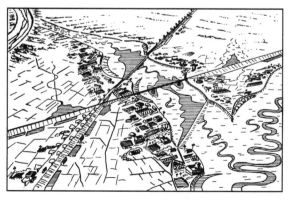

Figure 4.2 West Bengal (Learmonth, 1955, p.154, courtesy of A. Learmonth)

primitive, and the search for privacy often increases the chance of pollution.

Overcrowded housing also intensifies the impact of diseases present, which include tuberculosis, polio, smallpox, leprosy and cholera — Kalipura lies on the fringes of one of the world's endemic homes of cholera, and a notorious focus lies only 60 miles to the south east. The population at this time is stagnant: there is a tragic combination of a high birth rate and a high infant mortality rate.

Seventy per cent of the inhabitants cultivate their own land, usually as rice-growing and rice-eating subsistence farmers. As the land is in a 'dying delta', the fertile silt is no longer renewed and the soil is becoming exhausted. The stagnant pools encourage growth of the water hyacinth — the 'lilac devil' — which spreads into the paddy-fields and reduces the rice yields.

The people of Kalipura are also economically dependent on the great industrial conurbation of Calcutta–Hooghlyside, some 30 miles away, in two ways. First, some of the inhabitants travel daily to the city to work, or migrate there for shorter or longer periods, and send some of their earnings home to the village. And second, the great market there attracts much of the fruit, vegetables, milk and eggs from this countryside; this is a tragic instance of the economic influence of a great city, for all of these foods of high nutritive value are required just as much in the villages as in the city.

Figure 4.3 shows a good house in this area: the building materials are bamboo and thatch, though cement is beginning to be used. The courtyard may be covered by overhead trellis work on which a climbing plant (often a pumpkin) is grown. Near the house is the water tank and beside it the date palms to be tapped for syrup or toddy.

Figure 4.3 A house in West Bengal. (Learmonth, 1955, p.155, after A. Geddes, 1923; courtesy of A. Learmonth)

The village community in 1980

Let us look at the change in the fortunes of Kalipura since the earlier vignette based on data from just after Independence in 1947. The first post-Independence generation has seen many changes, good and bad.

First, some externals. Kalipura is largely tiled rather than thatched now. This is a sign of money coming into the village. Thatch remains on poorer huts, and some even have the flattened kerosene-can roofs of the Calcutta slum. Prosperity has come in two main ways. The rich have tended to get richer over the years. They have done so by money-lending and sometimes the acquisition of more land by foreclosing, along with skilful evasion of land reforms. In addition, the Green Revolution, less successful for rice than for wheat, has been profitable for those able to afford the capital inputs and to operate on a comparatively large scale. By the same process, diesel and electric pumps are now used for irrigation, and tractors have become important on larger farms, though they are less prominent than in the Punjab wheat farms. Some of these developments have worked against smaller landholders — pump irrigation tends to lower the water-table so that lift irrigation based on cattle or human power is no longer practicable. Some small farmers have perforce become landless labourers, joining the streams of labour migration to Calcutta, or to the industries of the Damodar coalfield or the Jamshedpur steel-based industries to the west.

However, on the whole the poor in Kalipura have tended to become a little less poor in absolute (not relative) terms, and this is almost entirely due to commuting, present in 1950 but immensely increased in recent decades. Roads are better — there are good dirt roads on embankments to the market town and railway and main bus station. One poor Muslim bread-winner has become almost middle-class by commuting daily by bus, train and bus again to work as an unskilled helper and messenger in the visual aids section of a research institute 15 miles north of Calcutta. Electric light gives some lighting to the main street and to the richer houses and village institutions. Some farmhouses cook by gas from cattle-dung, made by simple apparatus manufactured in a nearby village.

Bengali culture, always strong, has received an impetus from good lighting. As well as a primary school and middle school there is a flourishing library, including Bengali classics, as well as scientific and technical works. Harijans (Untouchables), now equal citizens in temple, school or voting-booth, may still find their children cold-shouldered by those from caste Hindu homes and (though rarely nowadays) even by teachers; but some win through, and there is positive discrimination in reserved places in universities and in some types of employment. Diet is traditionally less vegetarian than in many parts of India — fish is a favoured food though less available to poorer

Figure 4.4 Tiled and corrugated roofs in a West Bengal village in the 1980s. (Photo: A. Learmonth)

that are transmitted by mosquitos, and the introduction of the insecticides DDT and Dieldrin led first to the control and then the eradication of the disease. By 1965 Kalipura was almost totally free from new cases. Throughout India cases were reduced from 80 million to about 100 000, deaths from perhaps 3 million to almost none. Malaria, like some other infections, is believed by some to increase the rate of spontaneous abortion; one immediate and dramatic effect was an increase in live births and in the rate of population growth.

This increase in the size of the population of Kalipura led to an increased strain on food supplies, resulting in malnutrition, particularly affecting children in economically vulnerable groups. However, malaria increased again in India from 1965 to about 1976, apparently spreading back across much of the country from four or five residual strongholds, mainly in forested hill country with stream-breeding species of *Anopheles* mosquitoes. These mosquitos tend to rest between blood-meals in shady nooks and crannies in the jungle rather than on house walls where contact with the insecticides would be more likely. There has been some increase in malaria around the village, with some evidence of resistance to insecticides in the local hosts, *Anopheles philippinensis* and *A. culicifacies*. More serious in a way is that the malaria parasite associated with more violent symptoms (including cerebral malaria) *Plasmodium falciparum* has increased in proportion to *P. vivax* — the formerly dominant type which generally causes milder though lingering infections. *Plasmodium falciparum* is also developing resistance to anti-malarial drugs.

In addition to these changes, there is a strong possibility that another family of mosquitos, the Culicines, has moved in, partly to fill the ecological niche vacated by *Anopheles* at the peak of success of the DDT campaign, and partly because they are able to breed in quite strongly polluted water whereas *Anopheles* tend to prefer fairly unpolluted water. Certain of the Culicines carry the parasitic filarial worms which they introduce into the bloodstream (the most familiar symptom being swelling of the lower extremities, known as elephantiasis), whereas other species are hosts of Japanese encephalitis (infection of the brain). This last disease has spread rather rapidly over much of India in quite recent years, with pigs and various wild animals as the main hosts. It is known to villagers, and feared, for it not only causes death in about half its victims, but also leaves some of the survivors paralysed — a serious matter in any society and clearly a terrible burden in a poor farmer's or labourer's family.

Intestinal diseases are still a considerable burden on Kalipura's population, in terms of illness and suffering, loss of production, bereavement and orphaning. Polio remains an important cause of disability and death, especially in children. Typhoid frequently occurs: although water

groups than say in maritime or riverine Bangladesh. But in the poorest groups the one hot meal and cold rice breakfast of 1950 still obtains.

Health has its own balance sheet of good and bad over the first generation since Independence. The village doctor, trained in Calcutta in the western tradition, knows that he cares for only perhaps a fifth of the 5 000 people in the village. Traditional medicine is respected and the doctor is on good terms with a number of practitioners of Ayurvedic and Unani (Muslim) medicine. In 1950 endemic malaria meant that people were only able to work at limited efficiency. In addition, malaria caused many deaths in infants, children and adults. Malaria is caused by parasites

supplies have improved, the ritual bathing and mouth-washing in the tanks still goes on and the banks are still polluted by human excrement despite more families having latrines.

Only improved standards of housing, water sanitation and cooking facilities are likely to reduce the problem. Measles and influenza are still serious public health problems, with pneumonia often supervening, causing many deaths. Of the 'great' epidemic diseases — smallpox, plague and cholera — smallpox has been eradicated, and plague, never very serious as a public health problem in this part of India, has almost disappeared. Occasional outbreaks of cholera still occur.

However, there is a new epidemic on the way, of smoking-related diseases such as lung cancer, bronchitis and coronary heart disease. The last two decades have seen considerable increases in the prevalence of cigarette smoking in communities in Third World countries, partly as a consequence of massive advertising by multinational tobacco companies. This has included the promotion of high tar cigarettes, the sales of which have been banned in many industrialised countries. The worst effects of this will only become evident in the next few decades.

Changing patterns of health and disease

☐ What do you see as the outstanding differences in the pattern of health and disease between 1950 and 1980?

■ The retreat of the major epidemic diseases; the persistence of intestinal diseases; the retreat and partial return of malaria (with new problems of mosquitos'

resistance to insecticides); the appearance of Culicine-borne filariasis and Japanese encephalitis as responses to an ecological vacuum; and the emergence of a 'new' epidemic related to the consumption of tobacco.

The colonial age was only just over in 1950, so it is clear that such rapid progress in malaria and cholera control could not have occurred without a great deal of ground work having been done before Independence.

Even if the poor are generally a little less poor absolutely than they were at the end of the colonial era, differences between rich and poor still represent an enormous gap. In addition, some 'western diseases' are already appearing as causes of premature death, such as road accidents. Like most countries interested in industrialisation, India has pollution problems which always seem to be able to keep ahead of effective legislation, and some of Kalipura's migrants to the steel plants and coal mines will probably suffer from bronchitis, emphysema (loss of lung tissue), and silicosis, returning to the community in poor health.

Despite all these trends, there have been improvements in the health of the villagers. The expectation of life has risen to a level comparable with Britain's early in this century. But the tendency for different insect hosts to fill vacant ecological niches, for new diseases or old ones to wax as particular campaigns cause this or that disease to wane, the persistence of malnutrition in economically vulnerable groups because of poor diet, infections and parasites — all these suggest that all-round development is the change most likely to lead to better health, if not by AD 2000, then some decades into the new century. Just what is meant by 'development' is discussed in the following chapters.

Objectives for Chapter 4

When you have studied this chapter, you should be able to:

4.1 Describe how social and economic change in a particular community can affect the pattern of health and disease.

4.2 Give examples of how changes in the physical and natural environment may alter the pattern of diseases.

Questions for Chapter 4

1 (*Objective 4.1*) Explain how the introduction of electric pumps for irrigation schemes may indirectly lead to a higher prevalence of bronchitis in the village community.

2 (*Objective 4.2*) The introduction of DDT to control *Anopheles* mosquitos led initially to a dramatic decline in the prevalence of malaria. Give four reasons why the mosquitos have remained an important factor in the pattern of diseases in Kalipura.

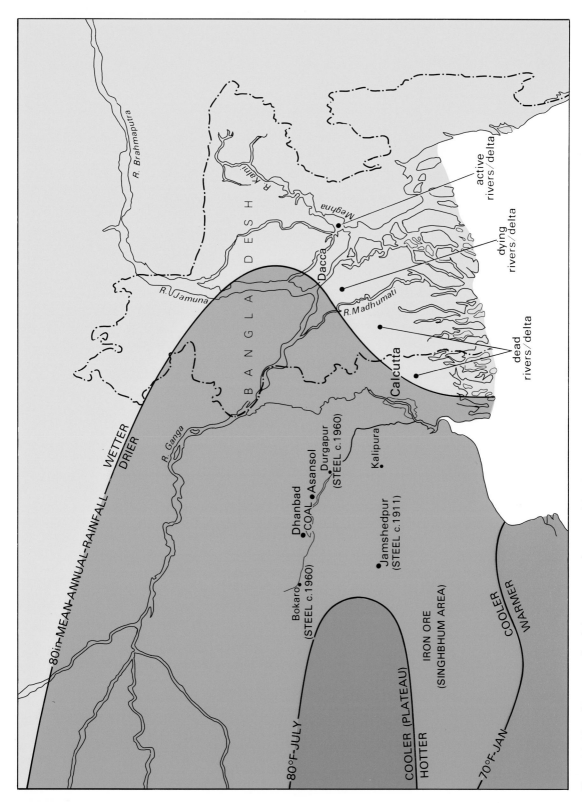

Figure 4.1 Map of West Bengal and the Ganges–Brahmaputra delta, showing climatic zones.

5

Health in a world of wealth and poverty

Look to your health; and if you have it, praise God, and value it next to a good conscience; for health is the second blessing that we mortals are capable of; a blessing that money cannot buy. (Izaak Walton (1593–1683), *The Compleat Angler*)

Amid all the various patterns of health and disease that we examined in Chapters 2 to 4 of this book, probably the most obvious fact to emerge was the degree to which the 'second blessing' of good health is not simply something enjoyed by some individuals and not by others, a biological roulette game where everyone starts more or less equal. In fact, health varies enormously from one society, nation or part of the world to another, such that it is possible to talk about the collective health of different populations: health seems to be a state that is socially shared as much as individually experienced.

Another important element of the material contained in Chapters 2 to 4 is that it questions the widespread assumption that the differences in health that now exist between different parts of the world are narrowing. Of course, because the further back in time we go the less reliable sources of information become, it is difficult to generalise over long historical periods. Nevertheless those measures of health available, such as infant mortality rates, indicate a relative widening of differences between a number of Third World countries and the industrialised countries.

Moreover, these contemporary international differences in health and disease, and the way they have evolved historically, seem to be related to patterns of social and economic development. Broadly, societies that are rich and industrialised also have comparatively high levels of health, and societies that are poor have a much poorer health experience. The period in which these health differences started to become more pronounced — the eighteenth and nineteenth centuries — was also the period when the Industrial Revolution began to transform a small but expanding group of countries.

In this and the following two chapters we shall be looking more systematically at the relationship between health and disease and social and economic development. In part this simply means trying to be more precise about what is meant by industrialised and Third World, and considering more carefully whether rich equals healthy and poor equals unhealthy: whether Walton was right or wrong in saying that money cannot buy health.

The following three extracts have been selected in order to illustrate different ways in which health and disease are related to social and economic factors. As you read them, make a note of the sequence of events in each extract. Try to define ways in which the sequences differ.

1 From *Mirage of Health*, by R. Dubos

The main reservoirs of the plague bacilli in nature are wild rodents which are infected but sufficiently resistant not to suffer from their infection under normal circumstances. They carry the plague bacilli throughout their life, just as so many healthy men and women are infected with tubercle bacilli or with viruses without showing signs of disease. Among the naturally infected animals are the tarabazan (Manchurian marmot), which has long been hunted for its fur. The professional Manchurian hunters carefully avoid any tarabazan which appears to be sick and in fact a religious taboo specifically instructs them in this regard. This taboo is probably related to the fact that the plague bacilli become active in sick tarabazans and therefore can more readily be transmitted to man. Around 1900 there occurred a change in women's fashion in Europe which increased the demand of the fur trade for the pelt of the tarabazan. Attracted by the high prices of the fur, inexperienced Chinese took to tarabazan hunting. Being ignorant of the ancient taboo, they did not hesitate to catch sick animals which proved the easiest prey. Several of the hunters caught plague from the tarabazans and transmitted it to the population of the inns of Manchuria. Thus began the great epidemic of pneumonic plague in Manchuria. (1979, pp.187–88)

2   From *Plagues and People*, by W. McNeill

Nearly twenty years ago . . . I was reading about the Spanish conquest of Mexico. As everyone knows, Hernando Cortez, starting off with fewer than six hundred men, conquered the Aztec empire, whose subjects numbered millions. How could such a tiny handful prevail . . .?

A casual remark in one of the accounts of Cortez's conquest . . . suggested an answer to such questions . . . For on the night when the Aztecs drove Cortez and his men out of Mexico City, killing many of them, an epidemic of smallpox was raging in the city. The man who had organized the assault on the Spaniards was among those who died on the *nocha triste*, as the Spanish later called it. The paralyzing effect of a lethal epidemic goes far to explain why the Aztecs did not pursue the defeated and demoralized Spaniards, giving them time and opportunity to rest and regroup, gather Indian allies and set siege to the city, and so achieve their eventual victory.

Moreover, it is worth considering the psychological impact of a disease that killed only Indians and left Spaniards unharmed. Such partiality could only be explained supernaturally, and there could be no doubt about which side of the struggle enjoyed divine favour . . . little wonder, then, that the Indians accepted Christianity and submitted to Spanish control so meekly. God had shown himself on their side, and each new out-break of infectious disease imported from Europe (and soon from Africa as well) renewed the lesson. (1976, pp.1–2)

3   From *Inside the Third World*, by P. Harrison

In a World Bank study in Indonesia, agricultural labourers and rubber tappers with hookworm-induced anaemia were found to be around twenty per cent less productive than their non-anaemic colleagues. Their foreman's views of which workers were 'lazy' or 'weak' were found to correspond closely to the incidence of anaemia. Workers with higher levels of anaemia earned less in incentive payments than their colleagues, and as a result of their lower income they consumed less calories, protein, vitamins, and iron than non-anaemic workers. This poorer nutrition contributed to their poor productivity and lowered their resistance to disease, hence they were more likely to lose time off work.

. . . Disease may also close up many areas that could be productive: river-blindness and sleeping sickness have emptied the river valleys in West Africa's Sahel region, while the tsetse fly has prevented the development of mixed agriculture in much of Africa. So disease creates poverty, while poverty, continuing the cycle, maintains the conditions that foster disease. (1979, pp.288–89)

☐   In the first extract, Dubos mentioned a social/ economic event, and a change in the pattern of health. What were they, and how were they related?

■   The event Dubos mentions was a change in fashion in Europe; the health change was an outbreak of pneumonic plague in Asia. Dubos is arguing that the change in fashion set off the change in health.

Even in quite unexpected or indirect ways, social or economic factors can have repercussions on health. In this first extract, the 'cause' of the pneumonic plague epidemic to which Dubos refers seems to have been these social and economic influences as much as the plague bacilli.

☐   Now consider the second extract. In what way does the sequence of events described by McNeill differ from that outlined by Dubos?

■   One way of interpreting McNeill's argument is as follows; if it had not been for the debilitating effects of disease on the Aztecs, it would have been much more difficult for the Spaniards to impose their cultural and economic domination. In other words, a change in disease pattern strongly influenced the social and economic history of the Americas.

The sequence of events described by McNeill seems in some way to be in the opposite direction to that in the first extract.

☐   Finally, how does Harrison's account construct a sequence of events?

■   In the extract from Harrison, the emphasis seems to be placed on interaction and interdependence. Health conditions are influenced by the social and economic environment, which in turn is influenced by the prevailing pattern of health and disease.

In practice, it is this more complex kind of relationship that is most frequently encountered. It is very seldom possible to attribute cause to a single factor. To return to the extract from McNeill, for example: the spread of disease assisted the Spanish conquest, but it could be argued that it was the overseas expansion of the Spanish that triggered the spread of disease. It could further be argued that the overseas expansion of Spain would not have been possible without the help of navigational discoveries and new ship-building techniques, and so on. In one sense all of these factors caused a change in disease patterns in America, but none was *the* cause.* The social and economic factors which this and the following chapters will be examining are not *the* cause of world health and disease patterns, but they are among the determinants of these patterns, and are one powerful way of trying to understand and explain how these patterns arose.

One way of looking at the world, already encountered in this book, is to draw up a list of countries and then order them into a league-table according to some indicator such as life-expectancy or infant mortality. International agencies such as the World Health Organisation present data in this way, and so also do organisations such as the World Bank, which publishes data on social and economic development. Such league-tables are therefore a convenient starting point, although they have limitations which we shall be discussing later.

One of the most commonly used indicators of social and economic development is *Gross National Product (GNP) per capita*. The GNP is a measure of the total output of a national economy expressed in money terms. It includes wealth produced abroad but brought into a country, and excludes wealth produced in a country but taken abroad. For example, millions of people — 'migrant workers' — go abroad to earn money and send remittances back to relatives in the country they left. Their remittances are included in the GNP of the country the remittances are sent to, and excluded from the GNP of the country the

remittances were earned in. Profits which companies earn in one country and move to another are included in the GNP of the country that recieves them. The GNP is thus an attempt to place a figure on the total wealth that accrues to the residents of a particular country, and *GNP per capita* is simply the total GNP divided by the number of residents in the country. One of the limitations of using GNP to measure wealth is that it tends only to include goods or services exchanged by a financial transaction in a market, and excludes goods and services which contribute to wealth but are not bought or sold.

☐ What common examples of goods and services can you think of that contribute to wealth but would be excluded from GNP?

■ In all countries of the world a great deal of cleaning, washing, cooking and other work is done by women in households. Because no formal payment is made for this work it is not included in the GNP. It is probably the largest single item excluded, and it has been estimated that including this sort of work might increase measured GNP by anything up to 30 per cent.

This kind of measurement problem can be found in all countries, but is particularly acute in Third World countries: subsistence farming, for instance, is by definition an activity in which food is consumed by the people who produce it. As they do not sell it in a market it is not included in the GNP. For these reasons, GNP measurements should not be accepted too uncritically as a measure of wealth: though like measures of health such as mortality they have the advantage of being relatively easy to arrive at, they present only one part of the story.

Figures for GNP per capita and various other social and economic measurements are published by the World Bank for 125 countries. (The countries excluded contain 34 with populations of less than a million, plus colonies and other occupied countries such as Namibia.) These 125 countries are grouped by the World Bank into 5 categories, and are shown in Table 5.1.

Table 5.1 World shares of population and GNP, 1980

	GNP per capita/US dollars	percentage of total world population	percentage of total world GNP
low-income countries	260	49.3	5.0
middle-income countries	1 400	25.0	14.1
high-income oil exporters	12 630	0.3	1.6
industrial market economies	10 320	16.3	64.9
non-market industrial economies	4 640	8.1	14.4

(data from World Bank, 1982, Table 1)

* Very similar issues are raised in the discussion of scurvy in Book I, *Studying Health and Disease*.

Thirty-four countries fall into the 'low-income' category, and in these countries the GNP per capita in 1980 was US$260. Another 62 countries fall into the 'middle-income' category, with an average GNP per capita of US$1 400. The four 'high-income oil exporters' had a per capita GNP of US$12 630, the 19 'industrial market economies' US$10 320 and the 6 'non-market industrial economies' US$4 640. As a working definition the non-market industrial economies are the countries of Eastern Europe plus the Soviet Union, where the ownership, planning and regulation of production and trade are centralised through the State, and the industrial market economies are the countries of Western Europe, North America, Japan, Australia and New Zealand, where ownership of production is largely in the hands of private companies or individuals, and where central planning and regulation is not widespread. Using these categories, Table 5.1 shows the way in which the world's population is distributed.

☐ If Third World countries are those with low or middle incomes, what proportion of the world's population do they contain?

■ Three-quarters of the world's population lives in these countries (mainly in the low-income countries), and the remaining quarter in the industrial countries.

The most striking thing about Table 5.1, however, is the final column showing the share of total world GNP taken by each group of countries.

☐ What proportion of world GNP is taken by the industrialised countries, and how does this compare with the share taken by the low-income countries?

■ The 25 per cent of the world's population living in the industrialised countries take about 80 per cent of the world's GNP, whereas the 50 per cent of the world's population in low-income countries take only a tiny 5 per cent of the world's GNP.

Preparing a mid-day meal outside the Durgarpur Steel Works, India. (Terry Fincher, Camera Press)

Table 5.2 Selected 'development indicators', 1980

	percentage of work-force involved in agriculture	percentage of population living in large towns and cities	percentage of population with access to safe water	percentage of adults who can read and write
low-income countries	71	17	31	50
middle-income countries	44	45	50	65
high-income oil exporters	46	66	88	25
industrial market economies	6	78	100	99
non-market industrial economies	16	62	100	100

(data from World Bank, 1982, Table 19, 20 and 22)

Table 5.2 shows a number of other measures often associated with development.

In low-income countries almost three-quarters of the working population are involved in agriculture, compared with only 6 per cent in the industrial market economies; most of the population in the industrial countries live in towns and cities, compared with fewer than 1 in 5 people in the low-income countries; access to safe water supplies is universal in industrialised countries, but in the low-income half of the world only three in ten of the population have access to safe water; finally, the table shows that although adult literacy is the norm in the industrialised countries, it is common to only half the population in low-income countries. These numbers and proportions reveal just some aspects of the many differences that exist between industrialised and Third World countries.

Clearly there are very wide differences in both wealth and health between industrialised and Third World countries. It could be argued, however, that this is the inevitable short-term consequence of some countries industrialising before others, that where there are pioneers there must also be late-comers, but in time the late-comers will catch up. It is possible to say something about the validity of this catching-up concept by looking at the relative rates of growth of GNP in different countries. The first column of Table 5.3 shows the average annual rate of growth of total GNP for each of the five groups of countries over the 20 years up to 1980.

☐ What light does the first column of Table 5.3 cast on the idea that the non-industrial countries of the world are 'catching-up' with the industrial countries?

■ Among the high-income oil exporting countries the average annual growth rate of GNP was much higher than those of the two industrial groups, although as we saw in Table 5.1 the former group of countries contains a tiny proportion of the world's population. Among the middle-income countries the average annual rate of growth of GNP was also above the rates for the two industrial groups. But in the low-income countries the average growth rate was well behind all the other groups of countries.

The half of the world's population living in the low-income countries is not only very much poorer than the rest, but also seems at present to be slipping further behind.

☐ Now look at the second column of Table 5.3, which shows the average annual rate of growth *per capita* over the same period. What is the reason for the difference between the first and second columns, and what does the explanation allow you to say about the differences between the groups of countries?

■ The *GNP per capita* is calculated by dividing the total GNP by the population. If the population is increasing, then GNP per capita will not grow as quickly as total GNP, and this accounts for the difference between the two columns. The bigger the difference

Table 5.3 World rates of growth of GNP, 1960–1980

	Average annual growth rate (per cent)	
	GNP, 1960–1980	GNP per capita, 1960–1980
low-income countries	3.3	1.2
middle-income countries	6.3	3.8
high-income oil exporters	10.8	6.3
industrial market economies	4.5	3.6
non-market industrial economies	5.1	4.2

(data from World Bank, 1982, Table 1)

between the two columns the higher the increase in population must be.

For the two groups of industrial countries the difference between GNP growth and GNP per capita growth is less than 1 per cent, but for the other groups of countries it is much wider: between 2 and 2.5 per cent. The effect of this difference is that in per capita terms the wealth of industrial and middle-income countries has been growing three or more times as rapidly as that of the low-income countries.

It is important to remember that by bundling 125 countries into 5 groups many differences will be lost among average figures. In the middle-income group, for example, 17 of the 62 countries included did in fact have average rates of growth in GNP per capita which were higher than the average for both industrial groups, among them some large countries such as Brazil, Nigeria, South Korea and Thailand. About 400 million people, or 9 per cent of world population, live in these countries, which are sometimes referred to as the 'newly industrialising countries', and if it could be assumed that the trends shown above will continue into the future, then some countries such as Brazil might be expected to have reached the present American level of GNP per capita in as little as 35–40 years. As we shall see later, however, this is a rather simplistic assumption to make. However, the picture is very much worse in the low-income group. Indeed with the exception of China, whose GNP per capita has grown quite rapidly since 1970, most of the population of this group has experienced little or no improvement at all in per capita GNP, and in some of them — for instance Chad,

Mozambique, Uganda, Niger, Sudan — per capita GNP was probably lower in 1980 than 20 years earlier. There is no single reason for the experience of these latter countries; in some, wars or revolutions have caused economic and social dislocation, others have been affected by droughts or other ecological changes to which they have been unable to respond unaided.

It can also be dangerous to generalise too much when looking at the way in which these broad measures of social and economic development compare with health indicators. National wealth might tend to be associated with health, but the pattern is not straightforward. Table 5.4 provides information on a sample of 20 countries; they are not meant to be 'typical' in any sense, but they have been drawn from each of the five groups we have been using.

☐ Look at the list of countries and try to decide which ones you would consider to be industrialised and which you would think of as Third World, i.e. low- and middle-income countries.

■ According to the World Bank categories we have been using, there are five industrial countries in the list: the UK, the USA, Sweden, Poland and the USSR. The low-income countries are Sri Lanka, China, Sierra Leone and Bangladesh; the middle-income countries are Kenya, Cuba, Brazil, Portugal and South Africa, and Saudi Arabia is the high-income oil exporter.

Bangladesh is one of the poorest countries in the world, and Sweden one of the richest. The per capita GNP in Sweden is about 100 times higher than in Bangladesh. In Bangladesh

Table 5.4 Health indicators and GNP per capita for selected countries, 1980

	GNP per capita, 1980/US dollars	Expectation of life at birth/years	Infant mortality rate (aged 0–1)	Child death rate (aged 1–4)
Bangladesh	130	46	136	20
Sri Lanka	270	66	44	3
Sierra Leone	280	47	208	50
China	290	64	56	5
Kenya	420	55	87	15
Cuba	N/A	73	21	1
Brazil	2 050	63	77	7
South Africa	2 300	61	96	18
Portugal	2 370	71	35	2
Poland	3 900	72	21	1
USSR	4 550	71	27	1
UK	7 920	73	12	1
Saudi Arabia	11 260	54	114	18
USA	11 360	74	13	1
Sweden	13 520	75	7	0

(data from World Bank, 1982, Tables 1 and 21)

the average expectation of life at birth is 46 years, 136 in every 1 000 people who are born fail to reach their first birthday, and a further 20 in every 1 000 die before they are 4 years old. In Sweden, the average life expectancy is almost 30 years longer, infant mortality is twenty times lower, and the child death rate is so small as to be officially counted as zero. At the two ends of the table, therefore, the association between wealth and health is strikingly clear.

□ Looking at the other countries in the table, what is the broad association between development and health?
■ It is approximately true to say that as GNP per capita increases, life expectancy rises and the infant mortality and child death rates decline.
□ Now see if you can spot any countries that diverge from this pattern.
■ Sri Lanka and China, for example, have per capita GNPs very similar to Sierra Leone and substantially lower than Kenya's but their health indicators are much better. Portugal has a GNP per capita similar to South Africa's, but life expectancy is 10 years longer and the infant mortality rate is only about a third of South Africa's. And Saudi Arabia has a per capita GNP as high as in the USA, but its life expectancy is much poorer than Sri Lanka's and it has one of the highest infant mortality rates.

Those countries which do diverge from the more general pattern of health and development give some first clues as to the limitations of the 'league-table' approach. In the first place, it can be grossly misleading to talk about national averages. South Africa, for example, had a per capita GNP of US$2 300 in 1980, putting it in among the 'middle-income' group of countries. But within South Africa the apartheid system means that four million whites have health and income levels comparable to Western Europe, while the 24 million black and coloured peoples have health

and income levels more similar to the pattern in low-income countries. Similarly in Brazil, over the period from 1960 to 1980, the share of national income taken by the poorest 50 per cent of the population fell from 17 per cent to 13 per cent, while the share of the wealthiest 1 per cent rose from 12 per cent to 18 per cent. Thus although the average per capita GNP of Brazil grew relatively rapidly, the distribution of income within the country became even more unequal. In turn, the average values of Brazil's health indicators conceal very wide variations between a wealthy elite and a great mass of rural poor and urban shanty-dwellers. By contrast, one of the reasons for Sri Lanka's relatively good health indicators is that, although per capita GNP is not high, attempts have been made to pursue a more equitable distribution. In particular, the Sri Lankan government has long operated a food-distribution programme, issuing ration books or coupons for essential commodities, and running a state system of food subsidies to the low-income sections of the population, and providing special protein-enriched food supplements to school children.

Distribution, therefore, is as important as any average figure or total amount of wealth, and although this is particularly so of poor countries, it is also true of industrial countries, as you will see when you look at the UK later in this book. A more fundamental issue, however, is that the league-table suggests a ladder of progress, with different countries on different rungs but all heading in the same direction and separated only by the time they set off. In fact we have already seen that some countries are not only a long way behind but seem to be slipping further back. Twenty years or so, however, is a very short period of time: it is only within a rather longer historical perspective that some of the reasons why these patterns have emerged can be considered.

Objectives for Chapter 5

When you have studied this chapter you should be able to:

5.1 Describe what GNP measures and what its main limitations are.

5.2 Describe how the distribution of world population differs from that of world GNP.

5.3 Evaluate the relationship between national wealth and levels of health.

Questions for Chapter 5

1 (*Objective 5.1*) In the Republic of Korea the total GNP increased over the past 10 years at twice the rate at which it increased in Greece. Why would it be incorrect to assume that the wealth of the average citizen of the Republic of Korea was also increasing at twice the rate of that of the average citizen of Greece?

2 (*Objective 5.2*) 'The Third World may be a lot poorer, but by sheer weight of numbers it must account for a big share of total world economic activity. After all, India is one of the top ten world industrial producers.' How valid is this line of reasoning?

3 (*Objective 5.3*) The World Bank's 1982 World Development Report noted that 'experience in improving nutrition, and reducing child mortality has varied widely among countries, a variation that mainly reflects the performance of government programmes in these fields'. What sort of programmes do you think this statement is referring to?

6

The world transformed: the rise of industrial society

During this chapter you will be asked to read an extract contained in the Course Reader. This is 'Health: 1844' by Frederick Engels, taken from his book *The Conditions of the Working Class in England*. It can be found in the Course Reader, Part 1, Section 2.1.

Subsistence or surplus? The Roman Pont du Gard aqueduct, Nimes, is typical of the massive building works that pre-industrial societies could produce. (Mansell Collection)

'The history of the world', claimed the nineteenth-century Scottish historian, Thomas Carlyle (1795–1881), 'is but the biography of great men' (*Heroes and Hero Worship: The Hero as Divinity*). When we turn to examine historical patterns of health and disease, and the social and economic changes with which they have been so closely associated, nothing could be further from the truth. Rather, what is of paramount importance and interest is the daily reality of existence for the mass of the population: how long they lived, what they died of, how hard they worked, how much food they had.

Unfortunately, Carlyle's remark was only too accurate as a description of the way in which history has often been written, and although our knowledge of populations has greatly increased in recent years there are still a sufficiently large number of gaps in that knowledge to leave room for disagreement and controversy.

Before addressing some of the questions which follow on from the previous chapter, it is worth trying briefly to sketch the kinds of diseases that are likely to have afflicted our early ancestors, and consider how these might have changed as human society evolved through different stages of development.

Disease in the pre-industrial world

Knowledge of the causes of illness and rates of death among our remote tree-dwelling ancestors is largely a matter of speculation. Comparison with the infections that currently prevail among monkeys and apes, which may resemble the sorts of diseases that affected prehumans, suggests that tree-dwellers would have been subject to mites, fleas, ticks and worms, and invaded by viruses carried by various insects, bacteria, fungi and parasites — such as that which causes malaria. A major threat to the survival of prehumans would have come from additional stresses such as injury and famine.

The first major change of habit and lifestyle that our ancestors underwent was the transition from heavily forested regions to more open grasslands. Although some infections and infestations would have remained the same during this change, it seems likely that humans would also have encountered new ones. Just what these were is uncertain. The adoption of a more carnivorous habit would have exposed them to such parasites as tapeworm, and close contact with species such as antelope may have brought them into contact with tsetse flies and thus sleeping sickness. In fact this disease would have limited the areas of grassland that were habitable by humans.

Despite the new dangers awaiting the early human *gatherers and hunters*, they came to dominate the food chain of the grasslands. Their development and mastery of hunting skills largely removed the threat of being preyed on by other species, but posed a new survival risk: slaughter by other humans. Additional stresses would have arisen regularly from food shortages and from changes in climatic conditions, such as the advance and retreat of successive Ice Ages, but human adaptability permitted a slow spread of the population to almost every part of the world. Viewed in the long term, these factors were probably largely in balance, preventing any rapid changes in total population size. This was a pattern that prevailed until the first *agricultural revolution*, in around 8 000 BC.

This first agricultural revolution transformed the social organisation of humans. Small, wandering groups who rarely came into contact with one another were replaced by much larger, settled communities in most (though not all) parts of the world. Gathering and hunting gave way to the cultivation of crops and the domestication of animals. This has been regarded by some commentators as the most significant change humans have ever experienced:

> For at least 99 per cent of the duration of their existence on Earth members of the genus *Homo* have lived by hunting and gathering. This way of life was presumably also shared by the preceding pre-hominids. Of the 50 000 odd generations in the last million years of history, only about 400 have occurred since agriculture was first adopted by one part of the human population. With agriculture came dramatic changes in diet, population density and patterns of daily life, and the human organism was exposed to stresses that were, in evolutionary terms, novel. It is unlikely that there has been major biological change

in man since the Neolithic revolution. Such change is highly improbable with respect to the more recent adoption of urban and advanced industrial patterns of life. (Powles, 1973, p.4)

As regards human disease, the agricultural revolution can be seen to have led to the rise of infectious diseases as the main cause of illness and death.

□ Why should infections have assumed such importance as a consequence of the social changes of the agricultural revolution?

■ The most important effect was the increase in both the total population size and the size of local groups living in close personal contact. Many infections require a minimum size of human population if they are to be maintained. Whereas some diseases depend on an animal host (e.g. rats in the case of plague), others, such as measles, are specific to humans. It has been suggested that measles requires a population of about one million to be maintained as an endemic (always present) infection.

Other less important reasons include the attraction of intruders such as rats and mice into human habitations, and an increase in food supplies — the latter because it would tend to lead to an increase in the size of the population which would then be more at risk of infectious diseases as discussed above.

Thus, though the agricultural revolution diminished the risk of death from starvation, predation and possibly violence, it led to an increased risk of infections, particularly those which are transmitted through the air (airborne) such as measles, mumps, smallpox, tuberculosis and diphtheria. Infections were to remain the predominant threat to human survival for almost 10 000 years. It is impossible to know what the mortality would have been during this period, but in the few such societies that exist today, the life-expectancy at birth is barely 25 years.

These different stages of development in human society are of course quite crude approximations to what was a long, complex and still poorly understood series of changes. However, it seems clear beyond reasonable doubt that major shifts in the experience of health and disease attended these changes. A second point to note is less obvious but equally important: each stage of development was characterised by a particular way of obtaining the means of subsistence, and scarcity or plenty in a society resulted from the relationship between that means of subsistence and the number of people. The agricultural revolution made it possible to produce more food but this increase in food was probably absorbed in part by an increase in population. Without one fact the other loses much of its meaning.

It is all too easy to lose sight of this relationship when we try to make historical comparisons, for it is difficult to resist the temptation of applying our own definitions and values as if they were absolute standards. For example, the traditional view anthropologists have taken of gatherer-hunter societies has been that they were characterised by permanent scarcity, meagre resources, hand-to-mouth subsistence, and a life of continual struggle for survival. This seems to be remarkably similar to the famous description of life without social organisation suggested by Thomas Hobbes, the seventeenth-century social theorist, as 'solitary, poor, nasty, brutish and short'.

However, as evidence has accumulated on such societies, it has become increasingly difficult to reconcile these views with their irregular and not prolonged hours of labour, the amount of time spent dozing, chatting, playing games or engaged in ceremonies, and the generally low esteem in which many material possessions were held. What could be the explanation for this anomaly? One possibility could be that the assumptions held and the standard applied by these anthropologists were quite inappropriate. Their point of reference was the present industrial societies, where it is held '... that man's wants are great, not to say infinite, whereas his means are limited, although improvable, thus, the gap between means and ends can be narrowed by industrial productivity'. But what if the premise were to be altered, such that 'human material wants are finite and few, and technical means unchanging but on the whole adequate'. Within this set of assumptions 'a people can enjoy an unparalleled material plenty — with a low standard of living'.

These quotations, and this hypothesis, come from the work of the American anthropologist Marshall Sahlins, who has gathered together a great deal of information on gatherer-hunter tribes and tribal economies. His evidence is drawn from many different sources: among the !Kung (sic) Bush-people of the Kalahari for example, there seemed to be little or no material pressure in life, and possession of objects conferred no status on individuals. Among Australian natives in Arnhem Land, work was intermittent and averaged around four hours a day, and dietary intake was more than adequate. Sahlins also wryly points out that the performance of the Dobe tribe in Botswana, where one person's work in gathering and hunting food yielded enough to support four or five people, was at least as efficient as the French agricultural industry up to 1940, where 20 per cent of the population were employed in providing for the rest.

A key characteristic of the agricultural revolution was the increasing division of labour and specialisation of tasks. In recent years, much attention has been directed in particular towards the *gender* division of labour in such societies. Some evidence has been accumulated that the gathering of food such as fruits, roots, berries and nuts and the collection of firewood and water, were at least as important as hunting game. Gathering was predominantly done by women and hunting almost always by men, and the responsibilities placed on women for cooking, child-rearing and making clothes would have reduced their available leisure time compared with that of men. For these reasons such societies, formerly referred to as 'hunter-gatherer' societies are more accurately described as 'gatherer-hunter' societies, the term adopted in this book.

This important qualification, however, does not alter the essential points being made by Sahlins. These are summarised in the following extract.

From *Stone Age Economics*, by Marshall Sahlins

One third to one half of humanity are said to go to bed hungry every night. In the Old Stone Age the fraction must have been much smaller. *This* is the era of hunger unprecedented. Now, in the time of the greatest technical power, starvation is an institution. Reverse another venerable formula: the amount of hunger increases relatively and absolutely with the evolution of culture.

This paradox is my whole point. Hunters and gatherers have by force of circumstances an objectively low standard of living. But taken as their *objective*, and given their adequate means of production, all the people's material wants usually can be easily satisfied. The evolution of economy has known, then, two contradictory movements: enriching but at the same time impoverishing, appropriating in relation to nature but expropriating in relation to man. The progressive aspect is, of course, technological. It has been celebrated in many ways: as an increase in the amount of need-serving goods and services, an increase in the amount of energy harnessed to the service of culture, an increase in productivity, an increase in the division of labour, and increased freedom from environmental control. Taken in a certain order, the last is especially useful for understanding the earliest stages of technical advance. Agriculture not only raised society above the distribution of natural food sources, it allowed neolithic communities to maintain high degrees of social order where the requirements of human existence were absent from the natural order. Enough food could be harvested in some seasons to sustain the people while no food would grow at all; the consequent stability of social life was critical for its material enlargement. Culture went on then from triumph to triumph in a kind of progressive contravention of the biological law of the minimum, until it proved it could support human life in outer space — where even gravity and oxygen were naturally lacking.

Other men were dying of hunger in the market places of Asia. It has been an evolution of structures as well as technologies, and in that respect like the mythical road where for every step the traveller advances his destination recedes by two. The structures have been political as well as economic, of power as well as property. They developed first within societies, increasingly now between societies. No doubt these structures have been functional, necessary organisations of the technical development, but within the communities they have thus helped to enrich they would discriminate in the distribution of wealth and differentiate in the style of life. The world's most primitive people have few possessions, *but they are not poor*. Poverty is not a certain small amount of goods, nor is it just a relation between means and ends; above all, it is a relation between people. Poverty is a social status. As such it is the invention of civilisation. (1974, pp.36–7)

In this extract, Sahlins is suggesting that the emergence of modern societies has created new relationships between members of society, one feature of which is the existence of poverty. The extract also contains certain clues about the emergence of *hierarchies* as societies evolved.

    ☐ Re-read the extract carefully, looking for words or phrases which indicate the emergence of *social hierarchies* or strata. What clues can you find?

    ■ Among the key phrases used, you might have noted 'social order', 'power', political and economic 'structures', and 'division of labour'.

The existence of social class, or *stratification*, or hierarchy, is one of the most important aspects of health and disease patterns. But it is useful to note from this extract that neither hierarchy nor stratification is unique to industrialised societies. In fact, it seems that every society which produces more than is immediately consumed, that can accumulate a surplus of food or other wealth, inevitably confronts the question of how that surplus should be used. Out of this develops conflict, and such conflicts are resolved within a hierarchical structure in which power is exercised. The emergence of poverty as an 'invention of civilisation' is therefore one feature of the power relationships between different groups in a hierarchical structure.

Although a hierarchical ordering emerges as a prime characteristic of all societies, at least from the agricultural revolution onwards, the form it takes will vary widely depending on the prevailing type of social and economic organisation. Poverty, for example, may be much more widespread in some societies than in others which are differently ordered. Going further, it may be that hierarchies exist not only within societies, but also between societies. For example, the question could be asked whether the particular forms in which scarcity and poverty exist in today's Third World — chronic, long-term and widespread malnutrition — may also be an 'invention of civilisation' reflecting an international hierarchical ordering. An examination of this question must begin with the person whose name is most frequently associated with the relationship between population and the means of subsistence — Malthus — and the light which his work casts on the pre-industrial world.

The Malthusian system

The Reverend Thomas Malthus was born near Dorking in Surrey in 1766 and died in 1834. As we shall see, the lifetime of 'Population Malthus' (as he was caricatured) covered a key period of history. Like Machiavelli, the first great modern political theorist, the name of Malthus has acquired a patina of unpleasantness. It is not always clear whether this is because he has been regarded as having made observations which were untrue, or simply unpleasant; certainly his work has at times been enlisted in unpleasant and repressive ideologies. In 1798 Malthus published the first edition of *An Essay on the Principles of Population*, which put forward the following views.

1 The survival and increase of a population is completely dependent upon the means of subsistence.

2 The 'passion between the sexes' is so strong and unalterable 'that population, when unchecked, goes on doubling itself every twenty-five years, or increases in a geometrical ratio'.

3 As a general rule it is simply not possible for the means of subsistence to grow in the same geometrical ratio as population: 'Taking the population of the world at any number, a thousand millions, for instance, the human species would increase in a ratio of — 1,2,4,8,16,32,64,128, 256,512, etc., and subsistence as — 1,2,3,4,5,6,7,8,9,10, etc. In two centuries and a quarter, the population would be to the means of subsistence as 512 to 10' (Malthus, 1970, pp.25–26).

4 This disequilibrium is prevented from arising by a set of checks, producing 'misery or vice', which are unfortunately to be found 'in ample portion' in 'the cup of human life'. The main checks which he identified were starvation and the outbreak of epidemics of infectious diseases.

    ☐ What strikes you about the kind of checks on population increase that Malthus identified?

    ■ In this first essay on population Malthus concentrated on checks which caused deaths among the existing population.

Malthus labelled such checks as '*positive checks*'. At this stage, he barely considered the possibility of checks such as coitus interruptus and other forms of contraceptive practice which were known and practised, abortion, infanticide and — perhaps most important of all — the pattern of marriage. He later styled these as '*preventive checks*'. The two key features of marriage patterns are (a) *nuptiality*, which is the proportion of the population who are married, and (b) the average age of marriage, which influences the potential childbearing years of women. Malthus initially took a view of this similar to that of Dr. Johnson: 'It is not from reason and prudence that people marry, but from inclination. A man is poor; he thinks, 'I cannot be worse, and so I'll e'en take Peggy'. Later, however, Malthus grasped more fully the importance of marriage patterns and other preventive checks, which he put under the heading of 'moral restraint'.

The overall scheme of Malthus's ideas is shown in Figure 6.1. Looking at this figure, you will see that there are two loops: the upper one deals with the positive checks on populations, and the lower one with the preventive checks.

The upper loop begins by showing a positive association between population size and food prices; that is, a *rise* in population size leads to a *rise* in food prices, a *fall* in population size to a *fall* in food prices.

The next part of the figure connects food prices and real wages. *Rising* food prices mean that the same amount of money buys less food, and so real wages *fall*. Conversely, if prices were to *fall*, real wages would *rise*; in other words, there is an inverse relationship between them.

As real wages fall so mortality starts to increase through starvation, malnutrition and disease. The rise in mortality is the final positive check on population size, cutting it back as 'Nature wields her red pencil', and as the population size comes down so food prices start to fall, and so on.

Following the lower loop, the effect of a fall in real wages brought about by population increase is to lower the nuptiality rate: to paraphrase Dr. Johnson, a man becomes poorer, realises things are worse, and postpones taking Peggy. As nuptiality falls, so fertility falls, and thus the population increase is thrown into reverse.

All of this of course is a hypothesis. How does it compare with what we now know of population history? Putting qualifications temporarily to one side, this harsh picture of human existence in the centuries preceding 1800 seems to be not all that far wide of the mark. A broad picture is provided by the modern French historian, Fernand Braudel, in *The Structures of Everyday Life* (1981), which is the first volume of a monumental and richly referenced history of civilisation and capitalism from the fifteenth to the eighteenth century.

What characterised this period, writes Braudel, was 'a number of deaths roughly equivalent to the number of births; very high infant mortality; famine; chronic under-nourishment; and formidable epidemics' (p.91). It was a precarious battle for existence 'waged on at least two fronts: against the scarcity and inadequacy of the food supply ... and against the many and insidious forms of disease that lay in wait' (p.90). Famine was ever-present: in France, for example, there were '10 general famines during the tenth century: 26 in the eleventh; 2 in the twelfth; 4 in the fourteenth; 7 in the fifteenth; 13 in the sixteenth; 11 in the seventeenth and 16 in the eighteenth' (p.74). In the 1696–97 famine in Finland a quarter or a third of the population perished. 'Things were far worse in Asia, China and India. Famines there seemed like the end of the world .... In 1555 and again in 1596, violent famine throughout north-west India resulted in scenes of cannibalism ...' (p.76) and on and on.

Moreover, 'famine was never an isolated event. Sooner or later it opened the door to epidemics'. Each fresh disaster, however, was followed by a reassertion of life, as the population bounced back: for example, when plague mowed down the population of Verona in 1637, '... the soldiers of the garrison, almost all French — many of whom had escaped the plague — married the widows and

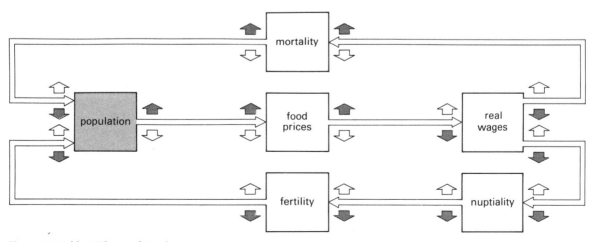

Figure 6.1 Malthus' Theory of Population.

life gained the upper hand again' (p.71). Rise and fall is the rhythm of population history and of 'standard of living', each cycle permeating the whole fabric of life: 'trees and wild animals overran fields that had once flourished. But soon the population again increased and had to win back the land taken over by animals and wild plants, clear the stones from the fields and pull up trees and shrubs' (Braudel, 1981, p.33). What evidence we have suggests that this rhythm stretched across the inhabited world, a procession of 'social massacres' and revivals that seems to confirm the Malthusian system.

However, some other points deserve to be made. First, the equilibrium between population and subsistence was far from perfect. Underlying the increases and decreases was a faint but perceptible longer-term trend, where 'revival ultimately had the last word. The ebb never entirely removed what the preceding tide had brought in' (p.92), and the population of the world slowly increased. Second, although famines were widespread and sometimes frequent, they were none the less periodic events with some respite allowed in between. The fact that specific dates of violent famines in North West India are recorded, for instance, could be interpreted as implying that chronic malnutrition and widespread starvation was not the *continual* norm in North West India. Third, we know from the monuments and relics of the past, that, whatever relationship existed between the mass of population and the means of subsistence, sufficient surplus was provided by the economic system to invest in mammoth schemes of building, often on a scale that might impose severe strains on not only the Third World countries of today, but also some industrialised countries. We are familiar with the vast temples, palaces and other buildings of Thailand, Peru, Mexico, Persia, Egypt and so on. In fact such works were always accompanied by complex and highly organised systems of irrigation, transport, food storage and distribution.

At least in certain parts of the world, the traditional view of subsistence farmers eking out a simple living was far from typical. In East Africa, for example, it has been claimed that, historically, agriculture was organised in a way that allowed the production, storage and exchange of a wide variety of foodstuffs; that shortages were exceptions rather than the rule, and that sufficient surpluses of wealth existed to enable the erection, for example, of massive temples and granaries in the ancient city of Zimbabwe (Kjekshus, 1977). Other evidence comes to us from the observations of travellers on the condition of the population and the wealth or poverty of the lands they visited. Most famous of all, perhaps, was Marco Polo, who in the late thirteenth century spent twenty years travelling widely throughout the Middle East and Asia taking notes on what he saw.

☐ Marco Polo was a merchant and a business traveller. Why might this background be of interest when reading his account?
■ Because he was a successful merchant and trader (a merchant of Venice, no less), he had a seasoned eye for the details of commercial life and the clues and signals of economic activity.

In his travels, Marco Polo was 'quick to notice the available sources of food and water along the route, the means of transport, ... and no less quick to observe the marketable products of every district, whether natural or manufactured, and the channels through which flowed the interlacing streams of export and import' (Polo, 1968, p.xix).

Following Marco Polo through his travels, the picture which emerges is not at all one that might be obtained today in the Third World, which now includes many countries he passed through: Armenia — 'a land of many villages and towns, amply stocked with the means of life'; Northern Persia — a ride 'through a fine plain and a fine valley and along fine hillsides, where there is a rich herbage, fine pasturage, fruit in plenty, and no lack of anything'; Cathay (North-East China) — where 'when harvests are bountiful corn is accumulated in huge granaries, along with wheat, barley, millet, and rice to be distributed when crops fail'; Bengal — 'the people live on meat, milk and rice. They have cotton in plenty. They are great traders, exporting spikenard, galingale, ginger, sugar and many other precious spices'; and Northern India — 'They live by trade and industry. They have rice and wheat in profusion. The staple foods are rice, meat and milk. Merchants come here in great numbers by sea and by land with a variety of merchandise and export the products of the kingdom'.

Venice may have been a 'jewel on the shores of the Adriatic', about to take its place in the forefront of the Renaissance, but Marco Polo at least gives no indication that it was unimaginably more advanced than many other places he passed through.

There are so many gaps in our knowledge of the pre-industrial world that there is ample room for disagreement. We have seen one picture of the world as essentially a procession of 'social massacres', of sweeping epidemics, famines, and 'die-offs' as the population seemed to collide with the subsistence barrier in the way Malthus expected. On the other hand there is evidence, at least in parts of the world, that to be poor did not imply continual misery and uncertainty about where the next meal was to come from. Both of these views are compatible with the possibility that the characteristics of Third World countries are not simply the continued existence of old patterns, but may be in part a feature of the post-industrial world. To examine this issue more directly, it is now necessary to look at the sequence of events and changes known as the 'Industrial Revolution'.

The Industrial Revolution

It is paradoxical that the first country in the world for which there is evidence that the Malthusian theory no longer applied was the same country in which the theory was formulated: eighteenth-century England. Here it seems that the population was not pressed hard against the basic means of subsistence, that bad harvests could be overcome without too much hardship or hunger, and that the population could slowly grow without causing real wages to slump. For example, one French traveller, the Abbé le Blanc, making his way from the south coast to London in 1747, was 'struck with the beauties of the country, the care taken to improve lands, the richness of the pastures, the numerous flocks that cover them, and the air of plenty and cleanliness that reigns in the smallest villages' (quoted in Hobsbawm, 1968, p.11).

Figure 6.2 shows changes in the population of England from the sixteenth to the eighteenth century, and changes in real wages over the same period. Some of the problems involved in estimating population size have already been discussed. The problems of estimating the average value of wages over such a long period are in many ways even more difficult to solve. The real wage index shown in Figure 6.2 is based on the work of two researchers who remarkably managed to trace the wage rates of builders and the price of various foodstuffs back to the twelfth century! (Phelps-Brown and Hopkins, 1956)

□ Look carefully at Figure 6.2. What are the main features of it that strike you as important? Does the figure fit the Malthusian system we examined in the previous chapter?

■ In the years up to 1600 we can see population increasing and real wages falling, a pattern that broadly fits in with the Malthusian theory. Around 1650

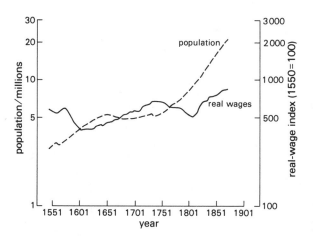

Figure 6.2 Changes in population and real wages, England. 1550–1900. (Wrigley and Schofield, 1981, p.408)

population growth is checked, while real wages are rising. Then from about 1700–50 population starts rising again (and this growth accelerates after 1800). Meanwhile, real wages decline very slowly, but around 1800 they start rising also: a sustained and rapid increase in the population has not set off the system of checks Malthus predicted.

England was the first country in the world to experience this pattern of development. This is why it is important to look closely at what happened before returning to a 'world-view'. The problem in explaining what happened is that it was a unique event, and cannot be repeated experimentally to increase knowledge of why — or even precisely how — it happened. The first key to understanding what was happening takes us back to Malthus and his geometrical versus arithmetical rates of growth of population and agriculture.

In eighteenth-century England agriculture was undergoing a whole series of changes which allowed it to expand at a rate that at least kept up with the increasing population. This expansion was made possible in part by new techniques such as crop rotation, stock-breeding and the famous seed-drilling machine invented by Jethro Tull. But these changes in technique and technology were encouraged and widely adopted largely because of other social and economic upheavals which were also taking place. For example, common land was taken over and enclosed by a new class of private landowners, and although this resulted in the size of fields and of farms being rapidly expanded, it also meant that the peasant subsistence farming which had been based on small plots of land, was completely disrupted and then painfully eliminated.

Thus Malthus's view that agricultural production could not increase at more than a slow, 'arithmetical' ratio of growth was made obsolete at the very time that he was developing his theory. Agricultural growth was fast enough to lift the check on population growth by facilitating both a reduction in mortality and allowing the birth rate to increase.

As we have noted already, there is no agreement over why this happened, or why it happened first in England. Some theories have laid stress on factors such as climate. For example, it has been suggested that weather conditions in the eighteenth century provided a long series of good harvests in England, and that the surplus produced triggered off wider changes. This argument, however, does not explain why previous runs of good harvests did not produce such changes. Other theories have focused on the values of the Protestant Reformation, arguing that Protestantism was ideally matched to the innovative and individualistic forces required to alter England's economic and social system. But again, this argument does not explain why Catholic Belgium was quicker to follow England's lead than Protestant Holland. The break-down of the Malthusian system, and agricultural and demographic changes were simply part of a much bigger set of changes occurring in England at that time, and attributing such changes to a single factor such as climate or religion ignores the many circumstances and combinations of factors which were undoubtedly present.

In fact, by the later years of the eighteenth century we have reached the beginning of that period referred to as the *Industrial Revolution*. What is meant by this? We commonly think of it in terms of a sudden increase in economic activity, and this is certainly part of it. The last quarter of the eighteenth century in England witnessed a boom in the construction of canals and roads, a flourishing of the cotton and textiles industries, a doubling of imports and exports, and a sudden increase in the size of towns such as Manchester.

However, to reach a definition of the Industrial Revolution that will help to understand what was happening we must think not simply in terms of quantitative change, of an increase in the *amount* of economic activity. The important point to grasp is that the Industrial Revolution was '... not merely an acceleration of economic growth, but an acceleration of growth because

of, and through, economic and social transformation', culminating in '... self-sustained economic growth by means of perpetual technological revolution and social transformation' (Hobsbawm, 1968, p.20).

This concept of transformation, or *structural change*, is the cornerstone of the process of development and social change. This process dramatically altered the everyday life of the population of England, and also altered the nature of the relationship between newly industrialised countries such as England and the rest of the world, with profound consequences for patterns of health and disease.

A good example of the structural changes occurring during the process of industrialisation in England was the sweeping away of the social structures that regulated the use of land and of labour. In pre-industrial society, land was in the gift of the Crown, held by the Church or the aristocracy, inherited by tenants in return for rent, or was simply 'common' land and not privately owned. Land ownership and use were decided by law and custom and the buying or selling of land in the way familiar to us today was not widespread.

By the late eighteenth century, however, land in England had been transformed into a commodity, an item bought and sold by private owners in a commercial market, and customs of access and use were renounced. Common land had been enclosed and had become private and the

The Industrial Revolution in full swing: view of a copper foundry in Swansea, 1862. Engraving after Durand-Brager. (Roger Viollet, Paris.)

'peasantry' had essentially disappeared. In the 34 years up to 1760, a mere 70 000 acres were enclosed, but between 1760 and 1792 the total jumped by half a million, and by 1812 had increased by a further million acres (Jones, 1967, p.13). In consequence, a large number of people no longer had any direct access to the produce of the land, their subsistence was thrown into doubt, and many became destitute paupers.

It would be impossible to put any figure on the mortality or morbidity that may have resulted from this dislocation, but it is quite plausible to argue that from being poor but relatively comfortable, large numbers of people became poor and frequently desperate about getting enough to eat. In 25 of the 37 years from 1811 to 1848, for example, the agricultural areas of England witnessed widespread rioting and disorder, and their plight is summed up in the words of a rioter from the Fens in 1816: 'Here I am between Earth and Sky, so help me God. I would sooner lose my life than go home as I am. Bread I want and bread I will have.' (Hobsbawm, 1968, p.74).

□ Think back to the discussion on agricultural production accompanying Figure 6.2. What strikes you about the above passage?
■ Earlier it was noted that by the nineteenth century agricultural production was expanding at least as quickly as the population. This suggests that there was no overall insufficiency of food.

What was being experienced by the Fens rioter and many others was a distributional problem associated with a social structure that had undergone a transformation. An extreme example of this occurred in mid-nineteenth century Ireland, which we shall look at in more detail in the following chapter. Suffice it to note that that event was referred to as the 'Famine' by the English, but as the 'Starvation' by the Irish.

Accompanying these changes in land ownership and land use, an entirely different kind of labour-force was created. In contemporary industrialised countries such as Britain, the great majority of people make a living for themselves and their dependants by obtaining work from an employer in return for a wage or salary. Such paid employment normally takes place separated from home and family in offices or factories where quite large numbers of people work. In pre-industrial England the contrast was striking. Although wage-labour was not uncommon, and even in Tudor times perhaps two-thirds of all households earned some part of their living from wages, nevertheless far fewer households were dependent on wages for all of their living all of the time. Instead, they worked the land tied to the home and exchanged the produce for other necessities. And in the home they carried out 'industrial' activities such as spinning or weaving.

Because agricultural work is seasonal, large numbers of people would have spent part of the year looking for other forms of employment, and some would fail to find any and become beggars. But as the British historian, Peter Laslett, has observed,

the trouble then ... was not so much unemployment, as under-employment, as it is now called ... the comparison is with the countries of Asia in our own century. Too many members of a family were half-busied about an inadequate plot of infertile land; not enough work could be found for the women and children to do around the cottage fire, in some districts none at all, for there was no rural industry in them. (Laslett, 1971, p.33)

□ What similarities strike you between this description of pre-industrial England and the cameo of Kalipura in Chapter 4?
■ Temporary migration to casual labouring jobs, pavement-dwelling in cities and short-term unskilled employment are features of life for this rural population in India and for pre-industrial England.

During the Industrial Revolution in England, therefore, another structural change was the transformation of the work-force into much larger groupings of employees dependent on wages. Without this transformation, it would not have been possible to organise production in factories and the industrial towns they gave rise to, to increase the specialisation of tasks and the division of labour, or to practice the rapid hiring and firing of labour that accompanied technical innovation. A mass of labouring people was created, depending for their livelihood on selling their labour. Only this wage relationship stood between the labourer and destitution, and if jobs were scarce destitution was rife.

These changes in the position of land and labour would not have been possible without a series of even more profound and subtle transformations. An economy based on commodity exchange and markets can only operate with the use of money, and the role of money had been increasing in English society since at least the Tudor period. Shakespeare frequently mentions the growth in the importance of money, and in *Timon of Athens* he was scathing about the 'common whore of mankind, that putt'st odds among the rout of nations': 'Thus much of this will make black, white; foul, fair; wrong, right; base, noble; old, young; coward, valiant ... This yellow slave will knit and break religions'. (IV. iii. 28–44)

A final example of the kinds of structural changes that occurred during the Industrial Revolution is provided by the historian Edward Thompson in a study of changing perceptions of time. Thompson begins by noting the way in which clock time was irrelevant and disregarded in any pre-industrial fishing, crafting or farming community, 'whose framework of marketing and administration is minimal, and in which the day's tasks (which might vary from fishing to farming, building, mending of nets, thatching, making a cradle or a coffin) seem to disclose themselves, by the logic of need, before the crofter's eyes'. His point is perfectly illustrated by an observation made by the Irish writer J.M. Synge on a visit to the Aran Islands, off the coast of County Clare:

> The general knowledge of time on the island depends, curiously enough, upon the direction of the wind. Nearly all the cottages are built ... with two doors opposite each other, the more sheltered of which lies open all day to give light to the interior. If the wind is northerly the south door is opened, and the shadow of the door-post moving across the kitchen floor indicates the hour; as soon, however, as the wind changes to the south the other door is opened, and the people, who never think of putting up a primitive dial, are at a loss ...
>
> When the wind is from the north the old woman manages my meals with fair regularity; but on the other days she often makes my tea at three o'clock instead of six ... (Thompson, 1967, p.59)

Clearly, such nature-dependent rhythms of life and work were incompatible with the operation of a large factory using powered machinery and employing several hundred workers, or with the running of a railway network or school. And so the Industrial Revolution witnessed a complete restructuring of the whole rhythm of life, with clocks and bells, timetables and schedules, set times for eating, sleeping, working and resting, and a sharp distinction between work and the rest of life.

In short, the whole process of industrial development meant much more than a growth in the national product: the kind of processes outlined above make it clear that development cannot be seen as simply a quantitative increase in economic activity brought about by technological changes. Development did eventually bring massive improvements in health to Britain, which will be looked at in much more detail in Chapters 8 and 9 of this book. But these were only one facet of a complete social, political, cultural and economic upheaval, which caused massive social dislocation, which did not happen overnight, and which was accompanied for a long period by great hardship and misery before general improvements in the standard of living and levels of health began to appear.

At the time, many people were horrified at the consequences of the Industrial Revolution in England. Some, like the Romantic poets, recoiled from it and wished to reject it completely. Others, like Charles Dickens and his illustrator, Paul Gustave Doré, devoted their lives to exposing its cruelties. And some, like Frederick Engels, condemned the conditions that the Industrial Revolution had created as part of a critique of the whole social order. An extract from the book he published in 1844, *The Conditions of the Working Class in England* is included in the Course Reader (Section 2.1).* This extract examines the results of the Industrial Revolution in terms of the health of city dwellers, and you should now read it.

☐ In the statistics he quotes, Engels concentrates on two particular aspects of the pattern of health and disease: class differences and differences between town and country. What findings does he make?

■ Engels notes that scarlet fever, rachitis (rickets) and scrofula were confined largely to the working classes, and did not seriously afflict the middle and upper classes. He also draws on evidence that the mortality rate in lower-class streets was up to twice as high as in upper-class streets. He then observes that the death rate in the industrial cities — at around one in thirty — was substantially higher than in rural districts — around one in forty.

☐ Within a historical perspective, what other dimension of health and disease patterns not considered in the extract would be of particular interest?

■ Perhaps the most important is some comparison of health and disease patterns around 1844 with patterns before the Industrial Revolution.

In fact intense controversy surrounds the question of the initial health consequences of the Industrial Revolution, and the limited data available will be considered in Chapter 8. This controversy is part of a wider dispute about trends in the standard of living of the population, for although it is plain that from the 1840s onwards standards of living were definitely rising, the pattern before then is not at all clear. The fact that there is no obvious answer to this question suggests that there can have been very little if any general improvement for at least half a century.

Whatever the short-term consequences of the Industrial Revolution in England, a giant break with the past had clearly occurred, involving among many other things health and disease patterns, populations and food. The next step, therefore, is to look at the implications of these changes for the Third World, and in particular for the patterns of health and disease that currently exist in Third World countries.

* Black, Nick *et al.* (eds) (1984) *Health and Disease: a Reader*, The Open University Press.

Objectives for Chapter 6

When you have studied this chapter, you should be able to:

6.1 Summarise the available information on disease patterns in early human societies up to the first agricultural revolution.

6.2 Understand the connection between the material wealth of societies and the emergence of hierarchical orders.

6.3 Sketch the outlines of the Malthusian population system, and be aware of evidence from the pre-industrial world about its validity.

6.4 Explain why quantitative change is an inadequate way of viewing the Industrial Revolution.

6.5 Describe the initial impact of the Industrial Revolution on the living conditions in English cities.

Questions for Chapter 6

1 (*Objective 6.1*) We have almost no hard data on how disease patterns altered during the first agricultural revolution. Why is it possible to state fairly confidently that infectious diseases were a much bigger threat after this revolution than before?

2 (*Objective 6.2*) Poverty is often defined as a state of scarcity or being poor. Why might you criticise this definition?

3 (*Objective 6.3*) In the Malthusian system, population and real wages are linked. Why is it important to be more precise about this link?

4 (*Objective 6.4*) In the eighteenth and nineteenth centuries many public buildings in England began to display clocks, and there was a big expansion in the manufacture of cheap pocket watches. What does this tell you about changes in English society at the time?

5 (*Objective 6.5*) According to Engels, life in nineteenth-century cities was one of 'toil and wretchedness, rich in suffering and poor in enjoyment'. And yet many people were migrating to the cities from rural areas. How would you account for this?

7

Population, food and development

During this chapter you will be asked to read an extract contained in the Course Reader. This is 'Entitlements and Deprivation' by Amartya K. Sen, taken from his book *Poverty and Famines: An Essay on Entitlement and Deprivation*. It can be found in the Course Reader, Part 2, Section 2.5.

There is a television programme and an audiotape sequence associated with this chapter. Television programme 2 deals with health in the Third World, and the audiotape sequence provides follow-up material to the programme. Details can be found in the Broadcast and Audiocassette Notes.

Only a few countries in the world were involved in the first wave of the Industrial Revolution, and the majority of the world's population still lives in countries that are not industrialised. As the example of Britain will show in Chapters 8 and 9, health and disease are intimately related to processes of social change and development, and it is clear that the solution to the health problems of Third World countries must involve some sort of social and economic change. How this might be done, however, is one of the biggest problems of our time, and raises a series of questions about the nature of development, the origins and present features of the Third World's problems, and the courses of action that might be taken to reduce these international inequalities.

Population

The rate of *population growth* in Third World countries is considerably more rapid than in industrialised countries: for example, in the years 1960 to 1970, the average annual rate of growth of population in the 'low-income' countries was 2.4 per cent, compared to 1.0 per cent in the industrial countries. For the period 1970 to 1980 the difference between these countries had widened, to 2.6 per cent annual population growth in the low-income countries and 0.8 per cent in the industrial countries (although population growth seemed to be slowing down in the 'middle-income' countries).

☐ In Chapter 5 another aspect of population growth was considered, when the growth in the total GNP for different groups of countries was compared with the growth in the GNP per capita. What did this comparison reveal?
■ It revealed that in many low-income countries there was little or no increase in the GNP per capita even where the total GNP was growing. Economic growth was barely sufficient to keep up with population growth.

Gerald Scarfe, 1970.

It has sometimes been argued that Third World countries cannot hope to improve standards of living without reducing their rate of population growth. According to this argument, death rates in Third World countries have fallen dramatically under the impact of Western medicine, but the failure of birth rates to fall accordingly had led to a situation of 'overpopulation' which has already reached crisis proportions. Especially in the 1960s, phrases such as the 'population explosion' and the population 'time-bomb' were applied almost exclusively to the Third World, and the clear implication was that population growth was a major obstacle to development and a cause of continued lack of development.

If this implication were correct, the overall picture would indeed be a gloomy one. On present trends it would be well into the twenty-second century before many countries reach a state in which the population is stable, by which time, for example, the population of Bangladesh would have risen from around 88 million at present to over 320 million, of Uganda from 13 million to 73 million, and of Ethiopia from 31 million to 160 million. We already know that as a result of these trends the total world population will increase from 1984 by around two thousand million by the end of the twentieth century, with 90 per cent of this increase taking place in the Third World.

There are some other aspects of population growth, however, that must also be taken into account. First, whereas the population density (that is, the number of inhabitants in relation to the land area) is very high in industrialised countries such as the United Kingdom (229 people per square kilometre), the Netherlands (346 people per square kilometre) or Japan (316 people per square kilometre), it is frequently much lower in Third World countries such as Pakistan, Tanzania, or China (with respectively 105, 20, and 103 people per square kilometre). Differences in climate and geography must be borne in mind – it would be a very boring and undesirable world that was uniformly like the Netherlands or the UK. Equally, it is not accurate to talk of 'overpopulation' in any absolute sense.

Second, population growth has not been associated with a decline in per capita food production in the world as a whole, suggesting that the previously discussed Malthusian pessimism over the ability to increase agricultural production has so far been misplaced.

Finally, the gulf in wealth between rich and poor countries is so great that the 10 per cent or so of total population growth attributable to the industrialised countries will consume approximately the same volume of the world's natural resources as the 90 per cent of the increase located in Third World countries. However, despite these important qualifications, it is clear that present rates of population growth cannot continue indefinitely. At a rate of 1.7 per cent growth per year, for

example, world population would double about every 40 years and increase 1 000-fold in 400 years: in 800 years there would be only one square foot of land per person!

There are abundant examples of the negative consequences of population growth to be used as ammunition by those who claim that population pressure is seriously handicapping economic development. In societies where land holdings are passed on through male inheritance, the size of holdings is repeatedly reduced and fragmented when several brothers inherit their father's land, resulting in hopelessly uneconomic field sizes. Overgrazing and other land pressures have led to land degradation, erosion, and sometimes the creation of desert. Unemployment and underemployment lead to migration to the cities and the break-up of families. Apart from the human costs, high birth rates in countries where child mortality remains high have economic consequences. These include the fact that a substantial portion of agricultural output is being consumed by people who die before reaching an age when they can contribute their labour. In pre-Independence India, for example, approximately one-fifth of total national income may have been used in this way.

□   Given that there are such obvious costs associated with rapidly growing populations, can you think of any reasons why people might continue to have large families?
■   There may be legal or religious obstacles to the use of contraceptive practices. Large families may also bring social or economic benefits.

There are many parts of the Third World where people face obstacles that restrict or prohibit the use of modern contraceptive practices. This is especially so in areas of the world where a substantial amount of political power is exercised by the religious hierarchies of Islam or Roman Catholicism: Central and Southern America, parts of North Africa and the Middle East, Pakistan, Bangladesh and the Philippines. In many of these countries, particularly in Central and South America, the prevalence of infanticide, of illegal abortion on a widespread scale, and of the abandonment of children, all suggest that difficulties in practising contraception may result in substantial numbers of unwanted pregnancies (Harrison, 1979, pp.240–245).

In addition to these obstacles, there are many cultures in which a large family size may bring greater social or political prestige in a community, and increase the likelihood of favourable settlement of disputes over land or water rights, legal disputes, or straightforward feuds. Economically, children may be highly valued from a very early age as agricultural and domestic workers. It must also be borne in mind that in many Third World countries social security provision against unemployment, old age, or sickness is either negligible or non-existent. Children may therefore be valued for the financial support they could eventually provide. In other words, large family size can be seen as a positive choice in many areas of the world, and not an accident or mistake. This view is supported by attitude surveys in Thailand, Chile, Indonesia, Korea, the Philippines, Nigeria, Ghana, Kenya and elsewhere. For example, a 1973 survey of Yoruba women in Nigeria, which asked what their ideal number of children would be, even if all were sure to survive to adulthood, found that the average number was 6 children (Harrison, 1979, p.222).

For these reasons, it would be quite wrong to conclude that people are necessarily being irrational or ignorant in behaving in ways which result in rapid population growth. High birth rates can be seen partly as a defence against high rates of mortality and morbidity, and partly as a result of lack of state provision of pensions or other forms of social security. Patterns of population growth in Third World countries are therefore more readily understandable as *symptoms* of low levels of development rather than as *causes*.

In the 1930s and 1940s attempts were made to construct a more formal theory linking population change to industrialisation. This theory of *demographic transition* was originally intended to fit the demographic experience of industrialised countries, but has been used to try to explain demographic trends in the Third World.

Figure 7.1 depicts the demographic transition for a hypothetical population before and after industrialisation. In this model, the demographic transition has four stages. Stage 1 is characterised by a high death rate and a high birth rate, so any population growth is very slow. This is the pre-industrial stage in the model. In Stage 2, the death rate starts to fall sharply, but the birth rate remains high.

□ What hypothesis could you suggest for this stage?
■ One hypothesis that could be supported from the

evidence in the previous chapter is that increases in agricultural productivity have removed the Malthusian 'checks' of famine and disease, allowing the population to expand.

By the third stage of the transition, the birth rate also falls sharply, while the fall in the death rate begins to level off. The fourth stage is reached when both the birth rate and the death rate have levelled off at a low level, and the total population size is again fairly stable, but much larger.

This four-stage theory of demographic transition has been criticised as some aspects do not fit the facts of population change in many of the now industrialised countries, and some of these criticisms will be raised when the demographic history of England is considered in the next chapter. The World Bank has assembled data on birth and death rates for the industrialised and Third World countries from 1775 onwards, and these are shown in Figure 7.2.

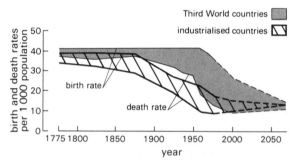

Figure 7.2 Demographic transition? (The World Bank, 1982, Figure 3.4)

□ Using the model shown in Figure 7.1, see if you can find different stages of demographic transition in Figure 7.2. Try to put approximate dates alongside the stages, first for the industrialised countries and then for the Third World countries.

■ For the industrialised countries, it looks as if Stage 1 is right at the edge of the figure, that is, up to the late eighteenth century. By 1800 the death rate is clearly falling while the birth rate remains high: this approximates to Stage 2. By around 1880 the birth rate has also started falling, while the decline in the death rate continues: this is the broad pattern of Stage 3. Stage 4 — low birth rates and death rates — is not clear in the figure. By 1960 the death rate has almost levelled off, but the birth rate is still falling. Among the Third World countries, it seems that high birth rates and death rates existed until around 1880. Then the death rate began to fall, but the birth rate remained high until about 1960, when it too started to fall.

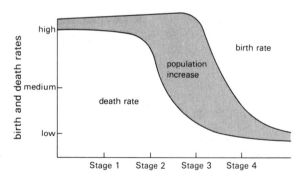

Figure 7.1 A model of the demographic transition. (The Open University, 1982, Figure 3, p.19)

On the evidence of Figure 7.2, Third World countries seem to have been in a situation corresponding to Stage 3 of the demographic transition for the last twenty or so years. As with all such models, however, the reality has to be considerably simplified to fit, and such simplification can be very misleading. A closer look at the trend of the death rate in Third World countries shows that the decline became much steeper after around 1950. A contributory reason, though not the only one, was the widespread use of insecticides in Third World countries after the Second World War. In particular, large quantities of DDT were used to reduce mosquito populations and hence malaria. This reduction in the death rate, however, was not directly linked to industrial and agricultural improvements in the way in which the model suggests for the now industrialised countries.

A further set of difficulties arise when attempts are made to fit the demographic transition model onto projections of future populations, as in Figure 7.2. The first problem is the accuracy of the projections.

□   How might you assess how good such population projections are?
■   There is no wholly reliable way (short of waiting the appropriate length of time!) but we can examine how good they have been in the past.

One example of this is that the projections made in the 1950s by the UN for the 1981 world population were too low. Since then the projection methods have changed and may have improved but any projections are bound to be uncertain. A comparison of past projections with actual outcome in the UK would show similar inaccuracies, the only difference being a tendency to overestimate rather than underestimate growth.

The projections shown in Figure 7.2 must therefore be treated with great caution. Nevertheless, they imply that the period of high population growth in the Third World which might correspond with Stages 2–4 of the demographic transition, will be considerably shorter than the period taken in the now industrialised countries.

□   Thinking back to Chapter 5, what factors might cause you to be surprised by this?
■   The rates of economic growth of many Third World countries are much lower than in the industrialised countries: large parts of the Third World, far from rapidly catching up, are falling further and further behind. And yet it is claimed that it is economic development that propels the demographic transition.

Clearly, therefore, the fact that some form of demographic transition occurred in the industrialised countries is no guarantee at all that the demographic changes occurring in the Third World are following the same path.

Famine

The image of Third World countries that comes most readily to mind is probably that of a black child with arms and legs of skin and bones and a swollen belly, caught in the middle of drought, famine or simply pervasive and chronic malnutrition and poverty. Insufficient food is a major contributory cause of much death and disease, and seems to be another defining characteristic of the Third World.

However, in Chapter 6 we hinted that in the example of one well-known, nineteenth-century famine — the potato famine in Ireland of 1845–1849 — there was room for more than one interpretation of its causes. In Third World countries of today, famines raise in a tragic and acute way the need to take into account the social and economic circumstances in which they occur. They have been the subject of recent research by the economist Amartya Sen, who is currently (1984) Professor of Political Economy at Oxford University. An extract from his book *Poverty and Famines* is included in the Course Reader (Part 2, Section 2.5).

□   Before reading this extract, write down as briefly as possible your own view of why famines occur. Read the extract before continuing with this chapter and then compare your view with Sen's comments on how famines occur. How does it differ?
■   Of course we can't claim to know what your earlier views were. But most probably you would have held to the common assumption that famines occur because of a shortage of food. However, Sen argues that it is quite misleading to focus on food supply; what is much more important, he argues, is the system of *entitlement* relations, which govern whether or not people can get hold of food.
□   Why does Sen claim that it is misleading to focus on the *supply* of food?
■   Famines can occur even if there is no overall shortage of food, as a consequence of some groups having no 'entitlement' to what is available.

During the potato famine in Ireland, between 1846 and 1849, it seems likely that the population of Ireland fell by almost one-third, from roughly 9 million to 6.5 million. Of this third, nearly one million people emigrated, and the rest died of hunger, disease and fever. A conventional view of this event would be that the potato crop, a staple in the diet of most of the Irish population at the time, had been ruined several years in a row by a blight or disease, leading to a straightforward food shortage.

The closer we look at this event, however, the more the facts seem to fit the 'entitlement' approach. In the first place, large quantities of cattle, corn and other foodstuffs were being produced normally throughout the famine years and exported to England in quantities that would have been

The famine in Ireland — a funeral at Skibbereen. From a sketch by Mr. H. Smith, Cork; *Illustrated London News*, 30 January 1847.

sufficient to avert the famine had the Irish population had the means to obtain them. Second, although the English Parliament cheapened the price of grain in 1846 by repealing the Corn Laws in a proclaimed attempt to make grain more accessible to the Irish, the reality of the situation was that the Irish tenant farmers grew grain to pay rent to the landowners, and the falling price of grain increased their rent and thus their poverty, and made them liable to eviction through an inability to meet the landowners' demands. Again, the social and economic organisation of Ireland, and its colonial relations with England, were of more importance than the absolute quantity of food being produced in Ireland at the time. Hence the Irish saying: 'God sent the blight; but the English landlords sent the Famine!'

A more recent example of famine occurred in Bangladesh towards the end of 1974. We have already seen that it is often extremely difficult to obtain reliable health statistics in Third World countries, and not surprisingly there is no agreement over how many people may have lost their lives as a consequence of this famine: the absolute minimum is approximately 26 000 deaths, but the estimates range up to 1.5 million deaths.

Between June and August in 1974 severe flooding occurred in northern Bangladesh as the Brahmaputra river burst its banks, and this event seemed to point to the common-sense conclusion that the food supply had been badly hit and people went hungry in consequence. Once again, however, a careful look at the data reveals a much more complex picture.

☐ Table 7.1 shows the average availability per capita of all food-grains in Bangladesh for the years 1971–75, measured in ounces per day. What do you notice about 1974, the year the famine occurred?

Table 7.1 Availability of food-grains in Bangladesh, 1971–1975

Year	Per capita availability per day/ounces
1971	14.9
1972	15.3
1973	15.3
1974	15.9
1975	14.9

(data from Sen, 1982, Table 9.5)

■ The availability of food-grain in this year was actually higher than in the surrounding years.

Not only was 1974 the least likely year for a famine to have occurred if we look at total food supply, but the districts of Bangladesh most seriously affected by famine tended to be those which if anything had increased their food supply in 1974 by more than the average for the country as a whole.

However, those most seriously affected by the famine were the wage-labourers, and their employment opportunities and therefore income had been severely reduced by the flooding. At the same time, the price of food rose very sharply in response to an expectation of a damaged harvest in 1975, and also perhaps because of panic buying or hoarding. This rise in price compounded the reduction in the entitlement of this part of the population to food, leading to destitution, famine, and, for many, death.

Famine, of course, is only the most spectacular instance of a breakdown in the system of entitlements to food, and these systems can vary widely from one country to another with correspondingly different consequences. In India, for example, periodic famine no longer occurs, but substantial sections of the population suffer from chronically inadequate access to food. In China, by contrast, the normal lot of the population is much better, and entitlement to food is comprehensive. But it now seems clear that occasional large-scale famines have occurred. In 1959–61, for example, it has been estimated that up to 15 million people may have died in China because of famine conditions to which the government was unable to respond rapidly. Sen has suggested that this difference may be caused by the political processes which affect and influence the system of entitlements. In India relatively independent media and competing political parties act to ensure that sudden famine is at least newsworthy and considered a political liability to be avoided, but chronic long-term hunger is neither newsworthy nor politically intolerable to the main parties. In China, the state is committed to and can ensure regular access and equal entitlement to food. But because its political system is centralised, he argues, it can pursue policies which may have completely unintended and (for a time) unknown consequences (Sen, 1981). Indeed not until 1983, over 20 years after this famine, was its occurrence officially acknowledged by the Chinese Government, following publication of a detailed account by a Chinese economist in the *New York Review of Books*.

One other aspect of entitlement that requires greater emphasis relates to gender. Evidence, particularly from India and Bangladesh, suggests that women and girls have much more restricted entitlement to food than men and boys. Surveys in West Bengal after flooding in 1978, for example, indicated a 60 per cent higher incidence of third-degree malnutrition among girls under 5 years old compared to boys under 5. This systematic preference given to males over females is reflected in the Indian demographic structure, where the ratio of females to males is 93:100. This ratio is one of the lowest in the world, and, although an extreme example, evidence of gender discrimination can be found in many other societies as well. In China, moves by the government in recent years towards a one-child family policy seem to have led to a resurgence in infanticide particularly of baby girls, at least in certain regions of the country. If only one child is allowed, males are most frequently favoured. In short, food entitlement seems to be a fundamental and pervasive influence on health and disease patterns.

Development and underdevelopment

As Chapter 6 showed, famines have been recorded throughout history but the world in which they occur has changed, particularly since the beginning of the Industrial Revolution. The first great change has been in international trade.

One of the most characteristic features of the Industrial Revolution was the degree to which it relied upon a great increase in trade and exchange between different parts of the world, and stimulated a great wave of *colonisation*, empire-building, and annexation of territories. As every schoolchild used to be taught, for a time the sun never set on the many countries of the world that were part of the British Empire, and there were very few areas of the world in which control or influence was not exercised or fiercely contested by the newly industrialised countries, including France, Germany, Italy, Belgium and Holland.

Overseas expansion was not of course a phenomenon new to the period of industrialisation. We have only to think of the Romans, whose influence and power in Europe and much of Asia is witnessed even today, not only by the many relics of buildings, but by the location of towns, the routes taken by roads, the language, laws, currencies and measurements that still mould our lives. We must also note that other examples of European conquest, which have already been mentioned (for example the conquest of the Americas by the Spaniards) occurred from the sixteenth century onwards, well before the Industrial Revolution reached full speed. The devastating impact on native populations of infectious diseases imported with the European conquerors has already been discussed.

In this first wave of colonial acquisition, it was already evident that once a European country had taken possession of a territory elsewhere in the world, key aspects of the political, social and economic system prevailing in that territory would be greatly altered in a way which was essentially geared to the needs of the colonists rather than the local populations. In the Americas and Caribbean the first major change introduced was the establishment of plantations to provide cotton, and later coffee and tobacco, for Europe. In the first instance, this required the importation of labour on a massive scale, in large part to compensate for the collapse of the native population through the epidemics. These were the origins of the slave trade, which not only dislocated the social and economic system of much of Africa, but again set off new waves of infectious disease. The other important aspect of this process was that the entire pattern of agriculture and farming was changed beyond recognition, with the most fertile land being devoted to the production of crops that were grown for export rather than to meet the needs of local populations.

With the Industrial Revolution, the speed of change

increased, the parts of the world unaffected by change shrank dramatically, and the economic, technological and political predominance of the industrialised countries was greatly strengthened. Many parts of the world were transformed into satellite economies producing the raw materials and foodstuffs required by the industrial countries: tea from India and Ceylon (Sri Lanka), coffee from Brazil and Kenya, rice from Burma and Thailand, rubber from Malaya, guano fertiliser from Peru, and so on. For these countries, whether formally administered as colonies or informally administered by European commercial enterprises, the needs of distant industrial economies were placed foremost, and the needs of the local populations and of indigenous development were very much secondary considerations.

This dependence on the export of raw materials has continued to the present day: 71 per cent of the exports of the low-income countries are raw materials and foods, compared with less than 30 per cent of the total exports of the industrialised countries. And one paradoxical aspect of this is that many Third World countries with insufficient food for their own populations are also exporting more food than they are importing: of the 77 net food-exporting countries in the world, 42 have inadequate food supplies for their own populations. (You may recall that Ireland was also a net food exporter throughout the potato famine, a fact which lent support to the entitlement argument.)

International trading in foodstuffs clearly reflects certain patterns of world wealth distribution, but the distribution of wealth within countries is also important. For example, many hundreds of thousands of acres of good land in the Indian state of Madhya Pradesh have recently been switched from coarse grain production to soya-bean cultivation. The soya beans are exported to the EEC as cattle fodder, and skimmed milk from the cattle is then imported to India for consumption by those wealthy enough to afford it. The coarse grain was a staple part of the diet of the Indian poor, but the landowners could make more profit by exporting soya extract (Gopalan, 1983).

The industrialised countries have thus exerted a powerful influence over agriculture around the world. But in addition to this role as producers of foodstuffs and raw materials, the colonised or partly-colonised countries of the world were affected in other ways as a world economy developed around the industrialised countries. In particular, they became markets for the industrial goods being manufactured in Britain and elsewhere. The frequent result of this need for new markets, and of the technological superiority of the industrial countries, was that traditional manufacturing industries in the colonised countries were destroyed. India's textile industry, for example, was dealt a death-blow as cotton fabric imports from Britain soared from one million yards in 1814 to 51 million by 1830 (Desai, 1971).

Recently an attempt has been made to calculate the effects of this process on the Third World as a whole. The economist Paul Bairoch has assessed changes in total world manufacturing production from 1750 onwards, and some results are shown in Table 7.2. The figures are expressed in terms of an index where the volume of production in the UK in 1900 is taken as equal to an index number of 100. Thus, in 1880 manufacturing production in the USA had an index number of 47, which means that it was approximately equal to 47 per cent of UK production in 1900.

☐ Look at the column for the Third World. What happens from 1750 onwards?
■ From 1750 to 1830 the Third World index rose from 93 to 112 (in other words, by 1830 it exceeded by 12 per cent the production of the UK in 1900). From 1830 onwards, however, as the process we have described gathered pace, manufacturing production in these countries started to fall, and by 1900 was barely half the level it had been at the beginning of the nineteenth century. Only by 1938 had Third World manufacturing production regained its earlier level.

Not simply in terms of food supply, therefore, but through a much wider process of economic and social change, it seems fairly clear that the characteristics of many Third World countries are not a straight continuation of old patterns, but are in part the direct and indirect results of the industrialisation that has occurred in other areas of the world. However, the degree to which this historical experience *explains* low levels of development is an area of intense controversy.

Table 7.2 The development of world manufacturing production, 1750–1980 (UK in 1900 = 100)

| Year | Industrialised countries | | | Third World |
	UK	USA	all	
1750	2	–	34	93
1800	6	1	47	99
1830	16	5	73	112
1850	45	16	143	83
1880	73	47	253	67
1900	100	128	481	60
1913	127	298	863	70
1928	135	533	1 258	98
1938	181	528	1 562	122
1953	262	1 373	2 870	200
1963	334	1 804	4 699	439
1973	471	3 089	8 432	927
1980	454	3 475	9 718	1 323

(data from Bairoch, 1982, Table 2)

Colonising Africa. A French colonialist exterminating 'natives'. From 'L'Assiette au Beurre', 1902.

A conventional argument, particularly among countries that are already industrialised, is that industrial development will eventually and inevitably spread to all parts of the world if allowed and encouraged to do so. This argument continues to be the guiding principle of Western governments, and of the main international banking, investment and trade organisations. Implicitly, it is an argument derived from the view that the Third World has simply been left behind and now has to catch up. A modification of this position, which was recently expressed in the 'Brandt Report' on international development (1980), is that it is not in the interests of the industrialised countries that so much of the world should be at low levels of development. The Brandt Report argued that positive steps of international redistribution and reorganised trading arrangements are required, and would be of benefit to the industrialised and Third World countries alike.

A third view, which has little in common with the previous two, is that the existing structure of the world economy actively promotes a state of 'underdevelopment' in some countries as the necessary consequence of development in other countries. From this perspective, the main feature of the world economy is not that it is dominated by industrialised countries, but that it is dominated by capitalist industrialised countries, whose primary motivation is not universal development but rather profit and private accumulation of wealth. Two well-known exponents of this view are André Gunder Frank, whose most influential book has related these arguments to the history of Latin America (Frank, 1969), and the Guyanese historian Walter Rodney, whose book *How Europe Underdeveloped Africa* (1972) is an important landmark in history written by the colonised, rather than the colonisers.

These conflicting views raise a number of questions concerning the meaning of 'development' and how much can be learnt by Third World countries from the experience of the industrialised countries. In England, industrial development was not planned, and the state played a relatively minor supporting role. The Industrial Revolution came about through the unhindered activities of private entrepreneurs pursuing profit: this was known as 'laissez-faire' ('leave well alone') capitalism. No other country could afford to follow the same policy, or else their own industrialisation might have been long-delayed by the competition from England. Other European states took care to protect infant industries against imports, and to direct investment into particular industries. The same was true in countries such as Japan and South Korea: they remain fundamentally based on private enterprise, but the state has also been directly involved.

The Russian Revolution, however, provided the first example of a state wishing to take control of the entire economy in order to promote industrialisation. Since then, a number of Third World countries have taken the same path of socialist revolution. These include China, Vietnam, Cuba, North Korea, Angola, Mozambique and Nicaragua. Some, such as China and Cuba, have attained rapid rates of industrial growth, whereas the others are at present still basically agricultural countries. Such countries, however, are good illustrations of the fact that development is not simply about economic growth, but about the kind of economic growth pursued and the way in which the benefits of growth are distributed. Just as Sri Lanka has managed to achieve a high life expectancy by food distribution policies, so the health experience of the Chinese and Cuban populations is much better than those of equally wealthy or wealthier countries: the wealth is less unequally spread. In countries such as Brazil, quite high levels of industrial growth have so far brought benefits only to a much smaller proportion of the population.

In examining some of the different ways in which the process of development has been viewed, we may seem to have travelled some distance away from our starting point of patterns of health and disease. However, this wider perspective on development and underdevelopment is a necessary step to understanding why these patterns of health and disease exist, for a number of reasons. The first main point to emerge from these chapters is that health and disease are intimately connected to levels of development, but not in a way that can be reduced to a formula of 'GNP = level of health'. To view things in this way is to completely omit the importance of internal distribution, social and economic policy, and political determination. Because a country is poor it does not follow that the only way health can be improved is to become richer.

Second, although there is controversy over the extent to which underdevelopment has been *created*, it seems clear that the present state of Third World countries is not simply the same as the past that the industrialised countries of the world have now left behind. Underdevelopment is in at least some respects a consequence of the rise of the industrialised countries, themselves never underdeveloped in the contemporary sense. If this is so, then it follows that the health problems that characterise Third World countries are not simply the same problems as those found in Britain 200 years ago, and are not open to the same solutions. We shall be returning to the solutions which have been proposed for the health problems of Third World countries later in this course, but in the next chapters we look in more detail at the United Kingdom, and by so doing may be better able to answer some of these questions.

Objectives for Chapter 7

When you have studied this chapter, you should be able to:

7.1 Discuss the concept of demographic transition and its relevance to the Third World.

7.2 Describe and illustrate the entitlement approach to famine.

7.3 Describe some of the main consequences of the Industrial Revolution for the Third World, particularly in industry and agriculture.

Questions for Chapter 7

1 (*Objective 7.1*) Figure 7.2 suggests that the death rate among Third World countries is already close to that of industrialised countries. Consider this in the light of the discussion of death rates in Chapter 3: how do your conclusions modify the Third World 'demographic transition' represented in the Figure?

2 (*Objective 7.2*) It seems that in 1925 a famine occurred in the Szechwan province of China after invading troops took away the food reserves of the area. How does this fit into the entitlement approach of Sen?

3 (*Objective 7.3*) The UK during the Industrial Revolution was often described as 'the workshop of the world'. Looking at Table 7.2, how true was this?

8
From infections to chronic diseases

During this chapter you will be asked to read an extract contained in the Course Reader. This is 'The Medical Contribution' by Thomas McKeown, taken from his book *The Modern Rise of Populations*. It can be found in the Course Reader, Part 3, Section 3.1.

So far in this book we have considered the variation in the distribution of health and disease in different parts of the world and some of the major historical events and trends that have shaped the contemporary pattern. This has, of necessity, been a fairly quick account. At this point in the book we turn our attention away from such global considerations to just one country, Britain. We have chosen to concentrate our discussion on Britain partly because it is the country with which we are most familiar, and also because it serves as an example of an industrialised society. As such, the pattern of health and disease in Britain can be compared with information on Third World countries that appeared in earlier chapters. However, just as the introduction to the description of a village in West Bengal (in Chapter 4) warned of the dangers of generalising from one case study, so the same applies in this and the following three chapters. Although Britain is, in many respects, a typical industrialised country, it is also in other ways unique — its central role in the Industrial Revolution is the most significant example of this.

The starting date for our discussion is that of the earliest available quantitative data on population size — the Doomsday Book of 1086. We have chosen to consider the history in two periods: from 1086 to 1680, and from 1680 to the present day. All such historical 'book-marks' are a little artificial, but the reason for picking 1680 is that it is believed that at around this time the population size started to increase rapidly, considerably faster than during the preceding centuries. The end of the seventeenth century also marks the start of modern industrialisation and the end of the second pandemic of plague (1666).

Infection, famine and mortality crises, 1086–1680
The period from the first agricultural communities to the start of modern industrialisation is significant for the consistency rather than the changes in the pattern of diseases that affected humans. Despite the passage of about

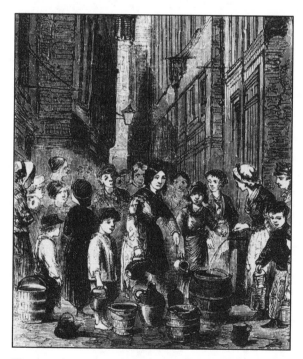

Water-supply — no supply. Fryingpan Alley, Clerkenwell. From *The Builder*, 6 July 1862. (Courtesy Wellcome Trustees)

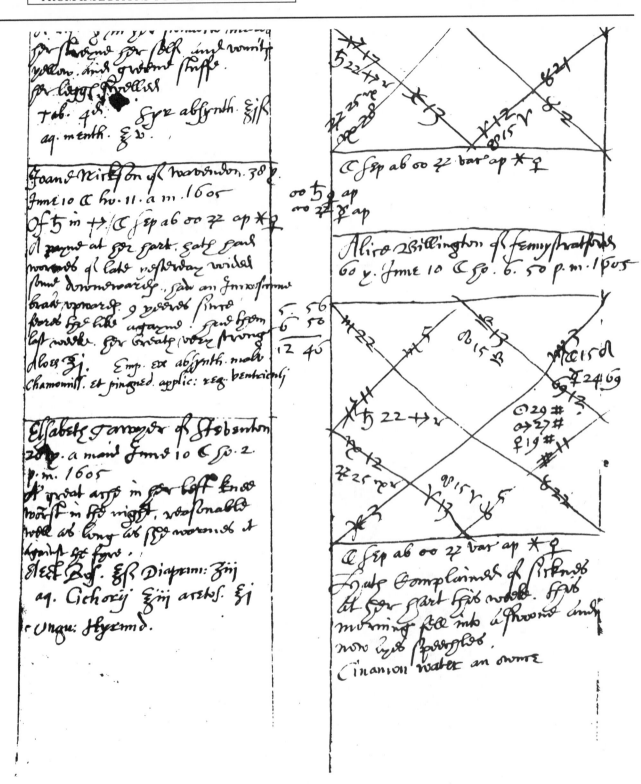

Figure 8.1 Extracts from the diaries of Richard Napier, seventeenth-century physician (Bodleian Library, MS Ashmole 216, Folio 116ʳ).

10 000 years, the main threats to health remained infectious diseases and food shortages. These two, together with violence both accidental and deliberate (such as warfare), accounted for almost all deaths. Their relative contribution and demographic impact are our main concern when considering this period. Much of our knowledge is speculative, based on a variety of different sources: from archaeology, ancient texts, Parish Registers of births and deaths since the sixteenth century, and Bills of Mortality from the following century. Most of the information on disease tends to be limited to records of mortality: the ages at which people died; the numbers dying at a particular time; and the cause of their deaths. This is a problem you have already encountered in earlier chapters, that our picture of the spectrum of disease is biased towards the more lethal ones. In addition, because of the limitations of epidemiological information on mental illness, throughout this chapter the emphasis will be on physical (often termed somatic) illness.

Patterns of morbidity

One of the few historical records from before 1680 that tell us about non-fatal diseases and conditions (ie. morbidity) is the diary kept by a country physician named Richard Napier, who lived and worked in the area approximating to modern Milton Keynes. His diary is not only a rich source of data on the prevalence of conditions but also of how people described their complaints. Uniquely amongst such diaries, Napier recorded his patients' own descriptions of their illnesses.

Two examples of consultations (from the many thousands he wrote) reveal both the ease and the difficulty of interpreting such data in modern terms. The first example is the case of Alice Billington of Fenny Stratford (Figure 8.1), sixty years old, who was seen by Napier on 10 June 1605 at 6.50 p.m.

> Hath complained of sickness at her hart this week this morning fell into a swoone and now lyes speechles.

This woman had probably suffered a stroke, and was prescribed 'cinamon water an ounce'. Contrast this with the case of Joane Nickson (also Figure 8.1) aged thirty-eight years, of Wavendon. Seen earlier the same day, she complained of:

> A payne in her hart
> hath had worms of late
> yesterday voided some downwards
> had an Impostume brake upwards 9 yeeres since
> feares the like agayne
> had them last week
> her breath very strong.

The worms were probably roundworms (still common throughout the Third World today), but the nature of the 'Impostume' she fears (some sort of abscess) is not clear to us. We should of course remember that random scrutiny of the present day records kept by a general practitioner could be equally puzzling!

☐ Before leaving Napier's diary, can you suggest what the strange diagrams in his records might represent? (Remember this was written in 1605 when medicine still contained many traditional beliefs.)

■ They are astrological charts. Napier used astrology to augment his clinical methods in deciding on a diagnosis and suitable treatment.

Unfortunately, few such records of morbidity before 1680 survive (or maybe ever existed). We therefore have to rely on the analysis of historical data on mortality and population size to construct a picture of the health and disease experience of that period.

Population 1086–1680

It is difficult to estimate the size of the population in Britain in medieval times. In fact, before the start of Parish Registers in 1538, the only quantitative demographic information generally available is that of population size — there is little information on such aspects as age and sex. On the basis of the actual figures recorded in the Doomsday Book, the population of Britain has been estimated as numbering about 1.75 million. Estimates of changes in the size of the population of England from 1100 to 1820 are shown in Figure 8.2.

☐ Consider Figure 8.2 and describe the features of population change during the years (a) 1100–1348, (b) 1348–1480, (c) 1480–1600, and (d) 1600–80.

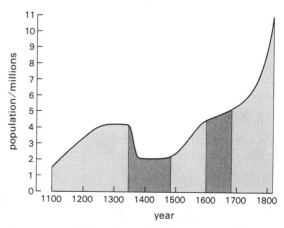

Figure 8.2 Population of England 1100–1820. (After Chambers, 1972, Figure 1).

■ You should have noted that from 1100 to 1348 the population appears to have trebled in size (a); from 1348 to 1480 there was an overall decline in size, including a possible fifty per cent reduction between 1348–75 (b); from 1480 to 1600 there was a rapid expansion of population (c); and that 1600–80 was a period of slow population expansion (d).

Though the population figures shown in Figure 8.2 represent the current view of most historians, it must be pointed out that some contemporary historians suggest that the population during the fourteenth century before the Black Death was as high as 5 to 7 million.

Mortality crises: subsistence versus infection
Although the population in 1680 differed only slightly in size from that in 1348, the intervening years saw repeated *mortality crises* — sudden, intense rises in the mortality rate of short duration. A doubling or more of the rate is usually regarded by students of demography as a 'crisis', an event that in the late sixteenth century occurred on average about every sixteen years in towns.

In the absence of records such as death certificates (not introduced until the nineteenth century), discovering the cause of a mortality crisis depends on the study of its demographic features. Two of the best sources of information have been Parish Registers and Bills of Mortality. The former were established in 1538 on the order of Thomas Cromwell, one of Henry VIII's chief ministers, in the wake of the Reformation. Unfortunately, only a few Parish Registers survive from the middle of the sixteenth century. Although most only inform us of a person's name and date of interment, some also recorded the age and supposed cause of death. Bills of Mortality were weekly, monthly or annual returns, by parish clerks, of information about the deaths occurring in their parish, including the cause of death. Unfortunately few remain outside London and the reliability of the diagnosis is uncertain. In addition the surviving examples may be atypical. Nevertheless the Registers and Bills are our main source of data for determining whether a mortality crisis resulted primarily from a shortage of food, an infectious epidemic or a combination of the two.

Evidence of the impact of food shortages and famine on the health of the population has been derived from studying the association between the occurrence of a mortality crisis and the success or failure of the preceding harvest. In this way many such crises have been shown to have resulted from harvest failures. Such findings tend to support one of the main theories of demographic change, first espoused by Malthus and already discussed in Chapter 6. In contrast, the occurrence of mortality crises at times of adequate food

supplies is one of the factors that has lent support to the notion of *autonomous* (or *exogenous*) *infectious epidemics**. Other factors include the seasonal pattern of deaths, the ages and social background of the victims and the size of the geographical area affected.

□ What evidence would suggest autonomous infections as the cause of a mortality crisis, rather than a shortage of food?
■ 1 Mortality showing a strong association with season (e.g. plague showing a rapid rise in summer and more gradual decline in late autumn and winter);

2 Deaths occurring in particular age groups: for example, deaths of more adults than children suggest typhus, whereas deaths occurring only among children suggest a smallpox epidemic in an area where smallpox was endemic (i.e. adults would have built up some resistance to the disease);

3 Deaths occurring in all social sections of the population and not just the poorest and weakest;

4 The crisis being restricted to a small geographical area, rather than a country or region.

No mortality crisis in this period seems to have been due exclusively to deaths from one or other cause, though it is usually possible to distinguish which was primarily responsible. In a few cases this is not possible, as a result of the two causes coinciding — a likely event given the frequency with which they both occurred, and the opportunity for a crisis of subsistence to fuel an outbreak of an infectious disease. This opportunity is thought to have been a result of famine and starvation causing an increased number of people to move from rural to urban areas; a situation that would clearly favour the spread of an infection. Similarly, if the population was weakened by an epidemic infection, this could lead to, or at least exacerbate, a failure to produce sufficient food (as was illustrated by the extract from McNeill (1976) in Chapter 5).

It is therefore difficult to assess the relative impact on mortality of infection and shortage of food. However, it has been estimated that the mortality rate in a crisis resulting from a lack of food tended to be about three to four times the 'normal' rate, whereas that resulting from an infectious disease outbreak was up to a twelve-fold increase.

The 'Golden Age of Bacteria'
Infectious diseases are caused by microorganisms such as bacteria and viruses. Although information is limited, we

---

* Autonomous and exogenous both refer to the theory that disease epidemics primarily arise independently of any internal features, such as the pattern of entitlement, of that society.

do know something about those diseases responsible for the epidemics during the five or six hundred years up to 1680; about earlier times, however, we can only speculate. One of the most dramatic causes of mortality has been discussed — plague. Although many recorded cases of plague were almost certainly not due to *Yersinia pestis* infection, this organism was responsible for many of the most devastating mortality crises between 1348 and 1666 in Britain.

The first hundred years of that period (1348–1448) is often referred to as the 'Golden Age of Bacteria' in recognition of the repeated infectious epidemics that held back any growth in population. It should, however, be noted that not all such infections were caused by bacteria — some were the result of viruses. Between 1348 and 1375 the population may have been reduced by half, as successive local epidemics occurred. Apart from plague, the other main causes are thought to have been smallpox, typhus and dysentery. There is considerable difficulty in recognising the true nature of past epidemics. Moreover, despite high death rates associated with epidemic infections such as plague, they may have had less effect on the general level of mortality than the constantly high death rate from endemic infections, such as tuberculosis. Unfortunately, the steady, unchanging impact of endemic infections makes accurate quantitative assessment of their contribution to mortality rates impossible.

The pattern of infectious diseases was not static in pre-industrial Europe: plague appeared suddenly in 1348 and disappeared just as suddenly in 1666. Another example is that of leprosy which appears to have been prevalent throughout Europe and the Mediterranean for many centuries, with around 19 000 leprosaria (institutions for sufferers of leprosy) in existence in 1300. The arrival of plague in Europe was associated with a massive decline in the number of lepers, an association that has given rise to a number of possible explanations, thus illustrating one feature of historical research — the difficulty of deciding on the most plausible explanation.

An example of the ability of microorganisms to adapt to changing circumstances, thus enabling them to maintain their dominance throughout this period, is that of the transformation of the contagious disease yaws into a venereally transmitted form known as syphilis. Yaws, a disease of tropical and sub-tropical countries, is spread by direct contact with the skin of a sufferer. In the temperate climates of Northern Europe, transmission of the bacteria in this way was limited by clothing. It is thought that in such circumstances the means of transmission of the bacteria altered from skin contact to penetration of the less resistant mucosa (or linings) of the mouth and genitals during sexual intercourse. Such an adaptation would explain accounts of the existence of syphilis in Europe

before Columbus returned from the New World in 1492 (though there is still some debate over these accounts).*

Historical accounts of some illnesses have proved insufficient to identify them in terms of modern categories of disease. The best example of this is the 'English Sweat' or 'sweating sickness' which occurred in five major epidemics between 1486 and 1551, then disappearing as mysteriously as it arrived. From contemporary descriptions it was probably a disease caused by a virus (some historians have suggested it may have been an early form of influenza) that affected the heart and lungs, causing rheumatic pains, fits of shivering and profuse sweating. Victims were often dead within hours of its onset, though in demographic terms it rarely caused more than a doubling of the mortality rate, compared with ten- to twelve-fold increases during plague epidemics. The appearance from contemporary records that the disease particularly struck the eminent and famous (unlike almost all other infections) probably reflects the chronicler's interest and concern rather than its true social distribution.

The sweating sickness first struck in London in 1486, and then spread across England, without ever reaching Wales or Scotland. In 1529 it crossed to the Netherlands, Germany and Switzerland, and by 1551 disappeared from England completely, its true nature lost in the mysteries of time. Indeed, the overall decline of the 'Golden Age of Bacteria' remains something of an enigma.

Local patterns of disease
A few Parish Registers survive that are complete enough to indicate the pattern of mortality in a whole community. One such example is for the parish of St Botolph without Aldgate in London for the years 1583–99. As the size of the population of the parish for this period is not known (the first census was not taken in England until 1801) it is neither possible to determine the incidence of deaths for specific ages and sexes, nor the mortality rates for specific diseases.

☐ How could the number of deaths from a particular disease in 1583–99 be meaningfully compared with the number occurring in the present day?
■ One way in which this has been done is to compare the percentages of all deaths that were caused by the particular disease. This is known as the *proportional mortality*. Note that this measure does not express the risk of dying from the disease, only the proportion of all deaths caused by that particular disease.

In a similar way the number of deaths occurring at different ages (Figure 8.3) can be compared with the present.

* Until recently, it has generally been considered that Columbus's expedition introduced syphilis into Europe from America.

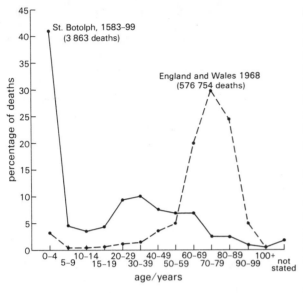

Figure 8.3 Percentage distribution of deaths by age-group; St. Botolph without Aldgate 1583–99 and England and Wales, 1968. (Forbes, 1979, p.124)

☐ What are the main differences between the mortality experiences at the end of the sixteenth century and 1968?

■ There was a much higher infant and childhood mortality, and a higher mortality in young adulthood during the earlier period. In contrast, most deaths in 1968 occurred in people aged over 60 years — an age that few people reached in the sixteenth century.

The high proportion of deaths in infancy and childhood in the sixteenth century is similar to the present-day experience of many Third World countries (as illustrated by Egypt in Figure 2.4).

Proportional mortality for the ten most common 'causes' of death in St. Botolph is shown in Table 8.1. These data present several problems of interpretation: plague was often used to denote any epidemic disease rather than

Table 8.1 Proportional mortality (per cent) from ten most common 'causes' of death at St. Botolph's, 1583–99

plague	23.6
consumption	22.2
convulsions	
[not stated]	14.1
pining, decline	13.2
ague, fever	6.1
flux, colic	2.5
smallpox	2.4
childbed	1.5
teeth	1.1

(data from Forbes, 1979, Table 2, p.127)

specifically that caused by *Yersinia pestis*; consumption and convulsions could be confused because records often only state the abbreviation 'Con'; and the meaning of a term such as 'Pining' is open to misinterpretation, though it is thought to refer to tuberculosis. The notion of 'cause' has also altered since the sixteenth century. 'Infancy' was seen as sufficient explanation for dying (though the current use of 'cot death' could be viewed as a modern equivalent, in the sense that the underlying 'biological' cause is unknown).

Although plague only occurred intermittently it was nevertheless responsible for almost a quarter of all deaths. The impact of plague epidemics at the end of the sixteenth century can be seen in the fluctuation in the annual number of burials at that time (Figure 8.4). No other disease caused such fearful loss of life in relatively short periods of time. In contrast tuberculosis, a chronic infection (recorded as consumption and pining), showed no epidemic pattern.

The dominance of infectious causes is striking, particularly when it is considered that the apparently non-infectious causes probably conceal an infectious basis. These include 'childbed' (maternal mortality) which led to the death of 23 women per 1 000 deliveries, and 'teeth' which denoted deaths in infancy. Of every 100 babies born in St. Botolph's parish, about 30 died before their first birthday, a further 22 died in the next 4 years, and only about 30 survived to the age of 15.

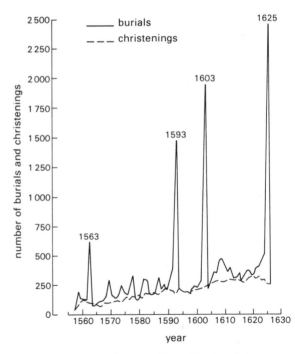

Figure 8.4 St. Botolph without Aldgate, burials and christenings 1558–1626. (Forbes, 1979, p.126)

Despite the existence of such records, it is clear that our understanding of pre-industrial society is still hampered by a lack of knowledge. What is surprising, however, is that our knowledge has deepened considerably in recent years. This suggests that lack of interest, as much as lack of data, has been a reason for our previous ignorance and doubts about the interaction of population, disease, and food. Peter Laslett, a contemporary historian who has done a great deal to assert the importance of such interactions, has summed up the position as follows:

> Why is it that we know so much about the building of the British Empire, the growth of Parliament, and its practices, the public and private lives of English kings, statesmen, generals, writers, thinkers and yet do not know whether all our ancestors had enough to eat? ... Why has almost nothing been done to discover how long those earlier Englishmen lived and how confident most of them would be of having any posterity at all? Not only do we not know the answers to these questions, until now we never seem to have bothered to ask them. (Laslett, 1971, p.134)

Population, 1680–1850

The transition from the disease and mortality patterns of pre-industrial society in which infectious diseases and food shortages were the main causative factors, to the present pattern dominated by chronic non-infectious diseases (such as heart disease and cancers) took place over a period of about 250 years. This was accompanied by an unprecedented increase in the size of the population, partly the result of an overall decline in mortality rates, but also a consequence of changes in the fertility rate.

As you have seen, the population of England in 1680 was steady at around 5 million (Figure 8.2): fertility and mortality rates were in balance. Over the following 150 years however, the population is estimated to have more than doubled (133 per cent increase), and in the later part of this period (from 1790–1830) the growth rate is thought to have been the highest in Europe, with the population expanding from 7.7 million to 13.3 million. Whether this surge of growth was the result of a fall in mortality, a rise in fertility, or both, has been the subject of much debate.

The decline in mortality 1680–1850

The crude death rate is thought to have declined during this period from 30.7 to 24.5 per 1 000. The historical demographer E. A. Wrigley has estimated that the expectation of life at birth rose from 32.4 years in 1670 to 38.7 years in 1810. Most of the improvement between the 1680s and 1850 occurred in the mortality of children under the age of five years. This can be seen in Figure 8.5 which

shows the proportion of the population surviving to different ages. The gradient (or slope) of the curves indicates the mortality rate at different ages — the steeper the gradient, the higher the mortality rate.

☐ At what age is the mortality rate highest (a) at the end of the seventeenth century; (b) in the mid-nineteenth century: and (c) in the present day?

■ The mortality rate is highest, (a) and (b) under 5 years; (c) over 70 years.

☐ How does the proportion of children surviving to five years of age in the mid-nineteenth century compare with that at the end of the seventeenth century?

■ Over 70 per cent survived in the mid-nineteenth century compared with less than 60 per cent at the earlier date.

The similarity in childhood mortality between Britain in the mid-nineteenth century and Third World countries today is striking.

The averages for the total British population mentioned above conceal substantial differences between social groups. For example, in the middle of the seventeenth century 80 per cent of the children of the British aristocracy survived to the age of five compared with only 60 per cent of children born to Lincolnshire villagers. Again, differences of this magnitude occur today in many Third World countries.

The main reason for the decline in mortality was a fall in the number of deaths from infectious diseases, though fewer deaths from starvation also contributed. Three

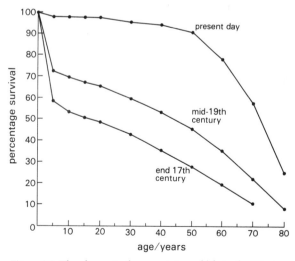

Figure 8.5 The change in the expectation of life in the Western world since the seventeenth century (data on seventeenth century from Halley's life table based on Breslau data; on nineteenth century and present day from English life tables). (Lowe, 1975)

possible explanations for the decline in deaths from infectious diseases have been proposed.

□ Can you suggest what these three may be?

■ These are the three types of possible explanation:

1 Biological — a decrease in the virulence of the microorganisms.

2 Environmental — less exposure to infections through improvements in social conditions such as housing and water supplies; or increased resistance to infection resulting from improvements in nutrition.

3 Medical — an improvement in the effectiveness of medical intervention in the treatment of infectious diseases.

As we have seen, biological explanations of historical changes in disease patterns are difficult to establish. The best evidence is often simply the failure to substantiate any other explanation. However, it is sometimes possible to provide circumstantial evidence, such as a decrease in the reported case-fatality rates, which may suggest that, for instance, the virulence of a microorganism had changed. This is thought to have been the case with the decline of scarlet fever, and may also have been true of plague and other infectious diseases.

The two main changes in the social environment which are thought to have been responsible for the decline in mortality were improvements in nutrition and in social conditions. The main advocate of the importance of nutrition has been Thomas McKeown, a doctor and the leading post-war medical sceptic about the impact of health care. He has pointed to the great increases in food supplies before 1850, due to a transformation in agricultural production affecting ownership, organisation, technology, and distribution. The gradual enclosure and commer-cialisation of land encouraged greater technical efficiency and provided a basis for exploiting technological develop-ments. The most important of these was the introduction of mixed farming (arable and livestock) which, along with crop rotation and the application of lime and urban waste products contributed to increasing the yield of the land.

However, some historians consider the most important development to have been the introduction of new crops: clover and hays (which provided winter feeds so that livestock could be fed over the winter months); root crops (such as carrots and parsnips from the Low Countries); and the potato, introduced in the sixteenth century from America by Walter Raleigh. There seems little doubt that the potato was the predominant influence on the growth of population in Ireland, and had a significant effect in Britain from about 1750.

Additional influences on agricultural yield are thought to have been improvements in seed production and the introduction of new farm implements, in particular a smaller, lighter plough and Jethro Tull's mechanical seed drill. Finally, as was seen in Chapter 7, food production and food supply are not necessarily synonymous. In the eighteenth century, the construction of canals in Britain is thought to have made a major contribution to improving the distribution of the increased amounts of food being produced, as did improvements in coast, river, and road transport.

Although Thomas McKeown has argued that other social improvements had little or no impact until after 1820, some people have suggested otherwise. They have pointed to such factors as the drainage of land which led to less malaria (though this was never more than a localised problem in Britain), the replacement of wooden with brick or stone buildings after the urban fires of the seventeenth century, leading to improved domestic hygiene and control of vermin; and the introduction of mechanised cotton cloth manufacture, which may have contributed to reducing the incidence of typhus (as a result of the greater availability of cotton clothes which could be boiled during washing).

The third possible explanation of the decline of mortality is an improvement in medical intervention. Most commentators have considered the contribution of eighteenth-century medicine to have at best been nil and at worst actually harmful. There have, however, been two alternative views. The historian Peter Razzell has argued that the introduction of smallpox innoculation in 1720, and its widespread use from 1760, helped reduce mortality from this condition. However, a problem with this argument is that by 1760 most people over the age of 5 years had been exposed to the infection in childhood and were therefore *naturally* protected against further infection in much the same way as contracting mumps in childhood protects most people for the rest of their lives. Suggestions have also been made that hospitals contributed to the falling death rate. This, however, has been based on the very low fatality rates experienced by people cared for in hospital — not a surprising finding given that it was not customary to be hospitalised during terminal illnesses at that time. In any case, hospital populations were so small as to be demographically irrelevant in the eighteenth century.

Before examining changes in the fertility rate during the eighteenth and early nineteenth centuries we must consider one particular non-infectious cause of death which may well have occurred on a large scale — *infanticide* (the killing of infants). Discussing this has two problems: is infanticide a cause of death in the same sense as tuberculosis or starvation, or should it be considered a form of population control similar to termination of pregnancy (induced abortion) nowadays? The second problem is the difficulty of quantifying its incidence. Thomas McKeown has summarised the extent of our knowledge:

In his survey of the history of infanticide, Langer concluded that it was practised on a substantial scale in both ancient and modern times. In the eighteenth and nineteenth centuries, 'the poor, hardly able to support the family they already had, evaded responsibility by disposing of further additions'. The same conclusion was reached by many contemporary writers, among them Disraeli who believed that infanticide 'was hardly less prevalent in England than on the banks of the Ganges'. (McKeown, 1976, p.67)

Whatever the actual incidence of infanticide — and although this is much debated it seems unlikely we shall ever know — our ignorance need not affect some of our calculations. As births resulting in infanticide went unrecognised in civil records (both as births and as deaths), they made no contribution to derived statistics such as mortality rates and life expectancy. On these grounds it is therefore possible to exclude consideration of the effect of infanticide, as a 'cause of death', in the overall statistics.

In summary, the decline in mortality during this period was probably mainly due to improvements in nutrition, which were themselves part of wider social and economic changes. Local environmental measures such as land drainage may also have contributed.

The rise in fertility, 1680–1850

Whereas the crude death rate declined during this period from 30.7 to 24.5 per 1 000, the crude birth rate (number of live births per 1 000 population) rose fom 30.7 to 39.6.

◻ List as many factors as you can think of that could have contributed to the rise in the crude birth rate.

■ Some of the factors are:

1 An increase in the proportion of women of childbearing age in the population.

2 Earlier age for marriage, leading to more pregnancies during a woman's reproductive life.

3 More women marrying and having children.

4 Shorter intervals between successive pregnancies.

5 Improvements in the health of women, leading to greater fecundity (reproductive capacity), earlier onset of menstruation (menarche), later menopause, and fewer stillbirths.

Investigation of Parish Registers and marriage documents have demonstrated that the rise in the birth rate was due to changes in *nuptiality*, that is earlier and more universal marriage. Mean age at first marriage in those parishes studied dropped from 26 to 23 years and the proportion of unmarried women fell from 15 to 7 per cent.

The reason for these changes in nuptiality was a rise in real incomes. Whereas in previous periods a rise in nuptiality initiated a sequence of changes in which higher fertility led to population growth, to higher food prices, to food shortages and finally to higher mortality (as discussed in Chapter 6), on this occasion something unprecedented happened. Contrary to the theories of Malthus, food prices did not rise. The old relationship between population and economy disappeared for a time as the country slipped the shadow that had inhibited population expansion for centuries.

It appears, therefore, that the expansion in population between 1680 and 1850 resulted from both a decline in mortality and a rise in fertility. It has been calculated that the rise in the fertility rate contributed two and a half times as much as the decline in the mortality rate.

The decline in mortality since 1850

The rise in fertility continued to be the principal cause of population expansion in Britain until about 1870 when a dramatic and unprecedented decline in mortality commenced. The social historian J.M. Winter has described the dramatic nature of this change:

In roughly three generations, crude death rates (deaths per 1 000 population per year) were halved, infant mortality rates were reduced by 80 per cent, and at all ages mortality due to infectious diseases was reduced by approximately 90 per cent. Another way of measuring this astonishing change is in terms of life expectation at birth, which in England and Wales in 1861 stood at 40.5 years for men and 43.0 years for women. Sixty years later, after the First World War, the 50-year mark was passed for women but not yet for men. Ten more years were added to the expectation at birth for both sexes by 1951. It was only in the 1960s that infants born in England and Wales were likely to survive to the Biblical lifespan of threescore years and ten. (Winter, 1982, p.100)

The decline in death rates for males and females at all ages can be seen in Figure 8.6. The reason we are able to be so precise about mortality rates from the 1840s onwards is because of the introduction of the routine collection of mortality statistics in 1838. In addition the establishment of a decennial (10-yearly) census in 1801 provided the means of determining mortality rates not only for the whole population, but for specific age groups, for each sex, and, from 1921, for social classes.

The difference in mortality rates between males and females is apparent in Figure 8.6. Although the rates have declined for both sexes, the decline for males has been slightly less than that for females. The consequence of this has been a widening of the difference between the sexes. The possible reasons for this will be discussed in the following chapter.

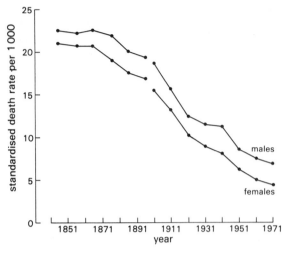

Figure 8.6 Death rates in England and Wales, 1841–1971. (McKeown, 1976, Figure 3.1, p.5.2)

Information on trends in mortality for different social classes is more difficult to determine. The available evidence shows that the mortality rate for people in social class V has always exceeded that for social class I and that this difference has widened over the past 50 years (Figure 8.7).

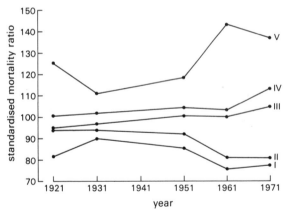

Figure 8.7 Male standardised mortality ratios (SMRs) by social class, England and Wales (Brotherston, John 'Inequality: is it inevitable?' in Carter, 1976, Table 8.1)

☐ Looking at both Figures 8.6 and 8.7 what has happened to the mortality rate for people in social class V since 1921?

■ The mortality rate has fallen. Figure 8.7 shows the *relative* changes in mortality not the absolute changes. For example, consider the change in the mortality rate of men in social class V between 1921 and 1971. In 1921 the rate for all men was about 12.5 per 1 000 (from

Figure 8.6), and the SMR for social class V was 125. The social class V male mortality rate was therefore 12.5 × 125 = 15.6 per 1 000. In 1971 the corresponding figures were about 7 per 1 000 and 140, thus the mortality rate was 9.8 per 1 000. The mortality rates for all social classes have fallen over this period, but fallen faster in classes I and II than in IV and V. This has led to a relative widening of the difference between the classes.

Information on social class and mortality in the nineteenth century is sparse and consists of the findings of a few surveys. One published by Edwin Chadwick, a social reformer, showed the differences between three social categories of people in London in 1840. The infant mortality rate for artisans and labourers (250 per 1 000) was two-and-a-half times higher than that for the gentry (100 per 1 000). As you will see in Chapter 9, such differences have persisted to the present day.

Changes in the cause of death since 1850
Unlike for the discussions of the causes of death before 1850, there is much more accurate and reliable information for the recent past as a result of the introduction of death certification in 1838. However, as Thomas McKeown has pointed out, this only represents a relative improvement in our knowledge of causes, and many problems can still arise unless care is taken in interpreting the evidence.

Problems arise both from vagueness and inaccuracy of diagnosis and from changes in nomenclature and classification. For example, there must be doubts about the diagnosis of tuberculosis at a time when it was not possible to X-ray the chest or identify the tubercle bacillus. In the Registrar General's classification scarlet fever was not separated from diphtheria until 1855, nor typhus from typhoid before 1869. Even the less exacting task, so important for the present discussion of distinguishing infectious from non-infectious causes of death, presents difficulties. For example, deaths attributed to diseases of the heart and nervous system included a considerable but unknown number due to infections such as syphilis. (McKeown, 1976, p.50)

Some of these problems can be avoided by adopting a simple classification based on groups of conditions rather than specific causes. This confirms that the major improvement in mortality rates was due to the decline in infectious diseases (74 per cent) rather than non-infectious conditions (26 per cent). Another difference between these two groups was that though half the decline in infectious causes occurred before 1901, most of the decline in non-infectious causes has taken place since 1901.

Within each of these groups there was considerable variation in the pattern of the decline of different diseases. Of the airborne infections, respiratory tuberculosis was the single most important disease to decline, accounting for as much as 17.5 per cent of the fall in overall mortality (from all causes) between 1850 and 1971. Whereas deaths from tuberculosis fell steadily throughout this period, the decline of other airborne infections such as bronchitis, pneumonia and influenza only occurred after 1901. Water-borne infections (such as typhoid) declined more before 1901 than those which were food-borne (such as dysentery). Though the mortality rate for *all* infectious diseases fell between 1850 and 1971, this was not true of all non-infectious causes of death (Table 8.2).

□ Look at Table 8.2. Which four non-infectious conditions showed the greatest decline, and which two the greatest increase between 1850 and 1971?
■ Old age (8.7 per cent), prematurity (6.2 per cent), digestive system diseases (3.6 per cent) and nephritis (kidney disease) (3.5 per cent), showed the greatest decline, and cardiovascular disease (6.4 per cent) and cancer (5.2 per cent) the greatest increase.

It is apparent from these data that the decline in mortality since 1850 has followed a sequence as regards the type of condition causing death: first water-borne and then food-borne infections declined, followed by airborne infections, and finally some non-infectious conditions. The timings of these changes have not of course been mutually exclusive,

and, as we have seen, within some categories the incidence of specific diseases has actually increased at times. However, the timing of these changes in mortality rates helps us to understand such improvements.

Explanations of the modern decline in mortality
Just as with the preceding period (1680–1850), the reason for the dramatic decline in infectious-disease mortality rates since 1850 has been a subject of much debate. The focus of the debate has been slightly different, concentrating on (i) the impact of medical intervention; (ii) the establishment of public health administration and legislation; and (iii) improvements in nutrition and standards of living. The influence of biological factors has largely been dismissed on the grounds that changes would have to have occurred in the virulence of *many* different microorganisms — an event that is regarded as most unlikely to have happened.

Until recently, the major contribution to the decline in mortality was considered to have been from medical advances. However, since the 1960s this view has been challenged, largely as a result of the work of Thomas McKeown. An account of his views on this subject appears in the Course Reader (Part 3, Section 3.1), which you should now read.

□ On what grounds does McKeown argue that medical measures made only an insignificant contribution to the overall decline of mortality from infectious diseases?

Table 8.2 Standardised death rates (per million) from conditions not attributable to microorganisms, England and Wales

| Condition | Period | | Percentage of reduction from all causes attributable to each condition |
	1848–54	1971	
congenital defects	28	237	0.6 increase
prematurity, immaturity, other diseases of infancy	1 221	192	6.2
cerebrovascular disease	890	603	1.7
rheumatic heart disease	64	88	0.1 increase
other cardiovascular disease	634	1 688	6.4 increase
cancer	307	1 169	5.2 increase
other diseases of digestive system	706	105	3.6
other diseases of nervous system	316	63	1.5
nephritis	615	46	3.5
other diseases of urinary system	107	23	0.5
pregnancy and childbirth (excluding sepsis)	130	3	0.8
violence	761	345	2.5
old age	1 447	16	8.7
other diseases	1 665	202	8.9
total	8 891	4 670	25.6

(McKeown, 1979, Table 3.6, p.38)

■ He does this principally by demonstrating that mortality had declined or was declining before the introduction of such measures (e.g. in the cases of measles and respiratory tuberculosis).

□ Despite this, medical measures appear (a) to have made a dramatic contribution to the decline of one infection, and (b) to have accelerated the decline in mortality from two others since the 1940s. Which diseases are these?

■ These are (a) smallpox — the decline was mainly due to vaccination, and (b) respiratory tuberculosis, with the introduction of chemotherapy; diphtheria, with the widespread use of immunisation.

□ As an assessment of the contribution that doctors have made to the overall decline in mortality, what are the main limitations of this article?

■ Quite explicitly McKeown is only concerned with the decline in *infectious* diseases, ignoring the possible effect doctors may have had on the other types of condition that account for 26 per cent of the overall decline. However, the more important limitation is that he concentrates on the biomedical role of medicine and ignores the preventive work carried out by doctors, both in the area of individual advice to people and in the establishment of public health measures.

J.M. Winter, on the other hand, is in no doubt of the importance and impact of such a medical role:

When a doctor advises a change in diet or the removal of unsanitary debris, he may very well improve the survival chances of his patients. Simply because doctors do not require a medical education to make such statements is no reason to conclude that such indirect medical intervention was unimportant in the process of mortality decline. (Winter, 1982, p.111)

In addition, he also challenges the conclusion that biomedical measures made only an insignificant contribution to the decline in mortality. As evidence he argues that while vaccines may not have been responsible for the decline in many infectious diseases, they may have prevented new outbreaks of these diseases in recent times. He also cites the impact that research into hormonal and dietary deficiency diseases has had on such conditions as diabetes and rickets. Though all these factors may have made valuable contributions, they do not seriously undermine McKeown's conclusion that medical treatment and immunisation made only a negligible impact on infectious disease mortality in Britain. The effective role of doctors in promoting prevention is one that McKeown himself would readily accept.

The second explanation for the decline in mortality since 1850 brings in the effect of public health legislation and administration, which probably contributed both directly and indirectly. Publicly enacted improvements in sanitation doubtless contributed *directly* to the decline in both water- and food-borne infections. However, in comparison, the *indirect* benefits resulting from establishing, in the political arena, an awareness of, and concern for, the social determinants of disease may have made a greater contribution than the direct improvements in sanitation. Since the nineteenth century, public health administration has played an indirect rather than a direct role in the decline of mortality. Although it is impossible to assess its impact quantitatively, its importance should be recognised.

The third and final explanation, however, is the one generally regarded as establishing the decisive factors — nutrition and standard of living. Although trends in standards of living in the early phases of the Industrial Revolution are still a subject of heated debate, it is agreed that the second half of the nineteenth century witnessed a sustained and significant rise in average real wages, a drop in fertility rates and, as a consequence, a greater provision of food for fewer children. Enhanced nutrition led to improved recovery rates from the common infections. Not only did children's resistance and ability to combat infections improve, but so did their growth. For instance, the mean height of schoolchildren in Glasgow increased between 1900 and 1950 by 2 inches for 5 year olds, 3 inches for 9 year olds and 4 inches for 11 year olds.

□ To summarise, place the three explanatory factors, previously discussed, in order of the impact they appear to have had on reducing mortality rates.

■ 1 Improvements in nutrition and standard of living.

2 Environmental improvements through public health legislation and administration.

3 Effects of medical interventions for some conditions.

The overall effect of all these changes in the causes of death can be seen in Figure 8.8. Infections (infectious diseases and tuberculosis) have undergone a spectacular decline and are now responsible for less than 2 per cent of all deaths. The decline of diseases of the nervous system was because of changes in diagnosis and classification: in 1851 many people were certified as dying from convulsions, others from insanity and delirium tremens, none of which would be commonly recognised as causes of death today.

These causes have been replaced by three categories in particular — heart disease, strokes and cancers. Though most of their increase is relative, due to the decline of other causes and the survival of more people to ages in which these diseases occur, some of the increase is thought to have resulted from an absolute rise in incidence. The current pattern of causes of death will be considered in greater

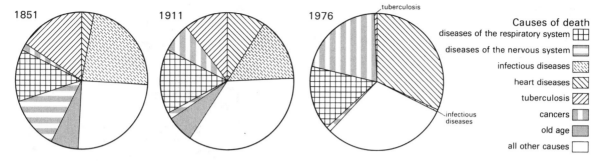

Figure 8.8 Causes of death, 1851, 1911 and 1976 in Britain. (Data from Registrar General England and Wales Report 1855, Statistic Abstract for the UK No. 70, '79 and Annual Abstract of Statistics, 1977; Hey, 1979, Figure 63, p.133)

detail in the next chapter.

A final comment on the historical changes in patterns of disease in Britain must be made. Most of the discussion has been concerned with *mortality* and changing causes of *death*. This is unfortunate as it provides only one indication of the *health* of a population. In particular it ignores two aspects of ill-health — morbidity and disability — which may be better indicators of the health of a population. The reason for their omission is simple and no doubt obvious — a lack of historical data. However, they are considered in the discussion of contemporary epidemiology in the next chapter.

Objectives for Chapter 8

When you have studied this chapter, you should be able to:

8.1 Explain what is meant by a mortality crisis and describe the features of (a) a mortality crisis caused largely by a shortage of food, and (b) one resulting from an autonomous infectious epidemic.

8.2 Discuss the difficulties of interpreting the cause of death and illness in historical sources such as Parish Registers and personal accounts.

8.3 Describe the main change in British population size since 1680, and the accompanying changes in life expectancy and mortality rate.

8.4 Explain why the mortality rate fell and the fertility rate rose between 1680 and 1850, and their relative contributions to population expansion.

8.5 Describe the main changes in the causes of death since 1850; how such changes affected different groups in the population as defined by age, sex and social class, and discuss what is thought to have caused such changes.

Questions for Chapter 8

1 (*Objective 8.1*) Looking at Figure 8.4 what do you think were the likely causes of the mortality crises in the parish of St. Botolph in 1593, 1603 and 1625? What features of these crises determined your answer?

2 (*Objective 8.2*) Can you suggest three reasons why it is impossible to compare meaningfully the prevalence of a condition such as hysteria in 1550 with its prevalence today?

3 (*Objective 8.3*) Throughout this chapter, references have been made to the expectation of life at birth in Britain. The following figures are for males:

Table 8.3

Year	Expectation of life/years	Year	Expectation of life/years
1670	32.4	1930	58.0
1810	38.7	1950	66.0
1861	40.5	1979	70.2
1901	46.0		

Draw a graph showing how the expectation of life has changed since 1670. Use the graph to determine: (a) which period has witnessed the fastest increase in life expectancy; (b) whether life expectancy is continuing to increase as rapidly as in former times.

4 (*Objective 8.4*) In the two later periods discussed (1680–1850 and 1850 onwards) mortality from infectious diseases declined. Describe the difference in the explanations offered for such a change in each of these periods.

5 (*Objective 8.5*) Looking at Table 8.2, can you suggest why mortality from 'old age' may have declined since 1850?

9

Contemporary patterns of disease in the United Kingdom

In Book I, *Studying Health and Disease*, Chapter 5, you were introduced to the epidemiological approach to the study of health and disease. In Chapter 9 we continue and develop the discussion of how epidemiology can help to explain the patterns and distribution of health and disease within a population. The chapter contains a considerable amount of data, presented in several different ways: tables, graphs, pie diagrams, histograms and maps. It is hoped that these data will be a useful source of reference as you study the rest of the course. However, it is important to realise that you are not expected to *memorise* the details — they have largely been included for illustrative purposes.

So far in this book we have described and discussed the differences in the pattern of health and disease between industrialised and Third World countries, and in the case of the latter, how health and disease are distributed between different social groups. In addition we have traced the historical changes in the health of the people of the UK, from a pattern which resembles a present day Third World country, to that of a modern industrialised state. We are now going to consider in some detail the patterns of health and disease experienced by different social groups in the UK today.

First we shall describe the overall pattern of mortality, morbidity and disability in the UK today. This is followed by a section that discusses both the nature of the epidemiological approach to understanding how such patterns arise, and some of the methodological limitations of which one should be aware when interpreting such data. In the remaining six sections we consider the main biological and social determinants of health and disease: age, gender, marital status, ethnicity, place of residence, and social class and occupation.

You may already be aware of some examples of the sort of approach to investigating disease presented in this chapter. A recent example which gained considerable attention was the report of a Department of Health and Social Security (DHSS) working group entitled *Inequalities in Health* (often referred to as the 'Black Report' after the group's chairperson, and at that time President of the Royal

College of Physicians, Douglas Black). That report, and other work on the distribution of health and disease in the population, have tended to concentrate on a single biological or social dimension. In the case of *Inequalities in Health* the dimension was social class, with less attention to such factors as gender, ethnicity and marital status. The approach adopted in this chapter is unusual in that several important kinds of inequality are considered alongside one another.

The main causes of mortality, morbidity and disability

Changes in the pattern of many diseases have gone hand in hand with alterations in the age structure of the population. The interrelationship of these two factors — epidemiology and demography — has already been discussed in the context of Third World countries in Chapter 3. The result of these changes in the UK can be seen in the increasing proportion of elderly people in the population. The continuing impact of these trends can be seen in the projected changes in the numbers of elderly people in England and Wales over the next few decades (Figure 9.1).

☐ Describe the changes up to the end of this century for the three population categories shown: all ages, 65–74, and 75 and over.

■ The size of the total population is projected to increase only slightly; the numbers of those aged 65–74 will decrease by about 10 per cent, whereas the 75-and-over group will increase by almost 30 per cent.

These trends are a reflection not only of survival but also of changes in the birth rate at the beginning of the century. For example, the relative fall in the number of people aged

65–74 years results from a fall in the birth rate during the years around, and following, the First World War.

You have already seen in Figure 2.4 how in England and Wales mortality rates remain low (after infancy) until late middle-age, and in Table 2.3 that males born in 1977–79 can expect to live about 70 years, and the life expectancy for females is about 76 years. Increases in the longevity of the population are also illustrated by the fact that, whereas in 1952 200 people celebrated their hundredth birthday, in 1982 no fewer than 1 750 people did so. One of the consequences of this improvement in survival has been the rise in importance of degenerative diseases (due to the wearing out of tissues). The main causes of death in England and Wales are shown by means of a pie diagram in Figure 9.2.

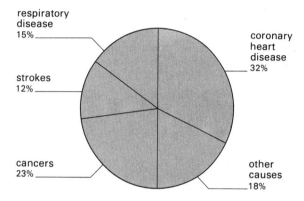

Figure 9.2 Causes of death in England and Wales, 1982. (OPCS, 1984, Table 3)

You can see the impact of chronic diseases associated with degeneration, and in particular those caused by deterioration of the arteries supplying the heart muscle (coronary arteries) and the brain (leading to strokes in which part of the brain is damaged or destroyed through losing its blood supply). Together these account for about 44 per cent of all deaths.

The next two largest categories identified in Figure 9.2 are those of cancers and respiratory disease, which account for 23 per cent and 15 per cent of all deaths respectively. The 'cancers' category includes a large number of cancers of different types and arising in different organs.* The numbers of deaths from different cancers are shown in Figure 9.3.

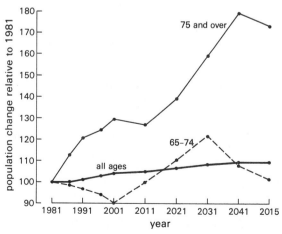

Figure 9.1 Projected population changes by age-groups (65–74 and 75 and over), England and Wales, mid-1981. (OPCS, 1983b)

---

* The biological differences are discussed in Books IV and VI. In the present context it is only necessary to appreciate that there are many forms of cancer with widely differing incidences. (The Open University Press (1985) *The Biology of Health and Disease*, and *Experiencing and Explaining Disease*, The Open University Press (U205 *Health and Disease*, Books IV and VI, respectively).)

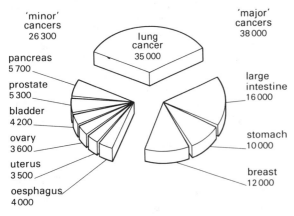

Figure 9.3 Commonest types of fatal cancers — numbers of deaths England and Wales, 1982. (OPCS, 1984, Table 3)

☐   Which four cancers are the commonest causes of death?

■   They are lung, large intestine, breast and stomach.

The distribution of cancer deaths by age and sex will be discussed later in this chapter. The main causes of death from respiratory disease (conditions affecting the lungs) can be seen in Figure 9.4.

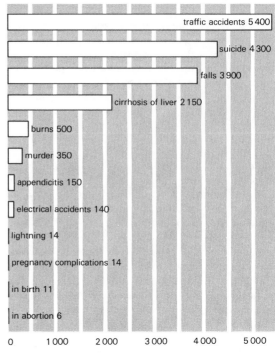

Figure 9.5 Some examples of deaths from 'other causes' (138 000), England and Wales, 1982. (OPCS, 1984, Table 3)

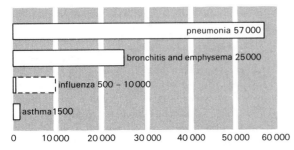

Figure 9.4 Deaths from respiratory disease, England and Wales, 1982, of a total of 80,000. (OPCS, 1984, Table 3)

You may be surprised by the high number of deaths from pneumonia. These mostly occur in frail, elderly people who are already suffering from chronic lung conditions. Deaths from influenza vary between 500 and 10 000 a year, reflecting the epidemic nature of this infection. 1982 was not an epidemic year, there being only about 700 deaths. The final category in Figure 9.2 is simply labelled 'other causes'. This includes numerous causes, some of which are shown in Figure 9.5. They range from six deaths a year in women undergoing an abortion to 5 400 deaths in traffic accidents.

☐   Consider the following pairs of causes of deaths. In each pair which cause is responsible for more deaths, and how much commoner is it?

(a) suicide and murder

(b) electrical accidents and burns

(c) cirrhosis of the liver and traffic accidents

(d) maternal death associated with childbirth and deaths associated with abortion

■   (a) Suicide is 12 times more common than murder.

(b) Burns cause 3 and a half times as many deaths as electrical accidents.

(c) Traffic accidents cause 2 and a half times as many deaths as cirrhosis of the liver.

(d) Almost twice as many women die in childbirth as from abortions.

Further information on the pattern of diseases can be obtained from studying morbidity. There are three commonly used methods of measuring morbidity: measuring the use of health services (such as the number of people admitted to hospital with a particular disease); screening, in which the whole population or a sample are investigated in some way to see if they have a particular disease; and self-assessment surveys in which people are asked about their own state of health.

Most available information on morbidity is based on the use of health services. Information derived in this way reflects not only the presence of ill-health and disease, but also such factors as the availability and accessibility of services, and people's knowledge, beliefs and attitudes about illness and health care. The influence of such factors on service use will vary with the type of condition suffered: almost everyone with a fractured leg will attend a hospital, whereas only some people with low back-pain or influenza will see their GP.

Another aspect of morbidity measures which are derived from health-service use is that different patterns of morbidity will emerge depending on which part of the service is studied. This can be seen in Figure 9.6 in which the top five groups of conditions resulting in hospital admission and use of hospital beds are compared with those seen by General Practitioners (GPs). (Note that mental handicap and pregnancy are not included as 'morbid' conditions despite that fact that health care is provided for both conditions.)

☐ By considering Figures 9.2 and 9.6, what can you conclude about the impact of cardiovascular disease (heart disease and strokes)?

■ Despite being responsible for 44 per cent of all deaths, it accounts for only about 15 per cent of hospital admissions and less than 10 per cent of reasons for GP consultations. This suggests it is a disease category of high mortality, but of intermediate morbidity.

This is in contrast to a category such as rheumatism which is rarely fatal or requiring hospital admission, but is responsible for about 7 per cent of all GP consultations. This demonstrates the importance of considering several different measures of the impact of a disease or group of diseases when assessing its importance on the health of a population. Consider, for example, skin conditions, which, like rheumatism, cause few deaths or admissions to hospital, yet are a common source of distress, and sometimes discomfort, for people. Some idea of the spectrum of common conditions can be obtained by considering how often they occur in general practice (Table 9.1 overpage).

☐ Which are the five most prevalent conditions seen in this general practice?

■ They are:

1 Upper respiratory infections (600): these include conditions such as tonsillitis and ear infections.

2 Skin disorders (350), such as eczema and warts

3 Psychoemotional problems (250)

4 High blood pressure (250)

5 Gastro-intestinal disorders (200), such as food-poisoning, diarrhoea and vomiting.

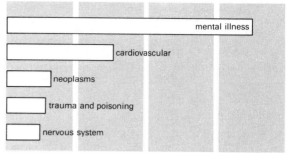

percentage of hospital beds occupied daily

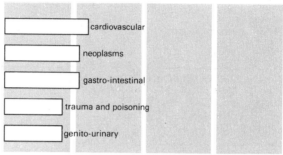

percentage of hospital admissions

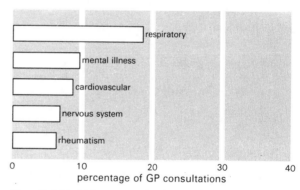

percentage of GP consultations

Figure 9.6 Morbidity patterns for the commonest five groups of disorders/diseases in each category. (Hospital beds and admissions: data from Hospital In-Patient Enquiry, England 1978; GP consultations: data from National Morbidity Survey, 1970/71)

These data reflect the everyday sorts of health problems which affect nearly all of us at some time or another. You should note that a General Practitioner would only expect to see one new case of breast cancer and ten heart attacks (acute myocardial infarction in the table) in a year, compared with hundreds of people with emotional problems, skin disorders and chronic conditions. However, as we have seen above, even data such as these from general practice may fail to reveal a considerable amount of ill-health and disability, such as simple foot-problems in the

Table 9.1 Annual prevalence of illness and other events in a primary care practice in a population of 2 500

Condition	No. of sufferers	Condition	No. of sufferers
1 *Minor illness*		asthma	30
upper respiratory infections	600	diabetes	30
skin disorders	350	varicose veins	30
psychoemotional problems	250	peptic ulcers	25
gastro-intestinal conditions	200	strokes	20
2 *Chronic diseases*		3 *Major acute diseases*	
high blood pressure	250	acute bronchitis	100
chronic rheumatism	100	pneumonia	20
chronic psychiatric	100	severe depression	10
ischaemic heart disease	50	acute myocardial infarction	10
obesity	50	acute strokes	5
anaemia	30	new cancers	5
cancers under care	30	acute appendicitis	5

(data from Fry, 1983, Table 1.4, pp.22–4)

elderly which cause difficulty with walking and even complete immobility. Information on the *prevalence* of such 'minor' conditions has to be obtained from special surveys such as that carried out into the dental health of adults (Figure 9.7).

☐ By what age had 50 per cent of the population of England and Wales lost all their teeth?

■ 55–64 years.

Information such as this cannot be obtained from routine health service statistics. This is true of most measures of *physical impairment*, that is, conditions in which some

bodily function is limited, such as having no teeth, or difficulty with breathing as occurs with chronic bronchitis. Frequently the impairment will cause some *disability*, that is, the person's physical functioning will be limited. With chronic bronchitis that may mean being unable to walk to the shops or climb the stairs. It is important to distinguish these terms from *handicap*, which is the result of the environment failing to accommodate a person's disability, with the effect that their social functioning is limited. The term 'environment' refers not only to physical structures, such as a lack of wheelchair access to a public building, but also society's attitude to disability which may either be welcoming and accommodating, or hostile and inflexible. In other words, disabled people may be handicapped by the able-bodied. Some indication of the prevalence of physical impairment is shown in Figure 9.8, which is taken from a large survey carried out by Amelia Harris in the late 1960s.

This shows that the three commonest causes of impairment in adults are diseases of bones and joints; of the circulatory system; and of the central nervous system (brain and spinal cord).

☐ Is there a consistent relationship between the mortality and the disability caused by a disease category?

■ No. Circulatory disease results in both high mortality and high disability, whereas diseases of bones and joints cause much disability but little or no mortality.

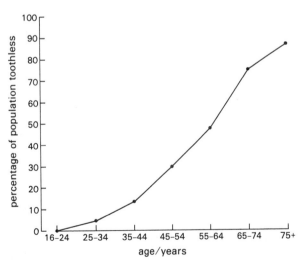

Figure 9.7 Total tooth loss for different age-groups, England and Wales, 1978. (OPCS, 1980, Figure 4.1, p.9)

Physical impairment is often thought to be largely a consequence of either congenital conditions (those which a baby is born with) and birth trauma (e.g. spastics), or of head and spinal injuries. As Figure 9.8 demonstrates,

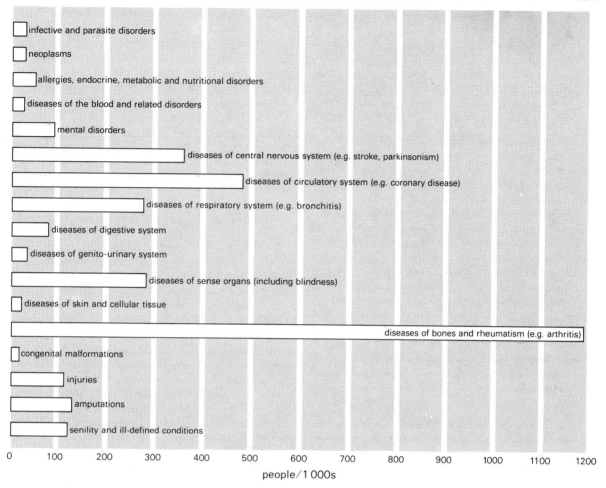

Figure 9.8 The main causes of physical impairment in adults in Britain. (*Note* This survey did not include those in institutions, and so may not reflect the impact particularly of neurological conditions such as strokes, parkinsonism and multiple sclerosis, which are likely to cause very severe disability.) (Harris, Cox and Smith, 1971)

common degenerative diseases affecting muscles and joints, the heart and circulation, and the respiratory system, are in fact responsible for the majority of disabilities. Another important category included in Figure 9.8, diseases of sense organs, is often referred to as sensory impairment and includes restrictions of hearing and vision. Approximately 60 per cent of men and nearly 70 per cent of women in Britain wear glasses for at least some activities. In addition some of those not wearing glasses are thought to suffer from some visual difficulty. Although we tend to think of disabled people as a minority group, in reality there are few, if any, *fully* able-bodied people.

To summarise: survival to middle and old age has led to a rise in the medical and social importance of chronic degenerative diseases (especially those affecting the cardiovascular and respiratory systems) and cancers. These conditions dominate the causes of both mortality and disability. Patterns of morbidity are dependent on how the measurements are made: for example, measuring the use of hospital services does not reflect the everyday experiences of distress and discomfort caused by upper respiratory infections, mental ill-health and emotional problems, and 'minor' conditions affecting the skin, muscles and joints.

Studying distributions of health and disease
Epidemiology addresses three types of questions.*

☐   Can you suggest what these questions are? And how might they be answered?

* Book I, *Studying Health and Disease*, Chapter 5.

■ Three types of questions important to epidemiologists are:

1 Who gets ill? — answered by describing the distribution of health and disease in the population.

2 Why do they get ill? — answered by investigating the aetiology (or cause) of disease.

3 How should they be treated? — answered by evaluating the effectiveness of different treatments.

This chapter is primarily concerned with the first question, though by describing how particular conditions are distributed in the population, it is possible to suggest explanations for such patterns, that is, to start to answer the second question on the causality of disease. There are many levels of causality: explanations of the cause of a disease may be offered in terms of chemicals and cells at one extreme, and in terms of politics and economics at the other. Epidemiology offers an explanation which takes into account both biological and social factors.

The study of biological and social characteristics requires populations to be stratified. While this may be straightforward for factors such as age and sex, it may present considerable difficulties in *operationalising** social factors such as class. One of the main purposes of describing how health and disease are distributed between strata is to suggest explanations of causality. However, there are two other potential benefits from this type of epidemiological study.

☐ Can you suggest what these two benefits might be?

■ Aiding the planning of curative and preventive action, and helping people to understand social processes and social structure (for example, the difference in the mortality rate between single and married people may tell us something about the social role of marriage) are possible benefits.

Operationalising social characteristics is not the only methodological difficulty faced by epidemiologists. There are four problems in particular of which you need to be aware:

1 The study of illness may be limited by defining conditions in terms of discrete diseases.

2 The value-laden nature of the choice as to which biological and social factors to study.

3 The need to simplify may fail to take account of interaction between factors.

4 An association between two factors does not necessarily imply that one causes the other.

Let us look at these four problems in more detail. The first is that epidemiology, like health care in general, depends essentially on measures of ill-health. Measures require definitions and classifications, and therefore the problems that are most feasible to study are, in general, those that have medical labels, definitions, and classifications attached to them. Though this has led to many advances in understanding illness, it can also limit the scope of epidemiology. It encourages epidemiologists to study those states of ill-health that are most easily measured, and discourages study of those that do not readily fit into the description of any disease. For example, consider the last time you felt 'under the weather': it is unlikely that you or anyone else attached a discrete disease-label to your state of ill-health. In addition, too rigid an adherence to the current range of diseases may actually limit advances in knowledge. For instance, the failure to increase significantly our understanding of the cause of coronary heart disease may be because the current disease definition actually comprises several different diseases, each with its own cause (or causes). In practice one of the roles of epidemiology should be to challenge such definitions and help to redefine diseases in more useful ways.

The second problem concerns the choice of factors with which to stratify the population. Epidemiology has always encompassed two main groups of variables, biological and social, though, in line with other medical approaches, it has favoured the biological. For instance, most studies of gastroenteritis (diarrhoea and vomiting) in infants have been concerned with whether or not the mother breast-fed her infant, rather than with social variables such as housing conditions and income. One consequence of this has been that studies of biological factors tend to result in policy recommendations for *individuals* to change their behaviour or lifestyle; in contrast, a social analysis would suggest the need for changes in *social conditions*.

☐ Can you suggest the likely recommendations to reduce infantile gastroenteritis arising from each of the approaches in our example?

■ The 'biological' investigation may suggest that the cause of gastroenteritis is mothers failing to breast-feed their infants. The recommended change would be to encourage mothers to breast-feed.

The 'social' investigation may suggest that gastroenteritis is associated with poor housing and social conditions. Recommended action would involve policy changes to redress inequalities in housing provision and to alter the social processes from which these inequalities spring.

Policy implications are, therefore, very much dependent on the factors chosen to be studied. While that choice is partly determined by practical considerations, it also reflects the

---

* Developing 'proxy' or indirect measures to quantify factors that cannot be measured directly.

interests and values of the investigator or the funding body behind the research.

The other two methodological problems are related to one another and are of a technical nature — those of interaction between factors, and establishing an association as being causal. Every individual is a member of many different social groups on the basis of age, sex, social class, ethnicity, etc. Epidemiology attempts to simplify the issue by separating out such factors for analysis. Although sophisticated statistical methods exist to cope with the interaction of factors, many epidemiological studies (especially much of the routine descriptive data) make no such attempt. This omission is important when assessing the nature of any association between diseases and variables, as it can only be assumed to be causal after an exhaustive analysis has considered all possible explanations of the association.

However, it is ultimately a matter of faith that all possibilities have been considered. For instance, in our infant feeding/gastroenteritis example we cannot be *certain* that the colour of the mother's hair, her astrological sign or her relationship with the infant's father are *not* relevant unless these are also studied. In practice, epidemiologists have to decide on which factors to study on the basis of currently held views of plausibility (both biological and social). The tendency of epidemiology to divide into two camps — the biomedical (or clinical) on the one hand, and the social on the other — means that each is liable to misconceive the plausibility of the other's factors. Thus there is a tendency for the more socially oriented work to ignore biological considerations and vice versa.

Despite these methodological difficulties, the epidemiological approach has made, and is likely to continue to make, a major contribution to the study of health and disease. The rest of this chapter is devoted to describing this contribution and discussing some of the explanations epidemiological work has suggested. Each of the six main characteristics (age, gender, marital status, ethnicity, place of residence and social class) is discussed below in terms of the following: (i) the distribution of mortality; (ii) the distribution of morbidity (and disability where appropriate); (iii) a discussion of explanations of such patterns, considering first biological ones then social ones, and finally the influence of personal life-histories.

Social factors may affect the distribution of health and disease in broadly two ways. First, social conditions such as housing may have a direct effect on the state of someone's health. Second, that person's use of health services may be affected by such conditions. This point has already been discussed in the context of interpreting morbidity statistics derived from health-service usage. Both of these potential effects will be considered in each of the six sections below.

There is one further facet of the influence of both biological and social factors that needs highlighting — that of discrimination. Stratification is the process of describing hierarchies, and one feature of a hierarchy, at least according to conflict theories, is discrimination against one stratum, or group, by another (usually a more powerful one). We are all familiar with some types of discrimination, such as those based on race and on sex. However, as you will see, discrimination can take many forms, for example, it can be based on age or marital status. By reinforcing the social structure, discrimination tends to exacerbate differences in health status between different strata. You will see examples of this in each of the six factors considered below.

Age

In Chapter 2 you saw how mortality rates in England and Wales vary with age (Figure 2.4). After early childhood the mortality rate increases with increasing age. Though this pattern is true for almost all causes of death, there are some notable exceptions.

The male mortality rate from road traffic accidents (Figure 9.9) shows two peaks, including one at 15–24 years of age. Whereas deaths from trauma (accidents and violence) account for only a small proportion of all deaths, their occurrence at relatively young ages means that they cause a disproportionately high number of lost years of life, as was demonstrated in Chapter 3, using similar data from Canada (Table 3.1). The second peak in the elderly largely relates to injuries to pedestrians.

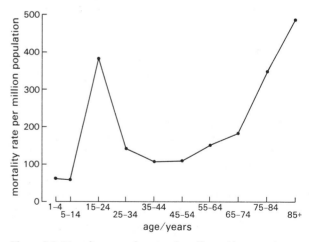

Figure 9.9 Mortality rates from road traffic accidents, males, England and Wales, 1980. (OPCS, 1982c)

The importance of trauma as a cause of death in young women can be seen in Figure 9.10. Note that this shows the proportions (not mortality rates) of different causes at each age. The proportion of each cause is represented by the *area*

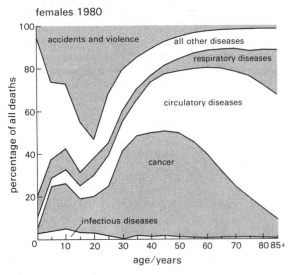

Figure 9.10 Selected causes of deaths by age, females, UK, 1980. (OPCS, 1983c, Chart 7.4, p.93)

of the graph occupied. Thus the increasing impact of circulatory diseases with age is shown by the area so labelled. (Note that the age/years axis denotes the first year of a five-year period, e.g. 25 denotes the age-group 25–29 inclusive.)

□ Approximately what proportion of deaths in girls aged 5–9 years are caused by accidents and violence?
■ About 15–20 per cent (obtained by measuring downwards from the top of the figure for the age group 5–9 years).

Interpreting data on mortality rates and age can be straightforward. For instance Figure 9.9 shows that as a man ages from 45 years to 75 years his risk of dying from a road accident increases in the manner represented by the graph. For most conditions, the association of morbidity with age follows a similar pattern to that of mortality — the older we become, the more ill-health we experience. This can be seen in the increasing incidence of most cancers with age (Figure 9.11).

□ Looking at Figure 9.11, what is the rather surprising exception to this association?
■ The incidence of lung cancer declines after the age of 70.
□ Approximately 90 per cent of lung cancers are thought to be due to smoking tobacco. How might you explain the apparent fall in the incidence of the disease after the age of 70?
■ There are three possibilities you may have considered:

1 Some men may have survived to later ages because of some form of resistance to the disease.
2 All the men who are at risk from smoking all their lives die of lung cancer (and other smoking-related diseases) by the age of 70, leaving few life-time smokers to survive into their seventies and eighties.
3 All the men born more than 70 years ago have some common experiences that make them less likely to develop lung cancer than younger men.

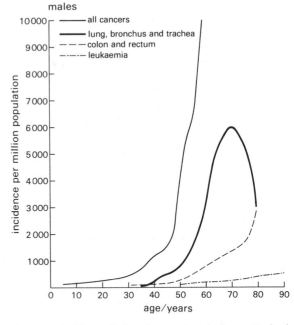

Figure 9.11 Incidence of selected cancers in males by age, England and Wales, 1970. (Open University, 1979, p.50)

The third explanation is known as a *birth cohort* effect. A cohort is a group of people who all share a common experience. In the case of a birth cohort the common factor is their year of birth. Such a group tends to share similar life experiences from birth to death. It is known that the prevalence of smoking has varied during this century. Suppose that men born around 1900–10 smoked more heavily throughout their lives than men born earlier. In 1970 (when the data in Figure 9.11 were collected) this cohort of heavy smokers would have been 60–70 years old, and would be expected to be suffering from higher lung cancer rates than the older group who had smoked less. The existence of a cohort effect can be assessed by comparing the mortality experience of cohorts of people born in successive years. This has been done in Figure 9.12 (though the data are restricted to men in social classes I and II).

The first point to note is that the rates of lung cancer

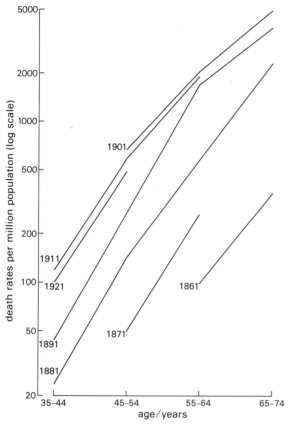

Figure 9.12 Lung cancer: death rates in birth cohorts, men aged 35–74 years, social classes I and II. (Logan, 1982)

increase with age in each and every cohort. In other words, when birth cohorts are studied there is *no* decline in rates in the oldest age groups. Second, men born in 1901 show the highest death rates from lung cancer at all ages, compared with earlier (1861–91) and later (1911–21) cohorts, thus supporting our speculative explanation of the findings of Figure 9.11. The importance of the cohort effect is that it can, as you have seen, distort the appearance of the relationship between mortality and age and lead to misinterpretation of that association. You should bear this in mind when you meet further examples.

Much of the reason for the observed age distribution of disease is the biological ageing of the cells, tissues and organs of the body.* However, social factors are also thought to influence the pattern. As you will see in the next

* This process is discussed more fully in Book IV, *The Biology of Health and Disease*.

chapter, the social position of some age-groups (particularly the elderly) means that they are more likely to be exposed to poorer, health-damaging conditions. This may be reinforced by *ageist* attitudes in society. Apart from biological and social causes, the influence of a person's life history — that is, the influence of past events on the present state of health — is particularly important in the context of age. The birth-cohort effect on the incidence of lung cancer illustrates the importance of considering this influence: in that example it was men's tobacco consumption. This is not to suggest that the decision to smoke was an entirely personal choice. In fact, many biological and social factors can influence our 'personal' behaviour. Another example of such influences may lie behind the high mortality rates in young men caused by road traffic accidents. This is normally ascribed to the high risk-taking behaviour of young adult males, in particular by those on motorbikes. However, additional factors include their social position which may preclude them financially from car ownership, and the behaviour of other road users. Recent filmed research has suggested that part of the explanation for their high mortality rate may be aggressive driving behaviour by car and lorry drivers in response to their risk-taking behaviour.

In summary, you should note the following points:

1 Mortality rates increase with age. This is true for almost all causes of death.

2 Morbidity rates also increase with increasing age.

3 Biological factors (cell and tissue ageing) are largely responsible for this pattern.

4 The health of some age-groups (such as the elderly) is adversely affected by their relative social disadvantage.

5 Health status at any age will be influenced by a person's life history (their experiences and the past events in their life), as well as their current behaviour (such as risk-taking).

Gender

From previous chapters you will be aware that on average males die younger than females. The annual death rates for England and Wales are shown in Table 9.2.

☐ Is there any age-group in which the male mortality rate is lower than that for females?

■ No. The male mortality rate is higher at all ages.

☐ Can you recall from previous chapters any exceptions to this finding?

■ In some Third World countries the female mortality rate exceeds the male rate (Chapter 2), and this was also true of industrialised countries until the nineteenth century.

About 40 per cent of the gender difference in overall mortality is accounted for by deaths from coronary heart

Table 9.2 Annual death rates per 1 000 people within each age-group for 1982, England and Wales

Age/years	Males	Females
less than 1*	12.3	9.5
1–4	0.5	0.4
5–14	0.3	0.2
15–24	0.8	0.3
25–34	0.9	0.5
35–44	1.8	1.2
45–54	5.9	3.6
55–64	17.5	9.7
65–74	45.8	24.3
75–84	105.5	65.8
85 and over	223.2	178.2

* Deaths under one year per 1 000 live births.
(data from OPCS, 1984, Table 3)

disease. The higher rate of deaths among men from coronary heart disease occurs all at ages, but is of greatest concern in late middle age when it accounts for 40 per cent of all male deaths, but less than 15 per cent in females.

Although there are several problems concerning the diagnosis and definition of deaths due to this cause, there is little doubt that both the incidence of myocardial infarction (heart attack) and the prevalence of coronary athero-

sclerosis (degeneration of arteries supplying the heart muscle) are higher in men than in women of the same age.

The overall cancer mortality rate is also higher in males than in females. The rates for the most commonly occurring sites for cancer are shown in Figure 9.13. The only sites in which the female mortality rate exceeds that of males (apart from exclusively female sites such as the uterus) are the breast (a few cases do occur in men), skin and large intestine and rectum.

The consistently higher overall death rates for males in the UK are not reflected in higher overall morbidity rates. Although the morbidity rates for many major chronic diseases are higher in males (e.g. coronary heart disease), for others there either does not appear to be any substantial difference or the female rate is higher. Studies have shown that the incidence of acute conditions, days of restricted activity because of illness, and visits to GPs tend to be higher in women than men. One disease that illustrates this is rheumatoid arthritis, a chronic disease of the joints resulting in stiffness, pain and loss of mobility. Not only is it more prevalent in women than in men, but in addition, the disease appears to advance more rapidly in women.

How can these gender differences in mortality and morbidity be explained? This question has given rise to considerable debate and speculation. Several biological explanations have been suggested for the lower mortality rate in females, including differences in the genetic material

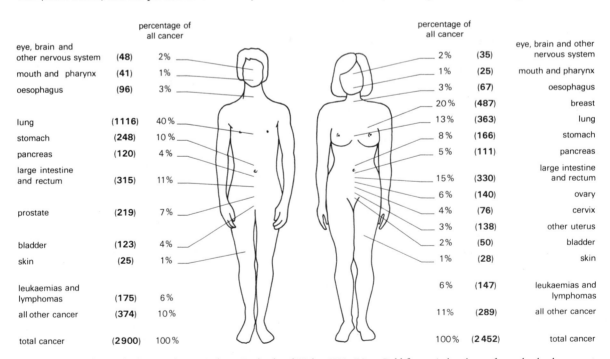

Figure 9.13 Death rates from cancer by site and sex, England and Wales, 1982. (*Note* Bold figures in brackets refer to the death rate per million population.) (OPCS, 1984)

between males and females. (The nature of genes and chromosomes is explained in Book IV, *The Biology of Health and Disease*. For present purposes it is necessary simply to note that such a difference exists, and that it has been suggested that this may result in greater resistance to infections in females.) Females may also benefit from hormonal differences from males. The higher levels of oestrogens in females may exert some protective effect, particularly against cardiovascular disease. In support of this view it has been suggested that the reason the female mortality rate from coronary heart disease increases sharply after the age of 50 years is because of the fall in the level of oestrogens around the time of the menopause. Finally, biological factors have been suggested to explain the higher female mortality rate noted in some Third World countries and in the past in the UK. These examples are thought to reflect the risks associated with pregnancy in such circumstances. The availability of contraception and improvements in the safety of childbirth in industrialised countries may have nullified this disadvantage, leading to a fall in female mortality rates.

In addition to these biological theories, a number of social explanations for the gender difference in mortality have been suggested. First, there are increased risks to men stemming from their higher rates of employment outside the home and, on average, in more obviously hazardous jobs. Second, there are systematic differences in behaviour between the sexes, partly resulting from social pressures operating from childhood, but also related to gender differences in the access to resources. This can be seen in the higher risk-taking behaviour of men: greater use of dangerous drugs, faster driving, higher smoking rates, less use of preventive services such as dentistry, and high accident rates.

□ The gender differences in mortality for several diseases have been described in this section. For which causes do you think the higher prevalence of smoking in men may be responsible?

■ You probably thought of lung cancer (Figure 9.13) and maybe also coronary heart disease. In addition, smoking is partly responsible for the higher incidence of cancers of the larynx, oesophagus and bladder.

Other behavioural differences, apart from smoking, which may contribute to the excess of male mortality, include the higher consumption of alcohol by men which contributes to the higher incidence of cancer of the larynx and oesophagus, and cirrhosis of the liver. It has been suggested that the gender difference in alcohol consumption patterns reflects men's recourse to alcohol in response to stress, anxiety and depression, whereas women are more likely to consume tranquillizers and sedatives (such as Valium). In this context, the latter *appear* to have the advantage of not causing physical disease, unlike alcohol.

Gender differences in behaviour have also been suggested as part of the explanation for the higher mortality from coronary heart disease in men. It has been suggested that this difference is due to a greater prevalence of a so-called 'coronary-prone personality' among men in white-collar jobs. Such people are seen as being hard-driving and competitive. The supposed preponderance of these characteristics among males is viewed as resulting from their adherence to a traditional, stereotyped version of the male role. This in turn arises from the social structure of the family, in which males have traditionally had a higher participation rate in employment outside the home and tended to be cast in the role of the main earner. However, despite a considerable amount of research in this area, the influence of personality types in general on the distribution of coronary heart disease (or any other disease) is still unclear.

How might the apparently paradoxical observation of higher morbidity rates for some diseases in women be explained? This finding may partly result from the method of measuring morbidity (based on health service use) and partly from gender differences in attitudes to health care.

□ Can you suggest how these two factors might explain some of the gender difference in morbidity rates?

■ 1 Methodological problems in the measurement of women's visits to a GP may arise as a result of the inclusion of consultations for contraception, antenatal, and postnatal care.

2 Women may be more predisposed to care for their health. This would contribute to their higher consultation rate and might also lower their mortality rate. They may also have greater access to health services, because they are less likely to be in full-time employment. In addition, women have traditionally cared for the health of male members of the family, which may have lowered the consultation rate of men.

Gender differences in psychiatric morbidity provide an example of how health-care factors may partly account for such differences. General practitioners report that many more women than men consult them for anxiety and depression. However there is also good evidence that in fact doctors are readier to diagnose women as suffering from psychiatric disturbance than men. Both may be true.

As with age, the patterns of gender and disease illustrate well the complex interaction between biological, social and life-history factors in determining health status. In particular, you should note the following:

1 Male mortality rates exceed those for females at all ages.

2 Gender differences in morbidity vary between

different conditions.

3 Biological factors, such as genetic and hormonal differences, are thought to account for some of the relative health advantages of females.

4 Social relations and structures, on average, place males in more hazardous work, and appear to influence their adoption of more health-damaging behaviour.

5 Some of the *apparent* differences in morbidity may result from systematic differences in measurement or in the use of health services.

Marital status

Marital status, like age, sex and social class, forms another pervasive personal and social characteristic. Marital state is a socially, and generally, legally defined condition, and serves to distinguish between currently married, never married (single) and formerly married (widowed and divorced) people. Although marital state is defined in terms of the presence or absence of a marital partner, it involves more than a personal relationship, for each marital condition is associated with socially sanctioned rights and obligations with regard to children, sexuality, kinship ties, property and domestic and economic services. (Morgan, 1980, p.633)

This quote from Myfanwy Morgan, a contemporary British sociologist, highlights both the social importance of marital status and the difficulties of operationalising it. By studying marital status, we are in fact attempting to investigate both the effect of a personal relationship on health status and the social consequences in terms of rights, obligations and resources such as income and housing.

☐ What two assumptions do you think there are in using a person's legal marital status in such investigations?

■ It assumes that people who are married enjoy the benefits of a close personal relationship; and it assumes single and formerly married people are not experiencing such a relationship.

Similarities to the difficulties in operationalising social class should be apparent to you. Nevertheless, the study of marital status reveals some clear patterns in the distribution of health and disease. The association between marital status and mortality was first demonstrated in the nineteenth century when it was shown that mortality rates were lowest for the married, higher for the single and highest for those widowed or divorced. This has been consistently found ever since. Married people experience lower mortality rates than non-married for all causes of death. The overall mortality ratios for men and women are shown in Table 9.3.

Table 9.3 Standardised mortality ratios (SMRs) for men and women by marital status

Marital status	Standardised mortality ratio	
	males	females
single	117	99
married	96	97
widowed	109	103
divorced	123	117

(data from Fox and Goldblatt, 1982, Table 4.2)

☐ Which sex appears to suffer higher mortality from being single?

■ Men. The SMR for single men (117) is much higher than for married men (96) compared with the equivalent figures for women (99 and 97). Similar differences occur in the formerly married groups, though these differences are not as dramatic.

Changes in marital status are also associated with mortality. The death rate among widowers during the first six months of bereavement was found to be 40 per cent greater than would be expected in men of that age, the main cause being cardiovascular disease. Divorce can have a similar effect, though usually during the later stages of marital breakdown rather than at the time of the divorce action. Although both bereavement and divorce most commonly have an adverse effect on health, they can be beneficial if they follow a period of stress such as a spouse's long terminal illness or in cases of domestic violence. As with single status, divorce appears to have a greater adverse effect on men than on women — compare for instance, the mortality experiences of divorced men and women in Table 9.3.

Comparative levels of morbidity suggest a different hierarchy from that of mortality. Whereas the widowed and divorced appear to experience the most morbidity, consistent with their position regarding mortality, the single appear to suffer less morbidity than the married in as much as this can be seen in general practice consultation rates (Figure 9.14). The minimal differences seen in 'all conditions' consultations conceal much more striking associations for three particular causes — mental disorders, musculoskeletal disorders (rheumatism, arthritis), and accidents — which are higher in unmarried people (i.e. single, widowed, divorced).

Rates of *self-reported illness** show the same relationship between marital status — highest in the widowed/ divorced and lowest in single people (although for chronic conditions there is no difference between married and

* Rates obtained from household surveys, for example, rather than rates derived from the use of the health service.

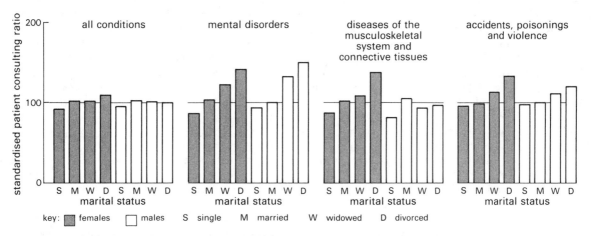

Figure 9.14 Standardised patient consulting ratios by marital status, men and women aged 15–74, England and Wales, 1970–71. (RCGP/OPCS/DHSS, 1982, Figure 3.1.2)

single). How can we explain these differences in the mortality and morbidity rates of different marital states? Though no biological explanations have been offered, several social factors have been suggested, and these will be discussed in a moment. First, though, it is necessary to consider the process of marital selection. In all the discussions in this chapter, it is assumed that health status is a *consequence* of the biological and social factor under investigation. However, it is possible that the reverse may be true, that is, states of health may influence social status.

☐ Can you suggest, how health may *affect* marital status?

■ People suffering from poor health may be more likely to remain single, and those bereaved or divorced who suffer poor health may be more likely to remain not married, than people enjoying good health.

Although this is probably a contributory rather than a major factor, it is one worth bearing in mind and considering for each of the factors discussed in this chapter. There are several possible social explanations of the pattern of health by marital status. The social conditions and position enjoyed by different groups will affect their health status: the widowed and divorced will tend to be less well-off financially than the other groups. In addition, the 'response to stress' theory suggests that the married state can be viewed as protecting against stress through providing the person with a well-defined and socially acceptable role.

Emile Durkheim, one of the founders of empirical sociology, concluded in 1897 in *Suicide: A Study in Sociology* that marriage reduced the chances of suicide by almost one-half, owing to the greater social integration of married people. In contrast, the anomalous social position of the single may serve as a source of stress. Just as was seen

with age and gender, some groups are discriminated against. In those instances we recognise the existence of ageist and sexist attitudes. Although it is less well recognised, those not married have tended to suffer in ways similar to the elderly and women. If this is an important factor, then changing perceptions of the family might alter the impact this has on health.*

Systematic differences in health service use by people of different marital status also need to be considered.

☐ Why is it important to do this?

■ As has been discussed previously in this chapter, differences in morbidity rates derived from health service usage may reflect systematic differences in the *illness behaviour* (how people respond to ill-health) of different marital states, and in the response they receive from doctors.

The highest consulting ratios for mental disorders, for example, are by divorced people, and the lowest by single people. This is true of both men and women. These may reflect, first, a real difference in the prevalence of morbidity between the groups; second, widowed and divorced people may be more likely to consult their doctor when depressed, anxious, etc., because they have no partner to confide in; or third, doctors may be more willing to label patients' problems as being psychological rather than physical in the knowledge of their marital status, particularly if the person is widowed or divorced.

Finally, the lifestyles associated with different marital conditions may contribute to the observed differences. Married people may have a stronger motivation to guard

* This is discussed in Book V, *Birth to Old Age: Health in Transition*, Chapter 4.

their health for the sake of their partner and dependants. The high mortality rates for road accidents and alcohol-induced cirrhosis of the liver among single men would support this theory. The existence of such equally plausible hypotheses underlines the need for more empirical evidence on the clearly important subject of marital status and health, and in particular the different experiences of men and women. However, the key points to remember are:

1 Mortality rates are lowest for married, higher for single and highest for those widowed or divorced.

2 Being unmarried has a greater adverse effect on male than on female mortality. Similarly divorce appears to be more health-damaging to men than to women.

3 Several social explanations of the apparent 'protective' effects of marriage have been suggested.

4 Unlike mortality differences, the single appear to suffer less morbidity than the married, though this is based on 'recognised' disease, and is therefore subject to the influence of systematic differences between marital states and illness behaviour.

Ethnicity and race

Another way in which the population can be stratified is on the basis of ethnicity or race. Over the past few years there has been much debate, at times heated and acrimonious, about which of these terms should be used. Many people have objected to the term '*race*' as its use in the past has suggested a biological basis for the differences between groups — an assumption that finds no support in genetic studies. It has therefore been argued that a social label, such as *ethnicity* is preferable. However, others have objected to the use of this term as they feel it infers that any difference between groups derives from cultural factors, rather than the social structures and relationships which determine the conditions in which people live. Currently, there is no agreement on this issue. We have chosen to use 'ethnicity' in preference to 'race' as it clearly establishes the social nature of the distinction. By using ethnicity we are not subscribing to the notion that any difference in the pattern of health and disease between groups is entirely culturally determined. In fact, as you will see in the following discussion, we consider that most of the differences result from the social structures in which people live and from discrimination on the basis of skin colour.

There are many difficulties in defining and operationalising ethnicity.* Despite the multiracial nature of British society, both today and in the past, the routine statistics on health and disease that are collected fail to provide adequate information for studying the health of different ethnic groups. We are therefore largely dependent

* See Book I, *Studying Health and Disease*, Chapter 10.

on special surveys and studies. These show that the majority of health problems experienced by minority ethnic groups in the UK are *different in degree*, but not in kind, from the majority ethnic group. This can be seen in Table 9.4 which gives an indication of the health concerns of a predominantly Asian community living in London. These data were obtained from a phone-in counselling service for health problems.

The main health concerns were not those perceived by the medical world, such as rickets and osteomalacia (softening of the bone leading to deformities and fractures), hypertension (high blood pressure) or tuberculosis. Instead, the concerns were similar to those found in a general practice serving a predominantly white community in Kent (Table 9.1), such as respiratory problems, mental health and skin complaints. Only 7 of the 3 679 callers were concerned about rickets and only 45 about tuberculosis.

Information on differences in the mortality and morbidity rates between ethnic groups in the UK is very limited at present. Two recent studies do, however, provide some useful, though small-scale information. The first was

Table 9.4 Reasons for 'phoning the counselling service

	No. of questions	Percentage of total
asthma, hay fever, breathlessness	479	13
family planning, fertility, infertility, psychosexual problems	408	11
diabetes	391	11
general nutrition and slimming (not rickets)	288	8
all mental health problems (ranging from mild depressives to those receiving hospital treatment)	282	8
homeopathic treatments/herbal treatments	271	7
skin complaints	252	7
back pain	138	4
child care	100	3
eye complaints	87	2
specific gynaecological problems	83	2
arthritis	82	2
queries concerning pregnancy	80	2
mild gastric problems	79	2
second opinions	79	2
minor ailments	67	2
headaches	59	2
others	323	12
total	3679	100

(data from Webb, 1981, p.144)

a study of tuberculosis, in which it was found that the annual incidence in white children was 3 per 100 000, that of British-born Asian children was 63, and that of Asian children born outside the UK was 114. It appeared that the majority of cases were contracted in the UK rather than in the Indian subcontinent. A second study considered the rates of admission to hospital for stroke and myocardial infarction (heart attack) for different ethnic groups: Europeans, West Indians and Asians (Figure 9.15).

☐ In men aged 45–54 years, how much greater is the incidence of (i) stroke in West Indians than in Europeans, and (ii) myocardial infarction in Europeans than in West Indians?

■ The incidence of (i) stroke is about 20 per cent higher (65 compared with 55 per 1 000) in West Indians, and of (ii) myocardial infarction is about 200 per cent higher (120 compared with 40 per 1 000) in Europeans.

Although these data suggest there are ethnic differences in the incidence of these two conditions, some care must be taken in drawing such conclusions. The incidence rates are based on the proportion of *all* admissions by each ethnic group. Thus, if the total number of admissions for other conditions fell, the rate for stroke and myocardial infarction would rise (despite there being no change in the incidence in the community). In this situation all that can be concluded from such studies is that they are consistent with more comprehensive data from other countries which have clearly demonstrated the overall higher mortality and morbidity rates suffered by minority ethnic groups. For example, in the USA the mortality rate for blacks is about 33 per cent higher than for whites (and 90 per cent higher in the case of infant mortality).

What could account for such differences? As in the previous sections on age, gender and marital status, we shall first consider biological explanations. There is a considerable amount of information on the *tiny minority* of diseases specific to certain ethnic groups. This reflects the dominant biological interest of scientific medicine. These diseases are genetic in origin and arise in specific ethnic groups because of a higher frequency of a particular gene. Two of the commonest and most important of these conditions — thalassaemia and sickle-cell anaemia — were discussed in Chapter 3.

Another example is called Tay-Sachs disease (progressive blindness and brain degeneration in childhood). Although found in most populations, 90 per cent of cases occur in Jews and in particular in those of Ashkenazi descent whose ancestors lived around the Polish-Lithuanian border at the end of the nineteenth century.

A final example is cystic fibrosis, a condition in which mucus produced by several organs in the body, but in particular the lungs and pancreas, is abnormally viscid

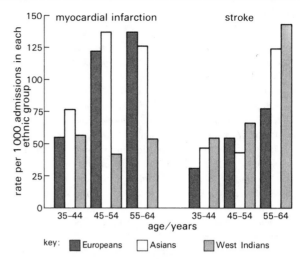

Figure 9.15 The proportion of admissions for myocardial infarction and stroke, males (rate per 1000 admissions). (Beevers and Cruickshank, 1981, Figures 1 and 2, p.764)

causing blockage and obstruction to the normal functioning of these organs. Cystic fibrosis mainly affects white people (in the USA this is true of 98 per cent of patients).*

These inherited conditions account for only a tiny proportion of the ill-health suffered by different ethnic groups. For instance, in 1977 in the USA, sickle-cell anaemia and thalassaemia accounted for only 0.3 per cent of the total excess number of black deaths compared to white. In fact most of the differences in the health status between ethnic groups results from social and life-history factors. For instance, the higher incidence of tuberculosis in Asians results partly from domestic over-crowding associated with poor inner city housing and poverty.

Members of minority ethnic groups in the UK tend to be concentrated in lower social classes and are therefore subject to the poorer health status associated with relative disadvantages such as lower income, poor housing, and inadequate health care.

These disadvantages are exacerbated by racism which may, for instance, limit employment and housing opportunities. In addition, racist attacks are likely to result not only in physical injury, but also fear and anxiety. Racism does not only affect health status but also the care that members of black and Asian communities receive from health services. In this context, the term *institutional racism* is usually used. What this means is that racist beliefs are accepted as factual evidence for differences between ethnic groups. The beliefs therefore become normalised, that is, they become incorporated into the belief system that

---

* The genetic aspects of all these conditions are discussed in greater detail in Book IV, *The Biology of Health and Disease*.

is a feature of any society (or section of society). These views then come to influence and determine the behaviour of the members of that society. In health care this is most obvious in psychiatric practice, some illustrative examples of which are contained in an article in the Course Reader by Littlewood and Lipsedge ('Ethnic Minorities and the Psychiatrist', Section 6.6, which is discussed in Book VI, *Experiencing and Explaining Disease*). You should note that the institutionalisation of prejudiced beliefs is not unique to racial views, but occurs with views of gender, age and the other factors being discussed in this chapter.

In summary the main points to note are:

1 Despite the lack of meaningful routine statistics on the health status of different ethnic groups, there is sufficient evidence to demonstrate the poorer health suffered by minorities.

2 These differences are almost entirely due to social factors, reinforced by a racist social structure.

3 Biological factors account for a tiny proportion of observed differences.

Place of residence

Variations in mortality rates between different regions of Britain have been noted since at least the last century. Figure 9.16 shows the standardised mortality ratios for males for 1972.

☐ How would you describe the regional pattern of mortality?

■ The highest rates are experienced in Scotland, Northern Ireland, Northern England and Wales. The lowest rates are in the area of England south of the line joining the Severn and the Wash.

A similar geographical distribution is true for the morbidity rates for those diseases for which regional variation exists. An example is dental decay in children. On average, fifteen-year-olds in Northern Ireland suffer from 9.2 decayed teeth compared with 5.6 in England — that is over one and a half times higher. Children in Scotland and Wales show intermediate levels of decay between these two.

What are the possible explanations for regional differences in age- and sex-standardised mortality and morbidity rates? Biological factors such as hours of sunshine, humidity and water hardness have been suggested as explanations for some regional variations. For example, it has been shown that deaths from cardio-vascular disease are partly associated with 'soft' water (containing low concentrations of calcium salts). Whether this association has any causal significance is still uncertain.

At a more localised level, there is considerable interest in biological hazards. For instance the association between lead in the environment and children's development has attracted much professional and public attention, leading

Figure 9.16 Standardised mortality ratios, males, 1972. (DHSS, 1976, Figure 4.4, p.49)

to a reduction in the lead in petrol. Another current example of concern over local health hazards is the risk of cancer (and in particular, leukaemia) occurring in people living near nuclear installations. Despite the risks such hazards might pose to local communities, the striking regional variations shown in Figure 9.16 are not thought to have arisen as a result of biological factors.

In contrast, there is considerable evidence to support social explanations of such differences. First, there are factors that are already known to be associated with the distribution of health and disease such as ethnicity and social class. For instance, it is known that the social class mix (or structure) varies significantly between regions, with a higher proportion of lower social classes in Northern England, Northern Ireland and Scotland (i.e. the regions with the highest mortality and morbidity rates). Variations in the social class structure will explain some, though not all, of the regional differences in mortality.

A second possible explanation is that of geographical mobility, that is, healthier people move to South-East England where there are more opportunities, for employment, for example.

The third type of explanation is concerned with

variations in the social environments of different regions and in particular, the degree of urbanisation. The difficulties of measuring the degree of urbanisation have already been encountered in the discussion of Third World countries in Chapter 3. Similar problems hold true for the UK. Nevertheless, it has been demonstrated that there are associations between urbanisation and ill-health. For example, by mapping the distribution of deaths from bronchitis, a clear association with housing density and level of industrialisation can be shown. Similarly, the incidence of perforated duodenal ulcer (an ulcer occurring in the first section of the small intestine) has been shown to be higher in urban than in rural areas. The reason for such a difference is not known, though it has been suggested that differences in occupations between urban and rural dwellers might be partly responsible.

Having discussed possible biological and social influences on regional differences, it is necessary to consider factors associated with the life histories of the residents of different regions. Consider Figure 9.17 which shows the regional distribution of deaths from cirrhosis of the liver (a disease largely caused by high alcohol consumption).

□ What are the likely explanations of the higher mortality rate in Scotland than the other areas, and the increasing rate in all areas?

■ Alcohol consumption per capita is higher in Scotland and consumption has risen throughout the UK.

Although it is recognised that there are social factors influencing alcohol consumption, these factors alone do not account for the mortality rate in Scotland (13 per 100 000) being over twice the rate in the other areas (6 per 100 000) in 1980. These differences, between areas and over time, almost certainly reflect differences in the life histories of the resident populations.

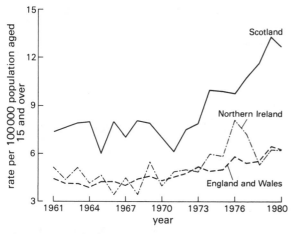

Figure 9.17 Deaths from cirrhosis of the liver, males. (OPCS, 1983c, Chart 7.9, p.96)

In summary, you should note the following:

1 Mortality and morbidity rates are highest in Scotland, Northern Ireland and Northern England and lowest in South-east England.

2 Though biological factors may be important in determining local differences in health status, they do not appear to have a significant influence on regional variations.

3 Regional variations appear to result from social factors (differences in social class structure; the effect of geographical mobility; the degree of urbanisation), and to a lesser extent from cultural differences.

Social class and occupation

In Chapter 8 you saw how the overall mortality rate of people in lower social classes has consistently exceeded that of people in higher classes (Figure 8.8), and, as you may know, the perinatal mortality rate (stillbirths plus deaths during the first week of life) in social class V is two to three times higher than in social class I. Similar differences can be seen in the mortality rates for men and married women aged 15–64 years in Table 9.5.

In addition to showing the mortality rates by social class for men and women separately, it also shows the differences between (a) men and women for each social class (the right hand column), and (b) social classes V and I for each sex (the bottom row). These differences are expressed as a *ratio*. If there were no differences the ratio would be 1.0. The ratio of social classes V to I, for men, of 2.5 means that the mortality rate for social class V (9.88 per 1 000) is two and a half times higher than that for social class I (3.98 per 1 000).

Table 9.5 Mortality rates (per 1 000 population) by sex and social (occupational) class for men and women aged 15–64 years, England and Wales, 1971

Social (occupational) class	Men (all)	Women (married)**	Ratio men:women
I (Professional)	3.98	2.15	1.85
II (Intermediate)	5.54	2.85	1.94
III(N)* (Skilled non-manual)	5.80	2.76	1.96
III(M)* (Skilled manual)	6.08	3.41	1.78
IV (Partly Skilled)	7.96	4.27	1.87
V (Unskilled)	9.88	5.31	1.86
Ratio V/I	2.5	2.5	

* Note that in this and some figures, data in social class III are divided into two categories, non-manual (N) and manual (M) skilled workers.
** In this table married women are classified by husband's occupation.
(data from DHSS, 1980, Table 2.1, p.24)

□ Does the association between gender and mortality vary with social class?

■ Only slightly — the ratios (far right-hand column in Table 9.5) vary from 1.78 to 1.96.

Similarly the association between social class and mortality does not appear to be influenced by gender (the ratio of social class V to social class I is 2.5 for both sexes). This relationship between social classes V and I is true at all ages (Figure 9.18).

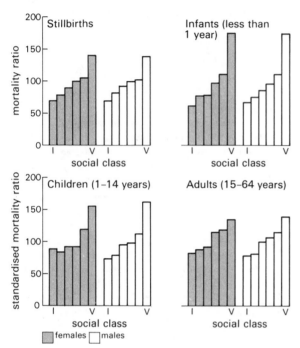

Figure 9.18 Mortality by occupational social class and age. (*Note* It is not necessary to age-standardise the data for stillbirths and infant deaths, as both categories refer to small age-ranges.) (DHSS, 1980, Figure 2.1, p.32)

□ At which ages are social class differences most marked?

■ They are most marked in infancy and childhood.

At birth and during the first month of life the risk of death in social class V is double that in social class I. From the end of the first month to the end of the first year the difference in mortality between social classes V and I is greater than at any other age — the mortality rate of infants in social class V is five times that of those in social class I. In children (1–14 years) the ratio drops back to about two.

The causes of death most strongly associated with social class are: infective and parasitic diseases; accidents, poisonings and violence; and to a lesser extent respiratory disease. If present patterns continue, a child born to social class I parents, and remaining in that class, can expect to live five years longer than a child born into social class V. Possible explanations for such differences will be discussed in later chapters.

Class differences in adult mortality are, as you have already seen in Table 9.5, less marked than those in childhood. However, this conceals a considerable difference for those in their twenties and thirties and a smaller difference for those approaching pensionable age. As with childhood, class differences in mortality vary between categories of disease, six of which are shown in Figure 9.19.

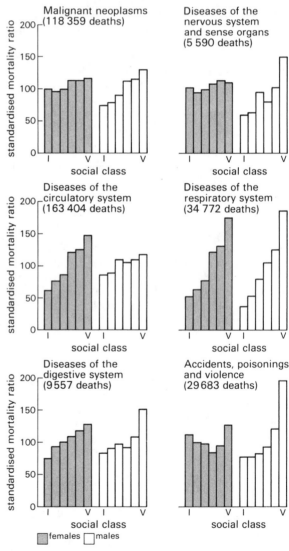

Figure 9.19 Mortality by occupational social class in adult life, men and married women (by husband's occupation), aged 15–64. (DHSS, 1980, Figure 2.4, p.40)

□   What categories of disease show the strongest class association, and for which sex?

■   The strongest class association is shown by respiratory disease (men and women); circulatory disease (women); accidents and diseases of the nervous system (men).

For some diseases the association with class is significant for only one sex. One means of attempting to understand class differentials better is to consider specific diseases rather than groups of conditions. Neoplasms (cancers) in women illustrate this well. It would appear from Figure 9.19 that these diseases are fairly evenly distributed across the classes. However, when the class distributions for three specific cancers are considered, some interesting patterns emerge (Figure 9.20).

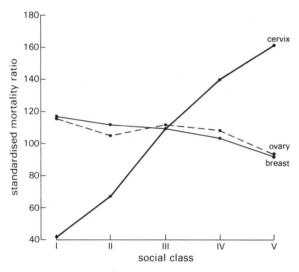

Figure 9.20 Standardised mortality ratios for cancers of the female reproductive system, by occupational social class (married women) England and Wales, 1971. (OPCS, 1978)

□   How much greater is the risk of death from cervical cancer in women married to men in social class V than to those married to men in social class I?

■   Four times greater (SMR of 160 compared with 42).

The staggering social-class difference in mortality from cervical cancer has given rise to several explanations. These illustrate how ideological considerations can influence the interpretation of epidemiological data. The first explanation to emerge was that cervical cancer is caused by a viral infection of the cervix and the reason the incidence of the disease is higher in women of lower social classes is because they are younger at the time of first intercourse, have more sexual partners and a poorer standard of personal hygiene. Though all these aspects of *women's* behaviour would

increase their likelihood of contracting a sexually transmitted infection, such an explanation fails to consider several other possibilities. First, if cervical cancer is caused by a sexually transmitted infection, then the sexual experience of *men* is equally important. Second, the assumption about social-class differences in sexual experience lack any reliable supporting data. And third, the higher risk of disease in lower social classes might result from men working in dirty occupations and, as a result, 'carrying' a carcinogen (cancer-causing substance) home from work. Whichever explanation is proposed will tend to reflect the ideology of the investigator.

Population surveys of morbidity reinforce the finding from mortality data, that people in lower social classes suffer from poorer health than those in higher social classes. An example is total tooth loss. You have already seen its association with age (Figure 9.7); in Figure 9.21 you can see the additional effect of social class.

□   At what age is there the greatest difference in the percentage of toothless people between upper social classes (I, II, III(N)) and social class III(M)?

■   At 45–54 years of age, 18 per cent of upper social classes are toothless compared with 34 per cent of social class III(M) (i.e. almost twice the percentage).

Another population-based survey was carried out into the social origins of depression in women. This revealed that psychiatric disorder, and depression in particular, was much more common in working-class women (23 per cent) than middle-class women (6 per cent) during a three-month period.

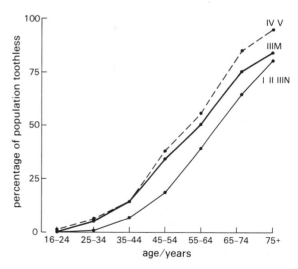

Figure 9.21 Total tooth loss in England and Wales by social class (of household) and age-groups, 1978. (OPCS, 1982, Table 4.5)

A third and final example of social class and morbidity comes from the General Household Survey in which people are asked to report on their own health status (Figure 9.22).

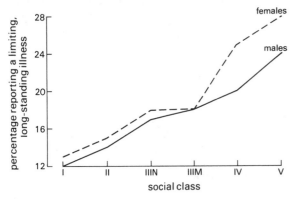

Figure 9.22 Chronic sickness: persons who reported a *limiting* long-standing illness by sex and social class, all ages, 1980. (OPCS, 1982a, Table 7.8)

☐ Bearing in mind the strong association between disability and age, why do you think the proportion of females reporting disability is higher than males?

■ These data are not age-standardised. This gender difference is due entirely to the larger number of elderly, infirm women than men included in the survey (because on average women live several years longer than men).

There is a clear association between self-assessment of both disability and ill-health, and social class. The strength of the association between health and social class is best summed up by a quote from the 1980 report, *Inequalities in Health*, referred to in the introduction to this chapter.

If the mortality rate of class I had applied to classes IV and V during 1970–72 (the date of the latest review of mortality experience) 74 000 lives of people aged under 75 would not have been lost. This estimate includes nearly 10 000 children, and 32 000 men (sic) of working age. (DHSS, 1980, p.356)

How can such social class differences be explained? A number of explanations have been put forward and they will be discussed in detail in the next chapter. However, it is appropriate to the nature of this chapter to consider one explanation now, that of occupational hazards. It is first necessary to distinguish between 'occupation' as a description of a job of work, and as an indicator of social class. In all the data you have seen on social class, occupation has been used to indicate the general social conditions experienced by particular groups of people. It may have already occurred to you that part of the difference in health status between social (occupational) classes may result from the higher risk to health and physical well-being

arising from many manual jobs. Those risks are manifold. They may result in direct loss of life, either suddenly in the form of accidents, or in an attenuated manner through exposure to damaging substances in the workplace over a long period. You may be aware of some of these, such as pneumoconiosis, a chronic lung condition suffered by coal miners.

One way of separating out the direct effects of occupation from those due to social class is by relating the mortality or morbidity of the workers in that occupation to that of their spouses. This process has suggested, for example, that leather workers are at increased risk of suffering from tuberculosis, chronic rheumatic heart disease, and bronchitis — all as a direct consequence of their occupation.

☐ Why do you think spouses are a good control group?

■ Spouses share most of the same social conditions as the worker (housing, income, etc.) and the same residential hazards (such as environmental pollutants), but not the working environment.

☐ For what factors can spouses *not* act as controls?

■ Biological and social factors relating to gender cannot be controlled for.

Care needs to be taken in making comparisons based on worker–spouse differences. This is well illustrated in studies of the dangers of asbestos. Not only were the male workers at risk of inhaling asbestos fibres, but so were their wives. This was because men took their contaminated clothes home to be laundered by their wives.

Finally, despite the importance of specific occupational hazards, many health risks associated with work are of a non-specific nature and arise from stress. Stress may arise in a number of ways but tends to originate from how work is organised. Some examples include low pay (leading to excessive overtime work), incentive payment schemes (speeding up potentially dangerous processes), shift-work (disrupting biological, psychological and social functioning), poor job design (producing boredom, and little satisfaction), and bad industrial relations. Such effects have been demonstrated in terms of accident and sickness absence rates associated with different work practices. Examples of the mortality and morbidity associated with various occupations will be discussed further in later chapters. Also, in Chapter 11, the consequences for health of unemployment will be considered.

In summary, the main points you should note are:

1 Mortality and morbidity rates in lower social classes are higher than in upper social classes. The magnitude of this difference varies with age, being greatest in infancy and childhood, and least in old age.

2 The association between social class and mortality

and morbidity varies with different diseases. For some diseases there is no association; for many the incidence and prevalence is highest in lower social classes, and for a few the rates are highest in upper social classes.

3 Health risks associated with different occupations account for some of the social class differences described. (Other explanations are discussed in the following chapters.)

In this chapter, the contemporary patterns of health and disease in the UK have been described in terms of the main biological and social determinants. The patterns that emerge can contribute to our understanding and explanation of the causes of ill-health. Thus, although biological factors may explain much of the age-related pattern, they appear to make only an insignificant contribution to the patterns associated with the other determinants. In comparison, social structures and conditions account for most of the observed differences, with the remainder resulting from variations in the life histories (or culture) of different groups. The importance and impact of social explanations is probably best illustrated by the example of inequalities in the health of different social classes — the subject of the following two chapters.

Objectives for Chapter 9

When you have studied this chapter, you should be able to:

9.1 Summarise the main diseases responsible for the overall patterns of mortality, morbidity and disability in Britain.

9.2 Describe the association of both age and gender with disease, and discuss the relative importance of biological, social and life-history explanations.

9.3 Describe the association between marital status and both mortality and morbidity; the different effects of marital status on men and women; and the social explanations for these differences.

9.4 Explain how the patterns of diseases affecting different ethnic groups differ mainly in degree rather than in kind; and how these differences arise from the social disadvantage suffered by minority ethnic groups.

9.5 Describe the main overall regional differences in health status in Britain; suggest some of the underlying factors that would explain some of the differences.

9.6 Describe the association between lower social class and higher mortality and morbidity rates, and discuss the contribution of occupational factors to this association.

Questions for Chapter 9

1 (*Objective 9.1*) How serious for the health of the population are skin diseases? To answer this, you will need to consider Figures 9.5, 9.6, 9.8 and Table 9.1.

2 (*Objective 9.2*) In 1978, 70 per cent of people aged 65–74 years had no teeth, while this was true of only 10 per cent of those aged 35–44 years (see Figure 9.7). Does this mean a further 60 per cent of the younger age group will lose all their remaining teeth over the next 30 years?

3 (*Objective 9.3*) Divorce appears to have a more health-damaging effect on men (SMR of 123) than on women (SMR of 117), as judged by mortality. Is the same true for morbidity, as measured by consultations in general practice (see Figure 9.14)? Is the gender difference the same for mental disorders as it is for diseases of the musculoskeletal system?

4 (*Objective 9.4*) Describe briefly the relative importance of biological, social and life-history factors in explaining the poorer health suffered by members of minority ethnic groups

5 (*Objective 9.5*) Suggest (i) biological, (ii) social and (iii) life-history explanations for the regional variation in SMRs seen in Figure 9.16.

6 (*Objective 9.6*) Overall mortality rates are higher in social class V than in social class I at all ages and for both sexes. Is the same class difference true for all conditions and for measures of morbidity and disability?

10
Explaining inequalities in health

At the beginning of this chapter you will be asked to read two extracts contained in the Course Reader. These are 'Deaths under 50', from a report by the Medical Services Study Group of the Royal College of Physicians, and an extract from *Inside the Inner City* by Paul Harrison. They can be found in the Course Reader, Part 2, Sections 2.7 and 2.2 respectively.

There is a television programme and an audiotape sequence associated with this chapter. Television programme 3, 'Salford: Dirty Old Town' looks at the living and working environment in a northern city over the last century and is accompanied by the audiotape sequence. Details of these can be found in the Broadcast and Audiocassette Notes.

Our concern is with the interaction of variables traditionally seen as directly implicated in illhealth (such as smoking behaviour and work conditions) with social variables. It will be necessary to examine the effects upon the health of social groups of a wide range of social and behavioural variables implying further work both on the development of health indicators and upon the way in which disadvantageous social and economic conditions may give rise to or exacerbate the effects of patterns of dietary behaviour, leisure behaviour, etc. (Townsend and Davidson, 1982, p.139)

In Chapter 9, the discussion of patterns of mortality and morbidity was structured around three sets of factors: the biological, the social and those associated with life history. These three dimensions are clearly interrelated, though in many instances we know little about the processes involved.

In this chapter we explore in greater detail the ways in which the social distribution of mortality and morbidity in contemporary times in the UK might be explained. We shall examine the nature of the variables that need to be considered and begin to tease out some of the ways in which they might interact. The different patterns of mortality and morbidity described in Chapter 9 — those associated with gender and ethnicity for example — will be referred to, but we draw primarily on data associated with occupational social class. We do this for three reasons. First, and perhaps most important, occupational social class is closely correlated with many different dimensions of inequality in society: differences in mortality and morbidity associated with occupational social class are the best available measures of socially structured inequalities in health. Second, and partly in consequence of the significance attached to occupational social class by researchers and policy makers, an extensive body of data exists. Finally, we have chosen to focus on occupational social class in the knowledge that other factors such as gender will be discussed in greater detail in other books in the course.

Whose responsibility is health?

Though we have stressed that the three dimensions of explanation — the biological, the social and the life-history — are interrelated, in practice emphasis is often placed on one particular approach. This is illustrated by two very different approaches to explanation included in the Course Reader, and you should now read the first of these, the report from the Medical Services Study Group of the Royal College of Physicians, 'Deaths under 50' (Part 2, Section 2.7).

☐ The Study Group paid particular attention to 98 cases from a sample of 250 patients who died. How did they label the cases, and why?

■ The 98 cases were described as cases of '*self-destruction*' because, according to the Study Group, 'the patients contributed in large measure to their own deaths'.

☐ In attempting to explain the 'causes' of these deaths, what factors did the Study Group emphasise?

■ In the article they emphasise self-poisoning, excessive smoking, drinking and eating, non-compliance with medical treatment, and failure to seek medical help.

☐ How did the Study Group seek to explain these aspects of individual behaviour?

■ They did this primarily by discussing existing mental illness, reckless or uncooperative attitudes, and a failure to heed health education and, specifically, doctors' advice.

☐ In relation to our three-fold classification of causal factors, what type of factors are the Study Group emphasising?

■ The Study Group are emphasising personal or behavioural factors that could be described as both social and life-history factors. But they give no information about the social or economic circumstances of the 98 cases of 'self-destruction', nor do they discuss the way in which behavioural factors may be influenced by other aspects of the individual's life history.

Now read the second extract, from Paul Harrison's book *Inside the Inner City* (Section 2.2).

☐ Paul Harrison is describing a particular situation in an inner city borough of London. He suggests that three factors which define most of the problems of this area are found in other inner city areas. What are these three factors?

■ He suggests that these are older declining industries; old Victorian housing and modern, badly designed council housing; and a higher than average concentration of unskilled and de-skilled workers, unemployed people and other disadvantaged groups

such as immigrants, single parents, people with mental and physical handicaps and the chronically sick.

☐ Does Harrison argue that these conditions are confined to inner city areas?

■ No. In fact he suggests that the bulk of poverty, bad housing and declining industries is *outside* the inner cities but that they are more concentrated in the inner cities and therefore more visible.

☐ Harrison argues that these problems are indicative of conditions, or what he terms 'diseases', spread throughout the British social, economic and political systems. What are these diseases?

■ A chaotic unplanned process of economic advance, the persistence of sharp class divisions between manual and non-manual workers and long-lasting inequalities in wealth and income; and the marginalisation of groups such as women, migrants, the handicapped, the mentally ill and the unskilled.

☐ How does Harrison relate all this to health?

■ For Harrison, personal health and the different health experience of different groups 'is one of the most telling and tragic indicators of the degree of inequality in Britain and of its consequence'. While he recognises many of the behavioural traits identified by the Medical Services Study Group and describes them as self-destructive, he stresses the interaction between factors. For Harrison, aspects of lifestyle such as smoking are influenced by stressful living and working conditions, diet is influenced by low income, and poor resistence to infection by low standards of living. At one point he notes that 'it is the entire complex of pressures acting on them that leads to their downfall'.

☐ Both the Study Group and Harrison argue that individuals may not make the 'best' use of health services. Their approaches to explaining this differ, however. How would you describe these differences?

■ The Study Group emphasised attitudes towards health care and noted that in a few cases lack of cooperation seemed to 'stem from fecklessness' or a 'psychopathic attitude to life and to doctors in particular'. No mention is made of the availability, accessibility or quality of care: three aspects of health care which Harrison (in contrast) emphasises. In essence, the Study Group emphasises individual characteristics, whereas Harrison focuses on the wider circumstances that constrain and influence characteristics and behaviour. In the language of much popular discussion, the Study Group are arguing that the individual is to blame, and Harrison that society is to blame.

These two explanations contrast sharply, but they are not mutually exclusive. Both authors recognise the importance of aspects of individual behaviour such as smoking, but they do differ profoundly in the way in which they apportion responsibility for the behaviour and in the attention they give to other factors.

The Study Group clearly feels that individuals are responsible for making choices that may adversely affect their health. Harrison, in contrast, is arguing that people do not necessarily have free choices, and that decisions such as whether to start or stop smoking, are influenced by a multitude of factors such as material disadvantage and discrimination. Thus, despite some superficial areas of agreement, the explanations of health and disease patterns offered in these two views are quite different. To evaluate these explanations it is therefore essential to consider the patterns of 'self-destructive' behaviour and inequalities in resources, power and status. In this way we shall be able to see how they might be related both to each other and to the patterns of mortality and morbidity described in Chapter 9.

Inequalities in health: a case of self-destruction

Smoking and the use made of health services may contribute to the patterns of mortality and morbidity with which we are concerned and are frequently described as aspects of lifestyle. Table 10.1 shows patterns of cigarette smoking in the UK in 1972 and 1982.

Table 10.1 Percentages of men* and women* in manual and non-manual classes smoking cigarettes, UK, 1972–1982

	1972	1982	Percentage reduction between 1972 and 1982
1 *Men*			
non-manual	40.6	26.3	− 35.2
manual	59.3	46.0	− 22.4
all men	52.0	38.0	− 27.0
2 *Women*			
non-manual	36.3	26.6	− 26.7
manual	43.6	38.6	− 11.5
all women	42.0	33.0	− 22.0

* All men and women aged 16 years or over. Women classified according to husband's present or last occupation.
(data from OPCS, 1983, Table 5)

☐ What has been happening to cigarette smoking among men and women in non-manual classes compared to those in manual classes between 1972 and 1982?
■ Cigarette smoking has fallen among men and women in both groups, but by different amounts. The fall among men in non-manual classes was over 35 per cent compared to a much smaller decline of around 22 per cent among men in manual classes. Among women

the picture was similar, with a fall of almost 27 per cent in the number of women smoking in non-manual classes compared to only around 11 per cent among women in manual classes.

☐ What proportion of men and women in non-manual classes smoked in 1982 compared to men and women in manual classes?
■ In 1982 just over 1 in 4 men and women in the non-manual classes smoked cigarettes compared to almost 1 in 2 (46 per cent) of men in manual classes and over 1 in 3 (38.6 per cent) of women in these classes.

The relationship between cigarette smoking and many diseases, especially lung cancers and other respiratory diseases, is now well established and it is therefore predictable that the different smoking habits illustrated in Table 10.1 will contribute to social-class differences in mortality and morbidity. It is also clear from these data that the higher rate of cigarette smoking among men may help to explain some of the gender differences in the incidence of specific diseases. But Table 10.1 also illustrates the way in which smoking among men is declining more rapidly than among women, and this may have important consequences for future gender-related mortality patterns. As the difference between the numbers of men and women smoking cigarettes has narrowed over the decade 1972 to 1982, so too has the difference in the amount they smoke.

The average weekly consumption of cigarettes among male smokers stayed about the same between 1972 and 1982 — about 120 cigarettes a week. Among women smokers, however, average consumption rose from 87 a week in 1972 to 98 a week in 1982, that is, 12 per cent higher than it had been a decade earlier.

Changes in the mortality rate for lung cancer among men and women may be reflecting these behavioural changes, for though the lung cancer rate for men increased by 8 per cent between 1969 and 1978, for women it increased by 50 per cent.

Smoking is not the only aspect of lifestyle in which there are social-class and gender differences. Another factor identified by both the Medical Services Study Group and Harrison was the use of health services, especially those concerned with prevention. Table 10.2 presents information on the use of selected services by children under seven classified by the occupation of their father.

The information in Table 10.2 is taken from a report of the National Child Development Study, a project that has followed a cohort of all children born in a single week in March 1958. The data in the table were collected in 1965 and are somewhat dated now, but they illustrate clear class gradients in the use of preventive services.

These differences appear to have persisted over time. In 1975, for example, a government survey of the use of dental

Table 10.2 Use of health services by children under 7 by occupational class (of father), Great Britain, 1965

	I	II	III(N)	III(M)	IV	V
per cent who had never visited a dentist	16	20	19	24	27	31
per cent not immunised against						
polio	1	3	3	4	6	10
diphtheria	1	3	3	6	8	11

(DHSS, 1980, Table 4.7, p.106; based on data from National Child Development Study, 2nd Report.)

services among five-year-olds found that 40 per cent of the children in social classes IV and V combined had never seen a dentist, compared to 18 per cent in social classes III non-manual, II and I combined. This might provide a partial explanation of social-class differences in dental decay.

More recent studies of vaccination rates also show clear social-class gradients, though overall rates of vaccination are far higher than they were in 1965. Failure to immunise children appears to be particularly high among groups defined as 'especially disadvantaged' according to 'composite' indicators which include such factors as housing amenities and parental education. Social-class differences in the use of health services, and especially the very low utilisation rates among particularly disadvantaged groups, are also apparent in relation to other preventive services, such as those for antenatal care and child health. The effectiveness of some aspects of health care is hotly disputed, but if we assume at this point that these preventive services do make a positive contribution to health, then the lower use of such services among the socially disadvantaged is a factor that must be considered when trying to explain differences in mortality and morbidity.

There are many other aspects of the lifestyle or the behaviour of individuals that we could have discussed: aggressive risk-taking behaviour among young people, for example; different patterns of alcohol consumption among men and women or between different social classes; differences in the use of contraception, in the lifestyles of many different ethnic groups or in the diets of different groups. The relationship between lifestyle and health and disease is often far from straightforward, but enough information exists to indicate that differences in lifestyles do contribute to the patterns of mortality and morbidity that were described in Chapter 9. The questions this raises include why such differences in lifestyle exist, and what other factors should be considered.

The Medical Services Study Group suggested that recklessness and irresponsibility are at the root of the problem. It has also been suggested that certain behavioural traits and attitudes, which may adversely affect health, are passed on from generation to generation, for example, through child-rearing practices. In this way, health disadvantage may persist despite considerable improvements in education, living standards, and other factors. There has in fact been a great deal of research focusing on the mechanisms by which disadvantage may be passed from generation to generation — a process often referred to as the 'cycle of deprivation'. Taken together this research, much of it done in the 1970s, suggests that the relationship between the attitudes and behaviour of parents and those of their children is far from straightforward. Though parental influences do play a part, it appears that one of the most powerful influences on an individual's health behaviour is the material environment in which they live as child and as adult. The way in which such factors can make their impact is vividly illustrated in the quotation below taken from a study of parents and children in the inner city.

> The children in the process of growing up have many shared experiences. They live in overcrowded conditions being members of large families; their homes are inadequate by current standards; the neighbourhoods are rough and disliked by most of those who have to live in them. They experience poverty ... Most if not all of the children have first-hand knowledge of illness, disability, accidents and mental stress ... They must learn, in growing, to come to terms with or contain the situations of stress to which they are subjected ... Events in these children's lives repeat themselves and form a pattern and thus become part of what appears to them to be the hazardous business of living ... the draining of human energy and potential is the element that outweighs all others and has an overpowering effect on the growth of children that no other element can counter. (Wilson and Herbert, 1978, pp.103–4)

As the quote suggests, there are strong reasons to believe that the distribution of material resources is as relevant to an understanding of patterns of mortality and morbidity in the UK as it is to an understanding of world patterns.

The distribution of wealth and income

Perhaps the most extreme example of the extent of material inequality in the UK is the *distribution of wealth*. This is illustrated in Figure 10.1 which shows data for personal 'marketable wealth', that is, the value of physical assets such as land, property and shares in companies. Incomes from these, such as rent, interest or dividends are excluded.

On the left-hand side of the horizontal axis of the figure is the 'top' 1 per cent of the population who are the greatest wealth holders. The height of the bar is an indication of how great their share of wealth is as a proportion of all

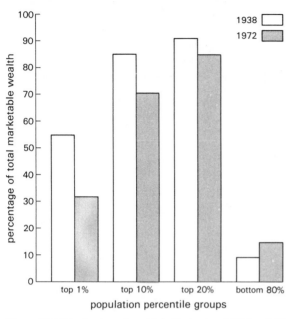

Figure 10.1 Distribution of wealth in England and Wales, 1938 and 1972. (*Note* 'Wealth' here does not include pensions and insurance policies.) (Data from Atkinson and Harrison, 1978, Table 6.5)

available wealth. Thus, in 1972, the top 1 per cent of the population owned just over 30 per cent of all marketable wealth. In contrast, the bottom 80 per cent of the population owned around 15 per cent. The figures also give some indication of how the distribution of marketable wealth has changed since 1938.

☐ What has happened to the share of marketable wealth going to the top 1 per cent of the population since 1938?

■ By 1972, their share had dropped from 55 per cent to just over 30 per cent.

☐ What was the share of the top 20 per cent of the population in 1972 compared to 1938?

■ The share of the top 20 per cent fell from about 91 per cent in 1938 to around 85 per cent in 1972.

Although there was, therefore, a redistribution of wealth between 1938 and 1972, much of this was redistributed among the top 20 per cent of the population. The share of wealth going to the bottom 80 per cent of the population only increased from 9 per cent to around 15 per cent.

Figure 10.2 shows the distribution of income after direct taxation, across the population. Income here includes salaries, social security benefits, rents, interest and dividends. Though the divisions between groups of the population are not so sharp as they were with regards to 'marketable wealth', the picture is still one of considerable inequality.

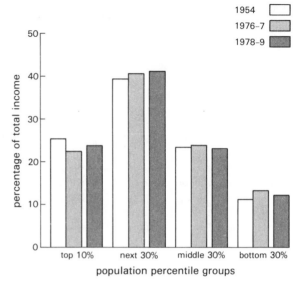

Figure 10.2 Distribution of income (after tax), UK, 1954, 1976–77, 1978–79. (Data from Atkinson, 1983, Table 4.1, p.63)

In 1978–79 the top 10 per cent of the population received almost a quarter of all income in the United Kingdom. In contrast, the bottom 30 per cent of the population received only 12 per cent. The figures given for the different dates are not directly comparable because of changes in the way the data are calculated. But they do give an indication of changes over time, and, as with wealth, the distribution of income across the population has been remarkably stable since 1954.

How different is the United Kingdom from other industrialised countries? Table 10.3 presents data on the distribution of pre-tax income in six capitalist industrialised countries including the UK.

Table 10.3 Distribution of pre-tax personal income of households (percentile of households)

Country	Year	Top 20 per cent	Bottom 20 per cent
Australia	1966/67	38.9	6.3
France	1970	47.0	4.3
Japan	1971	46.2	3.8
Republic of Ireland	1973	44.5	4.1
UK	1971	39.4	5.8
USA	1970	44.6	3.9

(data from Atkinson, 1980, Table 7.8, p.92)

☐ Look carefully at the table and suggest which two countries appear to be the least unequal with regard to these data.

■ Australia and the UK have the greatest share of pre-tax income going to the bottom 20 per cent of households, 6.3 per cent and 5.8 per cent respectively, and the smallest proportions, 38.9 per cent and 39.4 per cent, going to the top 20 per cent.

The income figures used in Table 10.3 are before tax, so the picture will change depending on how redistributive the tax systems are in the different countries. Nevertheless, the United Kingdom clearly is not unique among industrialised countries with regard to the unequal distribution of income, and is at least a little more equal than some other countries.

The distribution of income and the distribution of wealth have been treated separately in this discussion primarily because of the nature of the data that are available. But such a distinction is artificial. Income and wealth are merely different ways of expressing an individual's command over resources and they feed into each other. Wealth begets income and a high income begets savings and so more wealth.

Data on the distribution of wealth and income powerfully illustrate the scale of the inequality in access to material resources that exists in the UK, but they may seem a bit remote from issues of health and disease. In fact, however, the distribution of wealth and income is closely associated with many other dimensions of inequality — in the work environment, in access to housing, and in the experience of poverty. A closer examination of inequalities at these more concrete levels may reveal much more direct associations with the social distribution of ill-health and death.

The working environment and health

Occupations involve their own specific hazards to health. Industrial accidents and disease, for example, still take a considerable toll. We have used figures for one year, 1980, wherever possible, to show what the toll for accidents and diseases is in a year. In 1980, 276 100 accidents at work, resulting in 701 deaths, were officially notified to government agencies in the UK. But this is an under-estimate, for current legislation does not require that all accidents have to be notified. In addition to the many accidents that do not have to be notified, research suggests that as many as 25 per cent of accidents that should be notified to the official health and safety agencies in fact go unreported. More serious still, up to a quarter of these unreported accidents could give rise to serious injury such as the amputation or dislocation of a limb. Less serious accidents are far more likely to go unreported, yet even these might involve the loss of a joint from a finger for example, or concussion resulting in a hospital stay of up to 24 hours. These classifications of 'serious' and 'less serious'

accidents are currently under review, but you might like to consider whether you would regard losing a piece of a finger at work as serious or not!

Exposure to toxic substances such as chemicals, dust, gases or fumes, or to hazards due to excessive heat, noise or vibration may result in *industrial diseases*. Of the many different diseases that could occur under such circumstances, only sixteen are notifiable as officially recognised industrial diseases. These include infectious diseases such as anthrax (a risk to workers handling animal products such as meat, skins and bonemeal) and chemical poisons such as lead, cadmium and mercury. (Alice in Wonderland's 'Mad Hatter' was suffering from an occupational disease — mercury poisoning, from the materials of his trade.) In 1980, 64 cases of notifiable industrial diseases were notified to health and safety authorities. Surveys suggest however that only around 10 per cent of all cases are in fact notified, so that the figure is probably in excess of 600.

The sixteen notifiable industrial diseases do not represent a comprehensive list of all occupationally related diseases. A more important source of information about *occupational hazards* — the health hazards of work — comes from social security data. Injury, disablement and death benefits may be paid in respect of around 50 'prescribed' diseases or conditions, which include most of the notifiable industrial diseases.

Around twenty of these prescribed diseases involve poisoning from a variety of substances still found in certain industries. Pneumoconiosis, the chronic lung condition suffered by many miners, is included. So is asbestosis, a disease caused by inhalation of asbestos fibres, and byssinosis, a lung disease found among textile workers and caused by inhaling cotton fibres. Other prescribed conditions include inflammation of the tendons due to frequent or repeated movement of the hand and wrist, as on an assembly line for instance; dermatitis (inflammation of the skin) resulting from contact with substances such as mineral oil, soot or tar; 'beat hand', knee or elbow — a swelling of the affected area caused by prolonged or severe pressure associated with manual work; and occupational deafness.

In 1980, 799 death benefits were paid in relation to prescribed diseases of which around 80 per cent were associated with pneumoconiosis, asbestosis, and byssinosis, and 572 were paid in relation to fatal accidents at work. In addition, there were 509 000 new claims that year for injury benefit for industrial accidents and 10 214 for prescribed industrial diseases excluding pneumoconiosis and byssinosis. In 1979, 34 700 people were receiving benefit in relation to these two diseases.

But the figures do not tell the whole of the story: there are many conditions related to occupations which are not prescribed. One such is emphysema, a respiratory disease common among people working in dusty conditions. The difficulty is that conditions such as emphysema may be caused or aggravated by atmospheric pollution or smoking. A survey carried out for the Royal Commission on Civil Liabilities and Compensation for Personal Injury which reported in 1978 (The Pearson Report) suggested, however, that 'illness believed to have arisen at work but not presently prescribed may be of the order of five times as numerous as those which are prescribed'.

The effects of exposure to industrial hazards may also take many years to become apparent. The story of mesothelioma (a cancer of the chest lining caused by exposure to asbestos) illustrates this point. Between 1968 and 1981 the number of diagnosed cases of the disease rose from 154 to 445 and they are still rising. New regulations to control asbestos were introduced in 1969, but as this type of cancer may take up to forty years to develop, it will be many years before these improvements are reflected in lower mortality rates. Since the worst exposures occurred between 1935 and 1970 (many of them during the lagging of ships with blue and brown asbestos in the early years of the Second World War, and its removal when the hazards became known after the war), the peak of cases is probably still to come. Richard Peto, an epidemiologist at Oxford University, estimated in 1982 that at least 50 000 more asbestos deaths are to be expected over the next thirty years.

Work then can involve considerable direct hazards to health. However, not all occupations carry the same risks. Consider the data in Table 10.4 for example, which shows the number of days people had off work in different industries in 1979/80 because of industrial accidents alone. It only includes days for which a doctor's certificate was obtained.

Table 10.4 Number of days of certified absence from work due to industrial accidents

Industry	Days of absence in millions, 1979/80
construction	1.4
mining and quarrying	1.3
transport and communication	1.1
professional and scientific services	0.8
insurance, banking, finance and business services	0.1

(data from Health and Safety Executive, 1982, Table 9.3, p.49)

□ What does the table suggest about the risk of accidents in different occupations, and why do we need to be cautious in interpreting these data?
■ It suggests that the risk of being involved in an accident which is serious enough to require time off

work is far higher in manual occupations than in non-manual occupations. To say something definite, however, we should need to know what proportion of the work-force are employed in each of the sectors shown.

But who is responsible for industrial accidents? Opinion varies, and the debate may now be familiar to you.

□ Describe the two different perspectives on causality represented in the quotations below and how they relate to the articles in the Course Reader by the Medical Service Study Group, and Harrison (Part 2, Sections 2.7, 2.2).

> Everything possible is done to enable you to work in safety but your co-operation is essential.
> [and, under *Human Factors*]
> Accidents do not happen, they are caused; horseplay and tomfoolery, carelessness and thoughtlessness, lack of concentration, lack of respect for oneself and others, familiarity, drinking, fatigue, haste, working conditions, irritability and boredom. (From a Royal Society for the Prevention of Accidents booklet; quoted in Kinnersley, 1974, pp.194, 197)

> The 'attitude of the worker to safety' is no more the cause of industrial accidents today than it was in the days when little children were mangled in unguarded machinery in the cotton mills. Machines, buildings, and arrangements of work are still designed to the cheapest specifications that will produce goods at the greatest profits. Engineering design concentrates on the product and excludes the operator until the last moment. Safety, health and last of all comfort are treated as bolt-on goodies. (Kinnersley, 1974, p.195)

■ The first quote emphasises individual responsibility and carelessness much as the Medical Services Study Group did. The second stresses the influence of the actual conditions at work and the way work is organised, a perspective similar to that adopted by Harrison.

Research does suggest that the 'careless worker' approach is inappropriate in most cases. In a report published in 1971 describing 2 000 accidents observed over a 42-month period, the National Institute of Industrial Psychology concluded that:

> ... risks were so much an integral part of work systems as at present arranged, that the more work was done ... the more accidents occurred. ... It must follow that the two main lines of successful accident prevention policy must be a method of design and

layout which will eliminate hazards currently being built into systems of work and training to reduce the effects of inexperience. (quoted in Kinnersley, 1974, p.199)

The different risks to health associated with different occupations are reflected in overall mortality rates, some examples of which are given in Table 10.5. This table and much of the discussion in this section focus on the hazards facing men, which are much better documented than the occupational hazards of women's employment.*

The table reflects the very high risk of industrial injury and disease associated with manual jobs. Occupational mortality rates, however, do not only reflect these more obvious hazards. There are other dimensions to occupations that present hazards to health and which are also unequally distributed among the working population.

The graphs included in Figure 10.3 illustrate a number of these. They are based on data collected by the sociologist Peter Townsend in a national study of poverty in the United

* The latter is discussed in more detail in Book V, *Birth to Old Age: Health in Transition*, Chapter 12.

Table 10.5 Standardised mortality ratios for men aged 15–64 in selected occupations, 1970–72

Risk		SMR
Low	university teachers	49
	managers in building and /contracting	54
	local authority senior officers	57
	company secretaries and /registrars	60
	ministers and MPs and senior government officials	61
	medical practitioners	81
High	electrical engineers	317
	bricklayers, labourers	273
	deck and engine room ratings	233
	fishermen	171
	steel erectors/riggers	164
	machine tool operators	156
	coal miners (underground)	141

(data from OPCS, 1978, Appendix 2, Table A)

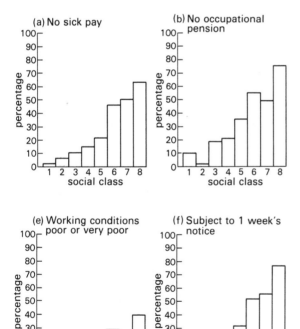

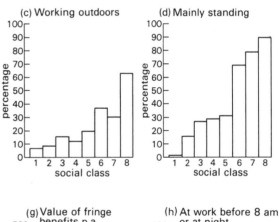

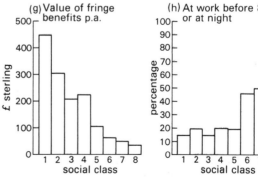

Figure 10.3 Inequality at work. (Data from Townsend, 1979, Table 12.2, pp.440–41)

Kingdom which he carried out in 1969, published as *Poverty in the United Kingdom* in 1979. The graphs demonstrate sharp differences in the character, security, conditions and fringe benefits of work available to men in different occupational classes. Manual workers are much more likely to work out of doors, to spend most of the day standing, to have insecure jobs with a high risk of unemployment, and to have shorter holidays and much less access to fringe benefits of various kinds. Whereas 81 per cent of male non-manual workers, for example, could expect to get full earnings as sick pay, 51 per cent of male manual workers had no entitlement to sick pay at all.

The index of poor working conditions illustrated in Figure 10.3(e) included, among other things, access to washing facilities, to a place of shelter from bad weather, to first-aid facilities and to a toilet. In all, 23 per cent of the men in this sample were working in poor or very poor conditions. For male unskilled manual workers the proportion increased to 40 per cent.

These aspects of occupation are clearly relevant to health and safety at work. It is probable, for example, that working long hours in poor conditions is stressful and may actually increase the risk of accidents, if not disease. Such conditions were an important focus of earlier reports from the Factory Inspectorates. In 1913, for example, sanitation, working facilities, meal facilities, lighting and temperature were all discussed. Today, despite improvements in some aspects of health and safety at work and the continuing campaign by some Trade Unions to improve their members' working conditions, these particular aspects are often given low priority by the official health and safety agencies.

There are also sharp differences in the earnings of different occupations, and it is through earnings in particular that occupation will influence the living standards of other members of a family. Figure 10.4 illustrates the differences in average weekly earnings before tax between manual and non-manual, male and female full-time workers in 1980.

□ Describe briefly the differences in earnings illustrated in Figure 10.4.
■ For both men and women, full-time non-manual workers earn more than full-time manual workers, though the difference is much greater for men than for women.
□ What does Figure 10.4 tell us about the earnings of women compared to men?
■ In both manual and non-manual occupations men earn far more than women.

Although less well documented, the health hazards associated with women's employment are considerable. You have already seen that full-time women workers are paid much less than men, but around 40 per cent of all

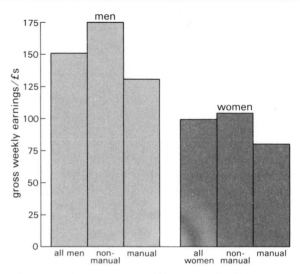

Figure 10.4 Average gross weekly earnings for full-time employees, men and women, UK, April 1980. (Data from *Social Trends*, 1982, Table 5.3, p.80)

women in employment work part-time. However, if the *hourly* earnings of *all* men and women in employment are compared, then in 1983 British women still earned only 66 per cent of the male wage per hour. In Sweden, in comparison, the difference is less acute: women earn 87 per cent of the male wage. Despite equal pay legislation in 1975 it seems that British women are still discriminated against in the labour market. They are certainly concentrated in low-status industries and occupations which are low paid. This concentration is illustrated in Figure 10.5.

□ In which three areas do women workers predominate?
■ Among female manual workers 57.5 per cent are working in catering, cleaning, hairdressing and other personal services. Almost 60 per cent of female non-manual workers are in clerical and related jobs, and a further quarter are involved in professional work in the 'caring' services — health, education, and welfare.

Though this figure does not show it, even within professional occupations women tend to be concentrated in the lower-grade posts. They are more likely, for example, to be social workers rather than Directors of Social Services. And even within a particular occupation, such as nursing, men are disproportionately represented among management posts.

Many women are under additional pressure because of the need to combine responsibility for work inside and outside the home — sometimes referred to as the 'double day'. In a recent study of women factory workers, for example, the researchers concluded that:

manual women workers

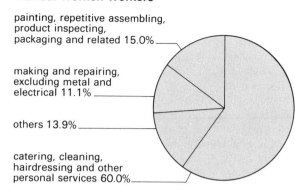

painting, repetitive assembling, product inspecting, packaging and related 15.0%

making and repairing, excluding metal and electrical 11.1%

others 13.9%

catering, cleaning, hairdressing and other personal services 60.0%

non-manual women workers

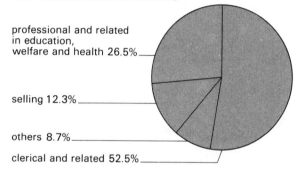

professional and related in education, welfare and health 26.5%

selling 12.3%

others 8.7%

clerical and related 52.5%

Figure 10.5 Women's earnings. (Equal Opportunities Commission, *7th Annual Report*, 1982; data from Department of Employment, *New Earnings Survey*, 1982, Part E, Table 136)

... women were caught in a constant and unremitting round of activity throughout their waking hours. Their day begins early, about 5 or 6 a.m. and finishes late, about 9 or 10 p.m. with little or no time for rest or relaxation, leaving them continuously tired and often emotionally exhausted. Many are responsible for the household budget and under financial pressure to make ends meet, which is a major factor in their going out to work. (Shimmin *et al.*, 1981, p.347)

Women are not the only group discriminated against in the labour market: disabled people and those in minority ethnic groups are also at a disadvantage. Recent data are lacking on the position of people with disabilities, but a government survey in 1969 found that half of a sample of disabled workers had incomes below 42 per cent of average earnings, and a quarter of the sample had earnings below 32 per cent of average earnings. Disabled people are therefore much more likely than the non-disabled to be low paid, but the disadvantage they experience in employment does not stop there.

In his national survey of poverty in 1969, Peter Townsend found that people with disabilities often had to work longer hours than the non-disabled to earn the same amount of money, and that disabled people in paid employment were more likely than the non-disabled to have to work in poor conditions, lacking sufficient heating, washing and toilet facilities.

Some minority ethnic groups also appear to be relatively disadvantaged within the labour market.

Table 10.6 Job levels of men by ethnic origin

Job level	European (white)	Pakistani/ Bangladeshi
professional/management/white-collar	40	8
skilled manual	42	33
semi-skilled manual	12	38
unskilled manual	6	20
not classified	1	1
total	100	100

(data from Smith, 1976, Table A26, p.64)

☐ Look at Table 10.6 and briefly describe the different employment patterns of white men, and men of Pakistani and Bangladeshi origin.

■ 40 per cent of all white men in this sample are in professional, management or white-collar jobs and 42 per cent in skilled manual. The proportions for men of Pakistani and Bangladeshi origin are 8 per cent and 33 per cent respectively — much lower in both types of jobs.

The study from which these data are taken was conducted in 1976 and was concerned with the disadvantage experienced by people 'who were black or brown by race and whose families originated from the West Indies, India, Pakistan, or Bangladesh'. It was concerned to explore the nature and extent of racial discrimination. But at least two other explanations have been offered for the data given in Table 10.6: first, that minority ethnic groups have fewer qualifications than white workers, and second, that they do not speak English fluently.

However, the 1976 study casts considerable doubt on both of these potential explanations. None of the white men with degree qualifications were doing manual jobs, in fact 79 per cent of them were in managerial or professional jobs. Among Asian men with the same standard of educational qualification, however, only 31 per cent were in professional or managerial jobs, and 21 per cent were doing manual work. The relatively low job levels of Asian men with academic qualifications are not easily explained by a lack of language competence, as nearly all those with degrees speak English fluently. However, language may be a significant factor at lower levels of the job hierarchy.

Language, skills, and qualifications all have some part to play in determining the job distribution of men from minority ethnic groups. But such factors still leave a great deal unexplained, and this suggests that racial discrimination continues to play a significant part in inequalities in our society. Whatever the explanation, the fact remains that people from minority ethnic groups are disproportionately represented in those occupational classes which experience the greatest hazards to health.

Explaining the labour market

The more one looks at the occupational and employment patterns summarised here, the more it seems that occupational divisions separate the working population into two distinct groups. In one group are those whose occupations provide the prospects of a high income, good working conditions, generous fringe benefits (including holidays and sickness benefits), security of employment and adequate provision for retirement. In another group, jobs provide poor wages and conditions, often involve hazards to health, and have few fringe benefits, poor prospects, inadequate pension provisions and a high degree of uncertainty. The first group are in 'good' jobs which have high status and tend to be the preserve of men and those from high social-class backgrounds. The 'bad' jobs are low status manual and clerical jobs, and are frequently filled by women, the disabled, young people without experience, and people from minority ethnic groups.

The existence of this division in the labour market is a challenge to orthodox economic ideas that people are free to move around a flexible and open labour market, looking for the best conditions and rewards. This has given rise to the idea that the labour market is in fact divided or 'segregated' into a primary and a secondary sector. A primary sector develops because firms need some workers to have specialised skills, and so invest heavily in training these workers. Having done so, they try to hold on to their investment in these workers by providing them with job security, good pay, and a proper career structure — 'good' jobs. However, because firms also need to adapt to changes in the markets for their goods, they need to complement their primary workforce with a more easily 'disposable' group of workers. Since this group need not be discouraged from leaving, pay and conditions are poor, little training is provided, and prospects for improvement are extremely limited. The divisions between these two sectors are so deep that it becomes very difficult to move out of the 'bad' jobs into the 'good' ones.

Moreover, firms with a predominantly primary-sector work-force are normally large and profitable (often having monopoly power) and maintain high levels of investment in up-to-date production techniques. On the other hand, firms with a mainly secondary-sector work-force are often very small and operating in conditions of intense competition — clothing and tailoring is a good example

— and tend to have low investment, outdated production techniques, and declining markets.

The existence of a segmented labour market is therefore likely to reinforce in a powerful way the health and disease patterns associated with inequalities in standards of living, conditions of work, and the many other factors this chapter has considered.

Wider dimensions of inequality

Precisely how much of the differences in mortality and morbidity can be explained by employment experience is hotly debated. As we have seen, occupational hazards do contribute to the differences in mortality and morbidity associated with gender, ethnicity, geography and social class. In addition to health hazards directly associated with work, there can also be ways in which work can indirectly affect the health of others adversely: for example, workers may take toxic substances, such as asbestos fibres, home on their clothes or bodies. Industrial waste may pollute the environment and so damage the health of people living nearby. Both of these processes linking work and health may be important. However, there are inequalities in health between social classes that cannot be explained by reference to occupational hazards, such as in the health of children or others outside the formal labour market. Other factors must therefore be considered. Perhaps the most obvious link between occupation and the health of these people is found in the access to material resources.

There are sharp differences in the earnings of different occupational classes; in their access to fringe benefits, sick pay and pensions; and in their ability to accumulate property, consumer durables, and other resources over the lifetime. There are also many people who are excluded from paid employment and who are thus dependent on social security benefits for their livelihood — benefits that, as you will see, provide a relatively meagre standard of living. Patterns of inequality within the sphere of formal employment are therefore paralleled by inequalities in many other spheres which can also contribute to our understanding of inequalities in health. We shall consider only two dimensions here: inequality in access to and quality of housing; and the nature and extent of poverty in the UK today.

Inequality, housing and health

Concern about the relationship between housing conditions and health goes back many years. T. H. C. Stevenson, who developed the Registrar General's classification of occupations, looked at the relationship between infant and child mortality and tenement size in the 1920s. He found clear associations between the child mortality rate and the number of available rooms, which he used as the index of overcrowded conditions. These are illustrated in Figure 10.6, Stevenson's original hand-drawn graph. The different lines on the graph relate to duration of marriage: the greater the duration of marriage (and therefore presumably the older the mother and/or larger the family), the higher the child death rate in that tenement size.

Since Stevenson drew his graph, housing standards have seen immense improvements. Between 1954 and 1973, for example, 1.5 million homes were demolished in slum clearances, and half of today's housing stock was built after 1948. These, however, include a large number of alienating and sometimes uninhabitable houses and flats. In 1981, 1.1 million dwellings in England (6.2 per cent of the total) were still classified as unfit for human habitation by the Department of the Environment. Additionally, in 1981–2 an estimated 75 000 households in England and Wales were accepted by local authorities as officially homeless. Townsend's study of poverty looked at a number of different indicators of housing disadvantage, including the traditional measures of structural defects and inadequate facilities and space. Some results are illustrated in Table 10.7. This table shows the proportions of people in the professional and managerial class and the partly skilled and unskilled manual class experiencing different types of housing disadvantage in 1969.

In all of the different categories of housing disadvantage, a larger percentage of people in the skilled and unskilled manual class were experiencing difficulties. Almost a third of the people in the unskilled manual class identified structural defects, and half of these felt they were a danger to health. Heating problems were common to both classes, but the figure for people in the partly skilled and unskilled manual class was double that of those in the professional and managerial class. Almost a third of the former group also felt they had insufficient space in the dwelling for children to play.

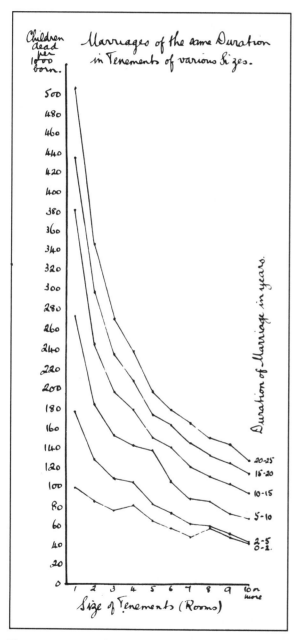

Figure 10.6 Diagram drawn by Stevenson to show child mortality, tenement size and duration of marriage, based on data from the 1911 Census. (Fox and Goldblatt, 1982, Figure 5.1, p.65)

Table 10.7 Inequality in housing: proportion of people living in inadequate housing by social class

Housing deprivation indicators	Professional and managerial class	Partly and un-skilled manual class
structural defects	18	31
poor housing facilities	4	29
no sole use of internal WC	2	23
no sole use of bath or fixed shower	3	22
no sole use of gas or electric cooker	1	6
overcrowded accommodation less than bedroom standard*	5	29
less than 40 per cent of accommodation heated	31	59
felt they had serious housing problem now	2	13
structural defects felt to be a danger to health	2	16
insufficient internal play space for children	1	31

* This standard depends on allocating bedrooms according to the composition of the household.
(data from Townsend, 1979, Table 13.1, pp.482–3)

Official figures show considerable improvements in some areas of housing deprivation since Townsend did his survey. For example, by 1980 only 1 in 17 households headed by an unskilled worker were in housing where bathing facilities were either shared or not available. However, some researchers have claimed that these improvements over time may be partly a statistical illusion: in 1981, for example, it was decided to revise upwards by nearly 50 per cent the number of unfit dwellings reported for 1976. Not all researchers were convinced by the reasons given for this revision, the result of which was inevitably to exaggerate the improvements that had occurred since then.

Townsend's study also found that large families, and elderly women living alone, experienced particular housing disadvantage. Almost a third of elderly women had poor housing facilities, as did 20 per cent of large families. Over half of both groups had less than 40 per cent of their dwellings heated and over a third of large families were 'overcrowded'. Those from minority ethnic groups also appear to experience greater housing disadvantage than white people. The study of racial disadvantage referred to earlier in this chapter found that on three separate indicators of disadvantage in housing — shared dwelling, numbers of persons per room, and lack of sole access to basic facilities such as an inside WC — the housing occupied by people from minority ethnic groups was much inferior to that occupied by white people. The proportions not having sole access to bath, hot water and an inside WC, for example, rose from 18 per cent of white people, to 33 per cent of Asians and 41 per cent of West Indians.

Inequality is also evident in relation to different types of housing tenure. The British housing market contains three main tenure types: owner-occupied, Local-Authority rented, and privately rented. In 1982, there were over 21 million dwellings in the UK, 59 per cent of which were owner-occupied, 29 per cent rented from Local Authorities and 12 per cent were privately rented. The pattern of tenure varies geographically with only 36 per cent of dwellings in Scotland being owner-occupied and 54 per cent rented from local authority. The percentage of owner-occupied houses is increasing rapidly at present (1984) as a result of recent policies regarding the sale of council houses to tenants.

Tenure type is not directly related to housing quality but traditionally, the worst housing of all was to be found in the privately rented sector. This sector is now a very small proportion of all dwellings. In 1969 Townsend concluded that with the decline in this sector, council housing was taking its place as the sector with the largest number of substandard houses. However, the incidence of different types of problems varies considerably between forms of tenure. According to the 1981 Department of Environment Housing Condition Survey, for example, more than 40 per cent of unfit dwellings were owner-occupied and 51 per

cent of the total number of dwellings in disrepair were in this sector. Although Local Authority housing contained a small proportion of unfit dwellings, over 65 per cent of all the post-1945 dwellings needing repairs costing more than £2 500 were in this sector. In addition, Local Authority tenants are also more likely to be overcrowded than people in any other sector except furnished privately rented accommodation. Owner-occupation does imply far greater control over where one lives and it is an important form of capital accumulation. It can, however, be a heavy liability to maintain an owner-occupied house on a low fixed pension.

As Figure 10.7 shows, there is considerable variation in the type of tenure held by different social classes. Households in lower occupational social classes were more likely to be in council housing in the late 1970s than those in higher occupational social classes, 85 per cent of which were in owner-occupied dwellings. Reflecting in part this social-class distribution Local Authority tenants are more likely than owner-occupiers to be unemployed, retired or receiving supplementary benefit and the household's gross weekly income more likely to be, on average, lower. The distribution of tenure by social class is also likely to change with the sale of council houses to tenants.

Privately rented

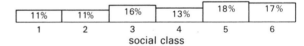

Council tenants

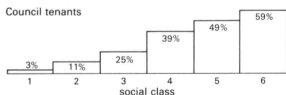

Owner-occupiers

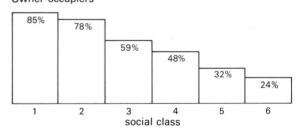

1 Professional
2 Employers and managers
3 Intermediate and junior non-manual
4 Skilled manual
5 Semi-skilled manual and personal service
6 Unskilled manual

Figure 10.7 Housing tenure by social class, Britain, 1977–79. (Data from Reid, 1981, Table 5.28, p.193)

Our knowledge about the relationship between housing and health is still limited. Attention has focused on aspects such as lack of amenities and overcrowding, the latter being associated with an increased risk of infection among children, for example, and the former with accidents when children have no protected place to play. Damp housing may cause or exaggerate respiratory diseases. Structural defects such as poor wiring may put children at particular risk. The psychological and practical difficulties associated with high-rise flats or isolated housing estates may also adversely affect the health of women or children at home or elderly people. There is a high incidence of depression among working-class women, for example.*

Factors such as these may partly explain the association between housing tenure and the risk of premature death illustrated in Table 10.8. These data are taken from the Longitudinal Study being run by the OPCS, in which a 1 per cent sample of the total UK population was drawn in 1971 and is being followed over time. This Longitudinal Study is already producing a great deal of data on topics which were previously surrounded by speculation, and is likely to prove invaluable to researchers, particularly social scientists.

Table 10.8 Standardised mortality ratios for men aged 15–64 in different occupational social classes and different tenure groups

Social class	Type of tenure		
	Owner-occupied	Privately rented	Local-Authority tenancy
I	79	93	99
II	74	104	99
IIIN	79	112	121
IIIM	83	99	104
IV	83	100	106
V	98	126	123

(Fox and Goldblatt, 1982, Table 13.5, p.210)

In each tenure group the risk of premature death is greatest in occupational class V and smallest in occupational class I, though the gradient between different occupational classes is not always clear cut. This is illustrated for example by the high SMRs for occupational classes II and III (non-manual) in the privately rented sector. What is interesting about the table, however, is that for almost every occupational class the risk of premature death is greatest in the council house sector and lowest in the owner-occupied sector. Though such differences will not be amenable to any simple explanation, it seems

*This is discussed in Book VI, *Experiencing and Explaining Disease.*

appropriate to question the quality of such council housing and the extent to which this sector provides a 'healthy' environment.

Poverty in the United Kingdom

How do we draw the line that defines when people are in *poverty*? You have already seen in Chapter 6 that scarcity and poverty are not absolutes that have always existed in the same form in different places and at different times. They may be viewed as relative both historically and culturally; neither need poverty be defined in purely financial terms. In practice, however, many studies of poverty have adopted what is essentially a *subsistence approach*, concerned with identifying 'an absolute level of need below which people are regarded as being poor and which does not change over time' (though the cost of meeting this need may rise with inflation, for example).

One of the most famous studies of poverty was that undertaken in York in 1899 by Seebohm Rowntree, a member of the Rowntree family, famous for the production of chocolate, whose firm is still based in York. Rowntree defined families whose 'total earnings were insufficient to obtain the minimum necessaries for the maintenance of merely physical efficiency' as being in *primary poverty* (*Poverty: A Study of Town Life*, 1901; quoted in Townsend, 1979, p.33). He formulated his poverty line by estimating the average nutritional needs of adults and children, translating these into quantities of different foods and hence into cash equivalents. To this he added minimum sums for clothing, fuel and household sundries according to family size. Rent was counted in full and a family was defined as in poverty if its income, minus rent, fell below this 'poverty line'. Rowntree carried out further studies in York in 1936 and 1950, in which the 'poverty line' used went beyond his earlier definition of 'merely physical efficiency'.

Subsequent studies in this and other countries have been deeply influenced by the concept of subsistence standards. This concept has also formed the basis for recommending minimum state social security benefits and minimum earnings in a number of countries. In the UK, Lord Beveridge, the 'architect' of the Welfare State, based his National Assistance allowances on a subsistence standard similar to the poverty standard of Rowntree and others. The actual levels were the result of negotiations with the Treasury and were in fact set below those recommended by Beveridge. Though they are now increased annually in line with prices, social security benefits are still implicitly based on a subsistence view. Since November 1980 Parliamentary Regulations have defined the items of normal day-to-day living that families are expected to meet from their basic supplementary benefit. Apart from housing costs these include:

... in particular, food, household fuel, the purchase, cleaning and repair and replacement of clothing and footwear, normal travel costs, weekly laundry costs, miscellaneous household expenses such as toilet articles, cleaning materials, window-cleaning and the replacement of small household goods (for example, crockery, cutlery, cooking utensils, light bulbs) and leisure and amenity items such as television licences and rental, newspapers, confectionary and tobacco. (From DHSS Supplementary Benefit (Requirement) Regulations; quoted in Burghes, 1980, p.6)

Although there is much discussion today concerning the extent to which benefits in the UK can actually meet these minimum needs, the level of supplementary benefit does provide one way of drawing the line below which people can be said to be 'in poverty' in the UK today. In the discussion that follows, we use data on the number of people living on incomes equal to or below the supplementary benefit level as a measure of the extent of poverty. However, quite different approaches to conceptualising and measuring poverty have also been suggested. Peter Townsend for example, argues that poverty is

... the absence or inadequacy of those diets, amenities, standards, services and activities which are common or customary in society. People are deprived of the conditions of life which ordinarily define membership of society. (Townsend, 1979, p.915)

In 1899, Rowntree defined clothing necessities for a young woman as:

... one pair of boots, two aprons, one second-hand dress, one skirt made from an old dress, a third of the cost of a new hat, a third of the cost of a shawl and a jacket, two pairs of stockings, a few unspecified underclothes, one pair of stays and one pair of old boots worn as slippers. (Quoted in Townsend, 1979, p.50)

Would this be an adequate definition of necessities in the 1980s? But Townsend also argues that 'needs' are not merely governed by the conventions or customs of the time, they are also defined by laws and regulations. There are, for example, state standards governing housing needs, though as you have seen many families are living below these standards. But if we adopt a relative approach to poverty we must still decide what level of resources is necessary to allow people to live 'as is common and customary in society'.

In his study of poverty, Townsend constructed a provisional index of *relative deprivation* by combining twelve summary indicators of style of living. These are shown in Table 10.9. Townsend calculated that the level of

Table 10.9 Townsend's index of deprivation, 1969*

Characteristic	percentage of population affected
1 Has not had a week's holiday away from home in last 12 months	53.6
2 *Adults only.* Has not had a relative or friend to the home for a meal or snack in the last 4 weeks	33.4
3 *Adults only.* Has not been out in the last 4 weeks to a relative or friend for a meal or snack	45.1
4 *Children only* (under 15). Has not had a friend to play or to tea in the last 4 weeks	36.3
5 *Children only.* Did not have party on last birthday	56.6
6 Has not had an afternoon or evening out for entertainment in the last two weeks	47.0
7 Does not have fresh meat (including meals out) as many as four days a week	19.3
8 Has gone through one or more days in the past fortnight without a cooked meal	7.0
9 Has not had a cooked breakfast most days of the week	67.3
10 Household does not have a refrigerator	45.1
11 Household does not usually have a Sunday joint (3 in 4 times)	25.9
12 Household does not have sole use of four amenities indoors (flush WC; sink or washbasin and cold-water tap; fixed bath or shower; and gas or electric cooker)	21.4

* This set of 12 summary indicators is drawn from a full list of 60 indicators of deprivation set out and discussed in Appendix 13 of Townsend's book.
(Townsend, 1979, Table 6.3, p.250)

income, below which the risk of being deprived of one or more of these items increased rapidly, was 150 per cent of the supplementary benefit standard.

Townsend's index has been criticised; first, because his list of indicators was arbitrarily selected, and second, because the lack of one of his twelve indicators could have as much to do with tastes as with poverty. More recently, however, a survey conducted by Market and Opinion Research International (MORI) for London Weekend Television has allowed an index of relative deprivation to be compiled of items people felt to be 'necessary and which all adults/families should be able to afford and which they should not be able to do without'. This index is illustrated in Table 10.10.

Further analysis of the data collected by MORI has shown that below a net income of about £70 a week at 1983 prices for a couple, the likelihood of families being without one or more of these items because they cannot afford them increased significantly — an income level equivalent to about 133 per cent of the supplementary benefit standard.

Table 10.10 MORI/London Weekend Television index of deprivation, 1983

Item	Percentage of population:		
	describing these items as 'necessary'	lacking these items	lacking as cannot afford them
heating to warm living areas	97	6	6
public transport for one's needs	88	9	3
a warm waterproof coat	87	10	7
3 meals a day for children*	82	7	4
2 pairs of all-weather shoes	78	15	11
toys for children*	71	5	3
celebrations on special occasions like Christmas	69	6	4
roast/joint equivalent once a week	67	12	7
new, not second hand, clothes	64	13	8
hobby or leisure activity	64	21	9
meat or fish every other day	63	17	9
presents for friends/family once a year	63	8	5
holidays away from home for one week a year	63	30	23
leisure equipment for children (bicycles, etc)*	57	17	13

* relevant for children only
(Lansley and Weir, 1983, Table 4, p.284)

You will see below that we have used data on people living on incomes up to 140 per cent of the supplementary benefit level. This figure is widely accepted as an indicator of 'low income' and is used in some official surveys. But people on incomes at this level are also often described as living 'on the margins of poverty' and these data are an indication of the numbers of people experiencing 'relative poverty' according to Townsend's definition.

This concept of poverty has been formally endorsed by the Commission of the European Community, who in 1975 adopted the following definition of poverty:

> *Persons beset by poverty:* individuals or families whose resources are so small as to exclude them from the minimum acceptable way of life of the member state in which they live....
> *Resources:* goods, cash income, plus services from public and private sources. (Commission of the European Community, 1981, p.8)

Poverty and health
The effects of poverty on health may be many and varied. Lack of money may affect the quantity and quality of goods that can be purchased or the environment in which one lives. It may profoundly restrict mobility and social life. Poverty also creates anxieties and stress which may themselves affect mental and physical health. In addition to any immediate effects these factors may 'cast long shadows forward' in the lives of the people involved.

There are clear differences in the pattern of expenditure between families living on different incomes. Among the richest households for example (those with an average weekly expenditure of £250 or more in 1981) 41 per cent of weekly expenditure went on the three basic necessities of housing, fuel and food compared to 50 per cent in households with an average weekly expenditure of less than £120. Among one-parent families the proportion rose to 54 per cent and to over 65 per cent among families experiencing long-term unemployment.

The greatest share of the financial resources of poor families therefore goes on these three necessities, leaving little to spare for clothes, outings, or other items. In some instances, in particular with regard to fuel, the costs involved are often prohibitive and fuel bills may cause considerable difficulties. In 1981, 137 000 households were disconnected from their gas and electricity supplies. In one study, 63 per cent of the families that were disconnected had children under 11. Disconnections have direct and obvious health risks. Cold homes may mean more condensation and damp, and cooking becomes difficult, if not impossible.

The elderly are at particular risk in cold conditions. In a UK national survey in 1972, 10 per cent of the sample of old people were at risk of experiencing hypothermia (low body temperature), which can be fatal. Though there was no simple relationship between low income and the risk of hypothermia, this group were generally disadvantaged; more likely to be living alone, on supplementary benefit and

Table 10.11 Meals for eight families living on supplementary benefit in England and Scotland, 1980

	Adults' meals				Children's meals			
Family	Breakfast	Lunch	Tea	Supper	Breakfast	Lunch	Tea	Supper
1	nothing	toast, coffee	rice and fish	milk, biscuits	cereal, egg toast	*School dinner* sausage and beans	rice and fish	hot chocolate biscuits
2	nothing	fish and chips	nothing	nothing	cereal	pie and chips	nothing	bread and butter
3	tea	nothing	*Mother:* sandwich *Father:* sausage, egg and chips	*Father:* boiled egg and tea	toast and tea	*School dinner* soup and yogurt	sausage, egg and chips	toast and tea
4	drink	soup	drink	drink	cereal, toast	fish fingers and potatoes	soup	beans on toast
5	nothing	nothing	nothing	egg salad	cereal	*School dinner*	nothing	egg salad
6	coffee	nothing	spaghetti	tea	cereal	*School dinner*	spaghetti	tea and sandwich
7	nothing	egg and toast	nothing	nothing	cereal	beans on toast	sausage and chips	nothing
8	tea and toast	tea and biscuit	tea and toast	nothing	cereal	*School dinner*	fish fingers, sausage and beans	orange juice

(Burghes, 1980, Table 7, p.34)

in poor housing. According to death certificates, there were 483 deaths from causes associated with hypothermia in the winter of 1980–81, an indication of the extreme difficulties some people face in relation to heating.

Research has suggested that poor families will try to make ends meet by cutting back on food. Though this is not likely to lead to absolute shortages in most instances, the effects on diet can be severe, as Table 10.11 illustrates. This information was collected from a group of families living on supplementary benefit in 1980 and illustrates the meals eaten by parents and their children in eight families over the course of one day.

In general, overall consumption is low, the meals are monotonous and nutritional balance is clearly lacking. (Fruit and vegetables of any form — fresh, tinned or frozen — are missing altogether.) It is much more likely that a parent than a child will miss a meal altogether, and for the children school dinners were an important part of the diet.

How many people are poor?

Table 10.12 provides figures for the number of people in Britain living on supplementary benefit or around the margins of this state standard. Perhaps the most dramatic facts to emerge from this table are that, according to this definition, 28 per cent of the population of Britain were living in or on the margins of poverty in 1981, and 2.8 million people, or around 5 per cent of the population, were actually living on incomes *below* the state standard.

In theory, at least, supplementary benefits have moved

Table 10.12 Numbers of people in or on the margins of poverty in Britain

	1960*	1981
below supplementary benefit (SB)/ National Assistance level (NA)	1 260 000	2 810 000
receiving SB/NA	2 670 000	4 840 000
at or up to 40 per cent above SB/NA level	3 510 000	7 350 000
total	7 440 000	15 000 000
percentage of the population	14.2	28.1

* 1960 figure relates to National Assistance.
(data from Townsend, 1981, p.67 and DHSS, 1983)

beyond providing for 'merely physical efficiency'. But the rates still only provide for a standard of living well below that enjoyed by others. In the financial year 1983–84, for example, a couple with two children under 11 received £61.80 a week on supplementary benefit plus a housing benefit. An income of 140 per cent of this rate would be equal to £86.52 a week. In contrast, the average spending of a two-child family (excluding housing costs) was approximately £147 a week.

Table 10.12 also illustrates the way in which the numbers living in or around the margins of poverty have changed since 1960: the proportion of the population in or on the margins of poverty increased from 14.2 per cent to 28.1 per cent over this period. Though changes in the way the data are collected mean the two figures are not directly

Table 10.13 Who are the poor? (Great Britain, 1981)

	Family type					Employment status		
	over pensionable age	families with children	one-parent families	single people	large families	in full-time work or self-employed	sick or disabled	unemployed for more than 3 months
1 Percentage of people in each group living on incomes of up to 140% of supplementary benefit	39.3	44.3	9.6	11.5	17.8	25.6	5.1	17.4
2 Percentage of total population in each group	16.5	49.3	4.8	16.3	12.5	67.1	3.0	6.5

(data from DHSS, 1983)

comparable, they do indicate the scale of change since 1960. Certain types of households are much more likely than others to live on low incomes. Table 10.13 gives the percentages of people living on incomes below 140 per cent of the supplementary benefit level by the type of family they live in and by their employment status. The column on the right shows what proportion of the total population lives in the different family types or falls into the different employment status groups. (The percentages do not add up to 100 as the categories overlap.) This table therefore illustrates which groups in the population are particularly at risk of experiencing poverty. For example, though only 16.5 per cent of the total population are over pensionable age, this group makes up 40 per cent of today's poor.

□   What other features of this table strike you as particularly interesting?

■   The issues you pick up will probably reflect your own interests, but you might have included one or all of the following:

1 Though families with children are not as a whole over-represented among the poor, some types of families are especially vulnerable. One-parent families and large families for example are particularly over-represented among the poor, and 44 per cent of today's poor are living in families with dependent children.

2 Almost one in five of today's poor have been unemployed for more than 3 months.

3 Though registered sick or disabled people represent only 5 per cent of those living in, or on the margins of, poverty they are over-represented among the poor for they form only 3 per cent of the total population. The registered disabled are also only a very small proportion of all people with some disability.

4 A quarter of the poor are in full-time work or self-employed. The fact that one in every four people in poverty are earning an income from employment reflects the extent of low-waged occupations in the economy.

The table fails to identify explicitly two other groups who are over-represented among the poor: women and minority ethnic groups. However, it does give some indication of the problems faced by many women, for almost 90 per cent of one-parent families are headed by women, and women make up 67 per cent of the elderly over 75 years of age.

The type of people experiencing poverty has also changed over time. For example, the numbers of elderly people and one-parent families among the poor has been increasing over the past decade or more. This partly reflects the increase in the number of pensioners in the population and the increasing rate of divorce. But their experience of poverty also reflects the inadequate provisions made for these groups. And in recent years the proportion of the poor who are unemployed has increased dramatically.

The increasing proportion of the poor who are of working age whether unemployed or in low-paid jobs, has inevitably meant that an increasing number of dependent children are exposed to the health hazards that poverty entails. Between 1979 and 1981 alone, the number of children living below the level of supplementary benefit nearly doubled. By 1981, 550 000 children were being raised on an income below the state standard and a total of 3.5 million on incomes of less than 140 per cent of supplementary benefit.

At the beginning of the chapter it was suggested that in seeking to explain patterns of inequality in health in the United Kingdom today we needed to look at the interaction of those 'variables traditionally seen as directly implicated in ill-health (such as smoking behaviour and work conditions) with social variables' (the 'Black Report'). We have not attempted to explore all of the possible variables. Rather, the material you have been studying has illustrated the types of variables that are important and has demonstrated that recurring patterns of inequality in, for example, access to material resources, exposure to hazards of various sorts, and, broadly, in the ability to control one's destiny, parallel many of the inequalities in mortality and morbidity with which we are concerned.

We have focused in particular on occupational class, but discrimination on the basis of gender, ethnicity and disability has also been discussed. The cumulative effect of these inequalities must be an important part of the explanation for the observable inequalities in health.

However, as we also suggested at the beginning of this chapter, in seeking to explain inequalities, emphasis is often placed on one particular type of variable rather than acknowledging the interaction between them. In apportioning responsibility for ill-health and the material disadvantage associated with it, much credence is given to explanations that stress the power of the individual — though this may be changing. Table 10.14 shows changes in public perceptions from 1976 to 1983 of why people are poor.

☐ Which explanations for poverty were given most and least support in 1976 compared to 1983 (excluding 'none of these' and 'don't know')?

■ In 1976, the largest group of people (43 per cent) felt that people were poor because of laziness and lack of will-power, whereas only 10 per cent suggested it was because of injustice. By 1983 the largest group of people (33 per cent) were suggesting that injustice was the most likely explanation, and less than a quarter stressed laziness and lack of will-power.

Popular perceptions of why people are poor have therefore changed fairly dramatically in recent years,

Table 10.14 Why are people poor?

Why, in your opinion, are there people who live in need? Here are four opinions — which is closest to yours?

	1976 (%)	1983 (%)
because they have been unlucky	16	13
because of laziness and lack of willpower	43	23
because there is much injustice in our society	10	33
it's an inevitable part of modern progress	17	26
none of these	4	5
don't know	10	3

(Lansley and Weir, 1983, Table 1, p.283)

perhaps reflecting the rising rate of unemployment, the focus of the next chapter. But the concern with how inequalities can be explained is not just idle academic curiosity. Different approaches to explanation have very different implications for policy decisions, and even when a particular perception of the causes is shared there may be no consensus about appropriate policies to reduce inequalities in health.

Objectives for Chapter 10

When you have studied this chapter, you should be able to:

10.1 Discuss the contribution of individual behaviour to contemporary patterns of health and disease in the United Kingdom.

10.2 Describe some of the possible health hazards attaching to different types of occupations.

10.3 Identify the different dimensions of inequality in the United Kingdom and comment on trends over time.

10.4 Describe two different approaches to the measurement of poverty, the 'subsistence' and the 'relative', and discuss some of the implications of these approaches.

Questions for Chapter 10

1 *(Objective 10.1)* The data in the table are taken from the annual General Household Survey. It shows the percentage of men and women in different socioeconomic groups who describe themselves as either infrequent/light drinkers or heavy drinkers.

Table 10.15 Type of drinker by sex and socioeconomic group

Socioeconomic group	Type of drinker (per cent)	
	infrequent/light	heavy
Men		
professional	16	10
unskilled manual	10	27
all men	12	23
Women		
professional	27	1
unskilled manual	15	2
all women	19	2

(data from OPCS, 1982, Table 9.5(b), p.159)

Comment briefly on the pattern of drinking habits revealed by the data in the table and how this might contribute to an understanding of patterns of mortality and morbidity, among socioeconomic groups and among men and women.

2 *(Objective 10.2)* Alice is a black nurse in a busy general hospital. Describe some of the general health hazards which she might face at work.

3 *(Objective 10.3)* The following quotation is taken from a study of attitudes to 'Welfare':

The higher income groups have been so badly knocked by taxation and contributing to the Welfare State. Professional people have been squeezed to help the poor. ('Mrs. Neil', 47-year-old teacher's wife. From Golding and Middleton, 1982, p.166.)

Comment briefly on Mrs. Neil's statement.

4 *(Objective 10.4)* In February 1980 a pressure group, The Low Pay Unit, published a report on the nature and extent of poverty in the UK. The day after, the following item appeared in the *Daily Express*:

If the hollow-eyed parents and hollow-bellied kids of Charles Dickens' world were alive today, they would have a good laugh at yesterday's news headlines. Statistics in a new report claimed that today's poor were more poverty striken than in 1886, when Queen Victoria still had a few years to reign. Do you believe such nonsense? Neither do I. Ah, but the statistics prove it! Statistics can prove anything. (*Daily Express*, 20 February 1980)

What two different approaches to poverty do you think may be implicit in the Low Pay Unit report and the Daily Express news item?

Health and unemployment

In 1933, three Austrian social scientists published the results of their research into the effects of widespread unemployment in the textile town of Marienthal. This study, *Marienthal: The Sociography of an Unemployed Community*, which was a pioneering application of social survey and participant observation methods, concluded with the following words: 'We entered Marienthal as scientists; we leave it with only one desire: that the tragic opportunity for such an inquiry may not recur in our time.' (Jahoda, 1982, p.33.)

For many years it seemed as if their hopes would be realised: mass unemployment vanished during the Second World War, and throughout the 1950s and 1960s full employment was maintained in most Western countries. In Britain, for example, the percentage of the work-force officially registered as unemployed never rose above 3.4 per cent in the years from 1948 to 1968, and averaged around 1.6 per cent or about 360 000 people. At times fewer than 200 000 people out of a work-force well over 20 million strong were unemployed, and for many the mass unemployment of the 1930s must have seemed as distant as gas lights and 'flappers'.

By 1974, however, the numbers of registered unemployed had risen to around 600 000 in Britain, a rate of 2.6 per cent; by 1979 the number was up to 1.3 million (5.6 per cent), and by 1983/84 to no fewer than 3.2 million, or around one in seven of the registered work-force. These figures must be regarded as minimum estimates of the number of people seeking employment in Britain, as many people who would take employment if it were available do not register as unemployed: non-registration is particularly high among women, for example. In consequence, many observers believe that the official statistics understate the true number of unemployed by up to 1 million people. Moreover, at the time of writing (1984) there seems to be little reason to expect a significant fall in these figures in the near future, and indeed much more evidence that unemployment may continue to increase here and elsewhere. Taking the 24 wealthiest Western countries who

together make up the membership of the Organisation for Economic Co-operation and Development (OECD), total unemployment rose from 16.5 million in 1975 to 23 million by 1981, and by 1983 the Secretariat of the OECD was predicting an increase to 35 million by the mid-1980s (in Merrit, 1982, p.16).

Mass unemployment, then, has once again returned to become a central problem of our time. It has also sparked off a major controversy in health research, the key question being whether or not unemployment causes poorer health. In this chapter we turn our attention to this controversy, and consider not only the available evidence, but also some of the difficulties in interpreting it.

The health of the unemployed

There seems to be little doubt that unemployment and health are in some way associated: ill-health, in fact, seems to be a feature of unemployment. For instance, the General Household Survey — one of the few sources of information on morbidity — reported in 1976 that long-standing illness was 40 per cent higher among unemployed males compared with employed males, and that long-standing illnesses causing a limitation to normal life were 80 per cent higher. Similarly, it has been shown that the standardised mortality ratios (SMR) of employed men are lower than expected, and, for those men out of work, higher than expected (these findings come from the OPCS Longitudinal Study, which was described in Chapter 10). It is also known that rates of disability are approximately twice as high among the unemployed compared with those in employment, and that psychological disturbance and mental distress are also more prevalent than among the employed. Many of these findings from recent years were also found during research conducted in the 1930s. Finally, research among males in Edinburgh has shown that men out of work for up to six months are six times more frequently admitted to hospital for parasuicide (deliberately self-inflicted injury) than men in work, and men unemployed for more than one year are nineteen times more likely to injure themselves (Platt, 1983).

☐ Consider the factual statement that ill-health and mortality are higher among the unemployed than those in employment. What interpretations could you place on this?

■ It could be that unemployment causes ill-health and mortality. However, it could also be that poor health leads to unemployment. Finally, there could be some other explanation in which both unemployment and poor health are independently related to some third factor or factors: this is called and 'artefact' explanation. Association and causality are not the same thing.

These differing interpretations lie at the heart of much of the controversy surrounding the subject and in fact raise issues relevant to much of the material in the preceding two chapters. In particular, the possibility that poor health might lead to unemployment is linked to the more general idea that the social position of individuals may be influenced by their state of health. This is referred to as 'social selection', to convey the notion that moves made by individuals into or out of occupations, social classes, or employment are partly determined by a process of 'selection' on health grounds. For example, people in poor health might move into lower, less skilled occupations if their health poses problems to themselves or their employers. Conversely, people in good health may be more likely to move into higher status and more skilled occupations.

If this were the case, and moves from one occupational class to another were influenced by health, then the lower occupational classes would have a growing proportion of members in poor health and the SMRs for these classes would be pushed up, while in the higher occupational classes SMRs would be pushed down by new class entrants in good health and class leavers in bad health. The consequence would be that the observed variations in mortality and morbidity between occupational classes would be a reflection of the influence of health on people's class position, rather than of the influence of class position on health.

There is a limited amount of evidence that this process of health-related social selection can occur. For example, one study of the relationship between schizophrenia and social class, was conducted in the UK in the 1950s. It examined the distribution of male schizophrenics by social class on admission to hospital.

☐ On what basis might you have predicted the social-class distribution of these patients?

■ One way would be to look at the social-class distribution of males of the same ages in the population as a whole. Another way would be to look at the social-class distribution of the fathers of the patients.

In fact the observed number of patients in social class V was roughly twice as high as would have been predicted using either of these two methods. This suggests that these males had fallen to the bottom social class because they had developed schizophrenia.

Another study conducted by the medical sociologist Raymond Illsley on a sample of women in Aberdeen, found that those who were taller and in better health than other women in their class of origin were not only more likely to marry into a higher social class, but also less likely to have premature births, stillbirths or babies who died within the first week after birth (Illsley, 1980).

For some people, therefore, social movement — social mobility — between social classes seems to be related to health. However, the importance of this process is hard to gauge, and it seems certain that no more than a portion of observed social-class differences can be explained in this way. For example, downward social mobility related to poor health is not an uncommon experience for manual workers: skilled miners with failing health are often moved from working underground to surface jobs, so moving from social class III to class IV. Many skilled manual workers start in lower social classes, work up to higher occupational levels and fall back again in later life. These processes may contribute to class differences in mortality among older age-groups, but they cannot explain the class differences in mortality for the age-groups 15–45, when in fact mortality difference between adults in different classes reaches a peak.

The influence of the 'social selection' process on unemployment is equally difficult to measure precisely. It is clear that some people do lose their jobs because of sickness or ill-health, and are more likely to have difficulty in finding employment. Evidence in support of this is provided by a DHSS cohort study, in which a sample of males who registered as unemployed in 1978 were followed over a period of years. One set of findings from this study showed that 53 per cent of those registered as disabled had worked at some stage during the 12 months following registration as unemployed compared with 83 per cent of those with no reported health problems. In other words, ill-health was associated with unemployment in a way that could fit the 'social selection' hypothesis.

Some attempts have been made to overcome the reluctance of employers to take on workers who are sick or disabled: for example, public-sector industries have operated a 'quota' scheme for many years in which a set proportion of all their employees should be drawn from the disabled population. However, although such schemes may be better than nothing, they are not widespread enough to alter the basic pattern of sick or disabled people having additional problems in obtaining employment.

Although more difficult to quantify, it is also likely that

employers laying off workers will tend to select those with poor health records or with disabilities, and this again would reinforce the observed association between unemployment and ill-health.

☐ Why might the 'social selection' argument be less important when unemployment is rising very rapidly?

■ During periods of rapidly rising unemployment whole factories and companies are closing down; it is not a case of just a few workers in an office or factory being made redundant, and it is therefore less likely that workers are being discriminated against on health grounds.

In the present phase of high unemployment, therefore, the 'social selection' explanation for poor health among the unemployed is likely to be fairly weak.

The other possible explanation noted above for the association between unemployment and ill-health was that it could be attributed to some 'artefact'. One form of 'artefact' explanation was suggested by the findings of Leonard Fagin, a London psychiatrist, in which a tendency was detected among his very small sample of 26 unemployed to exaggerate poor health as a way of justifying joblessness, maintaining self-esteem, or trying to cope with the social pressures to which unemployed people can be exposed.

A much broader form of potential artefact, however, arises from the fact that unemployment is far from being a random event, and the groups who are particularly prone to joblessness may also experience poorer health for reasons other than unemployment. In other words, it may be that poor health and unemployment are associated with another 'confounding' factor or factors. It is therefore important to pause for a moment and consider who the unemployed are.

Who are the unemployed?

The total number of people officially registered as unemployed in Britain in November 1983 was fractionally over 3 million, or 12.9 per cent of the total labour force. Each month, however, large numbers enter or leave the unemployment register — about 350 000 entered and similar numbers left each month throughout 1983, for example. About two-thirds of the total registered unemployed were male and one-third female, and the male unemployment rate, at 15.4 per cent in November 1983, was considerably above the female rate of 9.4 per cent. This difference, however, is exaggerated by the fact that a higher proportion of unemployed females than males do not register as unemployed and therefore are not recorded in official statistics.

Unemployment is not evenly spread across age-groups: in late 1983 the unemployment rate among females and males aged under 20 was over 27 per cent nationally, falling to 8.8 per cent in the 35-44 age-group and then rising to over 12 per cent among 55–59 year olds. In general, the likelihood of becoming unemployed decreases with age, but the likelihood of ceasing to become unemployed also decreases with age, so that younger age-groups tend to move into and out of unemployment at higher rates than older age-groups. Thus in 1983 around 25 per cent of all unemployed 25-year olds have been out of work for more than one year and 60 per cent for less than 6 months, whereas among the over-55-year-olds who were unemployed more than 50 per cent had been out of work for over one year.

In addition to these variations in the incidence of unemployment, there are extremely wide differences in unemployment rates between different parts of the UK. In the South-East, for example, towns such as Watford, Oxford, Reading and Guildford had unemployment rates in 1983 of approximately half the national average, while in Northern England, Wales and Scotland towns such as Whitby and Ormskirk, Ebbw Vale and Tenby, Irvine and Fort William had rates well in excess of 20 per cent. Worst of all was Northern Ireland, where the average unemployment rate was almost 22 per cent, and where in towns such as Strabane four in ten of the work-force were officially unemployed.

Striking differences in rates of unemployment are also apparent when we look at occupational groups. Information on this is not routinely collected, but Table 11.1 shows the percentage share of the total population taken by each of five occupational groups.

Table 11.1 The distribution of unemployment by occupational group

	Percentage of total population in 1971 census	Percentage of unemployed in 1981
professional/managers	23.0	9.5
clerical	11.9	6.3
craftsmen	28.5	18.8
semi-skilled	18.1	27.0
general labourers	8.6	35.5

(data from 1971 Census and Dept. of Employment Gazette, January 1982)

☐ Summarise the pattern shown in Table 11.1.

■ Unemployment seems to be proportionately higher among non-professional and less-skilled workers. For example, the semi-skilled and labourer groups comprise 27 per cent of the population but 62 per cent of the unemployed.

What is known about the living circumstances of the unemployed? A DHSS study has shown that in 1978 45 per cent of a sample of unemployed men were receiving in the form of benefits less than one-half of the net earnings they had obtained in employment. Moreover, the relationship between earnings and benefits has been weakened in a set of policy steps taken after 1979, so that in 1981 the Family Expenditure Survey showed that the average unemployed family lived on approximately 40 per cent of the income of the average family.

The civil (or marital) state of unemployed people is also rather different from the rest of the population: 80 per cent of long-term unemployed women, for example, were single, widowed, divorced or separated, compared with 38 per cent among women as a whole (although this reflects in part the fact that married women are least likely to register as unemployed). Unemployed men are also less likely to be married.

These differences are reflected in many other aspects of daily living: 60 per cent of the employed have a phone, but only 25 per cent of the unemployed; 66 per cent of those in work have a car, but only 11 per cent among the unemployed; over half the employed have central heating, but fewer than a third of the unemployed.

☐ Compare these social patterns of unemployment with the patterns of health and disease discussed in the previous chapters of this book. What do they have in common?

■ The social groups who are at present suffering the most from unemployment tend also to be the groups with relatively poor health.

Unemployment has hit hardest the lower occupational groups, whose overall morbidity and mortality rates are high anyway. Single, widowed and divorced people, who are overrepresented among the unemployed, also have a poorer health record than married people. Geographically, unemployment is most pronounced in areas which have a poorer health status than the national average. It is this correspondence between unemployment and poor health among particular groups and in particular areas that has provided the basis for claims that the association between the two is an 'artefact'. This has made the task of looking for evidence concerning the relationship between unemployment and ill-health so difficult. Of course, even if the observation that ill-health is particularly concentrated among the unemployed were not substantiated by any evidence of a causal mechanism, the problem of a deep social inequality would still be present. However, in this chapter we are interested in pursuing further the evidence concerning such a causal mechanism.

The health effects of unemployment

To examine the effect of unemployment on health it might help to begin by thinking of a chain or sequence of events affecting different individuals or groups in different ways, as in Figure 11.1.

The term 'unemployment' is not unambiguous. The figure distinguishes between the *threat* of job loss (that is, the possibility of losing a job), the *event* of losing a job, and the *state* of being out of work. This last category may include people who are unemployed without ever being made redundant, for at times of mass unemployment one of the most seriously affected groups are school leavers who have never experienced proper employment. The figure also identifies the different groups who may be affected by unemployment. The middle box in the diagram separates out two sets of potential effects of unemployment on these groups: the psychological effect, ranging from stress and worry through to loss of self-esteem, rejection, hopelessness, and chronic depression; and material consequences,

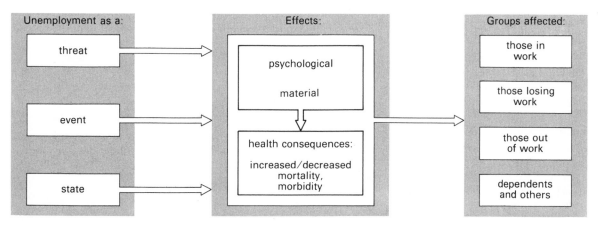

Figure 11.1 A model of the potential effect of unemployment on health.

including changes in income and wealth, leading to different consumption patterns, and change in the physical environment. Both these sets of potential effects have consequences for health. These can be measured in terms of morbidity or mortality. Most of the research we are considering is looking for evidence that unemployment causes deterioration in health. This figure also includes, however, the possibility that there may be an improvement in health.

◻ Why might unemployment improve health?

■ Some people in work are so exposed to occupational hazards or stresses that a major source of potential ill-health may be removed when they lose their job.

An example of this comes from the study of the effects of unemployment in Marienthal with which we began this chapter. The researchers found that the initial effect of unemployment was to improve health. The reason for this was that appalling working conditions in the textile factories had placed nine in ten of the workers at risk of contracting tuberculosis. Nor may such effects be restricted to the physical environment of work: many occupations may give rise to boredom, frustration, alienation and stress, as the following exchange between Senator Robert Kennedy and a firm's attorney in a 1957 Senate committee hearing makes plain:

MR KENNEDY   You say that the men can put the (enamel) equipment in the oven, then they can step back and eat their lunch during that period of time. How much time is there then before they have to do some more work?
MR CONGER   From 2 to 5 minutes, depending on the piece.
MR KENNEDY   So you feel they can step back from the oven, take off their masks, and have their lunch in 2 to 5 minutes?
MR CONGER   Mr. Kennedy, they have been doing it for 36 years.
(quoted in Jahoda, 1982, pp.39–40)

Although there is, of course, an unknown number of employed people who suffer material and psychological difficulties associated with working, this must be set beside the known, if relative, material deprivation caused by unemployment, as outlined above. Moreover, there is clearly an added dimension of psychological distress and frustration inherent in being unemployed, in that the vast majority are not unemployed by choice and would prefer to be in work.

Research into the psychological changes occurring among people (mainly men) who have lost their jobs has in fact been more common than any other form of research into unemployment and health. In 1938 two Austrian researchers, Eisenberg and Lazarsfeld, published an article summarising the results of no fewer than 112 such studies, and many more have been conducted since then (Eisenberg and Lazarsfeld, 1938). Such *surveys of the unemployed*, which tend to be based on interviews or questionnaires, throw a good deal of light on the social experience of unemployment: the stigma attached to job loss as some sort of personal failing rather than a social phenomenon, for example. They also bring out clearly the degree to which the work experience is central in establishing a personal identity, in terms both of the way individuals make sense of their own life — its meaning and direction or purpose — and of the way in which others assess a person's social identity by reference to that person's employment status and occupation.

◻ In terms of Figure 11.1, how would you characterise such studies? Which aspects of unemployment do they concentrate on?

■ They focus on the psychological effects of the event of job loss on those losing work, and do not, for example, address directly the material effects of unemployment and the potential health consequences.

It is not possible to say with any certainty precisely how such psychological stress may affect morbidity or mortality, although there is *some* evidence that such stress may have an adverse effect on clinical health. Clearly feeling depressed and perhaps distressed is an unpleasant experience in itself, regardless of whether there is any measurable influence on morbidity or mortality.

By surveying those people who had already become unemployed, studies such as those mentioned above can only assess the degree of change in health or psychological state arising from the event of unemployment by asking retrospective questions: by their very nature, it is difficult to make before-and-after comparisons. To do this requires a prospective study, and these are rare, not least because of the expense involved: it may be necessary to study a very large number of people in employment in order to have a chance of including some who later become unemployed. In one such study (Kasl and Cobb, 1977) it appeared that the threat and announcement of impending unemployment were of main importance to health, and that health deteriorated before redundancy actually occurred.

◻ What is the significance of this result for the surveys of the health of the unemployed mentioned earlier?

■ In the surveys, people were studied *after* they became unemployed, and so the effects of the threat of impending unemployment would have been missed.

Although the study by Kasl and Cobb was an impressive

and careful piece of research, some of the results do not lend themselves to simple interpretations. In particular, they selected changes in blood pressure as a key measure of health status, and although blood pressure may be relatively easy to measure, it is not an unambiguous indicator of health status in that a short-term increase in blood pressure does not necessarily lead to an increase in mortality risk.

A less ambiguous way of looking for the potential health effects of unemployment is to examine mortality rates among a specified sample of the population, allowing sufficient time for any serious illnesses to cause eventual death. A *cohort study* of this kind is being done in Britain by means of the OPCS Longitudinal Study, described in Chapter 10. This sample has been used to compare deaths among a cohort of people of working age, according to their economic position in 1971. Some of the results are shown in Table 11.2. Thus, 'unemployed sick' refers to people who in 1971 were unemployed for reasons of sickness, and 'unemployed not sick' to those who were unemployed in 1971 for other reasons and were fit to return to work. This distinction is clearly important in determining the health *effects* of unemployment rather than the health *causes* of unemployment, as we noted earlier. The death rates are shown as SMRs.

☐   What does a comparison of the SMRs of employed men and men unemployed but not through sickness reveal to you?

■   The former group has an SMR 14 per cent lower than expected, and the latter an SMR 30 per cent higher

Table 11.2 Deaths between 1971 and 1975 for persons of working age, according to their economic position at the 1971 census

Economic groups	Ratio of actual to expected deaths (SMRs)	
	men aged 15–64 years	women aged 15–59 years
Economically active		
in employment	86	81
unemployed not sick	130	80
unemployed sick	323	432
Economically inactive		
retired	153	141
permanently sick	393	500
student	82	94
others not in the formal labour market (most people so classified are housewives)	105	107

(data from Fox and Goldblatt, 1982, Table 3.3)

than expected. As those who are unemployed through sickness have been separately identified (as expected, they have a very high SMR of 323), this result does seem to suggest that unemployment may be a contributory factor in causing excess deaths among unemployed men.

If unemployment does cause an excess mortality among those out of work, what *kind* of effect does it have: is the mortality the result of psychological factors or of physical deterioration brought about by material loss? The Longitudinal Study, although giving some indication that the experience of unemployment may detrimentally affect health, cannot answer all these questions.

Correlational studies

A quite different way of examining the possible health effects of unemployment has been adopted by the economist Harvey Brenner, of the John Hopkins University, Baltimore; indeed, Brenner's research has tended to dominate discussion of the health effects of unemployment, despite the fact that his research method is only one among many. Brenner's work is essentially *correlational*: that is, it attempts to find some correlation or statistical association between changes in the overall unemployment rate and changes in population health indicators, and in particular mortality rates.

In his early work, Brenner claimed to show a close association between unemployment rates and first admissions to mental hospitals in New York: as unemployment rose, admissions rose and vice versa. The implication seemed to be that rising unemployment was sufficiently stressful to cause mental illness. He then examined cardiovascular mortality rates (that is, deaths from strokes and heart disease) in the USA and found that these rates tended to rise some 2–3 years after a rise in unemployment. This correlation between unemployment rates and mortality rates seemed to be sufficiently clear for Brenner to claim that a 1 per cent increase in American unemployment rates was associated with a 2 per cent increase in deaths over the following 6 years.

In 1979 Brenner published the results of a similar study of England and Wales. Looking at the period 1939 to 1976, he compared changes in the unemployment rate with changes in age-specific mortality rates and again claimed that the hypothesis that 'unemployment is positively related to mortality-rates trends is sustained for all age-groups' (Brenner, 1979, p.570).

We shall return shortly to these results, but what is the nature of the hypothesis Brenner is advancing? Essentially it is that unemployment, or the threat of it, is a 'life-event' that creates stressful effects, such stresses leading to increased morbidity and perhaps, after several years, increased mortality. The consequences for health of other 'life-events' such as divorce or being widowed are well documented, and Brenner draws a parallel between them and unemployment. However, whereas these other life-events have their health effects on the *individuals* concerned*, Brenner claims that the life-event of unemployment can be measured throughout the whole population as an effect on the health of a nation: the measures of mortality he uses are not rates for unemployed people, *but for the entire country*.

   □ In terms of Figure 11.1, how would you describe this approach?

   ■ The approach taken by Brenner is that it is the threat of job loss, or the event of job loss, which affects the entire population (all the groups mentioned in the figure) through a psychological stress effect, resulting in an increase in mortality.

A second part of the hypothesis being advanced by Brenner is that the stress induced by changes in the unemployment rate takes time to result in increased mortality. However, he does not predict how long this delay or time 'lag' might be using epidemiological data or the aetiology of particular stress-induced diseases, but instead chooses a 'lag' that gives the best statistical match between changes in unemployment and changes in mortality. Thus, because the best statistical match was found at lags 1, 2, and 5, Brenner concludes that it must be after 1, 2, and 5 years that the results of stress are most pronouncedly manifested in an increased mortality.

   □ What reservations might be expressed about this kind of hypothesis?

   ■ There seems to be an element of 'post-hoc' hypothesising, in which the details of the hypothesis are modified to fit the results. In consequence, it is not clear when the hypothesis might be agreed to have failed.

In our discussion of the work of Brenner it has been necessary to greatly simplify the whole battery of complex and at times obscure statistical methods he employs. Much of the argument over his work has focused on methods, and a number of researchers have attempted, not always successfully, to replicate his methods and obtain the same results. Most recently, however, an Irish economist has applied similar statistical methods to data for Scotland covering the years 1959 to 1978. Iain McAvinchey (1984) has shown that changes in unemployment rates do appear to be associated with subsequent changes in mortality rates among the population as a whole, but that these effects vary considerably between different age- and sex-groups. Among men, increasing national rates of unemployment

were associated with positive health effects in the 15–35 age group, but with negative effects for older age groups. Among women, older age groups appeared to experience decreasing mortality rates as national unemployment rates rose, whereas in younger age-groups unemployment was associated with an increase in infant mortality rates. Overall, the most vulnerable group seemed to be males aged between 35 and 65, where each 1 per cent rise in the unemployment rate for all males was associated with an increase of approximately 0.4 per cent in mortality rates over 10 years.

Such 'correlational' studies, therefore, have produced fascinating if controversial findings, and it is unfortunate that the debate they have engendered should be largely absorbed by the statistical methods they have employed. For example, the impact of unemployment on levels of income and many other aspects of the whole material fabric of life has already been noted. Given that such changes may take a lifetime or even more than one generation to reveal their health consequences, it seems inappropriate to concentrate on stress-induced increases in morbidity or mortality over relatively short periods of 5 years or less to the exclusion of the long-term material consequences of unemployment for those unemployed and their dependents.

In short, it is necessary to adopt a broader and more historical perspective, and to place short-term changes in their longer-term context. An example of this approach is provided by J.M. Winter, a social historian, who has studied the effects of the Depression on infant mortality in Britain. Winter characterises the whole period from 1920 to 1950 as one when there was a steady improvement in working-class living standards over their level in the previous century, coupled with better sanitation and standards of nutrition. Similarly, maternal mortality rates fell from the 1930s onwards, not least because of the introduction of sulphonamide drugs which led to the control of puerperal sepsis (childbed fever). These were long-term advances in working-class living standards, which were in some respects able to absorb short-term shocks: thus Winter concluded that 'these gains left (and still leave) a legacy that even foolish economic policies or politically imposed impoverishment cannot obliterate completely' (Winter, 1979). The essential point, therefore, is not that the effects on health of an event like the Depression (and perhaps of the current period of mass unemployment) are negligible or non-existent; rather it is that they are unlikely to be seen immediately or in isolation. This is perfectly illustrated by a set of classic studies conducted in Aberdeen under Sir Dugald Baird, who as Professor of Midwifery pioneered many aspects of social epidemiology and influenced a whole generation of obstetricians (Baird, 1974 and 1975).

* This is discussed in more detail in Book V of this course, *Birth to Old Age: Health in Transition.*

Baird and his colleagues noted a rise in the incidence of perinatal mortality in Aberdeen over the years 1968–72, and found it to be associated with low birth-weight. The mothers involved were mainly in the age-groups 15 to 19 and 20 to 24, and the periods when they themselves had been born — 1949 to 1957 and 1944 to 1952 — were also characterised by low birth-weight. The mothers of the survey mothers had almost all been born in the period 1928–32 (i.e. during the worst years of the Depression), had been exposed in infancy to malnutrition and poor health, and in consequence their adult 'reproductive efficiency' had been impaired with results carrying over to their children's children. The studies Baird initiated provide an excellent illustration of a cohort effect, which you have already encountered.

Clearly, the economic and social upheaval of the interwar years, of which mass unemployment was one aspect, had a long-term and deep effect on health, sufficiently powerful to interrupt the much longer-term decline in infant mortality. But equally clearly, the effect unemployment did have was not linked in any automatic or mechanistic way to health, and can not be discovered by using some kind of fixed 'lag' effect, as Brenner has attempted to do.

Many of the studies we have examined which attempt to identify the health consequences of unemployment are either inconclusive, or their conclusions are misleading. In large part, however, this seems to be as a result of the way in which the issue has been approached by researchers. The relationship between health and social and economic environment can very seldom be boiled down to a simple 'cause-and-effect' sequence. A theme running through this book is that by explaining the social and economic system as a whole, and its structural characteristics of power, ownership and inequality, patterns of health and disease become more readily understandable. Unemployment is one of these structural characteristics, and cannot easily be isolated from the many others discussed in Chapter 10. The studies we have considered here seem to suggest that it is most likely to be through these wider social and economic causes and consequences of mass unemployment that people today — or perhaps, as in Dugald Baird's study, their children's children — will discover the health consequences.

Objectives for Chapter 11

When you have studied this chapter, you should be able to:

11.1 Outline different ways in which unemployment and health may be associated.

11.2 Describe the main characteristics of the unemployed.

11.3 Demonstrate an awareness of at least three different kinds of research conducted in this area, and their limitations.

Questions of Chapter 11

1 (*Objective 11.1*) In the 1940s Richard Titmuss and Jerry Morris published a series of articles which showed that rates of unemployment and rates of mortality resulting from rheumatic heart disease across different county boroughs of England and Wales were closely associated. What explanations might exist for this association?

2 (*Objective 11.2*) Why is it important to consider not simply total unemployment but also flows into and out of unemployment?

3 (*Objective 11.3*) You have been given a small research grant lasting 12 months to look at the possible effects of unemployment on health. What kind of difficulties would be encountered in using the different research approaches?

12

Nutrition and health: a case study

So far in this book, we have compared the distribution of diseases between different parts of the world, and considered how these patterns have altered over time. You have seen the vast differences in life expectancy between people living in the industrialised world and those in the Third World, and the way degenerative diseases have replaced infectious diseases as the major threat to the health of people living in industrialised countries. For simplicity, these differences and changes have been considered separately; so have the social and economic factors influencing health and disease, and the way these factors have also changed over time. But such an approach carries a danger: it becomes difficult to appreciate the way these trends are all interconnected. For instance, it is only possible to explain the current state of health of people living in the Third World by understanding the contemporary economic relationship of the Third World with the industrialised countries, and also by examining the historical processes that have led up to the current position. It is therefore necessary in this final chapter to weave together the strands running through earlier chapters, and try to construct an account that integrates, rather than separates, historical and international comparisons. For this purpose we have chosen the topic of food and nutrition — a subject that has a far-reaching and universal impact on health but has also given, and continues to give rise to much controversy and debate.

Broadly speaking, there are two main categories of disease associated with nutrition — those arising from a lack of food and those arising from overconsumption. It is generally accepted that there are many diseases caused by an inadequate intake of certain vital nutrients. These *deficiency diseases* were formerly widespread in the UK, but with improvements in food supply and preservation

techniques, very few cases are seen in the UK today.

In contrast, our knowledge of the harmful effects of the overconsumption of food is much less extensive and less well understood. Although the *associations* between many foodstuffs and diseases have been demonstrated, the nature of many of these associations remains unclear: that is, there is uncertainty as to whether or not such associations are *causal*. Thus, at one extreme there is the association between sugar and dental caries which is generally accepted as being causal, whereas at the other extreme is the association between fat consumption and breast cancer, the nature of which remains a subject of much debate. Although many of the links between specific nutrients and specific diseases remain controversial, a consensus has emerged in recent years on what could be regarded as a prudent diet — that is, a diet that would tend to reduce someone's overall risk of developing the *degenerative diseases* that are so prevalent in industrialised countries.

Generally, such recommendations include a reduction in the consumption of animal fats (to less than 30 per cent of total energy intake), an increase in fibre content (mostly derived from plants), a reduction in sugar consumption, and a reduction in salt intake. It is widely believed that such changes would reduce the risk of coronary heart disease, stroke, diabetes, obesity, appendicitis, large bowel diseases, varicose veins, haemorrhoids (piles), tooth decay, gall-bladder disease and other, less common conditions.

It is not the aim of this chapter to examine the scientific basis for such a claim, nor to discuss the specific relationships between foodstuffs and diseases. Instead we shall look in the opposite direction and consider the factors that determine people's *diets* — both those that give rise to deficiency diseases in the Third World, and those associated with degenerative diseases in industrialised countries. The reason for looking in this direction is that what we eat is not the outcome merely of choices made of our own free will: it is constrained by a wide range of factors, from price (which explains why we do not eat much caviare), or custom (why we do not, like the Chinese, eat dogs) through ecological factors (which explain why Eskimos eat a lot of fish and no tropical fruit), to the host of social and economic pressures that restrict and direct our food choice.

In other words, diet is not what the theologians would call a 'First Cause' of disease. It is merely one link in the chain that relates disease patterns to the society in which we live. As such, it exemplifies many of the central themes of this book. Just as the epidemiology of world health patterns had to be accompanied by a look at the economics of world development patterns, so to understand diet-related disease we must look beyond the dinner-plate, into the super-market and over the farm gate, until eventually we see that the causes of individual diseases are bound up with the economic relationships between nations.

The growth of modern nutritional knowledge

The origin of modern nutritional knowledge some 250 years ago was the demonstration of vitamin deficiency disease.

> ☐ That work, which was to be ignored for so long, demonstrated the importance of diet in causing disease in the British Navy. Do you know what it was?
> ■ It was the study of scurvy in the British Navy conducted by Captain James Lind RN, and published in a book called *Treatise on the Scurvy* in 1753. Lind was able to relate scurvy to the poor naval diet of the British sailor of the period, and to cure it by administering a daily ration of fresh vegetables or lemon juice.

At the time, scurvy was pre-eminently a naval disease ('sea scurvy'), and was a more important cause of death among sailors than all other causes, including war and shipwreck, added together. Lind was influenced by Lord Anson's unsuccessful attempt to circumnavigate the globe in 1740–44, during which 1 051 of his 1 955 men died, mostly of scurvy. Such losses were not unusual, and served both to impair the development of British maritime power, and to inhibit the growth of the ability of the British mercantile marine to undertake the long voyages that were later to exploit its colonial empire.

> ☐ The problem of scurvy had increased in importance with the growth of the navy: the sailors of Henry VIII in the sixteenth century knew the disease, but predominantly as one that occurred in their com-munities at home. Can you think why the disease distribution changed?

> ■ Routine sixteenth-century voyages were shorter, confined virtually to European coastal waters, and no matter how poor the sea diet, it was not consumed for long. In fact in terms of deaths, there was probably more scurvy in Britain in 1573 than in 1753. But the deaths were of civilians — the village poor — during the winters when few vegetables were available in the diet. The navy had no special problem.

It was improvements in ship design and navigation that changed all this. The sixteenth-century voyages of discovery brought back the potato which soon became (and still is) both a major food of the poor and the principal source of vitamin C in our diet; scurvy, even winter scurvy, disappeared from the British mainland. But as the voyages got longer, ships' rations became concentrated around preserved foods, and once British sailors subsisted for longer periods on a diet of biscuit, salt meat, dried beans and rum, scurvy appeared at sea.

Lind showed that fresh lemons or vegetables would prevent or cure the disease, and after 1753 when he published his evidence and recommendations, some senior naval men began to take notice. Captain Cook was one. Cook's successful circumnavigation (1772–75) was due in no small part to the fact that he placed great stress on continually reprovisioning with fresh vegetables at every landfall. Consequently he lost not one man from scurvy on the entire voyage.

Scurvy was a particularly British problem. The major rival maritime and colonial power, the Dutch, had only a minor problem with scurvy, principally because they had sauerkraut among their rations. Such a British disadvan-tage eventually led even the highly conservative Lords of the Admiralty to adopt Lind's scheme in 1795 (the year after his death). The effect was the immediate eradication of the disease. For example, one naval hospital recorded 1 457 cases of scurvy in 1796 and a total of only 2 for the years 1806–10.

However, almost as soon as they had been accepted, Lind's results lost credence because they seemed to point to a disease whose cause was the *absence* of something (a constituent of the diet) whereas scientific progress at the time increasingly explained disease as caused by something *positive* (poisons, miasmas or later, bacteria).

Historians now say that this, and particularly the dominance of the germ theory of disease in the nineteenth century, is the reason why the implication of Lind's work — the existence of vitamins — was not fully realised for many years. Diseases, it seemed, were due to germs. The British navy seems to have continued with Lind's advice only because it was tradition. In fact it was modified crucially: his advice to consume lemons was abandoned in favour of limes (which could be cheaply obtained from the new West Indian colonies), which, ironically, though they gave the British sailor a longlasting nickname, provided so much less vitamin C that scurvy occasionally reappeared. No one took any notice because no one really believed that fruit juice was important. Indeed, though the army continued to be seriously afflicted by scurvy in long campaigns from the Crimean War until the First World War, they never even tried Lind's solution. And Captain Scott's 1912 expedition to the South Pole is said to have failed, in part, because members of his expedition suffered severely from the disease. Like other scientists of the time, Scott saw scurvy as an *infection*, and took no source of vitamin C with him.

The 'rediscovery' of deficiency diseases began in isolated observations made at the end of the nineteenth century, in which various scientists began to see poor diet as an explanation for diseases that the germ theory had failed to explain or cure. The modern concept of a collection of vitamins and deficiencies of vitamins was only put forward by the Polish biochemist Casimir Funk in 1912. (The acceptance of this concept only as recently as the First World War is illustrated in an article on the history of pernicious anaemia by Irvine Loudon contained in the Course Reader, Part 1, Section 1.6.) The hiatus that existed between Lind and Funk meant that nutritionists had virtually no role in attempting to influence the evolution of the nineteenth-century diet, as it related to *health*. The nineteenth century must therefore be seen as a period not merely of nutritional ignorance, but of stagnation in nutritional thinking. (Even Mrs Beeton's otherwise practical advice in choosing a wet nurse recommends a woman who doesn't eat greens (or drink) as it gives the baby wind.)

The discovery of the importance of vitamins some 70 years ago was the first of two important changes in scientific outlook that have created the modern understanding of nutrition. The second — the idea of a relationship between diet and the degenerative diseases — only developed after the Second World War, and is still developing and changing quite rapidly.

The social contexts of these two scientific changes are very different. There was little interest in the role of diet in the development of degenerative diseases in the first half of this century because, as you may remember from the evidence presented in Chapter 9, the diseases themselves were not seen as a major problem. For example, when a question on coronary heart disease was included in an examination for doctors in 1928, there was a professional outcry against the idea of requiring young doctors to learn about such an obscure disease, which it was felt they were never likely to see in practice.

It is curious to note, however, that when the sights of scientists were firmly fixed on the deficiency diseases, such diseases were a declining health issue in Britain, and had probably peaked in the nineteenth century. In contrast, the increasing interest in degenerative diseases has been much less to do with a conceptual change in scientific thought, and much more to do with changes in patterns of disease. (Indeed the study of diet and disease serves also as a vivid example of the complex forces that mould the process of scientific inquiry and understanding.) If we are to study the relationship between diet and disease then we must first look at what people eat and why.

The origins of the modern British diet

What we eat is the subject of marked regional and ethnic variation, and of individual preference. The idea of an 'average diet', therefore, can be misleading. Nevertheless, our *pattern* of eating, if not its *specific* content, is the product of our age. This pattern is shown in Table 12.1, which lists the foods consumed in contemporary Britain by an 'average person' during one week. This 'average' is simply taken from the total amount of all food consumed by the population, and it is almost certain that no-one actually has this one 'average' pattern of consumption.

What is of interest is that this is largely the pattern of consumption to which the Victorian artisan aspired, and a little less than the Victorian middle class probably consumed. It is the diet of the family of the post-Industrial Revolution urban worker, and as such its pattern makes sense, though this may seem strange in 1984.

How then does our present-day diet compare with that of the Victorians? In making comparisons we must constantly keep in mind the fragmentary nature of information on nineteenth-century eating habits: what was recorded is not necessarily what was typical.

☐ Figure 12.1 (p. 122) shows a typical dinner menu for Queen Victoria herself. Below, at a somewhat lower social stratum, is a restaurant 'Bill of Fare' priced at 2s. 6d (12½p). What is immediately apparent from them?

Hors d'œuvre variés
Consommé Caroline   Crème à la Reine
Sole Colbert
Filet Mignon Chasseur
Lasagne al Sugo
Bécassine Rôtie
Salade de Saison
Glace au Chocolat
Dessert

Food for a family of four for a year — the 'average' diet. (Andrew Davidson, Camera Press)

Table 12.1 Average food consumption per person per week, UK, 1981

Item		Quantity/ounces (except where stated otherwise)	Item		Quantity/ounces (except where stated otherwise)
bread:	white	22	dairy:	cheese	4
	brown/wholemeal, etc.	9		milk, cream	5 (pints)
flour		6		butter	4
cakes, biscuits, cereals		19		margarine	4
		—		fats, oils, lards	3
		57		eggs	4 (eggs)
					—
sugar and preserves		13			15
tea		2	vegetables:	fresh	28
coffee		1		dried, frozen,	
		—		canned	17
		3		potatoes	42
					—
meats:	poultry	7			87
	beef and veal	7			
	mutton, lamb, pork	8	fruit:	fresh	20
	bacon, ham	5		canned, bottled,	
	sausages	3		dried and frozen	8
	other	8			—
		—			28
		38	other pickles, sauces, jellies,		
	fish	5	spreads, salt, canned soups, ice-creams		10

(data from National Food Survey Committee, 1983)

Figure 12.1 Queen Victoria's dinner menu, 27 April 1882 (Burnett, 1979, p.182. Reproduced with the gracious permission of Her Majesty the Queen)

■ Simply the excessiveness. Both are characterised by the large number of separate dishes that are consumed, with a variety of fish and meat dishes, as well as both hors d'œuvre and soup.

The Royal example of lavish and extravagant eating was taken up as a model to be emulated by the Victorian middle classes. The culinary compendiums of Eliza Acton and Mrs Isabella Beeton, although claiming to be guides to plain and economical cooking, were full of six-, eight- or ten-course meals, and recipes including several pints of cream, thirty or more eggs, or even truffles boiled in champagne. However, as John Burnett has pointed out in his social history of the English diet (Burnett, 1979), Mrs Beeton's recommended ordinary family dinners, 'such as would be eaten by the professional man on his return from office or counting-house', tended to be a pattern of three or four courses which 'has not changed greatly in a hundred years'. Typical 'plain family dinners' were:

WEDNESDAY — Fried soles, Dutch sauce. Boiled beef, carrots, suet dumplings, lemon pudding.
THURSDAY — Pea soup, Cold beef, Mashed potatoes, Mutton cutlets and tomato sauce. Macaroni.
(Burnett, 1979, pp.223–4)

For information on the lower classes in industrial cities of Victorian England we owe a great deal to the surveys of the dietitian Dr Edward Smith. Table 12.2 shows a breakdown of the diet of three groups of industrial workers in 1863.

The needlewomen he reported to be in a 'feeble state of health'; the stocking weavers to be 'moderately fed, but do not exhibit a high state of health', and the shoemakers, who earned more than the other two groups, Smith considered, spent their earnings not very wisely and consequently had a diet little better than that of the other two groups.

□ Comparing Table 12.2 with Table 12.1, what main differences emerge?

■ In the diets of the workers surveyed by Edward Smith in the 1860s, bread and cheese consumption was much higher than now. Meat consumption was much lower. The other components of the diet are not greatly dissimilar, save that there was an absence of fresh fruit and vegetables in the 1860s diet.

The broad outlines of the modern British diet had been established by 1860. Its present shape can be explained only by looking at its origins, which are located approximately in the time in which Lind was working.

In mid-nineteenth-century Britain most people could not grow what they ate, had neither the facilities nor the servants to turn raw ingredients into foods, and were therefore at the end of a food-processing and retailing industry which drew on many parts of the world for its raw materials. These three factors do not *explain* the emergence of a different kind of diet during this period, but an examination of each of the main components of the emerging nineteenth-century diet repeatedly shows these same factors emerging and asserting themselves. The main components were wheat, sugar, tea, meat, dairy products and vegetables.

Wheat

As the urban population began to grow in the eighteenth century, British landowners began to meet the rise in demand by increasing agricultural production. Some factors associated with this increase were considered in Chapter 7: they included the enclosure of common land, and technical innovations. Up until the eighteenth century, barley, rye and oatmeal were the traditional food grains of all except the wealthy, but much of the newly enclosed land was given over to growing wheat (or 'corn' as it was then called). Modern estimates suggest that, by 1760, in the country as a whole, 60 per cent of the population consumed wheat-based bread, by 1820 it was 80 per cent, and by 1890 it had risen to 90 per cent.

Other changes in agriculture also began to exploit the growing market demand, noteworthy among which was the breeding and improved feeding of farm animals to produce bigger and fatter animals: Smithfield Market records indicate a doubling in size of the cattle sold there

Table 12.2 Nineteenth-century diets from the surveys of Dr Edward Smith (average consumption per person per week/ounces)

	London needlewomen, 1863	Derbyshire stocking weavers, 1863	Northampton shoemakers, 1863
bread	124	190	179
potatoes	40	64	56
sugars	7	11	10
fats	4	3	6
meat	16	12	16
milk	7	26	18
tea (for family)	2	2	3
cheese (for family)	—	12	14

(data from Burnett, 1979, pp.193–196)

during the nineteenth century. Nevertheless, the biggest change was in wheat production.

☐ Why do you think this was so?

■ It was among the poorer classes that the market was expanding, and they bought cheaper food. On land where there is a choice between arable and animal production, arable farming produces much higher yields per acre, so that the end-product can be sold much more cheaply and hence in greater amounts to the poorer consumer. Thus farmers had strong incentives to expand wheat production.

Food production was expanding quickly, but the growth of population was also rapid, and by the late eighteenth century Britain had become a net importer of wheat. This emerging dependence on imports was of the utmost significance, for it left the country under threat of one of the oldest of military weapons: the blockade. Thus when the Napoleonic Wars commenced in 1793, and just such a blockade of the British Isles was attempted, the resulting shortages of wheat pushed price levels up to nearly three times their pre-war level. For farmers it was a temporary bonanza but for the urban poor it was another blow to their standard of living. The possibility of such a blockade of food supplies became a recurring nightmare for agricultural planners.

When the Napoleonic Wars ended in 1815, the way was open to resume the importation of wheat. However, this would have struck a severe blow to the continued prosperity of landowners, and the government (itself largely composed of landowners) needed little persuasion to pass legislation to maintain wheat prices by banning or imposing taxes on wheat imports. These were the famous Corn Laws, which were the subject of intense political conflict, and were not fully repealed until 1849, during the disastrous famine in Ireland.

The repeal of the Corn Laws was a tacit acceptance that self-sufficiency in wheat was becoming untenable in the face of a continued growth of population. But the price of wheat continued to increase until a development on the other side of the Atlantic transformed the situation. This was the construction of the American railways connecting East and West, particularly in the 1860s. Suddenly the gigantic prairies of the Mid-West could be used to grow crops which could be moved cheaply to the eastern seaports.

By 1877 North American wheat imports to Britain stood at 2 549 000 tons, about 40 per cent of all wheat consumed. By 1914 imports were to comprise 80 per cent of British consumption. The scale of American production pushed the wheat price down markedly: it fell by 50 per cent between 1873 and 1893. Wheat bread became firmly established as the bread of poor as well as rich people, and increasingly dominated the diet of the poor.

Other technological developments played a major part in altering the role of wheat in the modern diet, and of particular importance was the roller mill, which was first used in Britain in Liverpool in 1878. Its technical advantages were two-fold. First, a larger scale of production was possible with steam-powered roller mills replacing the traditional water-mills or windmills with their grinding stones. Second, the nature of the roller mill made it easily possible to separate the husk of the wheat grain and the wheatgerm, from its starchy endosperm. The consequent flour was *white*, an attribute traditionally desired, because the whiter the bread, the more flour it contained. However, the prestige of white bread probably derived from its relative expense rather than its flour content. Suddenly the much-desired white bread was available to the poor, and, indeed, as milling switched totally to the roller mill the poor could buy little else. Meanwhile, the now more expensive brown breads such as the Hovis loaf (1892) became favoured by sections of the middle class for their reputed health properties.

Commercial milling and baking had of course been around long before the advent of the new technologies. Commercial baking was particularly popular among the urban poor; first, because it eliminated a long and tedious cooking chore, and second, because it saved fuel. The commercial baker's existence was further assured because many of the jerry-builders of the new nineteenth-century slums did not fit ovens into kitchen ranges. Thus in Manchester in 1800 there were no commercial bakers to serve a population of 70 000; by 1835 the population had swollen to 200 000, and 650 bakers were serving their needs. What the new technologies changed was not the dependence on commercially baked bread, but rather the nature of the industry. Milling and baking became increasingly dominated by a small number of very large producers able to take advantage of the new technologies to reap economies of large-scale production and therefore able to squeeze out smaller producers. Thus, though in 1935 there were still over 2 000 independent millers, by 1978 only *two* companies — Rank-Hovis-McDougall and Associated British Foods — accounted for over 75 per cent of milling output and 61 per cent of all bread production.

Sugar

Difficult as it now may be to believe, 500 years ago sugar was a sparsely used 'spice' imported to Britain at great expense from the Far East. The change came with the development of sugar plantations in the West Indies, following the expropriation of those islands in 1760 as part of the gains of the Seven Years War against the French.

With such plantations easily able to produce sugar, and with labour supplied by a slave trade from West Africa, the supply of sugar in Britain soon rose. Though slavery was abolished in 1833, the plantation system was by then established as the major employment outlet for local West Indian people. Low wages kept production costs down, and the competing beet sugar grown in Europe was excluded by duties.

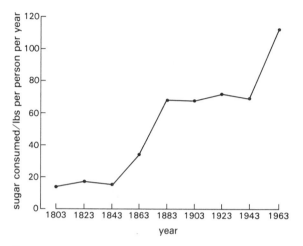

Figure 12.2 Per capita consumption of sugar in the UK, 1803–1963. (Data from Mitchell and Deane, 1971)

☐ From 1845 onwards such duties were progressively abolished and prices fell. What effect does Figure 12.2 suggest this had on consumption?

■ Consumption per head, which had remained static at about 16 lbs per year until then, began a rise that has virtually been uninterrupted.

This steadily rising consumption reflects the increasingly central role that sugar had come to occupy in the diet. One reason for this was that sugar is one of the few substances a strong enough solution of which can be made to prevent bacteria and mould growing on food. This property was put to work in making preserves such as marmalade and jam, the commercial manufacture of which began in the late nineteenth century. It also for a long time formed the basis of the only method of preserving milk in a sweetened, condensed form. These products were popular with poorer families because they were cheap, kept well and were one of the very few ways of making a diet dominated by bread palatable. Even more popular was a simple sugar solution which had the same advantage; this was sold as treacle, or in its decolourised form — golden syrup.

Cheap sugar supplies also formed the basis for new industries. Combined with cocoa, sugar led to the rapid development of the confectionery industry, started in the mid-nineteenth century by Quaker families such as the Frys, the Cadburys, and the Rowntrees. And combined with cheap flour, sugar formed the basis of the cake and biscuit industries. Both these industries, like milling and baking,

are now dominated by a small number of large producers.

The continued rise in sugar consumption after the 1940s shown in Figure 12.2 was in large part due to the increased use of sugar in food manufacturing. Some very unlikely foods now contain sugar for reasons not to do with its sweetness so much as its effect on other properties that add desirable characteristics to food, such as the viscosity of tomato ketchup, or 'mouth feel' to fizzy drinks.

Tea

Both wheat and sugar illustrate the way in which different components of the average diet have combined to produce new industries such as biscuit-making. A particularly good example of the influence of one item on another is the relationship between sugar and tea: the early stimulus for increasing sugar consumption was as a sweetener for tea, alongside other popular eighteenth-century drinks such as coffee and cocoa. All three drinks had become popular with the urban gentry from 1600 onwards, but cocoa suffered from the disadvantage that, until a process was invented in 1883 for removing cocoa butter, it caused intense flatulence when consumed, and supplies of coffee were unreliable. Thus tea gradually became the dominant drink.

What was the attraction of tea drinking? For the poorer people it seems clear from the rise in consumption as prices fell, that tea was consumed because it was a cheap, refreshing drink. The fall in tea prices is a story in itself.

The East India Company had until 1833 a monopoly on importing tea from China (the only place it was grown). The same ships took to China an export cargo from India of opium, and found a major market in the growing number of addicts. The Imperial Chinese Government not unnaturally wanted this trade ended, but could not persuade the British government to act against the East India Company, who were at the time the semi-official rulers of India. Finally in 1839, the Chinese attempted to solve the problem unilaterally, by cutting off all trade with foreigners. The response of the British government was to declare war on China, the infamous Opium Wars, after three years of which the Chinese were forced to submit and indeed to accept increased rather than decreased trade.

Already in the years leading up to the war, however, successful efforts had been made by the East India Company to free the growing of tea from the Chinese monopoly, and in 1830 tea plantations were started in India. The crop grew well and activities expanded, so that in 1870 other entrepreneurs developed plantations in Sri Lanka (Ceylon). In order to provide a work-force, Tamil labourers were transported from South India to Sri Lanka. As tea production from these new sources expanded, so prices fell, and by 1900 were around half the 1870 price.

The importance of tea in the British diet can be gauged by the leading role it played in revolutionising the retail trade. In 1889 Joseph Lipton, a Glasgow grocer, produced a mass-packaged brand of tea at only two-thirds the cost of its nearest rival: its success was phenomenal.

One important reason for Lipton's success was that by packaging his tea he greatly reduced the opportunity for adulteration by retailers, and thereby virtually guaranteed consumers pure tea at a low price. Before this, *food adulteration* was a widespread and well-organised mass fraud. In the early nineteenth century, for example, it seems that while around 6 million pounds of genuine tea were being imported and sold in Britain, a further 4 million pounds of 'tea' were being made and sold 'from native English hedgerows, the leaves of ash, sloe and elder, being curled and coloured on copper plates' (Burnett, 1979, p.103). In the 1840s, at least eight factories in London apparently existed to collect the used tea leaves of hotels, coffee-houses, and large private houses, then to dry, colour, and re-sell them. Poisons such as copper carbonate and lead chromate were among the colourants used in tea and many other foodstuffs at this time. Not until the late nineteenth century did packaging and stronger legislation begin to reduce gross adulteration.

Lipton proceeded to develop a grocery chain which by 1914 had more than 500 separate retail shops, and, for buying, 7 000 acres of plantation in Ceylon. By controlling everything from plantation to grocer shop, Lipton was a pioneer of a form of industrial organisation known as 'vertical integration'. However, the price-cutting policy he pursued and his development of the multiple shop were not his innovations, but were typical of the late nineteenth century, an era not only of growing output from the food industry but of increasing *size* of its retail units.

Many of the companies that came into existence in what has been called the 'retailing revolution' were to flourish until the rise of the supermarket in post-Second-World-War Britain. They included the Home and Colonial Stores, Lyons, and, most far-reaching of all, the Co-operative Movement. Begun in Rochdale, the movement's wholesaling organisation (the Co-operative Wholesale Society, CWS) was established in 1862. The Co-op movement dominated the retail trade until the First World War; indeed in 1914 it had 3.8 million largely working-class members (perhaps 20 per cent of the adult population) and an annual turnover of £100 million, mostly on goods sold under its own label.

Therefore, both the growth of branded packaged goods, and the growth of the grocery retail chain, were innovations in which the market for tea played a central role. Moreover, like wheat and, even more so, sugar, tea attained its importance in the national diet of Britain during a period when the British role in the world economy as the foremost colonial and industrial power was very different to its role in the 1980s.

Meat consumption

The usual view of meat consumption in Victorian Britain is of the rich eating vast excesses, and the poor eating none.

☐   What light do the menus and diets we quoted earlier cast on this? (Figure 12.1, Table 12.2)
■   Meat consumption by the affluent was certainly extraordinarily high, though such gargantuan menus must have occasioned considerable waste. However, the meat intakes of the workers surveyed by Edward Smith were not negligible. Broadly, consumption fell with income, but none of them actually ate a meat-free diet.

From 1850, British agriculture concentrated on increasing meat production because arable farming had been undercut by wheat imports. Estimates of meat consumption per head were 72 lbs per year in 1850, rising to 110 lbs per year by 1880. This occurred during a period when the population rose from 27 million to 35 million. The improvement in production in Britain began with the introduction of cattle breeding in the agricultural revolution of the mid-eighteenth century. Pig breeding for improved meat began somewhat later in the opening years of the nineteenth century, slightly after the start of breeding sheep for meat. But increases in production also depended on the growing use of feedstuffs produced from more intensive arable farming and from the wheat-grain by-products (bran and wheatgerm) of commercial millers who were increasingly making refined white bread.

The British farmer found these methods of meat production profitable because, apart from minor imports of low quality canned meat (they stood at only 2 per cent of home production in 1850), the market was protected by the perishability of meat. The situation began to change after February 1880 when the first cargo of refrigerated beef arrived in London on the S.S. *Strathleven* for sale in Smithfield market. Imports grew rapidly: by 1902 they were the equivalent of 56 lbs per person per year; by 1914 half the meat consumed was imported, and progressive improvements in refrigeration technique led to further rises. This ability to import meat led to a rise in supply and a fall in price in Britain, reflected in figures for meat consumption.

☐   Consumption estimates for the period 1880–1980 are shown in Figure 12.3. What do they indicate?
■   Average consumption reached a peak in the early twentieth century, and although it recovered from a fall caused by rationing during the Second World War, it has been declining in recent years. These figures of course tell us nothing about any narrowing of the difference in consumption between the social classes that may have occurred.

There are two discernible results from the change in production and imports. The first was an increase in the

Technological change — social change. The SS *Strathleven*, by carrying the first shipments of frozen meat from the USA to the UK in 1880, signalled a rapid change in eating patterns. (Science Museum)

supply of offal and carcass fat, not acceptable as such to the consumer but ideal for the development of meat products. Manufactured meat products such as pies and sausages began to appear in large numbers in the 1850s, together with shops that sold cooked meat products.

☐ These products were by all accounts very popular

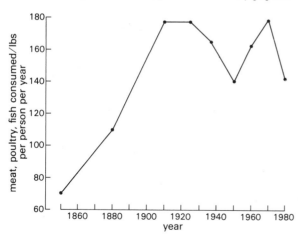

Figure 12.3 The consumption of meat, poultry and fish in the UK, 1850–1981. (Compiled from various sources)

with the poorer classes. What might have encouraged this?

■ First, the same factors that were involved in the growth of commercial baking: such meat products saved fuel in the home and, given the design of slum dwellings, roasting, for example, was often impossible because of a lack of ovens in the kitchen ranges. Second, being made from meat offcuts and cereals, pies and sausages were cheaper than raw meat. The sausage was often half cereal and mixed with very fatty meat. They could also be bought in small amounts.

The second result was the impact of imports on farming. Imported food did not merely supplement home production: the lower cost of imported meat from the large-scale ranching of cattle on the prairies of the New World meant that the British meat-producing industry declined, as had cereal farming before it. By the late nineteenth century, British agriculture had entered a slump, from which it was not to recover until the First World War when imports were drastically curtailed, and into which it was to return in the interwar years. Farming itself only survived with the help of subsidies and import restrictions, coupled with a change to two different crops that could not be imported in Victorian times: dairy products and fresh vegetables.

Dairy products and fresh vegetables

Dairying could in no way provide the sort of rewards for farmers that wheat and meat had previously supplied, simply because it was for many years technically difficult to get dairy products to urban markets in a fit state for consumption. The absence of home refrigeration and hygenic conditions for milk production and distribution made milk a perishable product, indeed a dangerous one. Until pasteurisation became widespread, milk carried diseases such as tuberculosis and salmonella. Only after the First World War were vigorous steps taken to bring milk up to its modern health standards.

Until the advent of the railway, milk distribution was non-existent, and in the towns and cities milk was purchased direct from squalid urban cowsheds where animals were kept in crowded conditions. Only in 1866 when, following an outbreak of cattle disease, the susceptibility of town animals to infection was realised, were the conditions of such sheds regulated.

Thereafter, milk production rapidly became rural, and the wholesale trade became concentrated into a few large firms who controlled conditions on the farms who supplied them. The product was not only perishable, it was relatively expensive, consumption being closely related to income: in 1902, middle-class families consumed 6 pints per person per week, lower middle-class 3.8 pints, artisans 1.8 pints and labourers 0.8 pints.

Changes in consumption resulted not only from improvements in milk hygiene and daily deliveries, but also from a concerted programme of propaganda for the virtues of milk, that was launched during the Second World War. But neither of the two milk products — butter and cheese — formed the basis of a major farming operation. The simple reason for this was that the very refrigeration that made imports of meat possible and undermined the meat producer, also made imports of cheese and butter at prices lower than home produce equally possible.

Increasing meat imports also encouraged a switch by British farmers to perishable fruits and vegetables. This, however, did not allay agricultural slumps, for although the acreages devoted to fruit-growing and vegetable-growing increased sharply, so too did imports, particularly of tropical fruit, made possible by the faster journey times of the new steamships. Bananas entered the British diet in the 1870s, and a variety of other fruits, both canned and fresh, followed. Products of the colonies, where production costs were low, became widely available in the late nineteenth and early twentieth centuries, and British farming was unable to compete.

By the end of the nineteenth century, therefore, the expansion in food supply needed to sustain the increase in population had been achieved principally by the importa-tion of foodstuffs — notably from the Empire. Changes in

British agriculture played a crucial role in developing food supplies at some points; for example wheat during the Napoleonic wars, and meat before refrigeration. However, the long-term effect of cheaper imports was to displace British agriculture, to cause it to adopt new crops, products, and methods, and to precipitate periodic slumps. These imports were obtained primarily from the colonies rather than wider world markets, and as the examples of tea and sugar illustrated, deliberate preference was given to production in the colonies.

The changes that occurred led also to the integration of the food production industry, for example in the use of bran and wheatgerm as farm animal foods, and in milk wholesaling. Food processing became important, and as it did so the food manufacturing industry became more concentrated in the hands of a small number of producers, who exerted greater control over retailing, and to a degree, over farming.

British agriculture, and in particular the farmworker, ended the nineteenth century in a worse state than at the beginning. The consumer, however, did not. The large-scale imports of wheat and meat, the new production techniques, and reductions in duties and taxes on foods, all brought the price of food down. In the 10 years from 1877 to 1887 alone, the retail price of food in the typical working-class budget fell by around 30 per cent. For the upper classes, new hotels, restaurants, cafés, and clubs provided for the first wave of eating-out fashion.

> For the lower middle classes probably more than for any other section of the community, the cheapness of food in the later nineteenth century had brought greater variety and interest to the diet. In particular, cheaper meat allowed the Englishman to indulge his liking for a joint at every meal, while technology also contributed an important service by bringing tinned fish and fruit out of season to those who could afford to live a little above subsistence level ... the world food market was so organised as to place the cheapest wheat and meat, the best fish, tea and coffee on English tables. (Burnett, 1979, p.237).

In short, by 1900 a pattern of diet and of food production and supply had emerged, which was to last, with only minor changes, right up until the present day.

Changes in diet from 1900 and the consequences for health

Given the far-reaching changes in food production and supply patterns which the nineteenth century witnessed, an obvious question to ask is what effect these changes had on the health of the British population. As has so often been the case, however, evidence was only gathered and action only taken because of military considerations.

The occasion was the Boer War, during which extensive army recruitment was required to meet the increased need for troops. A War Office memorandum of 1904 reported that in Britain as a whole over 60 per cent of volunteers had been rejected on the grounds of health, largely because they failed to meet the minimum height limit for a soldier of 5′ 3″ (160 cm). The only way of obtaining sufficient recruits was to reduce that criterion to 5′ 0″ (152 cm). This would have been bad enough, but the 5′ 3″ criterion had only been adopted in 1873 after a similar problem had necessitated a reduction in the minimum height, from 5′ 6″ (167 cm).

The idea that a national deterioration in physique might have resulted in a fall in male adult height of 6″ (15 cm) in 30 years, created a scandal, and though a government enquiry was unable to decide for or against 'deterioration', it did confirm an appalling situation among the poorer classes. For example, 10- to 12-year-old children at state schools were 5″ (13 cm) shorter than the same age group in public schools.

However, although the full nutritional implications of impairment of growth were not realised, the class ramifications of the problem were, and attempts were made to alleviate the lot of the poorer classes. Attention was paid to food in this regard because of the social surveys such as that produced by Rowntree in 1899 (discussed in Chapter 10) and the 17-volume survey of life and labour in London produced by his mentor Charles Booth between 1886 and 1902. Neither survey showed, or claimed to show, famine or conditions of outright deficiency disease. But both described inadequacy at a level where it was difficult to believe growth, health and resistance to disease could be unimpaired.

In response to these findings, from 1904 school meals began to be provided for poorer children, and in 1906 the National Insurance Act provided for unemployment and sickness benefit. In addition, funding of medical research via the Medical Research Council was begun, and one of the first projects undertaken showed that the widespread prevalence of rickets (softening of the bones) in poorer children was the result of poor diet, interacting with poor housing and atmospheric pollution.

As the complexity of nutritional needs was unravelled, increasing evidence was gathered concerning the inadequate diet and nutritional status of the nation's population. Some historians have been puzzled by this apparent paradox of an improving food supply alongside a rising concern about malnutrition. Part of the explanation may be that not all workers were benefitting from the rising *average* standard of living, and that incomes among the poor were still exceedingly low and liable to fluctuate. Edward Smith's studies of diet were discussed earlier. From other studies conducted between 1861 and 1863, the years of a depression in the cotton industry during the American Civil War, when cotton supplies from the Southern slaving states were disrupted (the 'Cotton Famine'), he demonstrated that consumption of all foods except milk fell, as the family income fell by nearly 70 per cent. Meat and potato consumption fell the most as families simply ceased to eat cooked meals. Bread, sugar and fat consumption fell less, as bread and tea became the predominant meal. Probably more cups of weaker tea were drunk, which is why milk consumption did not fall.

In 1935, seventy years later, another survey relating diet to family income brought out more clearly than ever how misleading an average can be. This survey into food, health and income was conducted by John Boyd Orr, a scientist whose views and work increasingly represented the most formidable source of criticism of the Ministry of Health (Boyd Orr, 1936). Boyd Orr classified the population into six income groups then worked out how many people were in each group and how much each group spent on food. Some results of this survey are given in Table 12.3.

Boyd Orr's survey, as had Smith's earlier, showed clearly that there was tremendous variation around the 'average diet' and that certain components of the diet were cut back more than others as average food expenditure fell. In particular, Boyd Orr showed great differences in protein

Table 12.3 Boyd Orr's survey of food, health and income, 1935

Income group	Income per head per week	Average food expenditure per head per week	Percentage of UK population in income group
1	< 50p	20p	10
2	50–75p	30p	20
3	75p–£1	40p	20
4	£1–£1.50	50p	20
5	£1.50–£2.25	60p	20
6	> £2.25	70p	10
average	£1.50	45p	

(data from Boyd Orr, 1936, reproduced in Burnett, 1979, Table 27)

and vitamin intake. Income group 1, the poorest, consumed an average 1.8 pints of milk per person per week, compared with 5.5 pints in income group 6, and spent only 1p on fruit compared with 8p. In fact Boyd Orr calculated that in none of the three poorest income groups — that is, half the population — was the diet adequate for perfect health in all its main constituents.

Boyd Orr's work brought forward two responses which are still affecting the diet of people today. The first came from the inevitable attempt to deny his findings. Although government ministers withdrew the Civil Servant who helped Boyd Orr in his work, the report still appeared. The second response came from a special committee of the British Medical Association, who had been asked to advise the government on the significance of Boyd Orr's results. This committee concluded that the several million people identified as being underfed because of low expenditure on food could be adequately fed if only they bought *different* foods. Malnutrition was defined by them as a problem of 'ignorance' rather than poverty. This view of course, was very favourably received by the government, and has become part of the orthodoxy on which the income supplements for the poor are still calculated. Social security payments are still based on a subsistence scale for the poor that implicitly assumes they eat a diet that, though nutritious, the rest of us would find unpalatable.

Despite this response, Boyd Orr's work did stimulate concern among people conscious of an impending second world war, and aware of the strategic issue of food supply such a war would raise. A steadily increasing flood of books on these strategic implications appeared in the years leading up to the War. On its outbreak then, there was an awareness of both the need to avoid civilian discontent owing to food shortages in the event of blockade, and a wish to eliminate the problem of malnutrition (which the social reformers had publicised). This awareness led to the imposition of both a food production policy *and* a policy of rationing and nutrition education to improve patterns of consumption.

The submarine blockade of Britain was very extensive, and home production became a dominant factor in the diet. Agriculture, which had been in decline since the 1880s, was actively stimulated by a variety of government grants. However, even with marginal land such as golf courses and parks being brought into use, Britain remained dependent on food imports.

Arable farming increasingly replaced livestock, and although meat allowances became extremely stringent, bread remained unrationed throughout the war. To avoid nutritional deficiencies in the face of falling imports of meat and butter, the production and consumption of milk was encouraged. Animal production in this country was switched to dairying and away from meat. Consumption in many ways reverted to the diet we associate with poverty:

less meat, more bread, more potatoes. At the same time intense efforts to increase the consumption of vegetables and dairy produce were successful. Consequently, though the diet was less palatable, it was probably less likely than ever before to result in deficiency disease. This is difficult to prove, however, as the international classification of diseases was revised at this time. Though food imports could resume at the end of the war, the shortage of foreign exchange actually increased the severity of rationing and, because of this, bread, for example, had to be rationed for the first time in the years 1947–49. Not until 1952 did rationing end completely.

Rationing left few marks on long-term patterns of food consumption. Production, however, increasingly reflected the policy preferences of the farmers. The growth in the power of the farming lobby during the period of the nation's dependence on farmers during the war, led to them forming a policy of expanding domestic supply and contracting the dependence on imports. Thus, whereas there was a close connection between food policy and health policy during the war, the two subsequently became almost completely divorced.

When the United Kingdom joined the European Economic Community (EEC) in 1972, this policy continued, but the level of government subsidy to agriculture rose as funds from the *Common Agricultural Policy (CAP)* became available.

The CAP was devised with many purposes in mind. It is a policy that involves a tariff barrier on foods being imported to the Common Market from non-EEC countries. This can result in higher prices for certain foods within the EEC than on world markets. Perhaps the most important aspect of the CAP is the price-support system, whereby food producers are guaranteed fixed prices for their produce, and any produce unsold at these prices on open markets is bought by governments. It is these surpluses bought at guaranteed prices that can result in the 'lakes' of wine or olive oil, and the 'mountains' of butter and beef. Indeed, some of the food produced at guaranteed prices is simply destroyed.

Within the CAP's price-support system it is still possible for individual member states of the EEC to pursue their policy objectives. The UK has consistently used the system to increase domestic production and to attempt to reduce the food import bill. This does not necessarily lead to cheaper food for consumers, however. And, as in France and West Germany, the large-scale mechanised farmers and 'agri-business' have prospered under the CAP, while the smaller farmers have been encouraged to leave the land.

Of course, the policies towards agriculture in the UK have varied, depending on the government in office. The 1974–79 Labour government, for instance, funded its own subsidy policy to try to keep food prices down, a policy abandoned after 1979. The central point, however, is that the CAP has accelerated agricultural changes in the UK that have been occurring since 1945, rather than initiating new policies. The United Kingdom pursues its own policy of self-sufficiency, exemplified by the fact that despite the butter mountain, despite the need for costly inputs into our dairying industry, despite our trade links with Ireland (which is ideally suited to dairying) dairy production has been encouraged in this country to achieve *internal* self-sufficiency. Such examples suggest that UK policy has increasingly been to exploit the opportunities offered by the CAP to expand our own agricultural production at the expense of both EEC producers and UK consumers and taxpayers.

Modern patterns of consumption and health

It is in the context of these deep-rooted and long-term trends in the UK agriculture and food industries that our modern patterns of consumption and health must be understood. For example, because our intensive agriculture takes animal growth rate as a primary target, it produces inexorably fattier animal carcases than pastoral systems in which animals, being fed less food, grow more slowly. Hence we have, since the nineteenth century, not only had a tendency to consume fatty meat, but also to have excess fat on our animals.

This has occurred despite some increase in consumer preference for leaner cuts of meat and an increasing medical concern about the harmful effects animal fat in the diet may have on our health, in particular cardiovascular disease. Although there has been some breeding of leaner carcases, CAP subsidies on sheep and beef tend to favour fattier carcases and therefore offset the trend towards lean breeds.

This excess of fat has been inherent in intensive agriculture since it began. It is reflected in the use of 'dripping' (beef or pork fat left over after roasting meat) which was both a cooking fat and a spread on bread for the poor. It is reflected in the rise of lard and suet as cooking fats. And it is reflected in the production of manufactured meat products.

Undesirable offal and excess fat was a primary product for the meat-processing industry, and foods like sausages — or more recently hamburgers — have always made use of such products.

☐ This can be seen from Figure 12.4, where the fat content of fresh and processed meats (measured by the percentage energy from fat) are compared. What is the difference between them?

■ Processed and cooked meat and meat products are higher in fat — sometimes remarkably so. For example, salami or frankfurters both provide over 80 per cent of their energy from fat, compared with less than 20 per cent from fresh turkey meat.

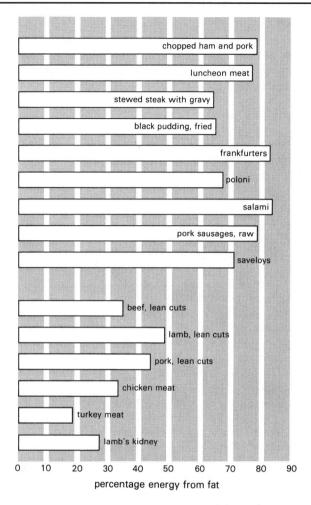

Figure 12.4 The fat content of fresh and processed meats, measured by the percentage energy from fat. (Compiled from various sources)

Sugar consumption shows many similarities. Though confectionery and soft drinks are well-recognised vehicles for sugar, together they make up less than half the sugar used by the food industry, and it is surprising perhaps that the baking industry uses almost as much sugar in its products as the confectionary industry. Because only 40 per cent of the sugar actually consumed is consumed as *visible* sugar, and given the high sugar content of many common foods, it is actually quite difficult to avoid fairly high levels of sugar consumption.

Changes in the agricultural and food industries have also led to a decrease in dietary fibre intakes. Before roller milling, dietary fibre intakes were very high, principally because of the high consumption of cereal fibre. They fell after roller milling arrived and although they may have risen slowly thereafter as more fruit and vegetables were consumed, particularly during the Second World War, this tendency has been counterbalanced by a fall in bread consumption.

□ Wholemeal bread has recently become much more popular. What difference will this make?

■ A great deal, if you eat it — but wholemeal bread is preferred by the middle classes, who do not eat much bread anyway. The poor, who eat more bread, eat less wholemeal, because it is so much more expensive. At Janaury 1984 prices, a wholemeal loaf cost about 55 per cent more than an equivalent white loaf.

Fibre consumption in the UK at present has been influenced by the fact that since the UK joined the EEC, bread has been made increasingly of mostly European rather than North American wheat. European wheat is softer (it has less protein) and also has less fibre in its white flour. This change is not just the result of the CAP policy: soft wheat is also now preferred by bakers as it suits some of the new industrial innovations in baking. A second contributory factor may be that though many people will eat brown bread for health reasons, not everyone will accept all pastry products (cakes and biscuits as well as pies) being wholemeal. The more these products dominate cereal consumption, the less impact brown bread has in the diet overall.

The relationship of fat, sugar and fibre to health is not clear-cut, although some relationships — for example between refined sugar and dental caries (decay) — seem to be undisputed. But whatever the precise nature of the diet–degenerative disease relationship, the development of the present UK diet has been influenced by factors which have also led to an industry which sustains that diet. If that diet has within it the seeds of degenerative disease, it is almost as difficult for the individual to change now as it was for the Victorian slum-dweller to avoid deficiency.

At the same time it is true that this diet has by and large led to the elimination of deficiency. By the end of the Second World War it was recognised that deficiency diseases in the UK had ceased to be the threat they were perceived as being ten years earlier.

□ The architects of the food policy claimed credit for this, but what else might have been involved?

■ First, the war meant an end to unemployment. In addition, many married women entered work for the first time, further increasing household incomes and real incomes of the workers also rose. As a result, class differentials in the growth of children narrowed.

Deficiency diseases have become very rare indeed. The sort of differences in the growth of children of different social classes that had been observed before the War were much smaller by its end, and continued to be reduced so that by 1974, though class differences in the height of young children persisted, it was only about 4 per cent of the difference that would have been reported 40 years before.

Discussion of diet-related disease in the UK today must therefore proceed from a recognition of the large improvements in nutrition that have undoubtedly occurred in the last two centuries, and perhaps particularly in this century. Nevertheless, there is evidence that deficiency diseases have not been completely eliminated, and that diet may have become increasingly implicated in the degenerative diseases that are now the main causes of death in our society.

Among the deficiency diseases that still occur in the UK are rickets and osteomalacia due to a lack of vitamin D. Rickets, a classical disease of the urban poor which was mentioned in Engels' account of nineteenth-century Manchester, had by the 1960s begun to be recognised again among some children from precisely the same urban areas it had been found in the nineteenth century. This time, however, the children affected have tended to be those of recent immigrants from the Indian subcontinent and the Caribbean. In addition, a deficiency of vitamin D in the elderly of all ethnic groups has led to increasing numbers of reports of osteomalacia. In both cases — immigrant children and the elderly — the occurrence of deficiency disease has been closely associated with poverty and poor, inner-city conditions.

□ The elderly seem to be vulnerable to a variety of dietary deficiencies and the problem has increased in its public health importance. Why might this be?

■ Diseases of the elderly are generally becoming of great public health importance because an increasing proportion of the population is elderly. Their nutritional vulnerability might relate to two factors. First, the elderly tend to be poorer than many other sectors of the population. Second, as the number of old people has increased, so has the extent to which they live on their own, rather than with their children. Hence they are more dependent upon their own resources for a good diet.

Despite these recent concerns for deficiency diseases in particular sub-groups of the population, the main worry about the influence of diet on health has centred on the apparent 'epidemic' of degenerative diseases. These include arteriosclerosis leading to coronary heart disease and strokes, cancers, various conditions affecting the large bowel, obesity and dental caries.

Although the associations between specific degenerative diseases and particular dietary factors have not, so far, been clearly defined, there is general agreement that the current pattern of such diseases in the UK is partly a consequence of the food we eat. Whether the importance some people attach to specific dietary ingredients turns out to be correct or not, there is little doubt that food is one of the most important determinants of our state of health.

Diet in the UK is a complex subject, and the dangers of over-simplifying the relationship between diet and health should by now have become obvious. But one central feature of it which has repeatedly emerged in this material is that our present diet has its origins in the nineteenth century, and in some ways made more sense then than it does now. Our diet no longer has the logic of cheap imports, but is sustained by the fact that those imports gave rise to an industry that was financially committed to a given diet, and by its nature acts as a brake on change. We now consume a diet that is manufactured from an agriculture which is funded to provide a pattern of consumption, thought to be traditional, but which makes less and less environmental, commercial or nutritional sense in the late twentieth century.

Nutrition and the health of the Third World

The nineteenth-century foundations of the modern British diet of cheap imports from the colonies have, as we have seen, had important implications for the development of the British agricultural and food industries. But these foundations have within them even more far-reaching implications for those colonies, that were the source of cheap food imports, and indeed for the Third World as a whole. As deficiency diseases virtually disappeared in industrialised countries, so it became increasingly evident that in the Third World deficiency diseases existed on a horrifying scale.

Initially, attention was focused on two deficiency diseases which affect children in the Third World: marasmus and kwashiorkor. The appearance of children with these conditions is a familiar sight in newspaper photographs, television documentaries and posters for development aid. The thin, skeletal child suffering from marasmus and the child with kwashiorkor, stomach swollen with excess fluid, are images that have haunted the conscience of industrialised nations over the past few decades. Since their first recognition, it has been realised that these two diseases were only the tip of a huge iceberg of what came to be called 'subclinical' malnutrition, which was associated with an increased susceptibility to infection and death. Estimates of the extent of this problem depend of course, on how big an impairment of growth is regarded as being within the normal range, but even the most conservative estimates are breathtaking. For example, the United Nations recently put the number of children suffering with moderate or severe malnutrition of this form at 200 million.

In the 1950s, the extent of this problem led to the apparently obvious deduction that if many individuals in

Third World countries were suffering from malnutrition, then such countries were not producing enough food. International agricultural statistics which the United Nations began to gather regularly, by juxtaposing the existence of food deficits with the extent of nutritional disease, lent evidence to the idea that there was a world food shortage.

□ Is this equation of widespread nutritional deficiency with inadequate food production a reasonable deduction to make?
■ Not necessarily. As was shown earlier, people often go short of food because they have no 'entitlement' to it, rather than because a food shortage exists. Widespread nutritional deficiency in some countries of the world might therefore be because of an 'entitlement failure' rather than the result of any overall world food shortage.

Whatever the underlying causes of nutritional deficiencies in the Third World, it was soon realised that they could not be ascribed to a vitamin or mineral deficiency, and because exact physiological causes could not easily be pinned down, the vague expression '*malnutrition*' came into colloquial usage. At first it was felt that because the characteristic of malnutrition is that children do not grow, and because the cells of the body are composed of protein, then the disease of malnutrition was clearly due to a lack of protein. As a result, from 1945 until the mid-1970s there was progressively expanding attempt to solve a world 'protein problem'. This involved in the main either sending high-protein foods such as dried skimmed milk as food aid to Third World countries, or developing new protein supplements which could be exported to, or be produced in the Third World.

□ Very little attempt was made to encourage such countries specifically to produce more protein-rich foods such as meat. Rather, solutions dependent on Western technology or food surpluses were promoted. What factors may have encouraged this?
■ First, it seemed plausible to conclude that if Third World countries produced insufficient food for their population, they could hardly be encouraged to concentrate upon producing animal products which yield less food per acre than plant foods. This was exactly the lesson that was realised during the Second World War in Britain. But there is a further reason: some protein foods were in surplus in the post-war American and European agricultural systems, and the world 'protein gap' was a useful sink for these surpluses.

The money spent on bridging the '*protein gap*', when the money spent on breeding high-protein cereals is included, has run into thousands of millions of pounds. Whatever the benefits in affluent societies, the impact of these strategies on malnutrition in Third World countries has been virtually zero. In fact it has been claimed that such strategies may have had some negative effects on nutrition. There are many reasons for this failure; sometimes it has been because the attempted solutions, though scientifically sophisticated, neglected simple social realities. Thus, for example, the defatted fish waste (fish heads and offal left over from the food-processing industry), which was developed as a protein supplement for Third World countries by the United States Government at a cost of more than US$60 million, has proved a total failure. Though the product was given the neutral name of 'Fish Protein Concentrate', its advocates did not consider the problem that the United States Food Labelling Laws required that foods containing animal offal be labelled as 'Filth', and 'Unfit for Human Consumption': in other words, the food being sent as aid for children in other countries was considered unfit for Americans.

But there is another reason why the protein strategies have failed. The supposed 'protein deficiency' does not exist. Attempts to induce malnutrition in animals experimentally by feeding them a low-protein diet has also failed. Attempts to cure children with malnutrition by feeding them very high protein diets have not been successful, and indeed in many cases more children were killed by such diets than would have died if fed only the traditional diet. Finally, despite many surveys, no good evidence has been produced to show that children who develop malnutrition eat less protein than those who do not. Just as James Lind's observations, though unchallengeable, were ignored, so the lack of evidence for protein deficiency did nothing for a long time to reduce the enthusiasm that existed for curing it. In the words of the title of a UN Special Report in 1969, there continued to be 'International Action to Avert the Impending World Protein Crisis'. Gradually though, as evidence has accumulated, the protein gap has come to be seen as a 'protein myth' and the crucial fact that even if fed enough protein children do not grow if they do not have a big enough energy intake (i.e. total food intake) has come to the fore. Malnutrition has ceased to be seen as protein malnutrition and has come to be described as Protein Energy Malnutrition. However, many nutritionists feel even this description is wrong, and that inadequate protein intake has little or nothing to do with this major disease. Since the mid-1970s some have advocated a switch from breeding high-protein crops or developing protein supplements towards proposals for increasing total food intake in Third World countries, and this has increasingly been reflected in official projects and programmes.

☐ What might the experience of nineteenth-century Britain tell us about the limitations of such procedures?

■ In nineteenth-century Britain rises in food production were sufficient to allow a rapid growth in population, but they did not eliminate the problem of malnutrition. This is because the disease was a particular problem of those who did not benefit to any extent from rising wages because their employment was intermittent, or because they were unemployed. More than anything else, it was growing employment, rising relative wages for poorer workers and unemployment and social security schemes that solved the problem. In other words, the extension of the 'entitlements' to food of the poorer sections of the population was as important as the expanding food supply.

The consequences of expanding food supplies without considering patterns of food entitlement can be witnessed in many Third World countries: some of these consequences were revealed earlier in this book as wide health inequalities within countries. Perhaps the most outstanding example of an innovation that has generated these consequences is the so-called 'Green Revolution': the introduction to the Third World of high-yielding crops specially bred by international research organisations funded by industrialised countries.

The Green Revolution has been hailed as holding out the promise to Third World countries of internal self-sufficiency in food (at least as long as their diet is heavily based on cereals). This doubling of crop yields that the Green Revolution promised is only available, however, to those who can afford the investment of buying the grain, adding the fertilisers that the fast-growing crops require, and if necessary also providing irrigation. In consequence, those who could afford this investment have done so, increasing their yields, their share of the market, and hence their profits, whereas those who could not afford the innovation have got relatively poorer. In some instances the disparity of incomes has become so great, and the value of land to the farmer who can afford high-yielding varieties so high, that the peasant farmer has been dispossessed, and though food production has risen, so has landlessness, destitution and, as a direct result, malnutrition.

These tendencies are not new. In the nineteenth century, as new lands in the colonies were utilised to produce foods for countries like Britain, the people who had previously used the land were simply evicted from it: the American Indians from the prairies, the native peoples from Australia and New Zealand. Where the new plantations needed labour, people were transported — West Africans as slaves to the West Indies, Indian Tamils as plantation workers to Sri Lanka.

These changes, which allowed the British population to grow, to become more wealthy and finally to be the victims of excess, were also the changes that established a pattern of relationship between what are today called the First and the Third World. The elimination of deficiency diseases in countries like Britain was accomplished despite the existence of the same problem in the very countries that provided the food. Consider just one example: Guatemalan sugar plantation workers. Recent surveys trying to explain why they have ten times the malnutrition rate of the rest of the population found the answer in the conditions of their way of life: low wages, long hours of labour, and housing provided by the plantation which had little land attached and thus little opportunity to grow food.

The worker's families are isolated from towns, and must buy food in company-run shops which are on the plantation and charge up to twice the normal price of food in the town. The sugar plantation owners provide only the schooling the law requires — three years elementary schooling, after which the children wishing to continue school must make the long and expensive bus journey to the nearest town. Most families cannot afford it, and anyway need the labour of their children to assist in the harvesting of grain, for wages depend on family size. So the children stay illiterate, and grow into adults who cannot escape, for leaving work on the plantation means losing not only the family income, but also the family house.

Life is lived on the edge of catastrophe, any event — the illness of an adult, the need to seek medical treatment for children — can and does tip life over the edge into the sort of chaos where children die. And even without such catastrophes, life is far removed from that state of physical, mental and social wellbeing defined as 'health' by the World Health Organisation. The situation, and its consequences, are little different to those earlier described by Engels, Rowntree, Booth and Boyd Orr in Britain.

The Green Revolution has gone part-way to meeting one of the needs of Third World countries, in that the introduction of new crops and techniques has frequently led to increases in food production. But the emphasis on a technological solution has averted attention from the distribution of land and food entitlement. In the same way as deficiency diseases could not have been largely eliminated in the UK without major changes in food entitlement as well as food supply, it seems clear that the deficiency diseases so common in the Third World cannot be tackled simply by concentrating on food supply. Indeed, there is a strong argument for looking much more closely at entitlement patterns between as well as within nations.

It was noted in Chapter 6 that foodstuffs and other primary commodities are a major part of Third World exports to the industrialised countries. In fact the export of such commodities is one of their main sources of foreign exchange. This is a pattern of trade which resulted from the nineteenth-century changes we described. It is not a pattern reflecting any real natural advantage held by Third World countries in producing the main cash crops, as is sometimes argued. On the land devoted to cotton or rubber or coffee production at present, it would be perfectly possible to grow many high-nutrition crops. The problem is that what might make nutritional sense to the rural populations of Third World countries often does not make commercial sense under present arrangements to 'agri-business' companies, Western food processors and importers, or the urban elites of those Third World countries.

The problems produced by this pattern of trade take many different forms. Populations like ours want low food prices, and if imports such as bananas become expensive we cease to eat them. Sugar producers have tried to form a cartel, but it is not successful. The countries that produce sugar, Guatemala, for example, are dependent for aid on industrialised countries and cannot afford the risk of reprisals. The industrialised countries have also developed extensive alternatives, such as artificial sweeteners, beet sugar, and corn-syrup made from maize. Sugar exports from the Third World continue only because the price is low, and for such countries it seems unlikely that their dependency will change unless their present role in the world economy also changes. In short, it is evident that the patterns of diet-related diseases in the industrialised countries and the Third World, although now very different, are inextricably linked. It is perhaps no exaggeration to say that the UK solved its problem of nutritional inadequacy by exporting it.

Conclusions

As this case study of nutrition has attempted to demonstrate, patterns of health and disease as related to diet in the UK, and other parts of the world, are complex, shifting, and subject to a wide number of influences. On a general level it is quite clear that nutrition is a major factor in understanding health and disease patterns, just as it seems quite clear that overall levels of economic development or the prevalence of poverty are also major factors. Moreover, there are some specific ways in which the influence of these factors is known to operate. Sugar, for example, is an important component of the modern British diet which has a clear association with diseases such as dental caries. Similarly, the lack of clean water that is a characteristic of the poorest segments of populations in the Third World is directly associated with infectious diseases such as bilharzia. A great strength of the comparative method used in this book is that the experience of different societies can be laid alongside one another, and the differences and similarities thus revealed can help us to reach an understanding of the factors that seem to be direct or indirect influences on health and disease.

An underlying theme of this book has been the need to distinguish between explanations focusing on social and economic structures and others emphasising the role of the individual. This theme surfaced directly at the beginning of Chapter 10, in the comparison of the Course Reader extracts by the Royal College of Physicians and by Paul Harrison. The stark contrast presented was between a view of people being almost entirely individually to blame for their experiences of ill-health, and a view which portrayed people caught up in a material environment over which they had little or no control. The same contrast can be found in almost any part of this book: the nutrition case study for example, showed that people can and must make decisions about the kind of diet they consume, and exercise choices that have some influence on the agricultural and food-processing industries. At the same time, however, the case study argued that these choices are constrained by many things, from the historical world role of the UK and the present world economy, to the technologies of food-processing and the nature of retailing. As we have noted, it would be difficult to avoid a substantial intake of sugar in one's diet even if one wanted to.

The same theme emerged in discussions of population change: people do make choices about family size or timing, and if modern contraceptives are unavailable or denied then other strategies are adopted, ranging from delayed marriage to infanticide. Again, however, these choices are often constrained, and the material environment sets these constraints, whether in the form of some variant of a Malthusian subsistence barrier or in the lack of social security provision for old age or infirmity.

On a grander scale, it could be argued that nations are also free to act and make choices, but again only within certain constraints. The historical development of the world economy has assigned a position of great influence to a small group of industrialised countries, and of weakness to the majority. Within these constraints, the ability of countries such as Sierra Leone to break out of a position of poverty and appalling ill-health is severely curtailed. Even so, countries such as Sri Lanka have managed to take initiatives despite their poverty which have resulted in well-above-average standards of health.

The book has ranged over a wide number of historical periods, from the gatherer-hunters to the present, and within that perspective the period of industrialisation during which health has so markedly improved is a relatively recent one. Even Britain, the first country to industrialise, did not reap many of the major benefits of increased life-expectancy and reduced mortality rates until the twentieth century. At the same time, however, the greater part of the world which is not industrialised cannot be expected to sit and wait for 'history' to propel them forward. As we saw in Chapters 5 to 7, there is no reason to *assume* that present trends will lead to the gradual global spread of industrialisation and the health improvements accompanying it. The sharply contrasting fortunes of different parts of the world are vividly stated in this passage written in 1967:

> In the sinking of the *Titanic*, in 1912, 3 per cent of the first class female passengers were lost, 16 per cent of the second class and 45 per cent of the third class. In the imaginary ship that is Latin America, there are 345 million passengers, subjected to differential roles by social class as cruel or even more so than those of the *Titanic*. Annually, almost a million bodies of children less than five years old, are thrown overboard; they come mostly from the 'third class' and, above all, they should not have died.
> (Antonovsky, 1967, p.153)

We have repeatedly stressed that there are no simple solutions to these inequalities in the health of nations. This fact, coupled to the complexity of the problems, can only serve to underline the need to more fully understand the issues involved.

Objectives for Chapter 12

When you have studied this chapter, you should be able to:

12.1 Outline the main components of the modern British diet, and the way this diet has evolved since the nineteenth century.

12.2 Provide examples of industrial and technological changes that have influenced the modern diet.

12.3 Describe the main changes that have occurred over the last century in diet-related disease in the UK.

12.4 Summarise the impact of diet on disease in the Third World, and discuss why policies to deal with these problems have had varying success.

Questions for Chapter 12

1 (*Objective 12.1*) According to Table 12.1, the average person in the UK in 1981 ate 22 ounces of white bread and 9 ounces of brown or wholemeal bread. What reasons can you give for doubting the value of these figures as guides to the average British diet?

2 (*Objective 12.2*) The following quotation, written in 1955, seems to suggest that there is little 'natural goodness' left in the modern diet:

Dear housewives, Do you know that there is hardly an honest food left to buy . . .? Nearly all the foods that go onto our table are so changed, so processed and chemicalised that all their original goodness is either removed or killed. They are bleached, dyed, dehydrated, frozen, synthetic, tinned, sulphured, pasteurised, iodized, refined, adulterated and too often unclean as well. It seems a wonder that we are alive at all. (Doreen Grant, quoted in Burnett (1979), p.357)

How does this conclusion strike you in light of your historical knowledge of some of the industrial and technological processes she mentions?

3 (*Objective 12.3*) Diet is thought to be in some way associated with the 'diseases of affluence'? Can you recall from Chapter 9 what the characteristics of these 'diseases of affluence' are? Are they in fact mainly found among the affluent?

4 (*Objective 12.4*) Children with vitamin A deficiency in Victorian England were normally significantly shorter than average. How would you interpret this statement, and what parallels can you draw from it with the debate over 'protein deficiency' or the 'protein gap' in the Third World?

References
and
further
reading

References

ANTONOVSKY, A. (1967) Social class, life expectancy and overall mortality, *Millbank Memorial Fund Quarterly*, Vol. XLV, No. 2

ATKINSON, A.B. (1980) *Wealth, Income and Inequality*, Oxford University Press, 2nd edn.

ATKINSON, A.B. (1983) *The Economics of Inequality*, Oxford University Press.

ATKINSON, A.B. and HARRISON, P. (1978) *The Distribution of Personal Wealth in Britain*, Cambridge University Press.

BAIRD, D. (1974) The epidemiology of low birth weight: changes in incidence in Aberdeen, 1948–1972, *Journal of Biosocial Science*, pp. 323–341.

BAIRD, D. (1975) The interplay of changes in society, reproductive habits, and obstetric practice in Scotland between 1922 and 1972, *British Journal of Preventive and Social Medicine*, pp. 135–146.

BAIROCH, P. (1982) International industrialization levels from 1750 to 1980, *Journal of European Economic History*, **11**, 2, pp. 269–333

BEEVERS, D.G. and CRUICKSHANK, J.K. (1981) Age, sex, ethnic origin and hospital admission for heart attack and stroke, *Postgraduate Medical Journal*, 57 (December), pp. 763–765.

BEHM, H. (1979) Socioeconomic determinants of mortality in Latin America: *Proceedings of the Meeting on Socioeconomic Determinants and the Consequences of Mortality*, UN/WHO, Mexico.

BLACK, NICK, BOSWELL, DAVID, GRAY, ALASTAIR, MURPHY, SEAN and POPAY, JENNY (eds) (1984) *Health and Disease: A Reader*, The Open University Press. The Course Reader.

BOYD ORR, J. (1936) *Food, Health, and Income*, Report on a Survey of Adequacy of Diet in Relation to Income.

'BRANDT REPORT' (1980) *North-South: A Programme for Survival. Report of the Independent Commission on International Development Issues*, Pan.

BRASS, W. (1982) Policies for the reduction of mortality differentials, *Population and Development in the Middle East*, UN Economic Commission for Western Asia.

BRAUDEL, F. (1981) *The Structures of Everyday Life: the Limits of the Possible*, Collins.

BURGHES, L. (1980) *Living from Hand to Mouth: A Study of 65 Families Living on Supplementary Benefit*, Child Poverty Action Group.

BURNETT, J. (1979) *Plenty and Want, A Social History of Diet in England from 1815 to the Present Day*, Scolar Press.

CARTER, C.O. and PEEL, J. (eds) (1976) *Equalities and Inequalities in Health*, Academic Press.

CHAMBERS, J.D. (1972) *Population, Economy and Society in Pre-Industrial England*, Oxford University Press.

COMMISSION OF THE EUROPEAN COMMUNITY (1981) *Final Report on the First Programme of Pilot Schemes and Studies to Combat Poverty*, COM (81) 769, December 1981.

DESAI, M. (1971) Demand for cotton textiles in nineteenth-century India, *Indian Economic and Social History Review*, 8(4), pp. 337–361.

DHSS (1976) *Prevention and Health*, HMSO.

DHSS (1980) *Inequalities in Health*, Report of a Working Group (the 'Black Report').

DHSS (1983) *Tables on Families with Low Incomes 1981*, October 1983 (based on Family Expenditure Survey data and Annual Statistical Enquiry of SB Claimants).

DUBOS, R. (1979) *Mirage of Health*, Harper and Row, New York.

EISENBERG, P. and LAZARSFELD, P.F. (1938) The psychological effects of unemployment, *Psychological Bulletin*, 35, pp. 358–390.

ENGELS, F. (1844) 'Health: 1844' from *The Conditions of the Working Class in England*, reproduced in Black *et al.* (1984).

EQUAL OPPORTUNITIES COMMISSION (1982) *Seventh Annual Report*, EOC.

FORBES, T.R. (1979) By what disease or casualty: the changing face of death in London, in WEBSTER C. (ed.) *Health, Medicine and Mortality in the Sixteenth Century*, Cambridge University Press.

FOX, A.J. and GOLDBLATT, P.O. (1982) *OPCS Longitudinal Study: Socio-demographic Mortality Differentials, 1971–75*, Series LS No 1, HMSO.

FRANK, A.G. (1969) *Capitalism and Underdevelopment in Latin America*, Modern Reader Paperbacks.

FRY, J. (1983) *Common Diseases*, M.T.P. Press Ltd, 3rd edn.

GHANA HEALTH ASSESSMENT TEAM (1981) A quantitative method of assessing the health impact of different diseases in less developed countries, *International Journal of Epidemiology*, 10, pp. 73–80.

GOPALAN, C. (1983) Development and deprivation: the Indian experience, *Economic and Political Weekly*, 18(51), pp. 2163–2168.

HARRIS, A.I., COX, E. and SMITH, R.W. (1971) *Handicapped and Impaired in Great Britain*, Part 1, HMSO.

HARRISON, P. (1979) *Inside the Third World*, Penguin Books Ltd.

HARRISON, P. (1983) *Inside the Inner City*, Penguin Books Ltd; extract reproduced in Black *et al.* (1984).

HEALTH AND SAFETY EXECUTIVE (1982) *Health and Safety Statistics, 1980,* HMSO.

HEY, JOHN (1971) *Britain in Context*, Basil Blackwell.

HOBSBAWM, E. (1969) *Industry and Empire*, Weidenfeld and Nicolson.

ILLSLEY, R. (1980) *Professional or Public Health? Sociology in Health and Medicine*, Oxford University Press.

JAHODA, M. (1982) *Employment and Unemployment: A Socio-psychological Analysis*, Cambridge University Press.

JONES, E.L. (1967) *Agriculture and Economic Growth in England, 1650–1815*, Methuen & Co. Ltd.

KASL, S.V. and COBB, S. (1979) *The Consequences of Job Loss*, USDHEW Publication No. 77–224, Washington.

KINNERSLEY, P. (1974) *The Hazards of Work: How to Fight Them*, Pluto Press.

KJEKSHUS, H. (1977) *Ecology Control and Economic Development in East African History*, Heinemann.

LANSLEY, S. and WEIR, S. (1983) Towards a popular view of poverty, *New Society*, 25th August, 284.

LASLETT, P. (1971) *The World We Have Lost*, Methuen & Co. Ltd, 2nd edition.

LEARMONTH, A.T.A. (1978) *Patterns of Disease and Hunger, A Study in Medical Geography*, David and Charles.

LEARMONTH, A.T.A. and LEARMONTH, A.M. (1955) Aspects of village life in Indo-Pakistan, *Geography*, Vol. XL, pp. 145–160.

LOGAN, W.P.D. (1982) *Cancer Mortality by Occupation and Social Class 1851–1971*, IARC Scientific Publications No. 39, OPCS/WHO/IARC.

LOWE, C.R. (1975) Health Needs and Health Services: a question of priorities, *Central African Journal of Medicine*, 21, pp. 229–235.

MALTHUS, T.R. (1970) *An Essay on the Principles of Population*, reprinted by Penguin Books Ltd, 1st edition 1798.

MCAVINCHEY, I.D. (1984) Economic factors and mortality: some aspects of the Scottish case, 1950–1978, *Scottish Journal of Political Economy*, 31(1), pp. 1–27.

MCKEOWN, T. (1976) *The Modern Rise of Population*, Edward Arnold; extract reproduced in Black *et al.* (1984).

MCKEOWN, T. (1979) *The Role of Medicine*, Basil Blackwell.

MCNEILL, W. (1976) *Plagues and Peoples*, Basil Blackwell.

MERRIT, G. (1982) *World Out of Work*, Collins.

MITCHELL, B.R. and DEANE, P. (1971) *Abstract of British Historical Statistics*, Cambridge University Press, 2nd edn.

MORGAN, M. (1980) Marital status, health, illness and service use, *Social Science and Medicine*, 14A, pp. 633–643.

NAPIER, RICHARD (1606) *Personal Diaries*, Manuscript MS Ashmole 216, Folio 116ʳ, Bodleian Library, Oxford.

NATIONAL FOOD SURVEY COMMITTEE (1983) *Household Food Consumption and Expenditure, 1981,* Annual Report of the National Food Survey Committee, HMSO.

OPCS (1978) *Occupational Mortality: Decennial Supplement, England and Wales 1970–72*, Series D.S. No. 1, HMSO.

OPCS (1980) *Adult Dental Health in England and Wales in 1978*, Vol. 1, HMSO.

OPCS (1982a) *Adult Dental Health in England and Wales in 1978*, Vol. 2, HMSO.

OPCS (1982b) *General Household Survey 1980*, HMSO.

OPCS (1983a) *GHS Monitor 83/3*, July 1983, Government Statistical Service.

OPCS (1983b) *Population Projections*, PP2 83/1, HMSO.

OPCS (1983c) *Social Trends*, HMSO.

OPCS (1984) *Mortality Statistics (cause), England and Wales, 1982*, Series DH2, No. 9, HMSO.

OPEN UNIVERSITY (1979) T101 *Living with Technology*, Block 6, *Health*, The Open University Press.

OPEN UNIVERSITY (1982a) D301 *Historical Data and the Social Sciences*, Units 5–8 *Historical Demography: Problems and Projects*, The Open University Press.

OPEN UNIVERSITY (1982b) U204 *Third World Studies, Third World Atlas*, The Open University Press.

PHELPS-BROWN, E.H. and HOPKINS, S.V. (1956) Seven centuries of the prices of consumables compared with builders' wage-rates, *Economica*, **23**.

PLATT, S. (1983) Unemployment and parasuicide ('attempted suicide') in Edinburgh, 1968–1982, *Unemployment Unit Bulletin*, **10**, pp. 4–5.

POLO, MARCO (1968) *The Travels of Marco Polo*, translated by R.E. Latham, Penguin Books Ltd.

POWLES, J. (1973) On the limitations of modern medicine, *Science, Medicine and Man*, Vol. 1, Part 1, pp. 1–30.

RCGP/OPCS/DHSS (1982) Morbidity Statistics from General Practice 1970–71 Socio-economic analysis, *Studies on Medical and Population Subjects*, No. 46, HMSO.

REID, J. (1981) *Social Class Differences in Britain*, Grant McIntyre.

RODNEY, W. (1972) *How Europe Underdeveloped Africa*, Bogle-L'Ouverture Publications.

ROMEDER, J.M. and MCWHINNIE, J.R. (1977) Potential years of life lost between ages 1 and 70, *International Journal of Epidemiology*, **6**, pp. 143–151.

ROYAL COLLEGE OF PHYSICIANS, MEDICAL SERVICES STUDY GROUP (1978) Deaths under 50; reproduced in Black *et al.* (1984).

SAHLINS, M. (1974) *Stone Age Economics*, Tavistock Publications Ltd.

SEN, A. (1981) *Poverty and Famines. An Essay on Entitlement and Deprivation*; extract reproduced in Black *et al.* (1984).

SHIMMIN, S. (1981) Pressure on women engaged in factory work, *Employment Gazette*, August, pp. 344–349.

SMITH, D. (1976) *The Facts of Racial Disadvantage*, PEP Broadsheet No. 560.

THOMPSON, E.P. (1967) Time, work-discipline and industrial capitalism, *Past and Present*, **38**, pp. 56–97.

TOWNSEND, P. (1979) *Poverty in the United Kingdom*, Penguin Books Ltd.

TOWNSEND, P. (1981) Towards equality in health through social policy, *International Journal of Health Services*, Vol II, No. 1, pp. 63–76.

TOWNSEND, P. and DAVIDSON, N. (eds) (1982) *Inequalities in Health: The Black Report*, Penguin Books Ltd.

UNITED NATIONS (1981) *Demographic Yearbook*, UN, New York.

WALDRON, I. (1983) Sex differences in illness incidence, prognosis and mortality: issues and evidence, *Social Science and Medicine*, **17**(16), pp. 1107–1123.

WALSH, J.A. and WARREN, K.S. (1979) Selective primary health care, *New England Journal of Medicine*, **301**, pp. 967–974.

WEBB, P. (1981) Health problems of London's Asian and Afro-Caribbeans, *Health Visitor*, **54** (April), pp. 141–147.

WERNER, D. (1978) *Where There is No Doctor*, Macmillan Publishers Ltd.

WESTOFF, C. F. (1974) The populations of the developed countries, *Scientific American*, Vol. 231, No. 3, September, pp. 108–22.

WILSON, H. and HERBERT, G. (1978) *Parents and Children in the Inner City*, Routledge and Kegan Paul.

WINTER, J.M. (1979) Infant mortality, maternal mortality, and public health in Britain in the 1930s, *Journal of European Economic History*, **8**, pp. 439–462.

WINTER, J.M. (1982) The decline of mortality in Britain, 1870–1950, in BARKER, T. and DRAKE, M. (eds) *Population and Society in Britain, 1850–1950*, Batsford Academic and Educational.

WORLD BANK (1982) *World Development Report 1982*, Oxford University Press.

WORLD HEALTH ORGANISATION (1958) *Constitution of the World Health Organisation*, WHO, Geneva.

WRIGLEY, E.A. and SCHOFIELD, R.S. (1981) *The Population of England 1541–1871: A Reconstruction*, Edward Arnold.

ZUNIGA, M. (1975) Parasitosis ey nival de salud en America Latina, *Salud Publica de Mexico Epoca*, V, XII, pp. 775–85.

Further reading

International Health by Paul F. Basch (1978, Oxford University Press, New York), although written primarily for American readers, is a wide-ranging and fairly recent book covering many of the topics discussed in Chapters 2 and 3. The medical geography perspective underlying Chapter 4 is much more fully developed in *Patterns of Disease and Hunger*, by A.T.A. Learmonth (1978, David & Charles). A comprehensive survey of Third World development, extensively referenced, is 'The Spread of Economic Growth to the Third World: 1850–1980' by Lloyd G. Reynolds, in the *Journal of Economic Literature*, Vol. 21, Sept. 1983, pp. 941–980. Fernand Braudel's *The Structures of Everyday Life: the Limits of the Possible* (1981, Collins) includes health, disease, population and much else in what is in effect an economic and social world history from the Middle Ages to the Industrial Revolution.

The definitive study of England's historical experience of mortality, fertility, population, famine, marriage, and related topics is *The Population History of England 1541–1871: A Reconstruction*, by E.A. Wrigley and R.S. Schofield (1981, Edward Arnold). At £45 it is too expensive for most private readers, but no library should be without a copy. Peter Laslett's *The World We Have Lost* (1971, Methuen) is very much cheaper and brings England's social history uniquely to life. An alternative view of the population history of England which pays particular attention to assessing the role of medicine is *The Modern Rise of Population* by Thomas McKeown (1976, Edward Arnold).

An epidemiological view of contemporary patterns of health in the UK is provided by Mark McCarthy in *Epidemiology and Policies for Health Planning* (1982, King Edward's Hospital Fund for London). *Inequalities in Health*, edited by P. Townsend and N. Davidson (1982, Penguin Books) also surveys a vast amount of epidemiological data, particularly with respect to social-class mortality differences, but accompanied by a discussion of potential explanations of these patterns.

Agribusiness in Africa, by Barbara Dinham and Colin Hines (1983, Earth Resources Research), while not directly concerned with health issues, does cover the main aspects of food and agriculture in the Third World. Finally, John Burnett's *Plenty and Want* (1979, Scolar) is a lively and judicious survey of the social history of the UK diet from 1815 to the present.

Answers to self-assessment questions

Chapter 2

1   Your answer should contain the following main points:

(a) The advantages of using mortality rates to measure health status are that countries with high death rates will also have high rates of non-fatal diseases, and mortality data are available for most countries.

(b) The disadvantage of the crude death rate is that it is dependent on the age structure of the population, which is very different in industrialised and Third World countries. In comparison, the infant mortality rate is, in general, a better measure of health status than the crude death rate: it does not need to be age-standardised; it can be estimated indirectly, while at the same time also being an indicator of general mortality in the population.

2   Given that the land area of the USA and Australia are similar and exceed that of India, the population density of India must be higher than the USA and far in excess of Australia.

3   The absolute difference between the infant mortality rate in Sierra Leone and the UK has hardly altered (falling from about 215 to 200 per 1000 live births). However, the *relative* difference has increased dramatically, from 10 times higher in 1950 to 15 times higher in 1980. In other words, the IMR in the UK has been falling considerably faster than it has in Sierra Leone.

4   (a) Expectation of life at birth in Bangladesh is greater for females (46.6 years) than males (45.8 years). In the UK the difference is greater — 76.4 years for females and 70.2 years for males.

(b) Female expectation of life remains greater throughout life in the UK, but not in Bangladesh. In Bangladesh, at the age of 1 year there is no gender difference (53.5 years) and by 5 years of age the expectation of life for males (54.5 years) exceeds that for females (54.2 years).

5   The data suggest that there were more people in the 'proletariat' and 'agricultural worker' groups than in the 'middle class' and 'bourgeoisie', or more precisely, that more children were born to people in these groups. The overall rate of 80 per 1000 is a *weighted average* of the class-specific rates 20, 39, 80 and 99, the weight being given by the numbers of births in the four social classes. Since 80 is near the upper extreme of these rates, the overall rate is clearly being weighted heavily by large numbers of births in the high mortality groups.

Chapter 3

1   In general, the chapter showed that the so-called 'tropical' diseases are not in fact a major cause of disease and death in Third World countries, and that the major diseases of the Third World also occur in industrialised countries — good examples are the respiratory diseases such as pneumonia, measles, bronchitis, whooping cough and influenza. The mortality differences between Third World and industrialised countries arise more from the very different *impact* these diseases have.

2   This method ranks diseases inversely according to the ages at which they occur. Infant and childhood deaths are so much more common in Third World than in industrialised countries, and the 'years of life lost' measure is very good at emphasising this difference.

3   Reductions in mortality have occurred particularly in numbers of deaths from malaria, smallpox, tuberculosis and measles. The area in which most improvement still has to occur is deaths from diarrhoeal infections, but these deaths can be traced directly to nutritional and sanitation standards. The problem is not ignorance of the origins of diarrhoeal infection, it is taking concerted action over these conditions.

4   (i) Pyramid (a) indicates a population with high fertility and high mortality, but the shape at the bottom suggests that child and infant mortality rates have been falling, and the indentation right at the bottom suggests a decline in fertility, perhaps as a result of a family-planning programme. These features suggest a Third World country which has quite a large and growing industrial sector. In fact the country is Singapore, 1968.

Pyramid (b) indicates a population in which birth and death rates have been low for many years, and in which the proportion in older age groups — particularly females —

is quite high. These features suggest a long-industrialised country. In fact it is Scotland.

(ii) Because of these age–sex structures, the crude death rate in Scotland (with large numbers of old people) might be expected to be quite high, but the age-standardised death rates to be low, as is typical of industrialised countries. In Singapore one might expect the reverse: low crude death rates because the population is young, but higher age-standardised death rates. (The Scottish crude death rate was in fact 12 per thousand, and the Singapore crude death rate 6 per thousand. But if Singapore had had the same age–sex structure as Scotland had, its death rate would have risen to 18 per thousand.)

Chapter 4

1 The introduction of electric pumps for irrigation has tended to lower the water table. As a result, simple lift-irrigation based on cattle or human power is no longer practicable. This has meant that some small farmers who cannot afford to invest in electric pumps have been forced to abandon agriculture and seek work in industrial centres, such as the coal mines or steelyards. These jobs expose workers to various hazards, among which are air pollutants that damage the lungs, causing bronchitis.

2 Mosquitos remain a serious health problem despite the introduction of insecticides because:

(i) stream-breeding species of *Anopheles* mosquitoes avoid insecticides by breeding in the forests;

(ii) some types of *Anopheles* are resistant to the insecticides;

(iii) a different family of mosquito, the Culicines, have 'moved into' the ecological niche vacated by *Anopheles*, and are spreading filarial worms and Japanese encephalitis;

(iv) the more serious form of malaria caused by *Plasmodium falciparum* has increased in proportion to *P. vivax*.

Chapter 5

1 There are two main reasons why this conclusion cannot be assumed. First, the growth of the total GNP does not take into account population growth. To do so it is necessary to compare the per capita GNP. The population of the Republic of Korea is growing at 1.7 per cent per annum, almost twice the 0.9 per cent per annum population growth rate in Greece. This means that the per capita GNP was growing at about the same rate in both countries. Second, national averages conceal the way in which wealth is distributed among different groups in the population: a comparison of changes in the standards of living in these two countries would have to taken in to account changes in the distribution of wealth. Unfortunately, no recent data on this are available for Greece.

2 The Third World does have a much larger population than the industrialised countries: in fact three-quarters of the world's population are in low-income or middle-income countries. But these countries are so much poorer that their share of world GNP is very small indeed: as the text noted, the poorest half of the world accounts for only 5 per cent of world GNP.

3 One example of government programmes to improve nutrition and reduce child mortality is food distribution, by means of subsidies, coupons, ration books and shops. The text noted that Sri Lanka has pursued such a policy, and despite being relatively poor has a good health record. (The same is true of Egypt.) Income distribution and land distribution programmes can also improve nutrition and health, while higher levels of wealth without such programmes may not bring these improvements.

Chapter 6

1 Infectious diseases such as measles cannot remain endemic in very small and scattered populations. The agricultural revolution raised food production and so populations increased and agricultural areas became more densely populated. This provided the conditions under which many new types of infectious diseases could have a fairly constant presence.

2 First, scarcity is not an absolute state but a relationship between wants or desires and means. Scarcity may therefore accompany great material wealth, or be absent where material wealth is extremely limited. Second, poverty is not so much a 'state' of existence as a relationship between different groups in a society. As noted in the text, it is one aspect of the hierarchical ordering that all societies seem to develop in one form or another as conflicts arise over the distribution of surplus.

3 Population and real wages are linked in two different ways in the Malthusian system. Changes in real wages can affect mortality rates, thus changing population size. But real-wage changes also alter *nuptiality*, and this affects the fertility rate and thus population size. In Figure 6.1 these two different links were represented by different loops in the Figure.

4 The Industrial Revolution was effecting structural changes in people's lives that greatly increased the importance of coordinated routines and time-keeping. Technological change was also cheapening certain goods such as watches, making them available to a mass market. Finally, many industrial towns were accumulating sufficient wealth to erect public buildings as symbols of civic pride and opulence.

5   Many people were being forced to leave rural areas as a result of landlessness due to enclosures or unemployment, and had nowhere to go but to the cities. Also, although conditions were appalling in the cities, they may have been no better in many rural areas because of the changes the Industrial Revolution was making to the country as a whole.

Chapter 7

1   The death rates shown in Figure 7.2 can only be *crude* death rates. As Chapter 3 showed, these are misleading because of age differences in the population structures of Third World and industrialised countries.

2   It doesn't. Like the example of looting mentioned in Sen's article, robbery by invading soldiers is a 'non-entitlement transfer' of food. Other examples include refusal to eat certain foods or refusal to take available work. As Sen notes, these instances are rare, but underline the fact that the entitlement approach is a *general* hypothesis.

3   In 1800 manufacturing production in the UK was only a small fraction of manufacturing production in the Third World. Even in 1850 UK production was half that in the Third World. In this sense it was not 'the workshop of the world'. However, the phrase is more accurate in conveying the notion of a great concentration of manufacturing production in one country. And, as the table shows, by 1880 the UK was producing more manufactures than the whole Third World, and continued to do so until the late 1950s.

Chapter 8

1   The most likely cause is autonomous disease — crises of subsistence only increase the mortality rate by three or four times, whereas these mortality crises are 6–10 times greater than the underlying mortality rate.

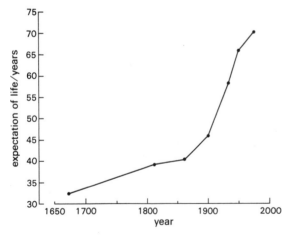

Figure 8.9 Expectation of life at birth for males, Britain, 1670–1979.

2   The problems are: (i) the changes in definition since 1550; (ii) the lack of qualified persons to make the diagnosis (few people had access to a physician in 1550); (iii) the lack of adequate and reliable records from the sixteenth century.

3   (a) The fastest increase in life expectancy occurred between about 1900 and 1935; this can be seen as the steepest part of the curve.

(b) Life expectancy is not increasing as rapidly as in former times. The increase has been slowing down since about 1945.

4   Between 1680 and 1850 the decline in mortality from infectious diseases is thought to have resulted from (a) improvements in nutrition, and (b) localised environmental measures, such as land drainage.

In contrast, the factors thought to be responsible after 1850 are (a) improvements in nutrition and general standard of living; (b) environmental improvements through public health legislation and administration, and (c) effective medical intervention in limited areas, such as some vaccines and anti-bacterial drugs.

5   This is because of a change in the medical definition of 'cause of death'. Old age is no longer viewed as sufficient reason for dying. Many deaths formerly classified as being caused by old age are now classified as due to heart disease, making interpretation of that category problematic.

Chapter 9

1   Although skin diseases are not apparently a cause of death (Figure 9.5) or a common reason for admission to hospital (Figure 9.6), they do cause considerable morbidity. They are one of the commonest reasons for consultations in general practice (Figure 9.6, Table 9.1). Skin diseases do not appear to cause much physical impairment (Figure 9.8), though people who suffer severe chronic skin conditions may well experience considerable social handicap.

2   Not necessarily. The younger cohort may not experience the same rate of dental decay suffered by the older cohort. For instance the younger groups may have benefitted from using fluoride toothpaste, eating less refined sugar and receiving better dental care, so that a higher proportion may retain their teeth than was true for the older cohort who were born around 1900–10 and have not enjoyed those same benefits.

3   No. The consultation ratio for divorced women is slightly higher for all conditions than for men. Although that is also true for diseases of the musculoskeletal system, the reverse is true for mental disorders, in which the ratio for men is slightly higher than that for women.

4 Most of the poorer health experienced by minority ethnic groups arises from their relative social disadvantage, that is, such factors as housing, employment and income. The contribution of life-history and biological factors is considered insignificant relative to the impact of social factors.

5 For a biological explanation, (i) you may have suggested climatic factors, such as hours of sunshine; for a social explanation, (ii) the variation in housing standards or income; and for a life-history explanation, (iii) alcohol consumption (although this is also a social explanation as levels of consumption will be affected by income).

6 The only exception mentioned in the chapter was that of breast cancer mortality (Figure 9.21), which is highest in social class I and lowest in V. Although this pattern is true for a few other conditions, the vast majority of diseases either show no social-class gradient or are commoner in lower social classes. This is true whether mortality, morbidity or disability is being measured.

Chapter 10

1 Men in the unskilled manual classes are almost three times as likely to be heavy drinkers as men in professional classes. Conversely there are more infrequent/light drinkers in the professional group than in the unskilled manual group. There are very few women in either socioeconomic group that describe themselves as heavy drinkers but there are twice as many among women in the unskilled manual group compared to the professional group. The pattern of heavy drinking among the unskilled manual group compared to the professional group could contribute to the increased incidence of certain diseases among this group — cirrhosis of the liver, for example. It might also be a factor in the differential accident rate in lower socioeconomic groups.

The table illustrates sharp differences in the drinking patterns of men and women, with a quarter of men admitting to being heavy drinkers compared to only 2 per cent of women. This might be expected to contribute to the increased mortality rates among men when compared to women.

2 Nurses are exposed to a wide range of direct health hazards at work. The risk of infection, for example, is obviously going to be higher than among other workers; working with sharp instruments such as scalpels and syringes involves risks, and chemicals may cause dermatitis. The actual job that nurses do — lifting and bathing patients, for example — may lead to back injuries, if proper lifting equipment is not used. A nurse's job may also be very stressful, for example, in dealing with anxious or distressed patients and relatives. Being in charge of a ward involves a lot of responsibility and this might also be a source of stress.

As a woman, Alice is likely to be less well paid relative to other skilled workers — some grades of nurses are poorly paid. She may also be trying to combine her paid employment with running a home. Although some hospital facilities are good, nurses do not always have access to adequate canteens or rest places, and work pressure may mean they miss breaks.

Finally Alice is black. She may therefore find that she is exposed to racial discrimination, either from other hospital staff or from patients, or within the career structure of nursing. You could probably have mentioned many other hazards which Alice might face.

3 Mrs Neil is expressing a common subjective perception that we are all taxed too highly to pay for the welfare services. Undoubtedly we are taxed to pay for these, but, as we saw from the data on the distribution of after-tax income, over the past years there has been very little redistribution of income from the top percentile groups of the population to the poor. Mrs Neil's perception that professionals are being squeezed in income terms for the sake of the poor does not fit with the evidence.

4 It seems fairly clear from the tenor of the *Daily Express* report that they are defining poverty in absolute terms as the satisfaction of the 'minimum necessaries for mere physical efficiency'. By this sort of standard there is of course no real comparison between most of the poor today and those of Dicken's time. It also seems that the Low Pay Unit must have been adopting a *relative* perspective. According to this approach, it is feasible that the relative standard of the poor today, especially those living below the state standard of supplementary benefit, may be in greater contrast with the customs and style of living of the rest of society than was the case when Queen Victoria reigned.

Chapter 11

1 It is possible that a causal relationship existed, so that unemployment resulted in higher rates of rheumatic heart disease mortality. However, as we said earlier in the chapter, unemployment is not random, either geographically or across occupational classes. The areas of high unemployment observed by Titmuss and Morriss may also have had generally poorer health records. This was in fact so: high-unemployment areas had above average proportions of the population in lower occupational groups, in poor housing, and in poverty. Thus although unemployment by itself may have adversely affected health, both unemployment *and* poor health were associated with other factors such as class structure, income and environment.

2 Large numbers of people move into and out of unemployment each month, but these flows are not even, particularly across age-groups. Therefore certain age-groups may be a small proportion of the total unemployed but experience much longer durations of unemployment because the outflow is slow. As we saw in this chapter, length of unemployment might have a significant association with state of health.

3 It would not be possible to conduct a cohort study without substantial resources and a long period of research time. This would circumscribe the research, because cohort studies are particularly well-suited to making before-and-after comparisons of employment and unemployment. Correlational studies tend to say more about association than causality, and surveys of the unemployed cannot answer questions about changes over time in the health of individuals, although they can provide useful comparisons of different groups of employed and unemployed people.

Chapter 12
1 Among the reasons you might have thought of are the following:

(a) consumption patterns vary widely by social class and also by region;

(b) the figures in Table 12.1 are simply total consumption averaged over the population, but it is likely that individuals will tend to eat white bread *or* brown bread, butter *or* margarine;

(c) most food information assumes that what is produced and bought is consumed, but in fact wastage rates may be quite high for some kinds of food: bread, for example, may go mouldy, the crusts might be left, or some might be thrown to the ducks or garden birds!

2 Tinning and freezing in fact transformed the average diet in Britain when they were introduced, and by expanding the range and convenience of foods and lowering prices they almost certainly were major factors in health improvements. Also, adulteration was much more blatant, widespread and responsible for immediate ill-health effects in the nineteenth century than now. Of course it is important to ensure proper precautions are observed about the use of additives, some of which have not been properly tested for their long-term safety. But modern urban populations would not be alive at all without some of the processes mentioned in the quote.

3 The 'diseases of affluence' are mostly degenerative diseases (ie., they are the result of the wearing out or deterioration of body tissue). In the main they are diseases of the middle-aged and elderly, and major examples are cardiovascular disease and cancer. They are 'diseases of affluence' in that they are most common in industrialised countries, whereas in the poor countries of the world deficiency diseases are much more common. But within the industrialised countries these diseases are most common among the poorest groups of the population. The fact that these population groups often cannot afford the money or time to have the 'prudent diet' outlined at the beginning of this chapter is an important clue about the association between health and diet.

4 Children with vitamin A deficiency in Victorian England would not have reached average height if their vitamin A intake alone had been supplemented: they were receiving insufficient food in general, and it was the overall shortage of food that was of most importance in reducing their growth. Similarly, most of the problems of deficiency diseases in the Third World are attributable to an insufficient overall level of food consumption, and it is normally misleading to focus on particular components of that overall food intake, such as protein.

Index

Entries and page numbers in **bold type** refer to key words which are printed in *italics* in the text.

Acknowledgements

Grateful acknowledgement is made to the following sources for material used in this book.

Figures

Figure 3.2 redrawn from C.F. Westoff, The populations of the developed countries, in *Scientific American*, vol. 231, No. 3, © Scientific American Inc., 1974, all rights reserved; *Figure 3.3* based on J.A. Walsh and K.S. Warren, Selective primary health care, in *New England Journal of Medicine*, vol. 301, 1979; *Figure 3.5* from D. Werner, *Where There Is No Doctor*, Macmillan, 1979; *Figure 6.2* from E.A. Wrigley and R.S. Schofield, *The Population of England 1541–1871: A Reconstruction*, Edward Arnold, 1981; *Figures 8.3 and 8.4* from T.R. Forbes in C. Webster (ed) *Health, Medicine and Mortality in the 16th Century*, Cambridge University Press, 1979; *Figure 8.5* based on C.R. Lowe in *Central African Journal of Medicine*, vol. 21, 1975; *Figure 8.6* from T. McKeown, *The Modern Rise in Population*, Edward Arnold, 1976; *Figure 8.7* courtesy of CSO, 1975, Crown Copyright; *Figures 9.1–9.5, 9.7, 9.8, 9.9, 9.13, 9.14, 9.16–9.22, 10.5*, Crown Copyright; *Figure 9.15* from J.K. Cruickshank and D.G. Beevers, Age, sex, ethnic origin and hospital admission, in *Postgraduate Medical Journal*, vol. 57, 1981; *Figure 10.3* adapted from P. Townsend, *Poverty in the United Kingdom*, © 1979 Peter Townsend, reprinted by permission of Penguin Books; *Figure 10.7* adapted from I. Reid, *Social Class Differences in Britain*, Blackwell, 2nd edn. 1981.

Tables

Table 3.1 based on J.M. Romeder and J.R. McWhinnie, Potential years of life lost between ages 1 to 70, in *International Journal of Epidemiology*, vol. 6, 1977, Oxford University Press; *Table 3.2* from Ghana Health Assessment Team, in *International Journal of Epidemiology*, vol. 10, 1981, Oxford University Press; *Table 8.1* adapted from T.R. Forbes in C. Webster (ed) *Health, Medicine and Mortality in the 16th Century*, Cambridge University Press, 1979; *Table 8.2* from T. McKeown, *The Role of Medicine*, Blackwell, 1979; *Table 10.9* adapted from P. Townsend (1979) *op.cit.*; *Tables 10.10 and 10.14* from S. Lansley and S. Weir, Towards a popular view of poverty, in *New Society* August, 1983; *Table 10.11* from L. Burghes, *Living from Hand to Mouth*, 1980, Child Poverty Action Group.